COOPERATING FOR PEACE AND SECURITY

Cooperating for Peace and Security attempts to understand – more than fifteen years after the end of the Cold War, seven years after 9/11, and in the aftermath of the failure of the United Nations (UN) reform initiative – the relationship between U.S. security interests and the factors that drove the evolution of multilateral security arrangements from 1989 to the present. The editors take as a starting point the argument that this evolution has occurred along two major lines and within three phases. Either existing mechanisms have been adapted to address emerging threats, or entirely new instruments have been created – and these changes have largely taken place within the timeframes of 1989 to 9/11, 9/11 to the invasion of Iraq in 2003, and 2003 to the time of this writing. Chapters cover a range of topics – including the UN, U.S. multilateral cooperation, the North Atlantic Treaty Organization (NATO), nuclear nonproliferation, European and African security institutions, conflict mediation, counterterrorism initiatives, international justice, and humanitarian cooperation – examining why certain changes have taken place and the factors that have driven them and evaluating whether they have led to a more effective international system and what this means for facing future challenges.

Bruce D. Jones is the Director of the Center on International Cooperation at New York University and Senior Fellow at the Brookings Institution. Dr. Jones's work focuses on the role of the UN in conflict management and international security, global peacekeeping operations, postconflict peacebuilding and statebuilding, conflict prevention, the role of the emerging powers in the contemporary security environment, and the regional aspects of the Middle East crisis. He is the author of *Peacemaking in Rwanda: The Dynamics of Failures* (2001) and coauthor, with Carlos Pascual and Stephen Stedman, of *Power and Responsibility: Building International Order in an Era of Transnational Threat* (2009).

Shepard Forman is Director Emeritus and Senior Fellow of the Center on International Cooperation at New York University. Prior to founding the Center, he directed the Human Rights and Governance and International Affairs programs at the Ford Foundation. Dr. Forman is coeditor of *Good Intentions: Pledges of Aid for Postconflict Recovery* (2000), *Multilateralism and U.S. Foreign Policy: Ambivalent Engagement* (2002), and *Promoting Reproductive Health: Investing in Health for Development* (2000), in addition to being author or editor of numerous books and articles.

Richard Gowan is Research Associate and Associate Director for Policy at the Center on International Cooperation at New York University. He works on peacekeeping, multilateral security arrangements, and the relationship between the UN and the European Union. He has worked with the Organization for Security and Cooperation in Europe (OSCE) Mission to Croatia and published on the political philosophy of Raymond Aron. Mr. Gowan is also a Policy Fellow at the European Council on Foreign Relations.

Cooperating for Peace and Security

EVOLVING INSTITUTIONS AND ARRANGEMENTS
IN A CONTEXT OF CHANGING U.S. SECURITY POLICY

Edited by

BRUCE D. JONES
New York University

SHEPARD FORMAN
New York University

RICHARD GOWAN
New York University

CAMBRIDGE UNIVERSITY PRESS
Cambridge, New York, Melbourne, Madrid, Cape Town,
Singapore, São Paulo, Delhi, Mexico City

Cambridge University Press
32 Avenue of the Americas, New York, NY 10013-2473, USA

www.cambridge.org
Information on this title: www.cambridge.org/9781107661318

© Cambridge University Press 2012

This publication is in copyright. Subject to statutory exception
and to the provisions of relevant collective licensing agreements,
no reproduction of any part may take place without the written
permission of Cambridge University Press.

First published 2010
First paperback edition 2012

A catalog record for this publication is available from the British Library.

Library of Congress Cataloging in Publication Data

Cooperating for peace and security : evolving institutions and arrangements in a
context of changing U.S. security policy / edited by Bruce D. Jones, Shepard Forman,
Richard Gowan.
  p. cm.
Includes bibliographical references and index.
ISBN 978-0-521-88947-6 (hardback)
1. Security, International. 2. Peace-building. 3. Security, International – Government
policy – United States. 4. Nuclear nonproliferation. 5. Terrorism – Prevention.
6. Humanitarian assistance – United States. 7. Humanitarian law – International
cooperation. 8. International courts. I. Jones, Bruce D. II. Forman, Shepard, 1938–
III. Gowan, Richard. IV. Title.
KZ5588.C66   2010
341.2 – dc22   2009014771

ISBN 978-0-521-88947-6 Hardback
ISBN 978-1-107-66131-8 Paperback

Cambridge University Press has no responsibility for the persistence or accuracy of URLs for
external or third-party Internet Web sites referred to in this publication and does not guarantee
that any content on such Web sites is, or will remain, accurate or appropriate.

In memory of Thomas Franck (1931–2009), an exceptional scholar of international law and inspiring believer in international institutions, who played an essential part in the establishment of the Center on International Cooperation at New York University

Contents

Contributors		*page* ix
Foreword		xiii
Acknowledgments		xv

I   FRAMEWORK

1	Introduction: "Two Worlds" of International Security *Bruce D. Jones and Shepard Forman*	3
2	"The Mission Determines the Coalition": The United States and Multilateral Cooperation after 9/11 *Stewart Patrick*	20
3	UN Transformation in an Era of Soft Balancing *Stephen John Stedman*	45

II   ADAPTING COLD WAR INSTITUTIONS

4	An Evolving UN Security Council *David M. Malone*	59
5	Too Many Institutions? European Security Cooperation after the Cold War *Richard Gowan and Sara Batmanglich*	80
6	Whither NATO *Mats Berdal and David Ucko*	98
7	The Evolution of Nuclear Nonproliferation Institutions *Christine Wing*	122

viii   *Contents*

8   9/11, the War on Terror, and the Evolution of Multilateral
     Institutions   143
     Eric Rosand and Sebastian von Einsiedel

9   Evolution and Innovation: Biological and Chemical Weapons   166
     Fiona Simpson

III   NEW TOOLS, NEW MECHANISMS

10   Normative Evolution at the UN: Impact on Operational Activities   187
     Ian Johnstone

11   Constructing Sovereignty for Security   215
     Barnett R. Rubin

12   New Arrangements for Peace Negotiation   227
     Teresa Whitfield

13   International Humanitarian Cooperation: Aiding War's Victims
     in a Shifting Strategic Environment   247
     Abby Stoddard

14   The Evolution of Regional and Subregional Collective Security
     Mechanisms in Post–Cold War Africa   269
     A. Sarjoh Bah

15   International Courts and Tribunals   291
     Cesare P. R. Romano

IV   CONCLUSIONS

16   Conclusion: International Institutions and the Problems
     of Adaptation   311
     Richard Gowan and Bruce D. Jones

Afterword   321

Index   333

Contributors

A. Sarjoh Bah is Research Associate and Program Coordinator for the Global Peace Operations program at the Center on International Cooperation at New York University. He was previously Senior Researcher with the Peace Missions Program at the Institute for Security Studies and has also served as a consultant to the Inter-Governmental Authority on Development and the European Commission. He was volume editor for the *Annual Review of Global Peace Operations* (Rienner) in 2008 and 2009 and also recently coedited *A Tortuous Road to Peace: The Dynamics of Regional, UN and International Humanitarian Interventions in Liberia* (ISS, 2005).

Sara Batmanglich is Senior Program Officer in the Preventing Conflict and Stabilizing Fragile States program at the Center on International Cooperation at New York University. Previously, she worked in media, focusing on youth culture and globalization. Her research interests include the Middle East, U.S. policy in the region, and Iranian domestic and foreign policy.

Mats Berdal is Professor of Security and Development in the Department of War Studies at King's College London. He was formerly Director of Studies at the International Institute for Strategic Studies in London. He is a contributor to and coeditor of *United Nations Interventionism 1991–2004*, published by Cambridge University Press in 2007.

Sebastian von Einsiedel is Political Affairs Officer with the UN Mission in Nepal (UNMIN). Previously, he worked on various aspects of the UN's role in peace and security at the International Peace Academy, an independent think tank in New York. In 2004–2005, he served as a researcher with the UN Secretary-General's High-Level Panel on Threats, Challenges, and Change and later on the follow-up to the Panel's recommendations in the UN Secretariat. Von Einsiedel has also worked with the NATO Parliamentary Assembly in Brussels and the German Parliament.

Shepard Forman is Director Emeritus and Senior Fellow of the Center on International Cooperation at New York University. Prior to founding the Center, he directed the Human Rights and Governance and International Affairs programs at the Ford Foundation, where he also was responsible for developing and implementing the Foundation's grant-making activities in Eastern Europe. He has served on the faculty at Indiana University, the University of Chicago, and the University of Michigan and authored two books on Brazil and numerous articles. He is coeditor, with Stewart Patrick, of *Good Intentions: Pledges of Aid for Postconflict Recovery* (2000), and *Multilateralism and U.S. Foreign Policy: Ambivalent Engagement* (Rienner, 2002).

Richard Gowan is a Research Associate and Associate Director for Multilateral Diplomacy and Conflict Prevention at the Center on International Cooperation at New York University. He was formerly manager of the Europe Programme at the Foreign Policy Centre (London), and he is the UN Policy Fellow at the European Council on Foreign Relations.

Ian Johnstone is Associate Professor of International Law at the Fletcher School of Law and Diplomacy, Tufts University, and Nonresident Fellow at the Center on International Cooperation at New York University. He has held various positions in the United Nations Secretariat, the Department of Peacekeeping Operations, and the Office of the Legal Counsel. In addition to publishing widely on international law and organizations, he was recently volume editor and lead scholar of the *Annual Review of Global Peace Operations 2007* (Rienner, 2007) and editor of a special issue of *International Peacekeeping, The US Role in Contemporary Peace Operations: A Double-Edged Sword?* (2008).

Bruce D. Jones is Director of the Center on International Cooperation at New York University, Senior Fellow at the Brookings Institution, and consulting professor at Stanford University. He served in UN political missions in the Middle East and Kosovo, in the Office of the Secretary-General, and as Deputy Research Director for the UN High-Level Panel on Threats, Challenges and Change. He is series editor, *Annual Review of Global Peace Operations*, author of *Peacemaking in Rwanda*, and coauthor (with Stephen Stedman and Carlos Pascual) of *Power and Responsibility: Building International Order in an Era of Transnational Threat* (2009).

David M. Malone was recently appointed President of the International Development Research Center. He was Canadian High Commissioner to India and Ambassador to Bhutan and Nepal, 2006–2008. A former Ambassador to the UN and President of the International Peace Academy (1998–2004), he has written extensively about the political economy of war and peace, decisionmaking in the UN Security Council, the past and future of Iraq, American foreign policy, and public international law.

Stewart Patrick is Senior Fellow at the Council on Foreign Relations, where he directs the Program on International Institutions and Global Governance. Previously, he was a Research Fellow at the Center for Global Development. During 2002–2005, he served on the Secretary of State's policy planning staff, helping formulate U.S. policy on Afghanistan and various transnational challenges. He is the author of *The Best Laid Plans: Identity, Ideas, and the Origins of U.S. Multilateralism 1940–1950* (Rowman and Littlefield, 2009). He is also coauthor of *Greater than the Sum of Its Parts? Assessing "Whole of Government" Approaches to Fragile States* and coeditor of *Multilateralism and U.S. Foreign Policy: Ambivalent Engagement* (2002).

Cesare P. R. Romano is Associate Professor of Law at Loyola Law School, Los Angeles, and a Director of the Project on International Courts and Tribunals. He has expertise in the law and practice of international courts and tribunals. His most recent publications include *The Sword and the Scales: The U.S. and International Courts* (with D. Terris and L. Swigart, 2009); *The International Judge: An Introduction to the Men and Women Who Decide the World's Cases* (2007); and *Internationalized Criminal Courts and Tribunals: Sierra Leone, East Timor, Kosovo and Cambodia* (with A. Nollkaemper and J. Kleffner, 2004).

Eric Rosand is Co-Director of the Center on Global Counterterrorism Cooperation in New York and a Nonresident Fellow at the Center on International Cooperation at New York University. Previously he served in the U.S. Department of State for nine years, including in the Office of the Coordinator for Counterterrorism. He is the coauthor of *Allied against Terrorism: What's Needed to Strengthen Global Commitment* (Century, 2006) and numerous articles, book chapters, and reports on multilateral counterterrorism efforts.

Barnett R. Rubin is Director of Studies and Senior Fellow at the Center on International Cooperation at New York University, where he directs the program on the reconstruction of Afghanistan. Previously, he was Director of the Center for Preventive Action and Director, Peace and Conflict Studies, at the Council on Foreign Relations. He has served as Special Advisor to the UN Special Representative of the Secretary-General for Afghanistan and advised the UN on the drafting of the constitution of Afghanistan. He has published extensively on Afghanistan, conflict prevention, state formation, and human rights.

Fiona Simpson is Research Associate for the Strengthening Multilateral Approaches to Nuclear and Other Weapons of Mass Destruction project at the Center on International Cooperation at New York University. Previously, she worked for the UN's Department for Disarmament Affairs and as an External Relations and Policy Officer at the IAEA in Vienna. Her recent publications include "IAEA Special Inspections after Israel's Raid on Syria," *Bulletin of the Atomic Scientists* (The Bulletin Online, February 11, 2008), and the coauthored "Atoms for Peace and the Nuclear Fuel Cycle," *Atoms for Peace: A Future after Fifty Years?* (2007, Joseph F. Pilat, ed.).

Stephen John Stedman is Senior Fellow at Stanford University's Center for International Security and Cooperation and professor of political science (by courtesy). He previously served as Research Director for the UN Secretary-General's High-Level Panel on Threats, Challenges and Change and has also been a consultant to the UN on issues of peacekeeping in civil war, light weapons proliferation and conflict in Africa, and preventive diplomacy. He has written extensively on international conflict management and war in the twentieth century and, most recently, is coauthor (with Bruce Jones and Carlos Pascual) of *Managing Global Insecurity* (Brookings, 2009).

Abby Stoddard is a policy analyst in international humanitarian affairs, conducting independent and commissioned research in association with the Center on International Cooperation at New York University and the UK-based Overseas Development Institute. She is a founding member of Humanitarian Outcomes, an independent research team that provides evidence-based analysis to governments and international organizations on improving humanitarian response. Her prior work as an aid practitioner throughout the

1990s spanned such crises as Rwanda and the former Yugoslavia. She is the author of *Humanitarian Alert: NGO Information and Its Impact on US Foreign Policy* (Kumarian Press, 2006), along with numerous articles and published reports.

David Ucko is a Trans-Atlantic Fellow at the Stiftung Wissenschaft und Politik (SWP) in Berlin and an Adjunct Fellow at the RAND Corporation. He is the author of *The New Counterinsurgency Era: Transforming the U.S. Military for Modern Wars* (Georgetown University Press, 2009) and coeditor of *Reintegrating Armed Groups after Conflict: Politics, Violence and Transition* (Routledge, 2009).

Teresa Whitfield joined the Center on International Cooperation in May 2008 as a Senior Fellow and Director of UN Strategy, having been Director of the Conflict Prevention and Peace Forum of the Social Science Research Council since early 2005. Her research interests include the United Nations, peace operations, and strategies to promote the resolution of internal conflict. Her most recent book is *Friends Indeed? The United Nations, Groups of Friends and the Resolution of Conflict* (United States Institute of Peace Press, 2007).

Christine Wing is Senior Fellow and Project Coordinator for the Strengthening Multilateral Approaches to Nuclear and Biological Weapons project at the Center on International Cooperation at New York University. She has a long history of nongovernmental organization (NGO)-based work on nuclear weapons issues, including as Program Officer for International Peace and Security at the Ford Foundation, and as coordinator of the National Disarmament Program of the American Friends Service Committee. She has also served as a consultant to the Nuclear Threat Initiative and the Ploughshares Fund and was Visiting Fellow at Princeton University's Center of International Studies.

Foreword

When I started the Center on International Cooperation (CIC) at New York University in 1996, I was seized by the problem of institutional, financial, and political impasses that precluded more effective multilateral cooperation in the post–Cold War world. From my perch as Director of International Affairs at the Ford Foundation, I had witnessed the failure of many donor governments to meet their international obligations, whether to international aid or to global peace and security. Time and again, the UN, the international humanitarian organizations, the International Court of Justice, and even the U.S. Department of State turned to private philanthropy (and increasingly, to the corporate sector) to seek funding for programs that were not only in the international public realm but basic to it. These programs ranged from humanitarian relief and resettlement efforts in the proliferating civil wars in Africa to clerkships, fact finding and translation at the World Court, and stabilization programs in the former Soviet bloc.

In those promising years between the end of the Cold War and the emergence of the preemptive "take the fight anywhere" Bush doctrine, the possibilities seemed ripe for improved multilateral cooperation to address the issues of poverty reduction, global health, cooperative security, environmental management, the expansion of human rights, and a comprehensive system of international justice. The premise was never a simple "all multilateralism is good," but an effort to examine deeply the political, financial, institutional, and legal underpinnings of multilateral cooperation to address critical transnational and global problems that no single nation or small grouping of nations could address on their own.

In an effort to deal with the overriding national interest question, we initiated several projects that reflected diverse national motivations: international justice, a matter of signatory obligation; pledges of aid to countries emerging from conflict, an urgent matter of regional and global security; the UN conference on development and reproductive health, a matter of moral commitment; and mobilizing resources for humanitarian relief, state altruism of the highest order. Of course, none of these motivations stood alone, and in none of these subject areas did a sense of common good prevail over national interests.

Each of our projects paired researchers from the United States and other countries to ensure multi-angled analysis of multifaceted issues and resulted in an edited volume of case studies and a set of policy recommendations. These ranged from the structure and staffing of the International Criminal Court and better distribution of international justice through ad hoc courts and tribunals to an improved architecture for postconflict reconstruction aid and peacebuilding. Given the overriding importance of the United States in a moment of unipolarity, we undertook a major study of multilateralism and U.S. foreign policy, with a set of recommendations on how the United States could better engage in the multilateral arena.[1]

Times have changed dramatically in the course of the Center's ten-year history, in terms of both the international environment for global policymaking and implementation and the proliferation of think tanks now devoted to the question of multilateralism. This book reflects both of these changes in its basic premise regarding the shifting dynamics of power and the two worlds of multilateralism, as described in the Introduction, and by including authors beyond the growing CIC family of researchers. Because of the overriding concern with global security and the changing nature of real and perceived threats, the Center's focus, apparent in this volume, has shifted away from a general concern with multilateralism per se to a tighter consideration of the link between broad areas of global concern and more traditional notions of political and military security.

I am extremely grateful to my initial partners in this effort – Rita Parhad, Stewart Patrick, Cesare Romano, and Abby Stoddard – and to our original supporters at the Ford and MacArthur foundations, who caught the vision and helped set in motion what has become an important inquiry into the workings (and failings) of multilateral cooperation. I am especially pleased to have passed on the Center's directorship to Bruce Jones, an accomplished scholar, a public policy expert and realist, and a person whose political antennae are constantly downloading the right signals. He and his team of able researchers and staff supporters are moving CIC ever closer to the practice of multilateralism while maintaining a high standard of policy analysis and increased cooperation with leading policy institutes and state parties around the world.

Shepard Forman, New York, 11 June 2009

---

[1] Stewart Patrick and Shepard Forman, *Multilateralism and U.S. Foreign Policy: Ambivalent Engagement* (Rienner, 2002).

Acknowledgments

The essays in this volume stem from a conference at the Center on International Cooperation at New York University in December 2006 to celebrate the Center's tenth anniversary. We thank all who participated, including our authors and Catherine Bellamy, Rahul Chandran, Feryal Cherif, Elizabeth Cousens, Victoria DiDomenico, Alex Evans, Trevor Findlay, Katherine Haver, Colin Keating, Edward C. Luck, Rita Parhad, Donald Steinberg, and Benjamin Tortolani. We also thank Thant Myint-U for his advice and Andrew Hart for his research assistance on the project.

The conference and this volume were supported by grants from the Norwegian Foreign Ministry and the Swedish Foreign Ministry, two of the Center's most supportive friends over the years. We are particularly grateful to Jan Knutsson and Jostein Leiro for their advice and support.

Our authors have tolerated a prolonged editorial process with humor and forbearance. John Berger at Cambridge University Press has been a gracious and tolerant overseer.

Finally, when three people get together to edit a volume of this type, they will almost certainly require a fourth person to keep everything in order. Sara Batmanglich has played this role superbly. Thank you, Sara.

I

Framework

1

Introduction: "Two Worlds" of International Security

Bruce D. Jones and Shepard Forman

SETTING THE STAGE: HEGEMON CONSTRAINED?

On March 29, 2005, to the delight of the assembled diplomats, UN Secretary-General Kofi Annan walked into the Security Council chamber and bested the United States.

It was fifteen years after the end of the Cold War, and ten years after France's President Chirac had termed the United States a "hyperpower."[1] In the previous two years, the United States had invaded Afghanistan and ousted the Taliban from its former safe haven and put on an extraordinary display of military might in the first phase of the Iraq war. The U.S. economy was operating with a massive surplus, and the U.S. military was not just unrivaled in contemporary terms but was realistically being described as the most powerful military force in history. In book after book, international relations scholars and historians eschewed the debate about whether there was an American Empire and turned their minds to such questions as: was the Empire good for American values and interests; was it liberal; was it stronger than the British Empire at its height; and how long it would last.[2]

Five years earlier, a confident American public, basking in eight years of prosperity and relative peace overseen by the Clinton administration, elected to office George W. Bush and the neoconservative wing of the Republican party, waving the flags of American dominance and contempt for multilateralism. "Nation building" was off the table, as was acquiescence to the belittling notion that the American superpower would submit its will to the vote and potential veto of the UN Security

---

[1] Chirac's Foreign Minister Hubert Vedrine first used the term "hyperpower" publicly in 1999. See, Craig R. Whitney, "France Presses for a Power Independent of the U.S.," *New York Times*, November 7, 1999, Section 1, p. 9.

[2] For example, see, Andrew Bacevich, *American Empire: The Realities and Consequences of U.S. Diplomacy* (Cambridge, MA: Harvard University Press, 2002); Niall Ferguson, *Colossus: The Rise and Fall of the American Empire* (New York, NY: Penguin Press, 2004); Chalmers Johnson, *The Sorrows of Empire: Militarism, Secrecy, and the End of the Republic* (New York, NY: Metropolitan Books, 2004).

Council,[3] a club of lesser states, weak-kneed Europeans, and dictators. China was to be contained, Russia managed, Europe directed, Africa aided; all from the enviable position of a power whose dominance was to be assured for the next generation.

This dominant, confident American government used its first weeks in office to repudiate the Clinton administration's decision, late and truculent though it was, to sign the Rome Statute of the International Criminal Court – the latest and arguably most daring innovation in international governance since the end of the Cold War. John Bolton, who was later to become Bush's ambassador to the UN, recalls in his memoirs that one of the happiest days in his career was in unsigning the Rome Statute.[4] Polite multilateralists like the amiable Secretary-General of the UN were to be treated in a manner reminiscent of a British diplomat's depiction of the late Qing dynasty's attitude to foreign envoys: "they were to be greeted with the utmost politeness, listened to with the utmost attention, and dismissed with the utmost courtesy." Later, he was to get rougher treatment.

If the tragic events of 9/11 shook the American public out of complacency and awoke the administration to the perils of far-flung corners of the globe, it certainly did not challenge the sense of the dominance of American power. So much so that when the North Atlantic Treaty Organization (NATO) reacted to the 9/11 bombing by offering to invoke, for the first time in the Alliance's history, the Article 5 provisions that compel its members to mobilize and to respond against an attack on another member, the administration (not very politely) turned down the offer. Several months later, the 2002 National Security Strategy, far from recognizing limits on dominance, articulated a policy of maintaining U.S. military dominance for the next generation. The result was what George Soros called "the bubble of American supremacy."[5]

And though events look different from the perspective of 2008, as we complete this volume, in the immediate aftermath of the U.S. toppling of the Taliban, Afghanistan seemed indeed to confirm, as did the early days of U.S. action in Iraq, that the United States had the will and power to project massive military and diplomatic might across the globe. The United States not only decided to launch a major military action without the support of the UN Security Council but actually did so defiantly against its expressed will. In fact, some within the U.S. administration had opposed the effort to gain Security Council backing, actively preferring to launch the attack on Iraq unilaterally, for the demonstration effect of U.S. power. The demonstration effect was there nevertheless, echoed in the administration's decision to entitle the first phase of their invasion the "shock and awe" campaign. The rapid destruction of Saddam Hussein's army by what many considered to be an undersized U.S. invasion force seemed to signal a triumph of American power projection.

[3] Condoleezza Rice, "Promoting the National Interest," *Foreign Affairs* 79, no. 1 (January/February 2000), pp. 45–62.
[4] John Bolton, *Surrender is Not an Option: Defending America at the United Nations and Abroad* (New York, NY: Threshold Editions, 2007), p. 85.
[5] George Soros, "The Bubble of American Supremacy," *Atlantic Monthly* (December 2003), pp. 63–66.

By mid-2004, falsely secure in victory in Iraq, the U.S. administration turned its attention to other troubles. First up was Lebanon, where Syria had earned U.S. ire by its opposition to the war and its actions in purported support of the ousted Hussein regime. Here, the United States scored another victory, using diplomatic pressure to compel a Syrian withdrawal from Lebanon, this time with the cooperation of France and the UN. Next on the list was Sudan, one-time safe haven for Osama bin Laden, oil supplier to China, and host to a Muslim dictator whose army was waging a brutal war on Christian groups – among others – in the south. Starting in 2004, the United States began to agitate for more assertive and more effective UN policy in south Sudan.

As in the case of Iraq, U.S. and UN policies had for some time been at odds. A particular bone of contention between the United States and the rest of the membership of the Security Council was the question of the International Criminal Court (ICC), John Bolton's bête noire. Established in 2002 after extensive negotiations, and against the negative vote of both the United States and China, among others, the ICC had come tenuously into existence at a time when the divisions in international politics revealed by Iraq were deepening and sharpening. In New York, Secretary-General Kofi Annan, with the support of most Council members and the broader "international community" – in this case, the middle powers, the signatories to the Rome Statute with which the ICC was established, and the human rights nongovernmental organizations (NGOs) – was seeking to wield the new tool of the ICC against the government in Khartoum, widely accepted to be barbarous in its policy in south Sudan and bloody-minded in its contempt for the UN.

UN policy put the United States into a dilemma. On one hand, it sought firm UN action against the Khartoum regime, which had not been deterred either by sanctions imposed (at U.S. instigation) in 1995 or by diplomatic pressure to rein in the Janjaweed and the other tribal militias waging a scorched earth campaign against civilians in Darfur. On the other hand, the United States had opposed the idea of the ICC, resisted its establishment, and had been working consistently to avoid being confronted by its application. In a display of diplomatic muscle, the United States had in fact sought and received in 2002, and again in 2003, a Security Council resolution exempting it from ICC jurisdiction on an annual basis.

Secretary-General Annan had used the unpopularity of U.S. policy on the ICC to his advantage before. In 2004, against the backdrop of the recently launched war in Iraq, Annan had opposed the third annual resolution granting the United States an exemption from the ICC, and got his way. And Annan had then cleverly taken U.S. Secretary of State Powell's statements in fall 2004 that the situation in Darfur constituted genocide[6] as an invitation to launch an international commission of inquiry into the killings in Darfur, which reported to the Secretary-General in January 2005.

---

[6] Glenn Kessler and Colum Lynch, "U.S. Calls Killings in Sudan Genocide," *Washington Post*, September 10, 2004, p. A1.

Although avoiding the word genocide, the report clearly established a pattern of large-scale war crimes and Sudanese government complicity therein.[7] Thus the stage was set for a confrontational meeting of the UN Security Council.

Secretary-General Kofi Annan had been buffeted in the preceding months by a deliberate campaign against him, accusing him first of corruption and malfeasance in the oil for food scandal and then (more tellingly) of mismanagement of the institution as a whole. Annan had been weakened by perceptions in Congress that he was acting against U.S. interests in Iraq; weakened among the UN's southern members by perceptions that he had caved into U.S. pressure by deploying a UN political office into Iraq; and had taken a blow to his standing within the UN Secretariat when twenty-one members of that office, including the charismatic Sergio Vieira de Mello, were killed by a truck bomb in their poorly guarded compound in Iraq. So it was that a weakened and bowed Secretary-General confronted a dominant United States in the UN Security Council chamber.

Annan was nothing if not a master of diplomatic maneuver. His aides leaked the rumor that he might introduce the notion of calling for the Sudanese to hand over suspects to the ICC, putting the dilemma confronting the United States into the public domain. Before the meeting, the U.S. Ambassador-at-Large for War Crimes Pierre-Richard Prosper said in a news conference that the United States does not "want to be party to legitimizing the ICC," clearly assuming that the Secretary-General would back down in the face of U.S. opposition. He did not; that March morning Annan took his seat in a tense Security Council chamber and called on the members to endorse a resolution referring the Sudanese suspects to the ICC. Faced with the prospects of vetoing fourteen other votes in favor of the motion, the United States backed down, allowing the resolution to proceed[8] and the ICC to come more actively into existence.

The Dilemma: Hegemony and Multilateralism in Conflict

If the Sudan/ICC vote had been the only instance in which the United States in its post–9/11 policy had found itself constrained by evolutions at the UN it neither sought nor supported, it could be written off as an aberration, an uncharacteristic moment. But in fact, despite the sound and fury of Ambassador Bolton's ringing condemnations of the vacuity and fecklessness of the organization, by mid-2005 the United States found itself reliant on or embedded with the UN in virtually every major issue on its agenda. As Stedman notes in Chapter 3, literally all of the top-tier security issues confronting the Bush administration in 2005 – from Iraq and Iran to

---

[7] Report of the Independent Commission of Inquiry into War Crimes in Sudan. Available at: http://www.un.org/news/dh/sudan/com_inq_darfur.pdf.

[8] The text of UNSCR 1591 is available at: http://daccessdds.un.org/doc/UNDOC/GEN/No5/287/89/PDF/No528789.pdf?OpenElement.

Introduction: "Two Worlds" of International Security

Afghanistan to North Korea and Sudan – had either a UN political or peacekeeping presence on the ground or a UN Security Council role.[9]

In several of these cases, the United States found itself needing more than it had thought from allies and multilateral institutions. By late 2003 in Afghanistan, the administration was forced to reverse its earlier positions and call on NATO to help stabilize the country, just as it found itself (rather more graciously) accepting the UN's help in nation building. U.S. policy still explicitly eschewed that notion until 2005, when it belatedly accepted that helping to build the core institutions of the Afghan state was a necessary corollary to defeating the enemies of that state, but it had given the UN's Lakhdar Brahimi both space and support in his efforts to play the role of tolerant but firm uncle to Afghanistan's maturing government.

Also, the United States found itself bested in negotiations on a major institutional shift at the UN, the establishment of the Human Rights Council in early 2006, following decisions of the 2005 World Summit to upgrade the functioning but increasingly discredited Human Rights Commission. In an astonishing failure of U.S. diplomacy at the UN, several months of active negotiations by the United States, led by Ambassador Bolton, took the starting position for the new body outlined in the 2005 Summit Outcome Document and watered it down disastrously, creating what even its supporters acknowledged was a far weaker body than had been called for or anticipated. Also in the realm of human rights, the United States pushed for a Security Council resolution in 2006 condemning human rights abuses in Myanmar, only to find this resolution the subject of a rare double veto by Russia and China, as well as negative votes by putative friendly states such as South Africa. Though subsequent events in Myanmar would lend credence to the U.S. position, the double veto was a humiliating defeat for the United States at the UN.

In Lebanon, too, the United States would find its position in 2006 resisted and its proposals rejected. Having taken a public stand against a ceasefire in the Israel-Hezbollah war of summer 2006 (a position quietly supported by many Arab governments, but universally rejected in public), the United States then pushed for the creation of a regional force to be followed by a NATO force to undertake stabilization operations – only to find both positions rejected in favor of the European/Arab preference for a UN mission, which was subsequently deployed in July 2006.[10]

Had the mighty fallen? Had accounts of U.S. power been hyperbolic? Could the dramatic decline in U.S. diplomatic prowess be explained only by its troubles in Iraq? Or was there more to the events of 2005 onward?

This volume argues that the explanation is more complex. If the United States was losing battles to the UN in 2005 and 2006, and if it was against the Bush administration that Kofi Annan had his public bouts, the roots of confrontation lay

---

[9] Stephen John Stedman, "UN Transformation in an Era of Soft-Balancing," *International Affairs* 83 no. 5 (2007), pp. 933–44. (Reproduced here as Chapter 3.)

[10] Technically, the force was not a new one but a remandated and reconfigured version of the preexisting UN force on the ground, the UN Interim Force in Lebanon.

deeper. And if Kofi Annan could best the United States at the Security Council in 2005, it was not a product just of a clash between the Secretary-General and the administration, but of the evolution of two distinct worlds of international security after the Cold War.

TWO WORLDS OF INTERNATIONAL SECURITY: BETWEEN BERLIN AND BAGHDAD

The story of the evolution of those "two worlds" of international security is a story of U.S. power, of international institutions, and of their evolution and adaptation after the Cold War. It is a story that has not yet been fully told, a story about the changing nature of power, and of careful adaptation and surprising innovation in international governance.

Since the end of the Cold War, conflict and cooperation among states on matters of peace and security have been increasingly managed, regulated, or implemented by and through multilateral security institutions. The most visible manifestations of this evolution in the practice and form of international politics have been the vast expansion of the work of the UN Security Council; the enormous expansion of tools such as international mediation, peacekeeping, and postconflict operations to manage civil wars; and the proliferation both of new instruments for tackling conflict and security challenges and of new mandates for older institutions to adapt themselves to changing security realities.

The literature on international security and international relations has not kept pace with the scale of these changes. Although numerous case study or comparative study volumes exist on the management of civil wars[11] and peacekeeping,[12] few if any have begun to assess the broader implications of the evolution of the international security architecture since the end of the Cold War. A separate literature examines the evolving (and arguably eroding) structures for the management of disarmament and nonproliferation,[13] though that literature largely underplays the role of such institutions as the International Atomic Energy Agency (IAEA).

So too the theoretical literature on international institutions and international regimes has with rare exception ignored the realm of security and conflict management. Haftendorn, Keohane, and Wallander's *Imperfect Unions*[14] is an important

---

[11] An early and still influential exemplar of the literature is Michael Brown, ed., *International Dimensions of Internal Conflict* (Cambridge, MA: MIT Press, 1996).

[12] Among the most influential in both research and policy terms are Stephen Stedman, Don Rothschild, and Elizabeth Cousens, eds., *Ending Civil Wars: The Implementation of Peace Agreements* (Boulder, CO: Lynne Rienner 2002); and William Durch, *UN Peacekeeping, American Policy and the Uncivil Wars of the 1990s* (New York, NY: Palgrave Macmillan, 2004).

[13] See, for example, Joseph Cirincione et al. *Deadly Arsenals: Nuclear, Biological and Chemical Threats* (Washington, DC: Carnegie Endowment for International Peace, 2005).

[14] Helga Haftendorn, Robert Keohane, and Celeste Wallander, eds., *Imperfect Unions: Security Institutions over Time and Space* (Oxford, UK: Oxford University Press, 1999).

exception, and one that has helped to shape the conceptual framework for this volume.

What is striking, historically and theoretically, is the limited extent to which the United States, for all of its unrivaled power, shaped the evolution of the multilateral security architecture in the post–Cold War era. The United States was influential, to be sure, and in some issue areas decisive. But in major arenas and areas of international security, U.S. influence was passive at best and allowed others to drive the significant evolutions that occurred.

This book charts the evolution of the multilateral security architecture, the evolution and adaptation of a host of international institutions to security functions broadly conceived. We argue that two processes have dominated the post–Cold War period: a U.S.-led process of adaptation of Cold War instruments to the challenge of embedding Russia in the Western order; managing post–Soviet nuclear and other weapons of mass destruction (WMD) arsenals; containing terrorism; and a U.S.-tolerated but not U.S.-led process of innovation to deal with "peripheral" or "soft" security threats, largely related to internal conflict and humanitarian crises. The result was the emergence of two worlds of international security.[15]

The First World: Adapting to the End of the Cold War

That the United States, an unrivaled power after the end of the Cold War, could drive international security arrangements if and when it devoted focused policy attention to the question, is evident in chapters that form the first part of this volume. In Chapter 2, Patrick sets the stage in his analysis of Clinton and Bush policies. Some of the weaknesses of Clinton policy are on display, notably its "cut and run" attitude to UN peacekeeping after the humiliation of Somalia and under siege in Rwanda – an issue to which we return. The Clinton administration of course did engage in a process of adapting Cold War institutions in order to manage the collapse of the Soviet Union. The institutional mode was not one of innovation, but of adaptation of existing instruments.

Of particular focus for the Clinton administration was the question of the nuclear weapons left by the collapse of the Soviet Union in the hands of Ukraine, Belarus, and Kazakhstan. As Wing (Chapter 7) argues, the United States was throughout the post–Cold War period the dominant actor in shaping the evolution of the formal nuclear nonproliferation regime. This role rarely took the shape of strategic leadership; much of it, rather, was tactical or reactive. The dominance of U.S. policy was evident also in the biological field (as noted by Simpson in Chapter 9).

U.S. policy was also decisive, unsurprisingly, in the reshaping of NATO after the Cold War. This had two phases: the first, designed primarily to deal with containment

---

[15] The two worlds described herein largely align with the two worlds described in a prescient article. See James M. Goldgeier and Michael McFaul, "A Tale of Two Worlds: Core and Periphery in the Post-Cold War Era," *International Organization* 46 no. 2 (Spring 1992), pp. 467–92.

of Russia; the second, to deal with terrorism. Gowan and Batmanglich (Chapter 5) discuss the first phase, setting out the impact of U.S. policy on NATO on the broader evolution of European institutions, caught as they were initially between U.S.-dominated mechanisms such as NATO, mechanisms in which both U.S. and Russian power were given institutional expression (the Organization for Security and Cooperation in Europe [OSCE]), and independent European mechanisms (especially the European Community/European Union [EC/EU]).[16] By the time the OSCE's early role in managing Kosovo had given way to the G8 and then NATO and the UN (and the EU, in an initially minor role), the U.S. impact on multilateral mechanisms in Europe seemed decisive. In fact, the U.S. emphasis on NATO as a U.S.-dominated tool for multilateralism within Europe actually helped drive a European movement toward a stronger EU, resisted for a time by the UK and some of the other strong U.S. allies on the continent but ultimately the dominant expression of multilateralism within Europe.

The more dominant Clinton administration approach of gradually evolving the institutional framework to shape the post–Cold War security landscape was evident in their approach to counterterrorism. As argued by Rosand and Einsiedel (Chapter 8), U.S. policy on international institutions' role in counterterrorism was shaped by three factors: the limitations on the bodies themselves, the limitations on multilateralism per se as an approach to deal with issues like intelligence sharing, and ideological predispositions of leading figures, in both the Clinton and Bush Jr. administrations. The net result was a policy of only gradual evolution of the UN's treaty regime and some modest innovations at the level of the Security Council, notably in the establishment of UN sanctions committees dealing with counterterrorism.

The policy of institutional evolution also shaped U.S. strategy on NATO in its second phase. As documented by Berdal and Ucko (Chapter 6), counterterrorism had been the increasing focus of U.S. policy for NATO since 2002. Events in Afghanistan brought the issue into closer focus. As noted earlier, the United States initially resisted a NATO role in Afghanistan, having learned in Kosovo that in circumstances short of a full-blown Soviet threat, the organization's decision-making structures were quite cumbersome, especially with the requirement for all members to approve all targeting decisions. (One Danish diplomat recounted spending much of his time during the 1999 bombing campaign driving back and forth between the Parliament and the Queen's residence getting royal assent to parliamentary decisions on new targets.) Nevertheless, by 2003 the strain on U.S. forces from fighting in both Iraq and Afghanistan contributed to a U.S. decision to accept a NATO takeover of the International Security Assistance Force in Afghanistan.

However, the lack of NATO preparedness for counterterrorism missions – an issue raised assertively by U.S. Secretary of Defense Robert Gates in early 2008 – meant that the Alliance was coming under increasing strain. Side missions like

---

[16] See *inter alia* Haftendorn, Keohane, and Wallender (1999).

counterterrorism duty in the Greek Olympics and counter-cyber-terrorism operations in Estonia in 2007 did little to bolster the Alliance against the strains of progressively losing ground to the Taliban in Afghanistan's southern provinces in 2006 and 2007.

Strikingly, it was in Afghanistan that the two worlds of international security were deployed in closest proximity. In addition to NATO's counterterrorism and stabilization function and the ongoing U.S. operation, the UN of course also deployed a large political mission to Afghanistan, which was also host to a vast array of UN agencies, European donors, and nongovernmental organizations – the shock troops of the evolving internal conflict management system that had been the focus of innovation in the "second world" of international security, to which we now turn.

The Second World: Innovation in Response to Crises

If Iraq (2003) was the stage on which the United States and the UN clashed during the Bush administration, Iraq (1991) was also the place where the "second world" of international security was born. The large-scale humanitarian response to Kurdish populations in northern Iraq following the abrupt conclusion of the first Gulf War laid the foundation for the creation of one of the more extensive international mechanisms for responding to internal conflict and crises, the UN's humanitarian coordination machinery. Together with the humanitarian response to crisis inside Afghanistan following the end of the Soviet occupation of that country, a new humanitarian architecture was born out of these two conflicts that saddled the collapse of the Soviet Union.

Indeed, given the importance of Bush Sr.'s decisions in shaping future directions at the UN, the 1991 moment stands as a road not taken – a road of progressive U.S. policy at the UN, marrying the power of the post–Cold War United States to the soon-to-be expanded institutions and energies of the UN. But this was not to be.

Humanitarian Crises. If Bush Sr.'s decisions in Iraq in 1991 set the stage for the creation of new UN humanitarian machinery, it was nevertheless not the case that the United States led the next stage of its development. As Stoddard documents in this volume (Chapter 13), the United States has since 1990 always been the largest financial donor to the humanitarian system, and in that sense has carried it; but it has never been in the lead in shaping either its institutional development or its policy formulation. That role fell primarily to the United Kingdom, frequently supported by the Scandinavian and Dutch governments, who have been major financial and personnel contributors to the humanitarian system.

Of course, the UN's humanitarian role is as old as the institution itself. The very first of the now myriad specialized agencies established by the UN was the UN Relief and Works Agency (UNRWA), created in 1946 to provide social support to the Palestinian refugee population in the aftermath of the first Arab-Israeli war. It was soon followed by the UN High Commissioner for Refugees (UNHCR), the better known refugee body and until the 1990s the largest of the UN's humanitarian agencies. Born out of the mass refugee movements that attended the end of the Second World War, by the 1950s and 1960s UNCHR was dealing with refugee populations globally.

The two main, and related, differences between the pre– and post–Cold War humanitarian architecture are, first, the ability of the post–Cold War instruments to operate inside government territory without formal authorization; and second, the extensive role of nongovernmental organizations in the response. In the days of the Cold War, UNHCR operated primarily along the borders of conflict-affected states – refugee status required, first and foremost, crossing a border. In northern Iraq, the UN found itself operating inside borders without the formal approval of the nominal sovereign, Iraq; the first but far from the last instance of the UN operating inside what would later become known by that maddeningly imprecise term "failed states." And it was operating alongside a host of nongovernmental organizations that would over the next ten years become a central part of the overall response.

At the UN, these two developments were driven by and encoded in the adoption by the General Assembly of Resolution 46/182, which established the position of Emergency Relief Coordinator, giving that official the authority to mount operations without prior authorization from any member state body, and also established for the first time in the UN a mechanism for coordination with the NGO community and the International Committee of the Red Cross (ICRC), the Inter-Agency Standing Committee. These technocratic terms masked the importance of the milestones they represented, the first step toward the now-expansive role that the UN plays in responding and helping states recover from internal crises, and the first steps toward the concept of a "responsibility to protect."

In Chapter 13, Stoddard makes a persuasive case that in this instance a backroom role for the United States was both positive and necessary, because it allowed the humanitarian system to retain a credible perception of impartiality vis-à-vis the major powers in a way that a U.S.-dominated system would not. The Western middle powers led where U.S. leadership would taint. That the UK has in the last several years been a close U.S. ally and operational partner in the Iraq invasion and subsequent occupation may cloud the useful role that the UK has played.

Mediation. It was not only in the humanitarian sphere that the international system witnessed substantial innovation in response to internal crises but also in the realm of political mediation. Here, however, the UN was not in the forefront in institutional terms, though the role of the UN Secretary-General was certainly more important during the post–Cold War period than it had been prior.

The backdrop was the changing landscape of the global security environment, which allowed a greater focus on small wars and on internal wars in nonpowerful states (many of which had raged during the Cold War, but unaccompanied by the now familiar panoply of international response mechanisms). The outcome was the emergence of a mediation system that rested primarily on mid-level powers, small coalitions of states and organizations, and sometimes use of "Friends" groupings that linked these coalitions with the UN.

Here too, as Whitfield points out in Chapter 12, the question of being seen as "disinterested" was an important factor in establishing a role for these second-tier actors. Together with a more expansive role of the UN Secretary-General in mediation (especially toward the end of mediation processes, in advance of the establishment of peace implementation mechanisms), and again with an important role for NGOs, such states as Norway, Sweden, and Switzerland, along with neighbors to conflict, took on a leading role in what the High-level Panel on Threats, Challenges and Change would later describe as a "sea change" in global governance – the emergence of a norm that internal wars would reach an end through mediation rather than through victory.

The role of such mechanisms was initially limited to Cold War carryover conflicts in Latin America and Africa (Guatemala and Mozambique being paradigmatic cases); it expanded most importantly with Norway's role in the brokering of the Oslo Accords in the Middle East. Over the decade since, the UN has also played an ever-larger role, though still hewed primarily toward the endgame, to the peacekeeping and peacebuilding functions.

Peacekeeping and Peacebuilding. The storyline of the evolution of the international system for peacekeeping and peacebuilding is more complicated. As told in this volume, the enormous expansion of peacekeeping and peacebuilding in the post–Cold War era is a story of successes and failures and changing concepts over time. Its evolution is importantly a story of the leadership of individuals, more than that of states. Specifically, the election for Secretary-General in 1997 brought Kofi Annan, deeply involved in early peacekeeping failures in the 1990s, into the office. There, Annan launched a multipronged initiative to revitalize peacekeeping. First, he commissioned two independent (or quasi-independent) and self-critical analyses of two key failures, in Rwanda and Srebenica. Second, he commissioned the diplomat Lakhdar Brahimi to lead an independent panel that produced the report that took his name, which is still the touchstone document of contemporary UN peacekeeping. Third, and most critical, when new missions in Sierra Leone and East Timor came under attack, Annan stood firm: ordering his in-country representatives to stand their ground; sending his Under-Secretary-General for Peacekeeping to the field at the moment of attack in the case of Sierra Leone; convincing the Security Council to take a mission to East Timor in that instance; and individually pleading with the Security Council for robust action in the face of the challenges – a call the UK took up in Sierra Leone and Australia (joined by Brazil and others) took up in East Timor. It was a decisive moment. In the subsequent seven years, UN peacekeeping would expand enormously, by 2009 topping eighty thousand troops in the field, and reemerging as the backbone of the global peacekeeping system.

As documented in this volume, the expansion of peacekeeping in both the UN and the European context has been matched by a tremendous expansion of peacebuilding capabilities, but in a far less organized manner. Rather than seeing one core department/institution leading the effort, as in peacekeeping, peacebuilding needs were met by a proliferation of postconflict or peacebuilding units among departments, agencies, institutions, and organizations. The result was a massive coordination challenge, as well as a lack of systematization or prioritization – only very partially ameliorated by recent innovations, such as the creation of the Peacebuilding Commission.

Overall, the story of peacekeeping and peacebuilding is one of innovation but not of vision.

The Secretary-General as "Norm Entrepreneur," and International Courts. The same could not be said about the emergence of an international justice sector since the end of the Cold War – a set of innovations that had everything to do with vision, and with normative entrepreneurship not by the United States or leading powers, but by middle powers and individuals, notably Secretary-General Annan.

As noted, the rebounding of UN peacekeeping from its failures in the 1990s was importantly a story of not only action by U.S. allies such as Australia and the UK but also of individual leadership by the Secretary-General. The Secretary-General's role in shaping the evolution of the UN in the 1990s has been underestimated in the literature. That role had two facets: driving organizational change and reshaping norms. As told by Johnstone (Chapter 10), the Secretary-General's role as "norm entrepreneur" was actually the more significant, though the two were closely interlinked.

Kofi Annan's normative innovations were also directly connected to the organization's experience in conflict management – but not to its successes. It is striking that Annan's main normative innovations, around the concepts of the protection of civilians, humanitarian intervention, and the responsibility to protect, were born out of failures – in Rwanda, in Bosnia, and importantly, in Kosovo. (In Kosovo the failure is differently interpreted – of a failure of the UN to respond or of the United States to be limited by the UN. From the editors' perspective, the failure of Kosovo was quite clearly one of the Security Council's inability to organize an effective response to Serbian aggression.)

Out of Kosovo was born a controversial Kofi Annan speech on humanitarian intervention – a speech that garnered a fierce negative reaction among the developing world's countries at the UN. And so here again, a U.S.-allied middle power – Canada – took the lead in pushing the innovation, this time outside of the UN through an eminent persons panel – while at the same time pushing a less controversial concept, about the protection of civilians, inside the UN. With backstopping by such leading individuals in Kofi Annan's cabinet as Sergio Vieira de Mello, the protection-of-civilians concept moved through the Security Council and the UN system, whereas the more controversial concepts were refashioned and reorganized by the Canadians into what emerged as "the responsibility to protect" – a concept later endorsed by the High-level Panel and then the General Assembly and Security Council.

Nowhere was the role of individuals as both normative and institutional entrepreneurs more important or more controversial than in the creation of the International Criminal Court (ICC). The ICC was not the only international court established during the post–Cold War period; far from it. Indeed, a panoply of international courts and adjudication mechanisms were established during this period, as documented in Chapter 15 by Romano. But it was certainly the ICC that was the most controversial of these, primarily because of opposition from both the United States and China: the current and the rising superpower. And as highlighted earlier, it was over the ICC that the two worlds of international security, the one driven by the United States, the other at the UN, came to a head.

BETWEEN TWO WORLDS: THE UN SECURITY COUNCIL

If the two worlds of international security described previously proceeded largely independently of each other in terms of operational institutions, they were continuously brought together in the UN Security Council. What is more, the evolution of the Security Council during the post–Cold War period was bracketed by two episodes in which the "first world" of post–Soviet WMD and terrorism control was interwoven with "second world" issues of conflict management and humanitarian crises – both in Iraq.

As Malone (Chapter 4) has documented in his scholarship on the Security Council, Iraq policy heavily shaped the evolution of the Council's practice and role in the post–Cold War era. In substantial part, that practice had to do with maintaining unity among the P5 even during periods of substantial policy difference and tension – often over Iraq containment.

One of the effects of the search for P5 unity was that in the face of energetic efforts by nonpermanent members of the Security Council such as Norway and Canada to push forward ideas like the protection of civilians and expanded mandates for peacekeeping, support for those efforts by the UK and often France tended to gain more acceptance by the United States than might otherwise have been the case. At the same time, both Russia and China largely avoided vetoes during most of the 1990s. The consequence of a series of Council decisions then, albeit unplanned and inconsistent, was the gradual strengthening of the multilateral system for response to conflict and with it the gradual erosion of "the foundations of absolute conceptions of state sovereignty."

The United States never led this process – indeed, it was unled, as Malone makes clear in Chapter 4 – but the fact that much of it occurred at the Council highlights the fact that U.S. policy was at least permissive to most of the evolution that occurred at and around the UN. This highlights an important point, which must temper the sense of limits on American power: that at any point in the 1990s the United States could have vetoed any of the evolutions, or most of them at least, that occurred in New York – in peacekeeping, peacebuilding, or in the humanitarian system. The creation of the ICC against American opposition (and similarly, with the establishment of the Landmines Convention in 1999) demonstrates that there were limits to American veto power. But it is perhaps not irrelevant that both the Landmine treaty and the ICC came at the tail end of that surprising era between the fall of the Berlin Wall and the fall of the Twin Towers.

AFTER 9/11: ROAD NOT TAKEN REDUX

If U.S. policy at the UN and in the second world of international security had been passive but permissive before 9/11, by 9/12 there was a sharp departure. Over the next three years, U.S. policy would prove to be active and constrictive, in the sense that the United States did not tolerate innovations or actions, that it did not drive – or sought not to. Moreover, the United States took a far more activist stance in pushing for both evolution and innovation in security policy, within the UN but more importantly outside of it.

For a brief moment after 9/11, it seemed like the two worlds of international security might be harmoniously united. Within days of the 9/11 attacks, France sponsored at the Security Council Resolution 1373 that not merely sharply condemned the attacks; it referred to them in terms that acknowledged an American right to self-defense in response, thus in effect pre-"approving" the U.S. war in Afghanistan.[17] As noted previously, NATO also offered its assistance, though that was declined, as did the UN Secretary-General, whose special envoy Lakhdar Brahimi did then work closely with the U.S. administration to craft the Bonn Accords, which provided the political framework for both international actions after the fall of the Taliban.

The moment was short-lived, broken by the clash of visions that was the diplomacy of the United States at the UN leading up to the start of the Iraq war. Here, it is difficult to isolate the impact of events from the fact of a U.S. administration ideologically predisposed to distrust international institutions. The effect, in any event, was that evolution and innovation in international security institutions after 9/11 were far more directly shaped by the United States than they had been pre-9/11, but as much outside the UN as within.

As documented by Patrick (Chapter 2), this innovation beyond the UN reflected both renewed interest on the part of the United States in the mechanisms of

---

[17] Under the UN Charter, of course, states do not require UNSC authorization to act in self-defense; they are merely required to inform the UN of the existence of an attack against them allowing them to act under the authority of Article 51, the so-called self-defense clause. However, because the Charter language is limited to attacks by states, it was arguably questionable whether Article 51 covered the issue of an attack on a state that was host to a terrorist organization that had conducted the attack in question. UNSC 1373 removed any doubt of the UN's attitude toward that position in the specific case of al Qaeda and Afghanistan, though the general issue remains mooted.

international security and distrust by the Bush administration of formal multilateral mechanisms. Thus we see such innovations beyond the UN as the creation of new "institutions" or arrangements as the Proliferation Security Initiative and the Container Security Initiative, initiated by the United States at the G8; the use of the OECD as a forum to initiate financial action against terrorist organizations (the Financial Action Task Force); and the drive to transform NATO into an operational capacity for counterterrorism (discussed earlier).

But it would be inaccurate to say that post–9/11 policy from the United States negated or neglected the UN; far from it. Indeed, in 2002 and 2003 the United States together with the UK and France (but against increasing resistance from Russia and particularly from a newly assertive China) drove ever-greater roles for the Security Council in the area of counterterrorism and nonproliferation. The distrust of multilateral institutions was evident even here, however, notably in the fact that in establishing the UN Counter-Terrorism Committee (CTC) as a subsidiary body of the Council, the United States insisted on the Secretariat for the CTC not falling within the UN Secretariat per se but being created as a stand-alone secretariat comprised of secondees from member states.

Since 9/11, and even more so (ironically) since the fall of Baghdad, the United States has also heavily shaped the evolution of UN and global peacekeeping: this, not primarily through the articulation of new doctrine, but simply through the initiation of new operations – especially in the Horn of Africa.

And indeed, as Jones, Pascual, and Stedman articulate,[18] for all of the anti-UN rhetoric of post–Iraq U.S. policy, the United States found itself by 2006–2008 deeply embedded within the UN and other multilateral security institutions, not only in "peripheral" cases but also in every major security crisis confronting it. This was true in Iran, where the IAEA was playing both an inspections and mediation role and where the UN Security Council plus Germany and the EU had taken on an important role in mediating between Iran and the United States; in Iraq, where the United States found itself belatedly pushing for a strong UN political role; in Sudan, albeit with important reservations as discussed previously; in Haiti, where the UN was in the lead on yet another crisis management initiative on that troubled island; and in Afghanistan, where in a major *volte-face* the United States actually placed 18,000 troops under the command of NATO in the International Security Assistance Force, at a stroke becoming the leading troop contributor to UN-mandated peace operations.

Different Worlds: The European Union, the African Union, and Asian Regionalism. The return of the United States to the role of prominent shaper of UN policy and operations was not the only reality of multilateral security after Baghdad, however. Indeed, the very assertiveness of U.S. policy was driving a second set of evolutions,

---

[18] In *Power and Responsibility: Building International Order in an Era of Transnational Threats.* (Washington, DC: Brookings, 2009).

namely, a movement to solidify regional structures that excluded the United States – particularly in Africa and Europe. In Europe, as Gowan and Batmanglich argue, governments have attempted to balance an organization explicitly intended to sustain U.S. involvement in the region (NATO) with an alternative that has the potential to reduce American influence (the EU). Both the outcome of this balancing act and the level of EU autonomy remain undecided, matters of deep political debate – this leads the authors to emphasize the extent to which individual governments may prefer to act through multiple organizational mechanisms rather than through a single framework. However, there can be no doubt that the EU has been transformed into a genuine and growing security actor since the Cold War.

Meanwhile the African Union (AU) had undergone its own important transformation. As Bah documents in Chapter 14, the transformation from the Organization for African Unity and the adoption of a Peace and Security Charter that contained important conceptual breaks from the past – notably in the form of a doctrine allowing AU intervention in member states' affairs when those members were failing to protect civilians – reflected African disillusionment with the evolution at the UN and beyond. In essence, African states had drawn the comparison between the UN Security Council's response in Africa and outside, and concluded that the continent could not trust external actors to manage their security. That this conclusion was actually slightly at odds with the UN's track record on peacekeeping since 1997 is moot; the fact is that the establishment of the AU as a more robust organization reflected a deepening lack of trust both in the response of the Security Council and indeed in its legitimacy.

Nor were these developments limited to Europe and Africa. Indeed, one of the most important developments in post–Baghdad international politics has been the evolution of Asian regionalism, in many cases specifically as a counterweight to U.S. policy. Here, however, we pause, for the question of the role of Asia in relationship to the United States, along with the evolving questions of European and African regionalism, forms the core of our conclusions – set out in Chapter 16.

CONCLUSION: THREE WORLDS OF MULTILATERALISM

Those conclusions describe the emergence of "three worlds" of multilateralism, or at least three pathways forward: a world of institutions driven by U.S. policy and politics; a world of institutions friendly to but not inclusive of the United States (especially in Europe and Africa); and a world of institutions specifically designed to contain or constrain the United States, both at the global level and in Asia.

Each of these pathways have this in common, though: U.S. policy remains the pivot around which these institutions are being formed or being shaped. In our last chapter, we explore the implications of various strands of U.S. policy on the continuing evolution of multilateral security institutions and, more importantly, on the prospects for cooperation for peace and security in an era of American

Introduction: "Two Worlds" of International Security 19

unpredictability. In particular, we explore the questions of whether we will see a return to unilateralism, the emergence of "democratic triumphalism," or the adoption of a cooperative framework for dealing with transnational threats.

In a cognate book, *Power and Responsibility: Building International Order in an Era of Transnational Threat*, Jones, Pascual, and Stedman make the case for the latter approach, for U.S. leadership in forging new cooperative mechanisms that can bring both U.S. power and the capacities of other major and rising powers to bear on tackling such threats as mass casualty terrorism, climate change, failed states, and biological insecurity. And as this volume was going to press, the recently elected Obama administration showed every sign of placing its emphasis on cooperative approaches – on diplomacy, on engagement with allies, on outreach to the emerging powers, and on what then-candidate Barack Obama called in his first major foreign policy speech, "a common security for a common humanity."

2

"The Mission Determines the Coalition": The United States and Multilateral Cooperation after 9/11

Stewart Patrick

A distinctive attribute of U.S. global engagement under President George W. Bush was skepticism of the capacity of standing international institutions and alliances to confront the main threats to national and global security, particularly terrorism, rogue states, and the proliferation of weapons of mass destruction (WMD). This attitude, apparent from the first days of the Bush administration, was accentuated by the terrorist attacks on the United States on September 11, 2001.

Although this sentiment was sometimes expressed through unilateral action, including decisions to act alone in pursuit of national objectives or to opt out of international agreements endorsed by the vast majority of other states, the more typical pattern was for the United States to turn to a more flexible form of multilateralism, by championing ad hoc and in some cases temporary coalitions of the willing that coalesced to address new issues. Such informal groupings of like-minded countries under American leadership – beyond avoiding the pathologies of formal multilateral organizations like the United Nations (UN) – promised to expand U.S. policy autonomy and freedom of action and provide greater control over the goals of collective action. The potential costs of this approach, in terms of squandered international legitimacy for U.S. actions and lost opportunities for sharing burdens – to say nothing of the eroded institutional foundations of world order – were only dimly appreciated, particularly during the first term of the Bush administration.

Of course, the United States has long had an ambivalent and selective attitude toward multilateral engagement, a function of its tremendous might, distinctive political culture, and constitutional separation of powers.[1] No American president, moreover, has ever placed the fate of the United States in the hands of universal collective security, nor has any administration defined multilateral cooperation as

---

[1] Stewart Patrick and Shepard Forman, eds., *Multilateralism and U.S. Foreign Policy: Ambivalent Engagement* (Boulder: Lynne Rienner, 2002).

being limited to action through the UN (or indeed any other standing organization like the North Atlantic Treaty Organization [NATO]). And yet from the presidency of Franklin D. Roosevelt to that of Bill Clinton, a recurrent feature of U.S. foreign policy was the promotion of international institutions as foundations of U.S. global leadership and a general (though hardly consistent) posture of self-restraint in the exercise of American power. From the moment it assumed office, however, the Bush administration signaled its desire to escape these historical constraints, portending a departure from fifty-five years of U.S. diplomacy dating from World War II.

The attacks of September 11, 2001, deepened these instincts by transforming the global threat environment and by stimulating a deeply nationalist reaction within American society that the Bush administration skillfully exploited. This chapter outlines the ensuing doctrinal shifts in U.S. national security policy; examines the implications of these shifts for U.S. efforts to prosecute the "global war on terrorism," deal with rogue regimes, and stem WMD proliferation; and assesses the impact of these dynamics on U.S. relations with NATO and the UN. It closes by offering an assessment of the relative merits and drawbacks of the Bush administration's preference for flexible coalitions in advancing U.S. foreign policy objectives and the larger goal of world order.

THE WELLSPRINGS OF AMERICAN AMBIVALENCE

When it comes to multilateral cooperation, and particularly engagement with the UN, the United States has long sent the world "mixed messages."[2] On the one hand, no country has done as much to promote one of the most profound global transformations of the past one hundred years: the proliferation of international institutions that today touch on virtually every aspect of world politics. In historical perspective, the U.S. turn to liberal internationalism during and after World War II (following an ill-fated effort a generation before under Woodrow Wilson) was unprecedented.[3] Never before had a globally dominant power chosen to organize its leadership and legitimate its power through consensual and mildly egalitarian frameworks that restricted, in some measure, its freedom of action.[4] On the other hand, few countries during that same time span have exhibited so much discomfort with the "movement to institutions" that America's own leadership inspired. This

---

[2] For an historical perspective, see Edward Luck, *Mixed Messages: American Politics and International Organization, 1919–1999* (New York: Century Foundation, 1999).

[3] Stewart Patrick, *The Best Laid Plans: The Origins of American Multilateralism and the Dawn of the Cold War* (Lanham, MD: Rowman and Littlefield, 2009).

[4] John Gerard Ruggie, "Multilateralism: The Anatomy of an Institution," in Ruggie, *Multilateralism Matters: The Theory and Praxis of an Institutional Form* (New York: Columbia University Press, 1993), pp. 3–47.

Stewart Patrick

dissonance arises from several factors, most notably from America's massive power, its "exceptionalist" political culture, and its unique constitutional structure.[5]

Power

All states naturally resist encroachments on their freedom of action, particularly in national security. Rule-based cooperation – based on the principles of equal treatment and self-restraint – is naturally attractive to smaller countries, because it promises to constrain and domesticate great powers and to provide the weak with diplomatic leverage lacking in conventional bilateral negotiations and frameworks. Great powers are more skeptical, having more unilateral and bilateral alternatives available. They can afford to shoulder the burdens and risks of going it alone, as well as impose their will on weaker states in unequal bilateral arrangements. Accordingly, the United States has long insisted on retaining freedom of action within international institutions.

During debate over the League of Nations, to cite an early example, Senate opponents of the draft League Covenant defended the U.S. liberty to act alone in defense of the Monroe Doctrine and refused to make any "automatic" commitment (under Article 10) to defend the security of other countries. As Senator Henry Cabot Lodge of Massachusetts explained in 1919,

> I want to keep America as she has been – not isolated, not prevent her from joining among other nations for these great purposes – but I wish her to be master of her fate.... I want her left in a position to do that work and not submit her to a vote of other nations with no recourse except to break a treaty she wishes to maintain. Let her go on in her beneficial career, and I want to see her stand as she has always stood, strong, alive, triumphant, free.[6]

Lodge's "reservations" were intended, in his words, "to release us from obligations which might not be kept, and to preserve rights which ought not to be infringed."[7]

The structural transformation accompanying the end of the Cold War, which inaugurated a "unipolar moment"[8] less fleeting than initially predicted, reinforced U.S. sensitivity to constraints. The vast concentration of power in U.S. hands was most palpable in the security arena, where by the year 2000 the United States

---

[5] For an extended discussion see "Multilateralism and Its Discontents: The Causes and Consequences of U.S. Ambivalence," in Stewart Patrick and Shepard Forman, eds., *Multilateralism and U.S. Foreign Policy: Ambivalent Engagement* (Boulder: Lynne Rienner, 2002), pp. 1–44.

[6] Cited in John Milton Cooper, Jr., *Breaking the Heart of the World: Woodrow Wilson and the Fight for the League of Nations* (Cambridge: Cambridge University Press, 2001).

[7] Similarly Senator (and former Secretary of State) Philander K. Knox believed that "America's general policy" should be "to regard with concern any threat of disturbance to world peace, but at the same time we should reserve complete liberty of action either independently or in conjunction with other powers in taking steps as we determine wise for preserving the peace." Cooper, *Breaking the Heart of the World*, p. 137.

[8] Charles Krauthammer, "The Unipolar Moment," *Foreign Affairs* 70, No. 1 (Winter 1990/Spring 1991).

was spending more on defense than was the rest of the world combined.[9] This asymmetric disposition of military capacity coexists uneasily with unchanged rules, enshrined in the UN Charter, governing the collective legitimization of armed force[10] – as well as with the formally egalitarian structure of the NATO collective defense pact. Moreover, American officials on both the right and the left maintain that this unchallenged power confers special responsibilities (and corresponding privileges) that are not shared by other states, even other permanent Security Council members. The United States, in this view, is the ultimate guarantor of global order, a benevolent hegemon or – to use Madeleine Albright's phrase, an "indispensable power." In fulfilling this custodial role, some argue, the nation cannot afford to be subjected to constraints binding on others. Such logic was invoked in the late 1990s to justify U.S. opposition to (among other things) the Rome Statute of the International Criminal Court and the Ottawa Convention banning landmines.

Political Culture

From the founding of the American republic, U.S. skepticism toward foreign "entanglements" has drawn sustenance from the nation's political culture, and particularly from the doctrine of American exceptionalism, which holds that the United States has a special place and destiny among nations.[11] An outward reflection of the country's Lockean liberal principles, expressed with the moral fervor of the nation's founding Protestant sectarianism, the exceptionalist tradition is a recurrent touchstone of American foreign policy. Although occasionally invoked (as by Wilson and Franklin Delano Roosevelt [FDR]) as an argument to remake the world in the U.S. image, it has frequently given ammunition to those who seek to preserve America's unique political values, domestic institutions, and constitutional traditions from external contamination and interference, and who insist that U.S. principles must not be compromised for the sake of a misguided international consensus.

Translated to the realm of international cooperation, American exceptionalism implies a vigorous defense of U.S. national sovereignty, conceived in terms not only of external freedom of action but also of domestic liberty. The emphasis is on protecting the U.S. Constitution from the growing reach of international law and restricting membership in any global body that could undermine democratic accountability.[12] Warren Harding raised such concerns in 1921, when he declared, "In the existing League of Nations, world-governing with super-powers, this republic

---

9 Larry Korb, "Force Is the Issue," *Govexec.com* (January 1, 2000), http://www.govexec.com/features/0100/0100s6.htm.

10 Ruth Wedgwood, "Unilateral Action in a Multilateral World," in Patrick and Forman, eds., *Multilateralism and U.S. Foreign Policy*, pp. 167–89.

11 The classic treatment remains Louis Hartz, *The Liberal Tradition in America*. See also Seymour Martin Lipset, *American Exceptionalism: A Double-Edged Sword*, new edition (New York: Norton, 1997).

12 Peter Spiro, "The New Sovereigntists," *Foreign Affairs* 79, No. 6 (November/December 2000).

will have no part."[13] Nearly eighty years later, Senator Jesse Helms (R-NC) echoed this theme in an extraordinary audience in New York before the UN Security Council, warning that "a United Nations that seeks to impose its presumed authority on the American people without their consent begs for confrontation and, I want to be candid with you, eventual withdrawal."[14]

The Separation of Powers

A third enduring source of U.S. ambivalence toward multilateral cooperation, particularly when it comes to formal international institutions and treaties, is the separation of powers enshrined in the country's constitution, which makes the legislative branch (in principle if not always practice) coequal with the executive branch in the shaping of U.S. foreign policy. From the Senate's failure to pass the Treaty of Versailles (including the League Covenant) to its rejection of the Comprehensive Test Ban Treaty eighty years later, one finds multiple instances in which Congress has exercised its veto prerogatives by declining to assume obligations favored by the White House. These dynamics are particularly common in highly charged partisan environments, when different parties control the two branches of government. Although the competition between executive and legislature often provides a creative tension, it can also complicate the U.S. commitment to credible multilateralism.

All three of these dynamics were on display during the 1990s, an era that began with high hopes – even euphoria – for multilateral cooperation after four decades of geopolitical and ideological competition between the United States and the Soviet Union. In the aftermath of the U.S.-led victory in the Gulf War, President George H. W. Bush articulated a vision of a "new world order," based on principles of collective security, the rule of law, democratic governance, and expanding trade.[15] His Democratic successor, Bill Clinton, likewise committed the United States to a path of "assertive multilateralism," in which alliances and international organizations would advance a new grand strategy, the "enlargement of the world's free community of market democracies."[16]

The dawn of multilateralism proved to be a false – or at least cloudy – one. The Clinton administration quickly discovered that implementing multilateralism was more difficult in practice than in theory, particularly when it came to the use of American military power. Following setbacks in Somalia and Bosnia, the administration faced a growing revolt from the Republican-led Congress and outside critics who charged it, in the words of Henry Kissinger, with "trying to submerge the

---

[13] Cited in Cooper, *Breaking the Heart of the World*, p. 395.

[14] Barbara Crossette, "Helms, in Visit to UN, Offers a Harsh Message," *New York Times*, January 21, 2000.

[15] Stanley R. Sloan, *The U.S. Role in a New World Order: Prospects for George Bush's Global Vision* (Washington, DC: Congressional Research Service, March 29, 1991).

[16] Douglas Brinkley, "The Clinton Doctrine," *Foreign Policy* 106 (Spring 1997) pp. 111–27.

The United States and Multilateral Cooperation after 9/11   25

national interest in multilateral ventures."[17] The administration quickly retreated to a more pragmatic internationalism, embodied in the phrase, "multilateral when we can, unilateral when we must." Following the Republican takeover of Congress in late 1994, the legislative branch opposed President Clinton's endorsement of a range of international treaty commitments, ranging from the Kyoto Protocol to combat global warming to the Comprehensive Test Ban Treaty.[18] Still, if the resulting U.S. posture was often feckless and episodic, the Clinton administration continued to see value in multilateral security institutions.

GEORGE W. BUSH: THE FIRST EIGHT MONTHS

The ascent of George W. Bush to the presidency in January 2001 sharpened this long-standing U.S. ambivalence toward multilateral cooperation into something resembling antipathy. The president's most influential foreign policy advisers, with the exception of Colin Powell, represented wings of the Republican Party skeptical of the value and sensitive to the constraints of standing international institutions and alliances. In contrast to the pragmatic internationalists who had dominated his father's administration, they were more apt to insist on the forthright and unapologetic use of the country's unmatched power in the service of American interests and values, heedless of the impact of unsettling longstanding institutional arrangements.

The new administration wasted no time in signaling a new course and tone, in a now-familiar litany of actions. In its first months in office, the White House abrogated the Anti-Ballistic Missile Treaty with Russia, "unsigned" the Rome Statute of the International Criminal Court, repudiated the Kyoto Protocol, blocked a verification protocol to the Biological Weapons Convention, opposed a draft UN convention to reduce illicit trafficking in small arms and light weapons, and reaffirmed the Senate's 1999 rejection of the Comprehensive Test Ban Treaty. Regardless of the merits of any particular case, Bush administration officials took to this task with a relish that signaled disdain for international institutions and constraints. This was not simply an assertion that unique power gave the United States unique interests, but also that there would be little compromise in the pursuit of those interests, even in return for legitimacy, to reach common ground with others.[19]

This was a significant departure in U.S. foreign policy. Since World War II, leaders of the two main U.S. political parties had often invoked the notion that the United States was somehow different among nations. And yet they had also sought to reassure partners that the United States would act alone or opt out of multilateral cooperation

---

[17] Henry Kissinger, "Foreign Policy is About the National Interest," *International Herald Tribune*, October 25, 1993.

[18] Eric Schmitt, "Senate Kills Test Ban Treaty in Crushing Loss for Clinton: Evokes Versailles Defeat," *New York Times*, October 14, 1999.

[19] Stewart Patrick, "Don't Fence Me In: The Perils of Going It Alone," *World Policy Journal* 18, No. 3 (Fall 2001), pp. 2–14.

only on an "exceptional" basis: that is, that there were limits to U.S. unilateralism. The United States had voluntarily accepted modest but real restraints on its national sovereignty and freedom of action within international institutions. This orientation required devoting significant time and energy to building diplomatic consensus, in return for the promise of greater international legitimacy and the prospect of real burden sharing.

This commitment to self-restraint appeared to diminish with the arrival of George W. Bush, whose administration chafed under the requirements of institutionalized multilateral cooperation. It was replaced by the robust pursuit of American primacy (a grand strategy that had been explicitly rejected during the tenure of the president's father[20]).

The New Approach Rested on Several Convictions

First, the administration insisted that *multilateralism must be a means to concrete foreign policy ends, rather than an end in itself.* During the preceding presidential campaign of 2000, the Bush camp had accused the Clinton administration of making a fetish of multilateral cooperation, or, in Condoleezza Rice's words, of holding "the belief that the support of many states – or even better, of institutions like the United Nations – is essential to the legitimate exercise of power."[21] The Bush administration promised a more discriminating approach that would assess proposed treaties and organizations on a hard-headed, case-by-case basis. And as Republican adviser Robert Zoellick added, "Every issue need not be dealt with multilaterally."[22]

Second, the new administration believed that many *standing international institutions, including the UN, were hopelessly dysfunctional, sclerotic, or obsolete.* By their very nature, they tended to diffuse responsibility and accountability and to encourage free-riding and buck-passing. Instead of focusing on concrete actions and results, such entities were preoccupied with the promulgation of high-sounding principles and norms divorced from reality (or incapable of being enforced), as well as with the generation of lowest-common-denominator decisions that diluted or departed from U.S. objectives. This was particularly true of universal bodies like the UN General Assembly or large groupings like the Commission on Human Rights, many of whose members did not appear to share a commitment to the principles on which the organizations were founded and, indeed, often tried to thwart their achievement. As

---

[20] The ascendancy under George W. Bush of advocates of primacy echoed the viewpoint expressed in an early draft of the U.S. Defense Planning Guidance for 1994–1999, leaked in March 1992. Drafted by Paul Wolfowitz and others, it recommended a vigorous effort to prevent the emergence of a new rival. Patrick E. Tyler, "U.S. Strategy Calls for Insuring No Rivals Develop," *New York Times* (March 8, 1992). Following an international outcry, the administration revised the document to give it a more multilateral thrust.

[21] Condoleezza Rice, "Campaign 2000: Promoting the National Interest," *Foreign Affairs* 79, No. 1 (January/February 2000), pp. 45–62.

[22] Robert Zoellick, "Campaign 2000 – A Republican Foreign Policy," *Foreign Affairs* 79, No. 1 (January/February 2000), pp. 63–78.

The United States and Multilateral Cooperation after 9/11

Robert Dole, the GOP candidate in 1996, complained, international organizations too often produced "a consensus that opposes America's interests or does not reflect American principles and ideals."[23]

Third, *the expanding reach of international law posed a growing threat to the domestic American sovereignty,* by undermining the supremacy of the Constitution and the democratic accountability of international organizations. The Bush administration took office alarmed at the expanding frontiers of international law and aware that many countries, particularly in the European Union (EU), were delegating powers to supranational institutions.[24] The administration made it clear that in the U.S. conception, the legitimacy of international institutions and of international law would continue to derive from domestic sources of political authority, not from the preferences of unaccountable international civil servants. To this end, it would resist the creation of any institutions (such as the International Criminal Court [ICC]) whose officials were given authority over member states.[25]

Fourth, growing asymmetries in military and technological capabilities between the United States and its traditional allies, as well as the transaction costs of multilateral alliance management, made the Bush administration *question the continued relevance of multilateral alliances, notably NATO, as a primary foundation for American national security policy.* Beyond criticizing the "war by committee" that the alliance had fought over Kosovo in 1999, Bush administration officials were dismissive of Europe's modest military spending, convinced that inadequate burden sharing undermined European claims to "decision sharing," and that accepting codetermination of alliance policy would undermine U.S. freedom without any appreciable benefit.

Fifth, the administration argued that *multilateralism comes in many forms and is most successful when it reflects a real convergence of interests and values.* Accordingly, rather than relying on standing alliances and formal institutions in a "one-size-fits-all" manner, the United States should *make greater use of flexible, ad hoc "coalitions of the willing"* that could be tailored to the specific challenge at hand. Such an "à la carte" approach would permit the United States to assemble individual countries for discrete tasks, on the basis of common principles and purposes.[26] Because such arrangements were selective, they could be restricted to like-minded countries with something to contribute, while excluding potential spoilers that did not share (and indeed hoped to subvert) collective objectives. Such exclusive coalitions promised prompt action, unlike large bodies that avoided hard decisions and took refuge in neutrality.

---

[23] Robert Dole, "Shaping America's Global Future," *Foreign Policy* No. 98 (Spring 1995), 29–43, p. 36.

[24] Jeremy Rabkin, "Is EU Policy Eroding the Sovereignty of Non Member States?", *Chicago Journal of International Law* 1, No. 2 (Fall 2000).

[25] Bartram Brown, "Unilateralism, Multilateralism and the International Criminal Court," in Patrick and Forman, *Multilateralism Matters,* pp. 323–44.

[26] The notion of "à la carte" multilateralism was advanced publicly for the first time by Richard Haass, director of policy planning under Secretary of State Colin Powell. Thom Shanker, "White House Says the U.S. Is Not a Loner, Just Choosy," *New York Times,* July 31, 2001. See also Andrew F. Cooper, "Stretching the Model of 'Coalitions of the Willing,'" CIGI working paper number 1, October 2005.

28 *Stewart Patrick*

Finally, beyond seeking new, more flexible forms of multilateral action, the new Bush administration was convinced that *unilateralism – or its threat – could in some circumstances be an essential catalyst for effective multilateral action.*[27] Given incentives toward institutional inertia, the only way to jump-start collective action might sometimes be a credible threat to go it alone if others bow out, a stance that Adam Garfinkle labels "uni-multilateralism." As he explains,

> In a unipolar world, the choice for the United States may come down to acting unilaterally in pursuit of its preferred goal, with fewer constraints but at considerable risk to itself; acting multilaterally, with the risk of getting constrained in exercise of power and achievement of ends; or threatening to act unilaterally to secure a multilateral outcome on its terms.[28]

Despite general agreement on the preceding points, one could detect two competing strains among the Bush administration's leading foreign policy voices. On the one hand were "neoconservatives," like Deputy Secretary of Defense Paul Wolfowitz and Richard Perle, the Chair of the Defense Policy Board, who believed that the United States should employ its overwhelming power to transform foreign societies in its own image, in the service of a worldwide democratic revolution. On the other were "assertive nationalists," including Vice President Dick Cheney and National Security Advisor Condoleezza Rice, resistant to entanglements in the internal affairs of other countries and particularly dismissive of nation-building exercises.[29]

These tendencies would compete for the first eight months of the Bush presidency, until 9/11 persuaded the White House that the neoconservatives were right: the security of the United States depended on U.S. willingness to use its might to transform the stagnant societies and failing states, particularly in the Muslim world, that had produced such evil. As an ideology of foreign policy, "neoconservatism" combined a moralizing belief in the special virtues and destiny of the United States with a resistance to any restraints on the use of U.S. power in realizing its global purposes. It was, in effect, Wilsonianism without international institutions. In embracing this ideology, the Bush administration transformed the United States from a status quo power into a revolutionary one.

THE IMPACT OF 9/11

In the absence of the terrorist attacks on the United States of September 11, 2001, it is conceivable that the Bush administration might have reverted gradually to a more traditional posture of ambivalence and selectivity toward multilateral cooperation. Instead, the catastrophic events of 9/11 accentuated the unilateralist thrust of its

[27] Charles Krauthammer, "The Unipolar Moment," *Foreign Affairs* (1990–1).
[28] Adam Garfinkle, "Alone in a Crowd," *The American Interest* 1, No. 3 (Spring 2006), pp. 132–40.
[29] Ivo H. Daalder and James M. Lindsay, *America Unbound: The Bush Revolution in Foreign Policy* (Washington, DC: Brookings Institution Press, 2003). The pragmatic internationalism advocated by Colin Powell's State Department could be considered a third vision.

foreign policy. Although the United States would occasionally turn to international institutions, and notably the UN, to achieve its national security objectives, it would brook little interference in the definition or pursuit of these goals.

The attacks reinforced the administration's skepticism of multilateral institutions in several ways. First, they redoubled the U.S. insistence on freedom of action by persuading the White House that it confronted a new era of catastrophic threats, in which other countries and international organizations could not be permitted to limit the use of America's awesome power. For the Bush administration, the rise of mass-casualty terrorism and the proliferation of WMD meant that massive dangers could arise with little or no warning, erasing comforts previously afforded by time and distance. In an age of transnational, networked threats, the United States could no longer place its faith in deterrence, tolerate time-consuming multilateral diplomacy, and accept the constraints of international legitimization. The emphasis must be on anticipation, speed, and flexibility. The fact that few of America's closest allies and partners shared this threat perception and its attendant obsession with terrorism and WMD complicated U.S. efforts to reach common ground on appropriate responses – with allies often favoring an approach based more on a model of law enforcement than on military action.

Second, the events of 9/11 aroused within the American body politic an outburst of nationalism reflecting what Walter Russell Mead calls the "Jacksonian" strain in U.S. political culture.[30] This is the tendency of America's largely inward-looking society to lash outward with "don't tread on me" ferocity in the aftermath of attack. In the dark days after the terrorist events, the Bush administration drew sustenance from – and skillfully exploited – the fear and grievous sense of injury of an American public united in a righteous quest for vengeance. The president, a religious and moralistic man, framed the "global war on terrorism" in Manichean terms as one pitting good versus evil, a formulation that resonated with broad swaths of American society while alienating many constituencies abroad. This framing helped erase the distinction (common in traditional Republican Party realism) between a foreign policy based on the sober pursuit of concrete interests and one based on the spread of American ideals. The resulting strategy envisioned the use of U.S. power in the service of universal values, *as defined and articulated by the United States.*

Third, besides emboldening U.S. insistence on freedom of action and deepening the ideological justifications for acting alone, the attacks of 9/11 effectively removed any legislative limits on the administration's conduct of its revolutionary foreign policy. In previous decades, the U.S. Congress had provided a cushion against any large deviations in U.S. policy toward multilateral institutions, ensuring that expressions of ambivalence and selectivity fell within a predictable range. After 9/11, the Republican-dominated legislature ceded the field to the president, abandoning its constitutional responsibilities of oversight. If America was truly "unbound"[31] in

---

[30] Walter Russell Mead, "The Jacksonian Tradition," *The National Interest* (Winter 1999/2000).
[31] Daalder and Lindsay, *America Unbound.*

30   *Stewart Patrick*

the Bush administration's first term, this was particularly true at the domestic level, as Congress gave the president a blank check and rubber-stamped the administration's major initiatives.

AVOIDING CARICATURE

Of the many epithets lobbed at the Bush administration, "unilateralist" has come closest to sticking. As a blanket indictment it is arguably unfair, however. Certainly, Washington assiduously resisted encroachments on its power after 9/11. But it also turned repeatedly to international partnerships in pursuit of the majority of its national security and foreign policy goals. The typical choice the administration confronted, in other words, was rarely between acting alone and acting with others, but between alternative forms of multilateral cooperation.

What was most problematic for champions of a UN-centered world order was the administration's apparent downgrading of standing organizations and formal international treaties and its greater reliance on ad hoc, flexible arrangements. The United States adopted a "horses for courses" approach to global challenges, mixing and matching among multilateral vehicles – some formal, some ad hoc; some global, some regional; some permanent, some transitory – to secure its goals. These frameworks ranged from the UN to NATO, the World Bank and International Monetary Fund, the African Union (in Darfur), the Economic Community of West African States (in Liberia), the G8, the Organization for Security and Cooperation in Europe, the Asia-Pacific Economic Cooperation forum, the "6 plus 2" framework for Afghanistan, the Six-Party talks on North Korea, the Financial Action Task Force, the "Quartet" in the Middle East, the Community of Democracies, and the Global Fund to Fight HIV/AIDS, Tuberculosis, and Malaria, among others. In this scheme, the UN became just one – and not necessarily the most important – arrow in Washington's foreign policy quiver.

Moreover, the United States approached the UN Security Council at key junctures to seek diplomatic support for its purposes. These included Resolution 1373, obliging member states to cut off terrorist financing; Bush's appeal to the UN on September 12, 2002, to enforce sixteen of its own resolutions on Iraq; Resolution 1441, of November 2002, offering Iraq "a final opportunity to comply with its disarmament obligations"; the pursuit of a second Iraq resolution in early 2003; Resolution 1483, in May 2003, lifting sanctions on Iraq; Resolution 1500 of August 2003, recognizing the Iraqi Governing Council and authorizing UN assistance for Iraqi elections; and Resolution 1540, designed to prevent WMD from falling into the hands of terrorists.[32]

And yet it was on several pivotal issues – including in declaring and prosecuting a "global war on terrorism" defined in Washington, in propounding a new doctrine

---

[32] Colin Powell, "A Strategy of Partnerships," *Foreign Affairs* 83, No. 1 (January/February 2004).

The United States and Multilateral Cooperation after 9/11   31

of preemption, and particularly in going to war in Iraq without an explicit Security Council mandate – that the U.S. penchant for unilateral action seemed most troubling.

DECLARING AND WAGING THE "GLOBAL WAR ON TERRORISM"

Two core foundations of America's Cold War leadership, beyond the military capacity to deter Soviet aggression against U.S. allies, had been the commitment of successive generations of U.S. administrations to a positive, broadly shared vision of world order and a generalized willingness to exercise restraint in the pursuit of U.S. national interests. The genius of America's containment policy had been to organize the country's free world leadership through consensual institutions, including the NATO alliance, the Bretton Woods Institutions, and the General Agreements on Tariffs and Trade (GATT). Despite periodic accusations of U.S. "unilateralism" and occasional fissures in the Atlantic alliance, the United States and its major Cold War partners possessed common threat perceptions, interests, and ideals.

This sense of common purpose, which had begun to crumble during the 1990s in the absence of a common enemy, was placed under further stress by the advent of George W. Bush to the presidency. But it was the U.S. response to 9/11, and particularly the White House's decision to pivot from Afghanistan to deposing Saddam Hussein, that marked a break point in the U.S. role in the world. The Bush administration's declaration of a "global war on terror" and its insistence on waging this struggle unencumbered by the requirements of multilateral consensus would shake the normative foundations of America's international legitimacy.

In the days immediately following 9/11, the new course of U.S. policy was temporarily obscured by the outpouring of global solidarity for the United States, as well as a number of U.S. actions that seemed to portend a more multilateral orientation. Washington worked to build a broad coalition to defeat the Taliban, to root al Qaeda out of Afghanistan, and to deal with the terrorist threat globally. The United States paid its outstanding arrears to the UN, took a more constructive approach to Organization for Economic Cooperation and Development (OECD) efforts to regulate offshore banking centers, worked within the UN to win broad support for resolutions designed to combat the terrorist threat, and committed itself to assist postconflict reconstruction and political stability in Afghanistan. Early press commentary remarked on this apparent U.S. return to multilateralism.[33]

On September 12, 2001, the UN Security Council met in emergency session and, invoking the UN Charter's inherent right of "individual or collective self-defense," passed Resolution 1368 authorizing "all necessary steps" against the perpetrators, organizers, and sponsors of these acts. The same day the North Atlantic Council

---

[33] William Drozdiak, "Crisis Forces Shift in Policy as Bush Assembles Coalition," *Washington Post*, September 17, 2001, p. A9.

invoked for the first time the collective defense provisions of Article 5 of the North Atlantic Treaty, promising material support for the United States. The administration returned to the Security Council to win Resolution 1373 of September 28, 2001, mandating that all member states take concrete steps to eliminate sources of terrorist financing, including providing regular reports on progress to a new UN Counter-Terrorism Committee (CTC).

Yet the Bush administration quickly made it apparent that Washington alone would define the nature of the new struggle and brook no interference in its prosecution. The president alarmed many allies by declaring a "global war on terrorism" – emphasizing the military dimensions of the struggle while downplaying its political, law enforcement, and socioeconomic components – and by painting it as a stark choice of good versus evil. As he told a joint session of Congress, "Either you are with us, or you are with the terrorists."[34]

Moreover, the broad antiterrorist coalition was less a genuinely multilateral undertaking – in which members accepted reciprocal obligations – than a classic "hub and spoke" arrangement, founded on bilateral deals between the United States and a large and heterogeneous group of countries, in which an American "sheriff" largely determined the actions of members of its "posse." From the administration's perspective, a flexible framework permitted the United States to deploy (others') assets in a manner that reflected immediate U.S. priorities and the perceived capabilities of its partners, rather than strain to reach consensus on a common strategy among numerous parties, or find its policy options constrained.[35]

Secretary of Defense Donald Rumsfeld captured this ethos in an interview with Larry King on December 5, 2001. As he explained, "Dozens and dozens of countries are helping with over-flight rights, with landing rights, with intelligence gathering, with law enforcement, with freezing bank accounts, with supplying troops in some cases and supplying aircraft and ships in other places." Asked whether it was critical that "the coalition hold" together, Rumsfeld tellingly responded "No."

> There is no coalition. There are multiple coalitions. . . . Countries do what they can do. Countries help in the way they want to help. . . . And that's the way it ought to work. I'll tell you why. The worst thing you can do is to allow a coalition to determine what your mission is. The mission has to be to root out the terrorists. It's the mission that determines the coalition.[36]

---

[34] The White House, "Address to a Joint Session of Congress and the American People," September 20, 2001.

[35] As Colin Powell reassured the Senate Foreign Relations Committee on October 25, 2001, "There are no arrangements within this coalition which in any way, shape, fashion or form constrain the President in the exercise of his constitutional responsibilities to defend the United States of America and to defend the people of the United States." "The Campaign against Terrorism," testimony to SFRC, http://www.state.gov/secretary/former/powell/remarks/2001/5751.htm.

[36] Secretary Rumsfeld interview with Larry King, CNN, December 5, 2001, http://www.defenselink.mil/transcripts/2001/t12062001_t1205sd.html.

The United States and Multilateral Cooperation after 9/11   33

As Colin Powell added several months later, the administration understood that the global war on terrorism would be prosecuted by "a fluid coalition" – a "coalition of coalitions that are constantly . . . shifting and changing as the needs shifted and changed."[37] The floating nature of this arrangement implied that reliance on standing multilateral organizations to fight the war on terrorism might be unwarranted, even counterproductive.

DOWNGRADING NATO

During the 1990s, a constant refrain among Atlanticists was that the NATO alliance must go "out of area or out of business," by expanding its membership and proving its relevance to post–Cold War security threats. The Alliance made progress on both fronts, spreading eastward even to the borders of Russia, assisting the stabilization of the Balkans following the wars of Yugoslavia's dissolution, and, most dramatically, intervening to stop Serb ethnic cleansing in Kosovo.

Despite NATO's invocation of Article 5 treaty obligations after 9/11, the Bush administration – recalling the cumbersome Kosovo arrangements, being skeptical of the value added of European military contributions, and reluctant to grant allies a fundamental say in its prosecution of the campaign – rebuffed any formal NATO role in toppling the Taliban and pursuing al Qaeda. The rapid triumph of technologically advanced U.S. troops and local Afghan allies appeared to validate this instinct. Subsequently, Washington rejected allied suggestions to create a countrywide multinational peacekeeping force, out of a general aversion for nation-building and a fear of complicating the pursuit of terrorists. The administration insisted on restricting the UN-mandated International Security Assistance Force (ISAF) to Kabul and its immediate environs.

It was not until September 2003 that Washington agreed to place ISAF under NATO and to permit its gradual expansion outside Kabul, including command of Provincial Reconstruction Teams involved in stability operations. From Washington's perspective, this enhanced NATO role remained a mixed blessing, requiring laborious negotiations with resource-strapped and casualty-averse allied governments that found it difficult to generate even modest forces, funds, and materiel; insisted on restrictive rules of engagement; and placed "national caveats" on the use of troops.[38]

American skepticism about NATO would only increase during the transatlantic crisis over Iraq, which made Washington doubt the Western alliance as an effective instrument of U.S. security policy. Although NATO would play a modest postwar role in training Iraqi security forces outside the country, the crisis suggested that the

---

[37] *Frontline* interview with Secretary of State Colin Powell, June 2, 2002, http://www.pbs.org/wgbh/pages/frontline/shows/campaign/interviews/powell.html.

[38] In one egregious instance, the Alliance spent several months trying to get Luxembourg to come up with several hundred thousand dollars to transport Turkish helicopters to Afghanistan.

United States would henceforth rely on like-minded coalitions for both war-fighting and postconflict stabilization. Rather than attempt to revitalize NATO, one senior State Department official predicted in early 2006 that the United States would seek to create a regular process for bringing informal groupings together and generating the forces required for unique contingencies. "We'd 'ad hoc' our way through coalitions of the willing. That's the future," he explained. "We are focusing on the enduring dynamics of coalition warfare."[39]

THE AXIS OF EVIL

On the evening of January 29, 2002, George W. Bush delivered his first State of the Union address, in which he identified Iraq, Iran, and North Korea as an "axis of evil" that had to be confronted: "By seeking weapons of mass destruction, these regimes pose a grave and gathering danger. They could provide these arms to terrorists, giving them the means to match their hatred. They could attack our allies or attempt to blackmail the United States."[40]

By early 2002 it was clear to outside observers that the administration was determined to remove Saddam Hussein from power in Iraq. In February the European Commissioner for External Relations, Christopher Patten, worried publicly that the United States was moving into "unilateralist overdrive."[41] Within the administration, debates erupted over whether even to pursue UN authorization before carrying out regime change in Iraq. On the one hand, there was Vice President Dick Cheney, who pointed to a decade of UN failure to enforce its own resolutions to ensure the verifiable disarmament of Iraq and kept up a steady drumbeat for war, with increasingly dire warnings about the degree to which Saddam had reconstituted WMD capability. On the other hand, there was Secretary of State Colin Powell, who advocated U.S. pursuit of consensus within the Security Council before taking any military action.

The crisis over Iraq came to the fore on September 12, 2002, when UN Secretary-General Kofi Annan and President Bush both spoke before the General Assembly. Annan, clearly speaking to the United States, implored member states that "choosing to follow or reject the multilateral path must not be a simple matter of convenience." Bush, for his part, threw down an ultimatum: "Will the United Nations serve the purpose of its founding, or will it become irrelevant? . . . The Security Council resolutions will be enforced . . . or action will be unavoidable."[42]

---

[39] Guy Dinmore, "U.S. Sees Coalitions of the Willing as Best Ally," *Financial Times*, January 4, 2006.

[40] It is noteworthy that Bush delivered his entire speech without mentioning the NATO alliance, even perfunctorily.

[41] Steven Erlanger, "Europe Seethes as the U.S. Flies Solo in World Affairs," *New York Times*, February 22, 2002.

[42] President Bush address to UN General Assembly, September 12, 2002.

DOCTRINAL INNOVATION: THE NATIONAL SECURITY STRATEGY OF 2002

The Bush administration codified a new post–9/11 approach to international security in September 2002, one year after the attacks, releasing its National Security Strategy of the United States (NSS). The two most distinctive innovations of this document, compared to previous installments, were an explicit enunciation of a right to preemption to forestall catastrophic threats and a defense of unilateralism in advancing U.S. national security. These twin themes were joined in a single sentence: "While the United States will constantly strive to enlist the support of the international community, we will not hesitate to act alone, if necessary, to exercise our right to self-defense by acting preemptively against such terrorists, to prevent them from doing harm against our people and our country."[43] The president had foreshadowed such arguments in June 2002, in a graduation speech to West Point cadets, when he argued that rogue states that could not be contained or deterred might have to be destroyed: "Our security will require all Americans to be forward looking and resolute, to be ready for preemptive action when necessary to defend our liberty and to defend our lives."[44]

Although the sections of the National Security Strategy (NSS) devoted to preemption and unilateralism constituted a small fraction of the entire document,[45] they quickly grabbed headlines around the world, just as intended. The fact that America's closest allies were not consulted in the drafting process – nor even provided advance copies of the document – reinforced the sense that U.S. national security policy was being driven entirely by internal U.S. dynamics, without much consideration as to how these changes would play internationally.

What was controversial about the NSS was less that it asserted a right to unilateral preemption in the face of imminent threats – something previous U.S. administrations had also claimed – but that it appeared to elevate this right to a doctrine,[46] at the expense of the traditional expedients of containment and deterrence, while expanding the definition of "imminence" to include threats that were emerging rather than fully realized. The administration was effectively contending that the magnitude of new security threats, and the difficulty in detecting them, rendered traditional security responses wholly inadequate. In an age of "shadowy" terrorist networks, rogue states, and proliferating WMD technology, in which attacks of unparalleled devastation could come with little warning from nonstate actors, the United States could no longer rely on the deterrent force of massive retaliation. It needed the

---

[43] The White House, *National Security Strategy of the United States of America* (September 2002).

[44] Norman Pohdoretz, "In Praise of the Bush Doctrine," *Commentary*, September 2002.

[45] The White House, *National Security Strategy of the United States of America*.

[46] James B. Steinberg, "Force and Legitimacy in the Post-9/11 Era: What Principles Should Guide the United States?" Paper prepared for Century Foundation/Center for American Progress conference on Power and Superpower, June 6, 2006, New York, p. 18.

flexibility to respond with dispatch, on its own if necessary, rather than wait until threats had become acute, by which time it might be too late to begin gathering a coalition or responding militarily.

There was much to be said for this diagnosis. The world *did* need new international norms defining circumstances and criteria for principled preemption.[47] But the administration's insistence on enunciating this doctrine, rather than attempting to build such an international consensus, raised fears that the United States was seeking the unbridled exercise of American power, further marginalizing the UN Security Council's authority to legitimate the use of force, as well as lowering the bar for armed action in a manner that could be exploited by others. To many member states – even close U.S. allies – the doctrine of preemption appeared an invitation to international anarchy.

There is widespread global agreement that use of force is legitimate when a threat is imminent. What was most novel and controversial about the administration's doctrine was its premise that the definition of "imminence" must be construed more broadly in an age of terrorism, rogue states, and WMD, becoming almost synonymous with "preventive" war. What was equally controversial abroad (though historically not within the United States itself) was the contention that the U.S. judgments about imminence, and any subsequent armed response, do not require prior ratification of the UN Security Council to be legitimate.

Faced with an international outcry, administration officials sought to reassure international audiences that the United States would use preemption only in rare circumstances – notably as a last resort, when the danger was grave, and when risks of inaction outweighed the dangers of war. National Security Advisor Condoleezza Rice outlined these criteria on October 1, 2002. Nevertheless, it would be left to the United States to determine the evidentiary criteria for preemptive action, as well as the ultimate choice to use it.[48]

THE UNITED STATES, THE UN, AND IRAQ

The showdown within the UN Security Council over Iraq would pit the United States (supported by Great Britain) against other council members, including Russia, France, and Germany. Washington was intent on bending the UN to its will; the latter, on obstructing the United States.[49] Among UN member states, the opponents of authorizing military action against Iraq were troubled by the implication of

---

[47] See speech by Richard Haass, "Sovereignty: Existing Rights, Evolving Responsibilities," Georgetown University, January 14, 2003.

[48] The White House, "Dr. Condoleezza Rice Discusses President's National Security Strategy," Waldorf Astoria Hotel, New York, October 1, 2002. Powell had previously stated, on September 6, 2002, that any such action "must be used with great care and judiciousness and with a clear understanding of the obligations that we have as a responsible member of the international community."

[49] Michael J. Glennon, "Why the Security Council Failed," *Foreign Affairs* 82, No. 3 (May/June 2003).

endorsing the American doctrine of preemption and at the same time alarmed at the explicit U.S. threat to act alone if necessary to remove Saddam Hussein from power. The apparent choice was between endorsing a doctrine that would undermine core charter principles or risking an abandonment of the UN by its most prominent member. During autumn 2002, one heard approving references among UN member states for a policy of "dual containment" – that is, of both Iraq and the United States. The quest for consensus was hobbled by very different perceptions of the nature and scope of the threat Iraq posed to international peace and security. To most members, there was no clear and present danger: sanctions were working, inspectors had found no unambiguous evidence of ongoing WMD programs, and deterrence, in the final analysis, remained valid.

Bush's address to the General Assembly was a rare and temporary victory for Powell over the vice president, who perceived the UN as a trap and warned against granting it legitimacy in the exercise of American power. In the short term, the gambit paid off. On November 8, 2002, the Security Council unanimously approved Resolution 1441, threatening unspecified "serious consequences" if the Iraqi government did not demonstrate that it had abandoned pursuit of WMD.

And yet the aggressive determination of the United States to employ its power alarmed even traditional allies and partners, some of which came to regard Washington (as much as terrorism) as a destabilizing global influence that had to be tamed. This was not lost on the Bush administration, which perceived much of the diplomacy in the run-up to the invasion of Iraq as designed less to ensure effective multilateral outcomes than to domesticate U.S. power. French Foreign Minister Dominique de Villepin reinforced this perception on January 20, 2003, by declaring, "Nothing would justify the use of force in Iraq." German Chancellor Gerhard Schroeder did likewise by stating soon afterward that Germany would oppose war even if the Security Council authorized it.

On February 5, 2003, Secretary of State Colin Powell presented to the Security Council evidence – since discredited – of Iraq's continued pursuit of WMD and links with al Qaeda. Despite uncertain prospects, Washington launched an intense, ill-fated diplomatic campaign to win support for a second resolution authorizing force against Iraq (in large part to placate British Prime Minister Tony Blair, who required one domestically). These efforts came to naught in early March 2003. In the absence of an explicit Security Council imprimatur, the United States and its coalition partners launched Operation Iraqi Freedom on March 19, 2003. The rapid fall of Hussein's regime three weeks later engendered a short-lived wave of American triumphalism.

It is intriguing to compare the policies pursued by George W. Bush with those adopted by his father in 1990–1991, when the latter sought an explicit Security Council mandate to go to war with Iraq. In their memoir, George H. W. Bush and his National Security Advisor Brent Scowcroft explain their rationale for seeking UN authorization: "We also believed that the United States should not go it alone, that a multilateral approach was better. . . . Building an international response led us immediately to the United Nations, which could provide a cloak of acceptability to our efforts and mobilize world opinion behind the principles we wished to project."[50]

One can contrast this with the response of White House spokesman Ari Fleischer on March 10, 2003, several days after it became clear that the Security Council would not authorize enforcement action against Saddam Hussein. The exchange began with a reporter's question: "You seem to be equating an ad hoc coalition that the United States has been able to form around one issue and one task with permanent bodies, like the UN and NATO, which have charters formed by treaties, have charters and structures." The reporter asked, "Does the president believe that international affairs can be conducted entirely through ad hoc bodies like the one he's putting [together]?" To which Fleischer responded, "The point I'm making here is that there are many ways to form international coalitions. The United Nations Security Council is but one of them."[51]

And yet it would be wrong to make too much of this contrast, for George H. W. Bush and Scowcroft also suggest that (like Bush 43) they were prepared to act outside the UN, if need be. As they describe it, "We would ask the Council to act only if we knew in advance we had the backing of most of the Arab bloc and we were fairly certain we had the necessary votes. If at any point it became clear we could not succeed, we would back away from a UN effort and cobble together an independent multinational effort built on friendly Arab and allied participation."[52]

THE AFTERMATH: NEGOTIATING A UN ROLE IN POSTWAR IRAQ

In the aftermath of the 2003 invasion of Iraq, the Bush administration was determined to marginalize the UN, in the interest of ensuring untrammeled U.S. control over political developments there and to avoid what administration officials presumed would be a "bloated, inefficient" UN peacekeeping operation.[53] The central locus of political authority during the postconflict transition phase (following the demise of the short-lived Office of Reconstruction and Humanitarian Assistance) would be the Coalition Provisional Authority (CPA), headed by Paul Bremer, who enjoyed the power of a Roman proconsul for the duration of the occupation.

At the same time, the Bush administration hoped to leverage the UN's specialized capacities in certain narrowly circumscribed areas, including refugees and reconstruction, and in providing political cover for potential contributors to the U.S.-led

---

[50] George Bush and Brent Scowcroft, A World Transformed (New York: Alfred A. Knopf, 1998), p. 491.

[51] White House, "Press Briefing by Ari Fleischer," March 10, 2003, http://www.whitehouse.gov/news/releases/2003/03/20030310-4.html#7.

[52] Cited in Edward Luck, "The U.S., International Organization, and the Quest for Legitimacy," in Patrick and Forman, Multilateralism and U.S. Foreign Policy, p. 59.

[53] Unidentified administration official, cited in Elizabeth Becker, "U.S. Plans to Run Iraq Itself," New York Times, March 25, 2003.

The United States and Multilateral Cooperation after 9/11   39

coalition. Washington thus welcomed Security Council Resolution 1483 of May 22, which called on the Secretary-General to appoint a special representative to Iraq, and it strongly supported UNSCR 1500, which established a UN Mission in Iraq (UNAMI). At the same time, the administration resisted transferring to the UN any significant authority over Iraq's political evolution.[54] Despite these obstacles, the UN Special Representative Sergio Vieira de Mello made headway in engaging leading Iraqi leaders, including Grand Ayatollah Sistani, on the country's political future. This era ended tragically on August 19, 2003, one of the darkest days in UN history, when de Mello and more than a dozen colleagues were killed in the bombing of the UN compound in Baghdad. The UN then temporarily withdrew from Iraq.

Over the next few years, the Bush administration would return to the UN on several occasions, typically grudgingly, in an effort to share some of the military and financial burden and obtain a modicum of international legitimacy it needed to succeed in Iraq. As initial U.S. plans for a gradual political transition in Iraq imploded in late 2003 in the face of a swelling Sunni insurgency and deepening sectarian violence, U.S. officials enlisted the aid of Algerian diplomat Lakhdar Brahimi, who skillfully negotiated with Sistani to accept the transfer of Iraqi sovereignty from the Coalition Provisional Authority (CPA) to an interim Iraqi government on June 30, 2004 (with elections to be delayed for several months). The Security Council ratified this decision on June 8, 2004. Resolution 1546 also authorized the U.S.-led multinational force to "take all necessary measures to contribute to the maintenance of security and stability in Iraq," in concurrence with the new interim government.[55] The UN would subsequently play a pivotal role in organizing Iraq's first post-Saddam national elections, in January 2005, as well as the preparations and holding of the October constitutional referendum and December parliamentary elections of that year. Over the next three years, the UN continued to soldier on, seeking to advance national dialogue and reconciliation in a deteriorating security environment.

THE UNITED STATES AND THE FUTURE OF THE UN

The collapse of Security Council diplomacy over Iraq during early 2003 had raised the question of whether the UN could serve as an effective collective security organization, capable of confronting the main threats of the twenty-first century – and whether the United States was willing to allow it to play such a role. Several years after the greatest crisis in UN history, the jury is still out. But at least three things are clear.

First, notwithstanding high-profile fallout over Iraq, the UN remains indispensable to the realization of U.S. foreign policy and national security objectives. The United States has returned to the UN and its affiliated agencies again and again to cooperate

---

[54] Larry Diamond, "What Went Wrong in Iraq," *Foreign Affairs* 83, No. 5 (September/October 2004), 34–56.
[55] S/Res/1546 (2004), http://www.un.org/Docs/sc/unsc_resolutions04.html.

with other nations on the major threats to global security, stability, and welfare. This includes, among other things, working with the UN's Counter-Terrorism Committee to eliminate the sources of terrorist financing; with the International Atomic Energy Agency (IAEA) to restrict the spread of fissile material; with the World Health Organization (WHO) to monitor and control potential pandemics like avian flu; with UN member states to craft a response to atrocities in Darfur; with the UN's Office on Drugs and Crime to attack illicit trafficking in drugs, goods, and people; and with the UN's new Peacebuilding Commission to stabilize postconflict and failed countries. Moreover, everyday technical cooperation between U.S. and UN officials, and with officials of other UN member states, is often very good.

Second, achieving a new partnership with the UN will require the United States to adopt an attitude quite different from the one that dominated the Bush years. Washington will need to give up its destructive habit of denying the world body support and resources while transforming it into – or allowing it to be treated as – a scapegoat for the inevitable failures of the international community,[56] even as it returns to the UN and its affiliated agencies to address pressing crises from Sudan to Lebanon to Iran. Washington must continue to demand accountability and performance, but it must also commit itself to sustained rather than episodic engagement and devote more vigorous attention to the requirements of multilateral diplomacy. In this regard, style will matter as much as substance. The United States will need to adopt consultation as a point of departure rather than as an afterthought and avoid the tendency to stake out maximalist positions without compromise.

Third, a more vigorous UN role in global security will also require a readiness from other UN member states to reach agreement on new norms to address today's most troubling threats. As Kofi Annan declared to the UN General Assembly (UNGA) on September 23, 2003,

> [I]t is not enough to denounce unilateralism, unless we also face up squarely to the concerns that make some states feel uniquely vulnerable, since it is those concerns that drive them to take unilateral action. We must show that these concerns can, and will be addressed effectively through collective action.

It was with this end in mind that Annan sponsored a High-level Panel on Threats, Challenges and Change to explore the institutional changes required for the UN to address the world's main security challenges. That process culminated at the UN High-level Event of September 2005, in which member states considered 101 recommendations put forward by the Secretary-General. Unfortunately (as described elsewhere in this volume) the ultimate summit outcome document was a far cry from early aspirations. Rather than take a strong leadership role on critical issues such as Security Council reform, the United States remained curiously disengaged until the

---

[56] Warren Hoge, "Official of UN Says Americans Undermine It with Criticism," *New York Times*, June 7, 2006.

last moment, when it insisted on multiple changes to a painstakingly negotiated text. One result was to empower "spoiler" countries in their effort to roll back reforms on issues from terrorism to human rights.

NONPROLIFERATION: OPTING OUT AND AD HOC ARRANGEMENTS

The Bush administration's preference for ad hoc security arrangements over universal institutions was nowhere more apparent than in its approach to weapons of mass destruction. Wary of protracted (and often futile) multilateral arms control negotiations and skeptical of existing nonproliferation regimes, it adopted more aggressive counterproliferation efforts undertaken through flexible coalitions.[57] This provoked anxiety among nonproliferation advocates and some other countries, because Washington sometimes treated these ad hoc and unilateral responses less as complements to existing treaty regimes – that is, intended to fill gaps in them – than as alternatives to them. The accompanying U.S. resistance to embracing disarmament and submitting itself to intrusive inspection regimes was particularly problematic.

These dynamics were most apparent in the nuclear field. Although the administration sought to strengthen export controls and restrictions on uranium enrichment and plutonium separation, it in practice undercut such efforts by seeking to reduce constraints on its own margin of maneuver. From the time it took office, for example, the administration sought to break the link within the Non-Proliferation Treaty (NPT) between nonproliferation and disarmament. This contributed to the collapse of the NPT review conference in May 2005, which occurred in part because of a dispute between the United States and other nuclear states, who wanted to focus on the threats posed by Iran and North Korea, and the nonnuclear states, which sought progress on the NPT's Article VI commitments to disarmament. The Bush administration's apparent disavowal of U.S. commitments made at the 2000 NPT review conference – which endorsed benchmarks toward the elimination of nuclear weapons – undermined the bargain at the heart of the NPT. The ragged regime frayed even further in 2006, when Washington welcomed India into the nuclear club.[58]

At the same time, the United States embraced an ad hoc approach, embodied most fully in the Proliferation Security Initiative (PSI). The brainchild of former Under Secretary of State for Arms Control and International Security John Bolton, PSI is an innovative partnership of like-minded countries designed to allow the United States and its allies to intercept illicit maritime and air shipments of nuclear, chemical, and biological weapons; and ballistic missiles and their related technologies. Although full details of the program remain classified, Secretary of State Condoleezza Rice

---

[57] The administration also continued working with supplier groups to strengthen export controls on dual use and missile technology, including the Missile Technology Control Regime and the Australia Group, which restricts the spread of chemical and biological weapons and know how.

[58] George Percovich, "The End of the Nonproliferation Regime?" *Current History* 105 (November 2006).

claimed in spring 2005 that the initiative had already resulted in eleven interdictions in the past nine months. The genius of PSI, to its champions, was that it permitted a nimble response to a growing menace. "Rather than rely on cumbersome treaty-based bureaucracies," Bolton noted, "the robust use of the sovereign authorities we and our allies possess can produce real results."[59]

Indeed, by 2007 senior Bush administration officials were touting PSI as a general model that might be extended to promote collective action in confronting other global threats. Unlike universal organizations, which permitted Lilliputians to gang up on Gulliver to thwart its purposes or exploit its resources, the PSI model would allow the United States to determine the agenda for collective action.[60] Washington would begin by issuing invitations to a small group of like-minded countries and drafting a set of principles that narrowly defined the mandate and scope of activities of the coalition. In U.S. eyes, this approach would strip the coalition of any bureaucratic capacity to reimagine itself later, for instance, by adopting a secretariat or a set of voting procedures that made the grouping something different than initially envisioned. Once a core group of critical nations had signed on to the narrow agenda and scope of activities, the United States would lead a global campaign to get others to join, on its own terms.[61] The Bush administration pursued a similar approach in several other issue areas, including the president's initiative to combat nuclear terrorism; the U.S.-led coalition response to avian flu; the Asia–Pacific partnership on climate change; and the Global Health Security Action Group (focused on biosecurity).

There was also a transformational agenda at work in the administration's calculations: as lean, functionally oriented multilateral groupings proliferated and proved their utility, states would repeatedly return to them, bypassing standing, bloated international organizations. As these frameworks attracted new members, they would gradually gain a legitimacy lacking in simple ad hoc coalitions of the willing. Over time, administration officials believed, states would increasingly come to rely on and invoke such frameworks to create legitimacy for their own actions – whether this involved boarding ships on the high seas (as in the case of PSI) or other such endeavors. Finally, in such a world of "overlapping and sometimes competitive international institutions" – or what Francis Fukuyama has termed "multi-multilateralism" – the United States would have new opportunities to engage in forum shopping, selecting the international framework or institution that responded best to the challenge at hand.[62]

[59] John Bolton, "An All-Out War on Proliferation," *Financial Times*, September 7, 2004.
[60] The coalition approach also reflected growing Bush administration frustration that many of the bodies that currently exist to legitimate international actions, such as the UN Security Council or IAEA, included countries (such as China and Russia) that lack democratic legitimacy in their own countries. Who are they, some Bush administration officials wondered, to sit in judgment on the legitimacy of U.S. actions? Personal communication with U.S. officials, late 2006.
[61] Scenario based on interviews with Bush administration officials, early 2007.
[62] Francis Fukuyama, "The Paradox of International Action," *The American Interest* 1, No. 3 (Spring 2006), p. 10.

STRIKING A JUDICIOUS BALANCE AMONG FORMS OF MULTILATERALISM

In an edited volume produced by the Center on International Cooperation in early 2002, I argued that the ambivalent and selective attitude of the United States toward multilateral cooperation carried potentially significant costs and risks for the United States. Among other negative consequences, I predicted, it could serve to thwart the pursuit of coherent and effective policies toward particular global problems, weaken multilateral institutions critical to U.S. national interests, slow the spread of useful international norms and regimes, undercut the credibility of the United States to lead on certain topics, hinder the U.S. ability to mobilize the support of other countries, and diminish the reputation of the United States as an enlightened world leader.[63] The overall record of the Bush administration provided ample evidence of the costs and limitations of going it alone, on issues ranging from terrorism to Iraq, climate change to nonproliferation.

In responding to terrorism and other transnational problems that define our global age, the United States has little choice but to combine its own efforts with those of other countries and international organizations. The challenge for Washington going forward will be to strike a more judicious balance between reliance on ad hoc arrangements and formal institutions in the pursuit of its national interests. Coalitions of the willing do bring distinct advantages, including flexibility, agility, and exclusivity. It may make sense to turn to them to meet discrete contingencies when no standing international framework exists; when permanent institutions are paralyzed by internal divisions; when consensual, egalitarian norms threaten the pursuit of vital U.S. interests or values; and when standard decision-making procedures or bureaucratic inertia prevents prompt decisions and rapid responses. By contrast, standing institutions can offer advantages when there is no time or will to assume the delays and transaction costs implied with creating a new coalition out of whole cloth, when the challenge at hand requires specialized technical expertise that is available only in permanent organizations, when the challenge is an enduring one that is likely to outlive the short time-horizon and half-life of any coalition and to imply heavy burden-sharing over a protracted period, and where the requirements of international or domestic legitimacy mandate the use of formal frameworks to give political cover to wavering states.[64]

In sum, it would be a mistake for the architects of U.S. foreign policy to ignore the standing capacity, legitimacy, and legal status of formal multilateral organizations or to imagine that these can somehow be reproduced through ad hoc arrangements. By themselves, coalitions provide a thin reed for the pursuit of U.S. foreign policy goals, much less a foundation for global order. As James Traub has written, "If everybody

---

[63] Stewart Patrick, *Multilateralism and Its Discontents*, pp. 22–25.

[64] "Pragmatic Multilateralism: Strategies for Engagement in an Age of Interdependence," Final Report of Council on Foreign Relations Term Member Roundtable, chaired by Suzanne Nossel (2002).

accepts the constraints of multilateral bodies but the United States insists on playing by its own ever-shifting sets of rules, then the 'international order' is a will-o'-the-wisp. Multilateralism cannot simply mean 'acting with others'; it must also mean 'acting through rule-based institutions.'"[65] The challenge for the United States is to ensure that its coalitions reinforce – rather than undermine – the institutions and alliances that it needs over the long haul.

[65] James Traub, *The Best of Intentions: Kofi Annan and the UN in the Era of American World Power* (New York: Farrar, Strauss and Giroux, 2006), pp. 403–4.

3

UN Transformation in an Era of Soft Balancing

Stephen John Stedman*

From 2003 to 2006 Secretary-General Kofi Annan pursued the most ambitious overhaul of the United Nations since its inception. This chapter is written from the perspective of the team working with Kofi Annan on the reform agenda and reflects on the issues faced and choices made. In reviewing this experience, the chapter seeks to inform future choices on substance, politics, management and process that must be addressed in future reform efforts.

The 'Kofi Annan agenda' included:

- a redefinition of collective security to bridge the security–development divide;
- policy recommendations to strengthen existing security regimes (e.g. non-proliferation and disarmament) and to explore new regimes (e.g. on biotechnology);
- the creation of new intergovernmental organs on peacebuilding and human rights;
- expansion and reform of the Security Council;
- new norms to govern the use of force by member states and the Security Council;
- a new norm, the responsibility to protect, to legalize humanitarian intervention;
- a definition of terrorism and the first UN strategy for counterterrorism;
- new Secretariat offices for peacebuilding, conflict mediation and counterterrorism;
- new member state commitments of resources to fight poverty and deadly infectious diseases;

---

* This article first appeared in *International Affairs* (London), volume 83, number 5, September 2007. The author and editors of this volume wish to thank *International Affairs* for permission to reproduce it here. The original article is a revised text of a public lecture given at the London School of Economics and Political Science, London, on March 1, 2007.

Stephen John Stedman

- a new policy committee for the Secretary-General to improve the quality of executive decision-making;
- a thorough overhaul of UN budgeting, management and personnel rules.[1]

Some UN watchers, especially in New York, have criticized this effort as too ambitious, too divisive and fundamentally unnecessary.[2] They argue that the time for such an effort was not propitious; that some of the recommendations, especially regarding Security Council expansion, were misguided; and that the Secretary General was incorrect to take the lead in such a campaign, as prior experience shows that change at the UN usually comes when it is driven by member states.

To be sure, the effort *was* ambitious; the politics *were* divisive; and the membership *was* and still *is* polarized. Two intertwined crises, however, made it imperative to try. First, the Secretary-General feared that in the aftermath of the Security Council's refusal to authorize the US-led invasion of Iraq in March 2003, and in the shadow of the Bush administration's National Security Strategy that embraced preventive war and American primacy, the United States would walk away from the United Nations.[3] This is as close to an existential crisis as one gets in an international organization, as without U.S. leadership, engagement and support, the UN is a hollow shell. Second, the terrorist attacks of 9/11 revealed that the basic precepts of traditional collective security were out of touch with the threats and challenges of the twenty-first century. Either the UN would change itself fundamentally to address new threats and challenges, or it would be irrelevant.

The Secretary-General felt that in order to persuade the United States to re-engage with the UN, a credible case had to be made to build UN capacity to address real and pressing global threats. As for whether the Secretary-General erred in leading the charge, the question was whether there was an alternative. The most powerful member state was alienated and would not lead. The other member states were divided; no state or coalition sought to lead. The presidents of the General Assembly during that time, Jean Ping and Jan Eliasson, drove the negotiations at key points, yet they were not in a position to lead the international community. Meanwhile, as late as the autumn of 2003 there was a sense of urgency among member states that some kind of reckoning was due. When Kofi Annan created the High-level Panel on Threats, Challenges and Change (HLP), the first reaction of many member states

---

[1] The agenda was shaped by the Report of the Secretary-General's High-level Panel on Threats, Challenges, and Change, *A more secure world: our shared responsibility* (New York: United Nations, 2003) and revised in Kofi A. Annan, *In larger freedom: towards development, security and human rights for all* (New York: United Nations, 2005).

[2] See e.g. Edward C. Luck, 'How not to reform the United Nations', *Global Governance* 11: 4, Oct.–Dec. 2005, pp. 407–14; Thomas Weiss, 'The UN post-Kofi', paper presented at the annual meeting of the International Studies Association, San Diego, California, 22 March 2006; Mats Berdal, 'The UN's unnecessary crisis', *Survival* 47: 3, Autumn 2005, pp. 7–32.

[3] For a discussion of the background to the Secretary General's decision to initiate the transformation effort, see James Traub, *Best Intentions: Kofi Annan and the UN in the Era of American World Power* (New York: Farrar, Straus & Giroux, 2006).

was relief and support. Twenty-nine countries, from every continent, contributed financially to underwrite the Panel's work.

GLOBALIZATION AND COLLECTIVE SECURITY

Globalization both necessitates and complicates creating a new vision of collective security to underpin UN reform. On the one hand globalization creates interdependencies, some powerfully obvious, others of which we are only dimly aware. At the same time, globalization heightens our consciousness of inequalities, double standards and different ways of life. For all of our interdependence, globalization can also make us aware that in fundamental ways we live on different planets.

One must address this paradox to breathe life into a traditional concept like collective security. The idea itself is premised on a shared threat perception. In 1945, states forged the UN in response to the common threat of international aggression by other states and to the conditions which underpinned this threat: economic insecurity, beggar-thy-neighbour trading policies, ultra-nationalism and human rights violations. To update perceptions of 'shared threats', the High-level Panel began its work in 2003 by asking a simple question in every part of the globe, of governments and civil society organizations alike: 'What are the most salient threats to your security?' Depending on power, privilege and region, people articulated a world of very different threats: HIV/AIDS, malaria and deadly poverty in Africa; crime, economic crisis and lack of confidence in democracy in Latin America; catastrophic terrorism in the United States; and so on.

For any UN reform effort, one of the first critical choices will be how to act on these threats and the differing worlds they reflect. Do we prioritize among the threats? Do we simply say that some threats may be economic or social, but not threats to security? Do we acknowledge a world with differential threats, and seek to accommodate such diversity? The High-level Panel chose this last option, and defined threats to security as events or processes that lead to large-scale death or diminishment of life chances, and that undermine states as the basic unit in the international system.[4] It identified the following as threats to international security: poverty, deadly infectious disease, environmental degradation; civil war and violence within states; conflict and violence between states; nuclear, chemical and biological weapons; terrorism; and transnational organized crime.

The transnational nature of these threats underpins the case for a new understanding on collective security. First, all of these threats defy unilateral solutions and no state can defend against them without sustained, international cooperation. Second, these threats are probably more interconnected than many governments and people believe; and if this is so, what threatens humans in faraway countries and regions also threatens us. Third, even if one does not believe that these threats

---

4 High-level Panel, *A more secure world*, p. 23.

48   *Stephen John Stedman*

are interconnected (and with some, the empirical jury is still out), nations should still cooperate with others on 'their' threats in order to gain their cooperation in addressing what threatens them.

SECURITY COUNCIL REFORM

The Secretary-General was criticized widely by UN watchers for including Security Council expansion in the agenda for change. Had the High-level Panel and the Secretary-General ignored the issue, they would have felt the wrath of some important member states, such as India, Germany, Japan and Brazil (the G4). Including Security Council expansion as part of the transformation programme, however, made it highly likely that those same countries would focus on that issue to the detriment of other reforms. Complicating matters further, a coalition of mid-level powers arose against the G4, holding the whole reform agenda hostage to this single issue.

The arguments for and against Council expansion are straightforward. Supporters argue that the Council should accommodate the new rising power of India, an economically vibrant democracy of over a billion people; Germany and Japan, global economic powers that make great financial contributions to the functioning of the United Nations; and Brazil and South Africa, rising powers from regions not represented on the Council. An expanded Council with these states playing a greater role would bring more resources to the organization and provide greater legitimacy to the Council and therefore prompt greater compliance with its decisions. Opponents point out that it is extremely difficult to get the Council to take decisions under current circumstances, and that expanding the membership from 15 to 21 or 24 members would more likely produce paralysis than 'prompt and effective action' – the Council's mandate under the Charter.

The opponents of the Council's expansion ignore the possibility that excluding these powerful countries would produce a different kind of paralysis. These countries are almost always consulted on key issues, but at present they do not have the responsibility that comes with power. Moreover, the single most important determinant of the Council's effectiveness is not its size, but the *sustained* attention, investment and leadership of the United States in the diplomacy necessary to make the Council work. Given a commitment by the United States to make the Council work better, the addition of Germany, Japan, India, Brazil and South Africa – all democracies – could increase US leverage in getting the Council to act.

Regardless of the pros and cons, the attempt at Security Council expansion failed. Japan, Germany, India and Brazil aspired to permanent membership, and expansion of the permanent membership of the Council is a zero-sum game. For each country that gains, another loses (Germany v. Italy, Japan v. Korea, Brazil v. Mexico, South Africa v. Nigeria and Egypt, India v. Pakistan). Moreover, China let it be known that it had serious problems with Japan becoming a permanent member, just as it privately let it be known that it would not countenance India as a permanent member. German aspirations split the EU, as many European countries would prefer an EU seat eventually. The UK and France supported German aspirations, perhaps as a way of putting off future demands that they give up their seats for a united EU seat. The Bush administration was never going to accept a German seat, as its memories of Germany's tenure in 2002–2004 were not fond ones. The Bush administration did want Japan to have a permanent seat, but had no policy that could make that happen.

The High-level Panel proposed a new kind of seat: longer-term, renewable through re-election, and open to a small set of states which had to be among their region's top contributors to the UN financially or militarily. As Kofi Annan's special adviser on follow-up to the HLP, I argued with the G4 (Japan, Germany, India and Brazil) that they did not have the votes to achieve permanent membership, and that this new kind of seat would at a minimum give them greater influence and continuity on the Council, and might even provide them with de facto permanent membership. Moreover, these new seats would have greater legitimacy than that enjoyed by the P5, because they were earned through contributions to the organization and through election.

But as long as the G4 believed that they could attain their top preference, they were not willing to consider a second-best that was attainable and much better than the status quo. On this they blundered terribly, for they could have achieved this option on extremely favourable terms. The problem was that in the bargaining between the G4 and the Uniting for Consensus Group (those who opposed expansion in the permanent members, led by Italy and Pakistan), there was only one moment of possible compromise – when the G4's prospects for getting permanent seats, through a two-thirds election in the General Assembly, looked promising in March 2005. The Uniting for Consensus Group proposed in writing a willingness to negotiate over the length of tenure of renewable seats, and the proper qualifications for candidacy to such seats. This made the G4 overconfident that they had the votes for permanent membership; in their estimation, the Uniting for Consensus Group was running scared.

But G4 overconfidence was out of order. The United States had no policy on expansion and the Secretary-General did not take a stand. Only a few in the Secretariat were advising the G4 to negotiate. They did not, and when it dawned on Beijing that Japan might actually get permanent membership, China panicked and mobilized a heavy-handed public campaign against a Japanese seat. One can trace the decline in G4 fortunes to that moment. It took several months for the G4 to realize that they did not have the votes, at which point Uniting for Consensus had no interest in reviving its earlier offer.

RESULTS, 2003–2006

What was accomplished in trying to bring the United Nations up to date? More than is commonly realized, yet far less than could actually have been attained. Here is the agenda described above. Text in italic denotes where decisions were actually taken, definitions endorsed and institutions created:[5]

- a redefinition of collective security that attempted to bridge the security–development divide;
- policy recommendations to strengthen existing security regimes, for example in non-proliferation and disarmament, and *recommendations to explore new regimes, for example to address safety of biotechnology*;
- the creation of new intergovernmental organs to address peacebuilding and human rights;
- expansion of the Security Council;
- new norms to govern the use of force by member states and the Security Council;
- a new norm to legalize humanitarian intervention;
- a definition of terrorism and, for the first time, a United Nations strategy for counterterrorism;
- new Secretariat offices to address peacebuilding, mediation support and counterterrorism;
- new member state commitments of resources to fight poverty and deadly infectious diseases;
- a new policy committee for the Secretary-General, to improve the quality of executive decision-making;
- a thorough overhaul of UN budgeting, management and personnel rules.

The shortfalls reflect paralysis among the members on key issues. There is not a single word in the 2005 summit outcome document on disarmament and non-proliferation; member states refused even to reaffirm existing obligations under international treaties. Security Council expansion stalled because of the continuing conflict between those countries that seek permanent membership and those that oppose expansion of the numbers of permanent members in the Council. Although member states endorsed the need for a common UN strategy of counterterrorism (and subsequently adopted one in September 2006),[6] they once again could not agree on a definition of terrorism. Although member states agreed on the need for budget and management reform, their attempt to negotiate it grew increasingly polarized in 2006, and ultimately failed.

Member states created new intergovernmental organs – the Peacebuilding Commission and Human Rights Council – but compromises in the negotiation process diluted these bodies' potential efficacy. If there were a modicum of trust and good faith among the member states, such dilutions might not handicap the institutions.

---

[5] Most of the decisions are captured in what was known as the summit 'outcome document': General Assembly Resolution 60/1, 2005 World Summit Outcome.

[6] General Assembly Resolution 60/288, The United Nations Counterterrorism Strategy.

UN Transformation in an Era of Soft Balancing

But both institutions continue to feel the after-effects of the polarization of 2006 and, to put it charitably, are underachieving.

Finally, the General Assembly endorsed what is known as the responsibility to protect, the first time it has acknowledged that sovereignty is not sacrosanct and that how a nation treats its own population is not simply 'an internal matter'. At the same time, continued inaction on Darfur breeds international cynicism as the organization does not live up to its norms, indeed patently lacks the capacity to do so.

And what of showing the relevance of the organization to the United States? The work of the Secretary-General's High-level Panel on Threats, Challenges and Change was instrumental in setting the agenda and shaping the conclusions of the Gingrich–Mitchell Panel on U.S.–UN reform.[7] That bipartisan panel's message that the UN was a useful tool for American foreign policy, and that it needed to be strengthened, helped to turn back a rising tide in Congress and in the right-wing media that sought to delegitimize the UN as an institution in the wake of the 'oil for food' scandal.

Given how quickly the scandal sank in the media once the Volcker Commission published its final conclusions, it may be difficult to remember the atmosphere in the autumn of 2004, when the High-level Panel issued its report. At the beginning of December there were calls by several U.S. newspapers and members of Congress for Kofi Annan to resign. For the next two weeks, the Bush administration made no statement in support of the Secretary-General. When the Secretary-General visited Washington that month to give a speech on the HLP report, he asked for a meeting with President Bush and was refused. Instead, the Secretary General met with Condoleezza Rice, who was both Secretary of State designate and National Security Advisor.

Perhaps the strongest case for the importance of the UN to the U.S. came in that meeting between Kofi Annan and Condoleezza Rice. The UN Secretariat crafted the agenda of the meeting to highlight the areas where the UN was playing a useful role in furthering U.S. foreign policy goals. The meeting focused on:

- Afghanistan, where the UN had mediated the Bonn process and created the framework under which Hamid Karzai was able to create a government that unified disparate anti-Taleban factions; where the UN had played an instrumental role in helping to produce the constitution and a popular consultative process to legitimize the constitution, and had organized the national elections; and where the UN continued to shepherd political negotiations through two of their best mediators, Lakhdar Brahimi and Jean Arnault;
- Iraq, where the UN was preparing to carry out the 2005 national elections, and where Brahimi had, at the request of the Bush administration, generated

---

7 Report of the Task Force on the United Nations, *American Interests and UN reform* (Washington DC: United States Institute of Peace, 2005).

support for the elections with Grand Ayatollah Sayyed Ali al-Sistani, and had quietly tried to bring various insurgents into political negotiations;

- Lebanon, where the UN was responsible for implementation of Security Council Resolution 1559, charged with getting Syria to withdraw from the country;
- the Middle East peace process, at that time paralysed, but in which the UN was one of the Quartet, with one of its most respected diplomats, Terje Roed-Larsen, stepping down as the UN's special representative;
- Sudan, where the UN was to put in more than 12,000 peacekeepers to implement the North–South peace agreement, mediated in part by Republican Senator John Danforth, and much supported by the Bush administration;
- Darfur, where Kofi Annan had been a vocal proponent of a robust reaction to stop the killings and atrocities;
- Liberia, a country in Africa with important cultural and historical ties to the United States, where the UN had 17,000 peacekeepers and was preparing the country for new elections to replace Charles Taylor;
- Haiti, where the UN had more than 6,000 peacekeepers, once again trying to bring some stability to that troubled island close to the United States.

That meeting helped restart the Bush administration's engagement in UN affairs. Parts of the bureaucracy proved very supportive, but there was still a void in top-level political engagement. The administration's ambassador to the UN, John Danforth, resigned in early 2005. John Bolton was nominated in March, but his confirmation process was long and bruising, and he was finally appointed without confirmation in August 2005, in the last four weeks of negotiation before the World Summit in September.

In Bolton's absence, the U.S. mission was led by Anne Patterson, who worked hard on the reforms. The State Department engaged on recommendations concerning counterterrorism and peacebuilding, but not on issues of non- proliferation and disarmament. Discussions on recommendations concerning rules governing the use of force revealed a set of American red lines that could not be crossed. Recommendations on the responsibility to protect garnered support at the State Department, the National Security Council and Capitol Hill, but not at the Department of Defense.

When Bolton arrived, all of this work was shoved aside and previous understandings were off the table. The reform package still had supporters in the State Department and the NSC, but they had to cede much of the negotiation to Bolton, who pursued a strategy of 'harm minimization'. Viewing conference diplomacy as a threat to U.S. bargaining positions in a host of different fora, he set out to reach a short, vague, non-committal, anodyne outcome that would not constrain or put obligations on the United States in any way.

There is much to criticize about how Bolton did his job. One of the unfair criticisms was that he forced a line-by-line negotiation of the outcome document (a draft that ran to over 40 pages). At some point, such a negotiation was going to have to take place; there was too much that was controversial and consequential in the document. It is true that many of his early brackets (for example, deleting every single reference to the Millennium Development Goals and global governance; walking back from language on rights of peoples to self-determination that the U.S. government had accepted in other fora; and deleting every reference to disarmament) seemed designed to inflame the negotiations and raised doubts about U.S. sincerity at a time when the administration professed to want a constructive outcome. It is also true that in the negotiations he seemed unaware that the U.S. government had publicly supported a Peacebuilding Commission, and certainly ignored advice on details that would make the PBC a stronger or weaker body.

Bolton also refused to work with allies and members of the Secretariat who had engaged in a two-year process of developing the reform recommendations, with cooperation from some of the United States's closest allies, and with the Secretariat. His three weeks of negotiating the summit were punctuated with frequent asides about the illegitimacy of the Secretariat having a voice in any of the proceedings. This would not have been too harmful to the process had Bolton had a good working relationship with the ambassadors of those countries and groups that were active in the reform (the UK, France, the EU, the Nordic countries, and many of the African and Latin American countries). But they too found that Bolton had little interest in crafting common strategy for the negotiations, and many understandings worked out with the US mission over the course of 2005 fell apart.

That in the end there was a summit outcome document at all was a small miracle. The story has now been told and can be recapitulated briefly. The World Summit was to begin on the morning of 14 September, with more than 175 heads of state in attendance. By the evening of Monday, 12 September, the negotiations had run their course and the outcome document still had over 160 brackets in the text. With permission from Jean Ping, then General Assembly president in his last two days in office, and with strong encouragement from Kofi Annan, a small group from the Secretariat worked throughout the night playing Solomon – in essence removing brackets or making compromises on proposed language – in order to give Jean Ping a clean document that he could propose to the membership on a take it or leave it basis. On the morning of 13 September, Bolton learned what was happening and tried to stop it, only to be overruled by Secretary of State Rice, who had been briefed by the Secretary-General on the text. At 1 p.m. the text was presented to the General Assembly, with overwhelming support from the membership. At 4 p.m. it was accepted by acclamation and consensus. In the end there was a deal in spite of John Bolton.

Left to their own devices, the member states would not have reached an agreement in September 2005. The Secretariat, well placed to see possible compromises, was backed into a process of circumventing member states. This produced more hostility and suspicion than gratitude, as ambassadors and their staff pored over the outcome document looking for signs of imbalance, partiality and favouritism. This bred distrust among many member states and between the members and the Secretariat. The job of picking up the pieces in this poisoned environment and implementing the pledges and commitments in the outcome document fell largely on the shoulders of Jan Eliasson, Jean Ping's successor.

EVALUATING MIXED RESULTS

On the one hand, the three-year effort fell short of what was proposed and what was expected. On the other hand, it achieved much more than the media reported, because they were primed for total failure and were unaware of the last-minute rescue.

To the question why the effort did not yield greater results, the best answer is Johnson's comment to Boswell about 'a dog's walking on his hinder legs': 'It is not done well; but you are surprised to find it done at all.' This was an effort led by the Secretary-General and a small part of the Secretariat. Key states defined the effort solely as one of Security Council reform and tried to hijack the whole effort to achieve or forestall that goal. The United States, the single most important member state, was at times feckless, antagonistic and schizophrenic, and often clumsy and episodic, in its engagement. The reform effort coincided with the oil for food scandal, which cost the UN and Kofi Annan dearly in terms of their reputation within the United States. The U.S. never led; it never devoted sustained energy, attention and purpose to the effort. Its permanent representative, John Bolton, had his own agenda which was only partly related to the agenda of his nominal bosses. These are all parts of the answer.

Another part of the answer is that the process to achieve the outcome document placed real brakes on what was accomplished in the following year in terms of implementation of the outcome's decisions. The G77 and Non-Aligned Movement became hyper-vigilant about the prospect of losing clout in the post-summit negotiations. Combined with their suspicion towards the Bush administration and especially John Bolton, and their belief that the Secretary-General had gone too far towards mollifying the United States, many countries began to oppose reforms because of the possibility that they might further American interests.

Faced with the choice between having a more effective UN that furthered American interests and continuing with an ineffective UN, many countries chose an ineffective UN. In the parlance of international relations theory, faced with a sole superpower that holds a strategy of primacy, and whose actions on the international stage have been unpopular, some countries chose 'soft balancing' to deny American policies legitimacy and legality, and undermine American attempts to forge cooperation on its terms. Translating this to the UN, many countries voted for the UN to be a great global encounter session rather than an effective problemsolver, especially if it is the United States that chooses the problems.

Finally, a part of the answer of why the glass was half full was that the Secretariat itself did not have the right strategy to fill it further – or to put it more accurately, that it had the right strategy and did not implement it with full force. The Secretary-General's inclination was that if far reaching, transformative decisions were to be taken, heads of state would have to be the key decision-makers. He based this assessment on two considerations. First, numerous expert and ambassador-driven venues had produced protracted stalemate across a wide set of issue areas: counterterrorism, disarmament and non-proliferation, and Security Council reform. If new initiatives were to be set in motion, if bold decisions were to be taken, if deadlocks were to be smashed, it would have to be heads of state taking the decisions. Second, the transformation effort was produced as a package. Single issues may produce winners or losers, but compromises across issues could provide win–win solutions. Cherry-picking had to be discouraged, trading across issues encouraged. To do this required leaders to engage with the big-picture vision and establish command across parts of the bureaucracy to enable a security–development–human rights package to go forward.

All of this meant stepping on the toes of Secretariat officials tied to the issue venues and of New York-based mission staff and ambassadors, and preventing collusion between them. To get attention from the top, capitals had to be engaged and heads of state had to direct staff to get results.

This was the strategy, but it was pursued only intermittently and half-heartedly by the Secretary-General and his staff. In the absence of a concerted global effort to persuade world leaders to engage and lead on this issue, the reform fell captive to New York-based politics and dynamics. As many with experience of the UN can attest, there is often a serious principal–agent problem in the relationships between capitals and their permanent representatives to the UN, with UN ambassadors often given large degrees of freedom to pursue their preferences. This is not just a problem for small countries in lands far away from Turtle Bay. It was at the heart of American diplomacy at the UN from August 2005 until December 2006.

FINAL THOUGHTS*

Is the UN transformable, or are we stuck in an equilibrium that ensures that it underachieves? To ask the question somewhat differently, what would it take for most member states to prefer a UN and international order in which international institutions were effective and could provide the kind of collective security envisioned in the High-level Panel Report?

Key variables will be the language and deeds of the next administration in Washington DC. In 2009 the next American president will have the opportunity to repudiate the failed strategy of primacy and acknowledge that American security is dependent on global security. He or she can commit to putting effective multilateralism and international institutions at the front and centre of how the United

---

* These paragraphs should be read as an argument of early 2007.

States gets things done. The new president can also take some early actions to regain international credibility, and there is no better place to start than in the area of disarmament.

Will he or she do so? Possibly not; on the Democratic side there are pundits who suggest that the whole international architecture is broken and speak blithely of alternatives such as a concert of democracies, a classic version of American escapism that underestimates the low regard that much of the democratic world has for American foreign policy and assumes that the United States need not negotiate with countries that hold different values and political systems.

At some point there must be a reckoning of America's foreign policy leadership with a few basic facts: that it is the strongest military power on earth, but unable to translate that power into achieving any major foreign policy goal; that the United Nations has never been more important to its security goals; that America's reputation as a democracy and as an international power is at its lowest. Only a president willing to acknowledge these facts will have a chance of re-establishing American leadership.

And what, then, of the rest of the world? Were a new American president to put forward a new vision of multilateral engagement, would others respond? Some believe that after eight years of the Bush administration, the world will embrace a new American president and follow his or her lead. I, for one, am sceptical. There is too much distrust of American leadership, and too much potential for countries to hedge their bets. If a shared commitment to rebuilding multilateralism and the United Nations is to come about, it will be a lengthy, incremental process.

A new American president should not assume that the world is holding its breath waiting for American leadership to create a new world order. One must avoid setting up multilateralism to fail. It is all too easy to imagine a new president, believing that America's good intentions can be taken at face value, rushing headlong into reforming the international architecture, only to find few takers, arduous negotiations and intermittent cooperation. Aggrieved, the new president turns again to unilateralism, labouring under the delusion that he or she tried hard and failed because no one else wants effective multilateralism.

II

Adapting Cold War Institutions

4

An Evolving UN Security Council

David M. Malone

The chapter argues that the Security Council's decisions over the past twenty years, largely improvised and inconsistent though they may be, have, for good or ill, eroded the foundations of absolute conceptions of state sovereignty, allocating to the Council itself powers that fundamentally alter the way in which relationships among international organizations, states, and citizens are likely to be ordered in decades ahead.[1]

INTRODUCTION – THE P5 IN FIRM CONTROL

One important signal of the thaw in the Cold War was a noticeable improvement in the climate among the Permanent Five (P5) members of the United Nations Security Council (UNSC). The first serious evidence of the relaxation in East–West tensions within the Council was their ability, at the invitation of UN Secretary-General Javier Perez de Cuellar, in 1987, to tackle resolution of the murderous Iran–Iraq war.[2] The war came to an end in mid-1988 on the terms laid out in Security Council Resolution (SCR) 598.[3] The post–Cold War era at the UN had started.

The ability and disposition of the five permanent members, those holding veto power, to cooperate with one another seriously diminished the margin for maneuver

---

[1] The most useful reference book in print today on the UN Security Council is the magisterial *The Procedure of the UN Security Council*, 3rd ed., by Sydney D. Bailey and Sam Daws (Oxford, UK: Clarendon, 1998). A fourth edition is promised in years to come. See also *The UN Security Council: From Cold War to Twenty-First Century*, David M. Malone, ed. (Boulder, CO/London: Lynne Rienner Publishers, 2004). See also the compact and authoritative *The UN Security Council (A Primer)* by Edward C. Luck (London: Routledge, 2006). For a firsthand account, see Chinmaya Gharekhan's interesting *The Horseshoe Table: An Inside View of the Security Council* (Delhi: Longman, 2006).

[2] See Cameron R. Hume, *The United Nations, Iran and Iraq: How Peacemaking Changed* (Bloomington, IN: Indiana University Press, 1994).

[3] SCR 598 of July 20, 1987.

of other Council members. Now nonpermanent members grumbled that they were systematically marginalized, a complaint lent more weight by a tendency of the Secretariat to consult privately with some or all of the P5 before advancing recommendations to the Council as a whole.[4]

The post–Cold War period has been marked by the Council's disposition to tackle many more conflicts than it had been able to earlier, when it was stymied by Cold War animosities and the plethora of vetoes (cast and threatened) by the permanent members. Since 1990, there has been a sharp drop in the use of the veto, accompanying the introduction of a culture of accommodation among the P5, and substantive shifts in the Council's approach to conflict and its resolution. Factors held by the Council as constituting a threat to international peace expanded to include a coup against a democratically elected regime (in Haiti); a range of humanitarian catastrophes, particularly those generating large exoduses of displaced persons and refugees, internally and internationally; and acts of terrorism. This, in turn, allowed the Council to address a range of conflicts, mostly internal in nature, which it most likely would have avoided in the past when the Cold War antagonists often played out their hostility through regional proxies and were prepared to frustrate Council involvement. The Council's decisions in the 1990s proved highly innovative in shaping the normative framework for international relations.[5]

Council Dynamics

It may be useful to look more closely at recent dynamics within the P5. In the face of continuing North Korean provocations, the Council in October 2006 adopted a unanimous resolution of exceptional severity calling on North Korea to rejoin the Six-Party talks to defuse the crisis surrounding its nuclear weapons program, which doubtless contributed to Pyongyang's decision to do so and to a deescalation of the crisis in early 2007.[6] And the Council, not least through a process of intensive consultations in capitals, managed to retain unity on Iran's nuclear program.

Although the United States, the United Kingdom (UK), and France work closely with one another on most issues before the Council, and their differences are often a matter of nuance (e.g., during 2006 and 2007 on Iran's nuclear programs), they do occasionally part company, most spectacularly on Iraq in 2003. In that instance, France aligned itself with China and the Russian Federation, with fatal

---

[4] See C. S. R Murphy, "Change and Continuity in the Functioning of the Security Council since the End of the Cold War," *International Studies* 32, No. 4 (1995), p. 423.

[5] See David M. Malone, "The UN Security Council in the 1990s: Boom and Bust?", Keynote Address, From Territorial Sovereignty to Human Security, Proceedings of the 28th Annual Conference of the Canadian Council on International Law (1999) (The Hague: Kluwer Law International, 2000), pp. 35–52.

[6] See SCR 1718 of October 14, 2006.

consequences for the quest by the UK and the United States for Council authorization to use force against Saddam Hussein. As well, on Middle-East-related votes, the United States is sometimes isolated within the P5, not least in its willingness to veto some draft resolutions critical of Israel.

China, although formally championing traditional conceptions of sovereignty and nonintervention by the Council in the internal affairs of member states, in fact has displayed subtle and creative diplomacy within the Council practiced by accomplished recent Chinese ambassadors, notably by the remarkable Wang Guangya. When its own positions come under attack, it has shown itself capable of shifts that align it more closely with other countries, as was the case in 2007 on Darfur.[7] Its lead role in the Six-Party talks on North Korea boosted its profile and added to its luster. The emergence of China as a skilled sophisticated player within the P5 at a time when U.S. diplomacy has been much criticized internationally (and, increasingly, domestically) is a striking development at the UN.

Another striking development at the UN has been the Russian Federation's more assertive recent tone. Indeed, Russia has affected a growing sourness and abrasiveness in debate (but often quietly has proved quite collegial on issues such as Iran and Lebanon). In 2007, Kosovo emerged again as a bone of contention within the P5. The permanent status of Kosovo, a delicate diplomatic challenge deferred in 1999, came to a head in early 2007 with publication of a report by UN Special Envoy Martti Ahtisaari essentially arguing that Kosovo's independence should be recognized by the Council.[8] Moscow balked, threatening a veto, which prompted other Council members to defer action on a draft resolution endorsing the Ahtisaari approach that had been tabled by the Western powers on May 12, 2007. Late in that year, in spite of pressure from these countries, the Council still seemed deadlocked on the issue, while debate moved on to disagreements within the European Union (EU) over whether Kosovo's independence should be recognized without a Council decision and over the implications of a possible de facto partition of Kosovo.[9] Meanwhile, President Bush signaled that the United States was prepared to recognize Kosovo's independence unilaterally if discussions with Moscow failed to yield a constructive outcome.[10] This set the stage for Kosovo's contested declaration of independence in February 2008, which Hoscow still refuses to recognize.

Thus, although P5 cohesion remained a pillar of the Council's approach to most issues, geostrategically significant splits occasionally emerged and may do so with growing frequency in the future as the balance of great power relations evolves.

---

[7] See SCR 1769 of July 31, 2007.

[8] See UN Document S/2007/168.Add.1 of March 27, 2007.

[9] See "EU states reject 'very dangerous' Kosovo partition," Reuters dispatch by Ingrid Melander and Mark John, September 7, 2007.

[10] See, "Washington prêt a reconnaître unilatéralement l'indépendance du Kosovo," AFP dispatch, September 7, 2007.

U.S.–UN Relations

One of the major challenges facing the Council in recent years has been the often-parlous state of relations between the United States and the UN.[11] As explored more fully elsewhere in this volume, a misconception existed that the George H. W. Bush administration had been uniquely inclined to tangle with other countries at the UN and with the UN Secretariat. But, in fact, the Clinton administration's instinctive penchant for UN-bashing whenever in a tight spot from which blame might be delegated, first on view following the Mogadishu fiasco of October 4, 1993, belied its commitment to the assertive multilateralism advocated early on by Madeleine Albright. Relevant to the Council's agenda were legislative strictures introduced in the mid-1990s requiring the administration to consult Congress prior to the launch or expansion of any UN peacekeeping operations (PKOs), and a congressional proclivity for withholding U.S. dues for UN PKOs earlier approved by the U.S. government.[12] (The administration was much less constrained in its leadership of, or participation in, multinational coalitions not under the UN flag.)

No question, though, that tensions between the United States and the UN characterized the early years of the Bush administration. In particular, Iraq proved to be a highly divisive issue in the Council after 9/11, with the United States seeking authorization to use force to remove Saddam Hussein from power, on the grounds that he was harboring weapons of mass destruction (WMD), a claim not widely credited elsewhere. After a deadlock developed in the Security Council in March 2003, a U.S.-led coalition of countries acted militarily anyway to overthrow the Saddam Hussein regime, confirming fears that the United States was embarked on a new, unilateralist course in which forcible preemption was the preferred policy.[13]

However, with U.S. troops in Iraq soon tied down by an expanding insurgency and other sources of violence, Washington during the second term of George W. Bush, as of 2005, hewed to a fairly prudent line aimed at generating international company for its policies and initiatives. After several years during which the United States, driven by the shock of 9/11, had been inclined to act unilaterally sometimes seemingly as a matter of preference – thereby incurring serious costs and ultimately facing serious difficulties in Iraq – the role of the Security Council not only in conferring legitimacy on certain forms of international intervention but also in providing a mechanism for burden-sharing of expenses and risk is clearly once again valued to an extent by Washington. Critics sometimes complain that this new policy may not be "sincere," but that should not obscure the welcome nature of the shift.

[11] This is not new. See Boutros Boutros-Ghali, *Unvanquished: A U.S.-U.N. Saga* (New York: Random House, 1999). See also Madeleine Albright, *Madam Secretary* (New York: Miramax Books, 2003), pp. 127–215. Also, David M. Malone, "Goodbye UNSCOM: A Tale in UN-US Relations," *Security Dialogue* 30, No. 4 (December 1999), pp. 393–411.

[12] The repayment of a significant portion of U.S. arrears to the UN, amounting by the UN's account to roughly $1.7 billion in late 1999, was conditionally authorized by Congress in November 1999.

[13] See Malone, *The International Struggle over Iraq*, pp. 222–64.

An Evolving UN Security Council 63

A reflection of this, the appointment of the emollient (if tough-minded) Zalmay Khalilzad to succeed the combative, sometimes counterproductive John Bolton as U.S. Permanent Representative at the UN in early 2007 was widely welcomed.[14]

Structure of the Chapter

Rather than analyze all that the Council seeks to do, the remainder of the chapter examines in-depth changes affecting the Council since the end of the Cold War under several headings: the nature of its decisions, including a greater willingness to resort to coercive measures[15]; the drivers behind Council decisions; new fields of Council endeavor; new methodological approaches and some concerns relating thereto – including a shift by the Council to a more legal and regulatory mode of decision making; its waxing and waning role in the fight against terrorism; a new focus on transnational crime; and its important, sometimes critical, role in the development of international criminal law. The chapter's conclusions return to the influence of Council decisions on conceptions of sovereignty in the post–Cold War era.

THE NATURE OF THE CONFLICTS ADDRESSED BY THE COUNCIL AND OF ITS DECISIONS

Internal Conflicts and the Challenge of Compliance

An early consequence of the end of the Cold War among the P5 was the Council's new-found attention to internal conflict. The Council's willingness to involve itself in a broad range of internal conflicts, encompassing intercommunal strife, crises of democracy, fighting marked by a fierce struggle for control of national resources and wealth, and several other precipitating causes or incentives for continuation of war, forced it to confront hostilities of a much more complex nature than the interstate disputes with which it had greater experience.

Chapters 1 and 11 in this volume highlight that international efforts to mitigate and resolve these conflicts frequently involved the Council deploying peacekeeping operations. Unlike their Cold War-era predecessors, these missions required complex mandates significantly more ambitious than the modalities of "classic" peacekeeping were designed to meet.[16] The most striking features of "new generation" PKOs were

---

[14] Khalilzad's immediately previous tenure as U.S. Ambassador in Iraq had been widely judged a uniquely successful one by many Iraqis to whom I have spoken.

[15] See Thomas M. Franck, *Recourse to Force: State Action against Threats and Armed Attacks* (Cambridge, UK: Cambridge University Press, 2002), particularly pp. 5–9. Professor Franck, Simon Chesterman, and I revisit this view in *The Law and Practice of the United Nations* (Oxford: Oxford University Press, 2007).

[16] See the Center on International Cooperation's comprehensive report, *Annual Review of Global Peace Operations 2006*, Ian Johnstone, ed. (Boulder, CO/London: Lynne Rienner, 2006). See also Thomas G. Weiss, David P. Forsythe, and Roger A. Coate, *The United Nations in a Changing World*, 2nd ed. (Boulder, CO: Westview Press, 2004).

not so much the large numbers of military personnel involved but the important role and substantive diversity of their civilian and police components, which often focused on humanitarian, human rights, rule of law, and other good governance questions.[17]

The complexity of these internal conflicts was evident in the fact of parties to them frequently ignoring or skirting Council edicts. The Council's inability to induce compliance with its decisions fueled two apparently contradictory, but all-too-frequent responses: on the one hand, it moved to enforce decisions that had failed to generate consent in the field, notably in the former Yugoslavia,[18] Somalia,[19] and Haiti[20]; on the other, in the face of significant casualties, it cut and ran, as in Somalia at a later date and at the outset of genocide in Rwanda.[21] In two of these cases, Rwanda and the former Yugoslavia, it covered its own failed strategies by creating international criminal tribunals to address individual responsibility for heinous crimes.

Enforcement: Resort to Chapter VII

The compliance challenge pushed the Council toward ever-greater use of its enforcement provision, Chapter VII of the UN Charter. Resort to the provisions of Chapter VII of the UN Charter and to enforcement of Council decisions was not new: Council decisions were enforced in Korea and to a much lesser extent in the Congo during the UN's early years, whereas a naval blockade against Rhodesia proved largely unconvincing.[22] But the extent to which the Council has adopted decisions under Chapter VII since 1990 is wholly unprecedented. And it has proved addictive. By 2004, fully a third of the Council's resolutions were adopted explicitly under its provisions.

The Council also sought to ensure compliance by mandating enforcement operations. Some of these were entrusted to "coalitions of the willing" such as Operation Uphold Democracy (in Haiti, 1994–1995) and the International Security Assistance

---

[17] See Michael C. Williams, *Civil-Military Relations and Peacekeeping* (London/New York: Oxford University Press, 1998). See also Steven R. Ratner, *The New UN Peacekeeping: Building Peace in Lands of Conflict after the Cold War* (New York: St. Martins Press with the Council on Foreign Relations, 1996).

[18] See Adam Roberts, "Communal Conflict as a Challenge to International Organization: The Case of Former Yugoslavia," *Review of International Studies* 21 (1995), pp. 389–410; International Crisis Group, "Kosovo: Let's Learn from Bosnia – Models and Methods of International Administration," Sarajevo, Bosnia, May 17, 1999.

[19] See John L. Hirsch and Robert Oakley, *Somalia and Operation Restore Hope: Reflections on Peacemaking and Peacekeeping* (Washington DC: United States Institute for Peace Press, 1995).

[20] See David M. Malone, *Decision-Making in the UN Security Council: The Case of Haiti* (Oxford: Clarendon Press, 1998).

[21] See Bruce D. Jones, *Peacemaking in Rwanda: The Dynamics of Failure* (Boulder, CO/London: Lynne Rienner, 2001); and Michael Barnett, "The UN Security Council, Indifference and Genocide in Rwanda," *Cultural Anthropology* 12 No. 4 (1997), p. 551.

[22] UN Department of Political Affairs, "A Brief Overview of Security Council Applied Sanctions," *Interlaken 2*, 1998.

Force (ISAF) in Afghanistan since 2002, whereas others were assigned to the UN itself as UN PKOs.[23]

More common than military enforcement decisions by the Council was the resort to economic (and, increasingly, diplomatic) sanctions under Chapter VII of the Charter.[24] It is worth remembering that, at the time of the terrorist attacks on the United States, al Qaeda had already for two years been struck by Security Council-imposed sanctions.[25]

During the post–Cold War era, the deployment of the UN's own peacekeepers expanded dramatically, from Central America to Cambodia and from all parts of sub-Saharan Africa to the Balkans. The drift into "mandate creep," under which more robust mandates, often under Chapter VII of the Charter, were assigned to UN PKOs without necessarily providing the troops or equipment required to fulfill them, marked the era. By late 2006, the Security Council had authorized the deployment of 115,665 UN peacekeepers in 16 missions, the troop figure about 40 percent higher than only two years earlier, with 37,242 added in August 2006 alone for Sudan, East Timor, and Lebanon.[26] Police deployments amounted to 15,621.[27] With more robust mandates and operating in rough neighborhoods often engulfed by civil wars, UN peacekeepers increasingly came into contact with war crimes and crimes against humanity, as evidenced by the creation of or preparations for special courts to address the commission of such crimes in Cambodia, Sierra Leone, East Timor, and other places in which the UN had deployed and in some cases continues to maintain a peacekeeping presence.[28]

As explored more fully elsewhere in this volume, the Council has also supported in qualified terms enforcement activities by regional bodies, notably the Economic Community of West African States (ECOWAS) in Liberia and Sierra Leone. Indeed,

---

[23] See Oliver Ramsbotham and Tom Woodhouse, *Encyclopedia of International Peacekeeping Operations* (Santa Barbara, CA: ABC-CLIO, 1999).

[24] The Security Council invoked economic sanctions only twice prior to 1990, against Southern Rhodesia in 1966 and against South Africa in 1967. See Office of the Spokesman of the Secretary-General: The Use of Sanctions under Chapter VII, at http://www.un.org/News/ossg/srhod.htm. For an in-depth discussion of the Council's experience with sanctions regimes since 1990, see David Cortright and George Lopez, *The Sanctions Decade* (Boulder, CO/London: Lynne Rienner, 2000). See also their *Sanctions and the Search for Security: Challenges to UN Action* (Boulder CO/London: Lynne Rienner, 2002).

[25] See SCR 1267 of October 15, 1999.

[26] See Security Council Report's "Twenty Days in August: The Council Sets Massive New Challenges for UN Peacekeeping," Special Research Report No. 5, September 8, 2006, at www.securitycouncilreport.org.

[27] Police are generally very difficult to recruit for international operations as they mostly are employed at municipal or regional levels within member states, although some countries operating under the French *gendarmerie* or Italian *carabinieri* models can more readily supply units of police to PKOs.

[28] The most dramatic recent such case is centered on the UN-backed Special Court for Sierra Leone, to which Charles Taylor, former warlord in and later president of Liberia, surrendered in March 2006. See SCR 1688 of June 16, 2006. For more detail, see an excellent Human Rights Watch report at http://www.hrw.org/backgrounder/ij/ij0606/2.htm.

66   David M. Malone

the Council has increasingly both shaped and adapted to the role of regional organizations in seeking to prevent and resolve conflict, in such places as Haiti, Bosnia,
Kosovo, and Sudan, although reserving for itself the power to invoke force and
impose mandatory sanctions.[29] (However, with the exception of NATO, regional
bodies generally command even scarcer resources and offer even more limited
capacities than the UN, a serious problem for the African Union mission in Sudan,
2004–2007.)

SOME DRIVERS OF COUNCIL DECISION MAKING

The impact of Council decisions in transforming the framework for international
relations was in part a function of the issues that drove its decision making – including
humanitarian, human rights, and democratization concerns.

The Humanitarian Imperative

An innovative feature of the Council's decisions on a number of crises after the end
of the Cold War has been its concern over the humanitarian plight of civilian victims
of conflicts, particularly refugees. Refugees were hardly a new topic of concern for
the Council.[30] The fate of Palestinian refugees proved a continuing spur to the Arab-
Israeli dispute following Israel's war of independence in 1947–1948, leading also to
the creation of a UN agency (United Nations Relief and Works Agency [UNRWA])
exclusively dedicated to their welfare. Those displaced by war, particularly where
mass exoduses of the population occurred, had long been seen as deserving of care
from the international community and were among the prime "clients" of both
the Red Cross system (ICRC and the Federation of World Red Cross and Red
Crescent Societies) and the UN High Commissioner for Refugees. Nevertheless,
in the 1990s as never before, the Security Council invoked the plight of refugees
and their implied destabilizing effect on neighboring states as grounds for its own
involvement in conflict. Early Council resolutions on the former Yugoslavia[31] and on
Somalia[32] illustrate this development. Any threat that the Haitian crisis of democracy,
1991–1994, may actually have posed to international peace and security only arose

---

[29] For the Council's complex relationship with the African Union over Darfur and related issues, see
UN Document S/2006/433 of June 22, 2006, "Report of the Security Council Mission to the Sudan
and Chad, 4–10, June 2006." On Bosnia, see Elizabeth M. Cousens and Charles K. Cater, *Towards
Peace in Bosnia: Implementing the Dayton Accords* (Boulder, CO/London: Lynne Rienner, 2001). On
Kosovo, see Simon Chesterman, *You, the People: The United Nations, Transitional Administration,
and State-Building* (Oxford: Oxford University Press, 2004).

[30] See Francis Kofi Abiew, *The Evolution of the Doctrine and Practice of Humanitarian Intervention*
(The Hague; Boston: Kluwer Law International, 1999); Stephen A. Garrett, *Doing Good and Doing
Well: An Examination of Humanitarian Intervention* (Westport, CT: Praeger, 1999).

[31] See SCR 713 of September 25, 1991, and SCR 733 of January 23, 1992.

[32] See the Secretary-General's report requesting the Security Council to take up the case of Somalia
(UN Document S/23445, 1991).

from the outflow of Haitian boat-people threatening to engulf a number of Caribbean countries and the shores of Florida.[33] The newly widespread acceptance that refugee flows could actually be a major catalyst to conflict, rather than merely an outcome of it, was striking.

Furthermore, the intensive, if highly selective, media – particularly television news – scrutiny (the so-called CNN effect) of horrendous conditions endured by victims of war impelled populations worldwide to press their governments to alleviate suffering arising from a variety of conflicts.[34] Several factors conspired to focus attention on the UN to act on behalf of the international community: the limited impact of most bilateral assistance in these dramatic circumstances, the existence of several UN specialized agencies with the skills and "critical mass" required, and the possibility for the UN to deploy peace missions of various types and sizes with mandates focused on humanitarian objectives or at least including them. The most important consideration for many governments was that in delegating to the UN the responsibility to act, mostly in situations where few vital national interests were at stake, the costs and risks of response were shared.

At the peak of media and public fervor for humanitarian initiatives in the early 1990s, a lively debate unfolded over not only the international right to intervene in the internal affairs of countries to save civilian lives but also a purported duty to do so.[35] UN Secretary-General Kofi Annan proved a lively promoter of this debate, staking out new ground in championing human rights and concern for civilians in war as key themes.[36] His advocacy of humanitarian intervention was articulated most unambiguously in a speech to the UN General Assembly on September 20, 1999.[37]

This debate culminated in 2002 in a report of the International Commission on Intervention and State Sovereignty, sponsored by the government of Canada, "The Responsibility to Protect."[38] In 2005, the UN Summit endorsed the concept, as did, subsequently, the Security Council. However, the Council has been slow to come to grips with the operational implications of the concept, most notably in

[33] See Diego Arria, "Diplomacy and the Four Friends of Haiti," and Andrew S. Faiola, "Refugee Policy: The 1994 Crisis," in Georges Fauriol, ed., *Haitian Frustration: Dilemmas for US Foreign Policy* (Washington DC: Center for Strategic and International Studies, 1995), pp. 83–98.

[34] See SCR 688 of April 5, 1991, on humanitarian protection in Iraq; and James Cockayne and David M. Malone, "Creeping Unilateralism: How Operation Provide Comfort and the No-Fly Zones in 1991 and 1992 Paved the Way for the Iraq Crisis of 2003," *Security Dialogue* 37, No. 1 (March 2006), pp. 123–41.

[35] See Jonathan Moore, ed., *Hard Choices: Moral Dilemmas in Humanitarian Intervention* (Lanham MD: Rowman and Littlefield Publishers, 1998).

[36] See James Traub's excellent *The Best Intentions: Kofi Annan and the UN in the Era of American World Power* (New York: Farrar, Straus and Giroux, 2006), pp. 91–109.

[37] See the *Economist*, "Two Concepts of Sovereignty," September 18, 1999. But, in spite of his Nobel Peace Prize of 2001, differences among UN members over Iraq were to bedevil Annan's second term. See David M. Malone, *The International Struggle over Iraq: Politics in the UN Security Council, 1980–2005* (Oxford, UK: Oxford University Press, 2006), pp. 296–9.

[38] See the complete report at www.iciss.ca. See also Gareth Evans and Mohamed Sahnoun, "Responsibility to Protect," *Foreign Affairs* 81, No. 6 (Nov/Dec 2002), pp. 1–8.

its cautious and agonizingly slow approach to the political and humanitarian crisis affecting Darfur, on which, only late in 2007, it allowed itself to be backed into a more forward role, taking over the lead from an ambivalent African Union that had earlier (with UN support and the support of individual UN member states) fielded a monitoring mission of its own (African Union Mission in Sudan [AMIS]).[39]

Human Rights

Human rights, long cloistered within intergovernmental machinery and Secretariat bureaucracy designed in part to keep the topic at a safe distance from those responsible for international peace and security at the UN, burst onto the Security Council's agenda with the realization that civil strife was not amenable to negotiated solutions as long as human rights continued to be massively violated. For this reason, the protection, promotion, and monitoring of human rights formed an important part of the mandates of several UN peacekeeping operations, notably in El Salvador and Guatemala.[40] Where this was not the case, as in Rwanda and Haiti, the UN General Assembly often deployed parallel human rights missions. The salience of human rights at the UN was reinforced by the appointment of a UN High Commissioner for Human Rights as of 1994.

The quandaries faced by the Council in factoring human rights considerations into its decisions were highlighted when the parties to Sierra Leone's civil war reached a peace agreement in mid-1999 including sweeping amnesty provisions against which Mary Robinson, then High Commissioner, sharply protested (and over which the UN Secretary-General's representative at the peace pact's signing ceremony had registered a formal reservation). On the one hand, Sierra Leone's population was clearly eager for peace on virtually any terms; on the other, the agreement's amnesty provisions patently ran against long-standing and emerging human rights norms. Thanks in part to strong UN resistance to sweeping amnesties for those involved in war crimes, it was subsequently possible to create the Special Court for Sierra Leone to try several of these individuals, including Charles Taylor, former president of Liberia.[41]

More broadly, with successive High Commissioners for Human Rights playing an assertive role in the promotion and protection of human rights in conflict situations (while the new UN Human Rights Council slumbers, alas), UN human rights monitoring missions have emerged that are sometimes loosely tied to UN peace or

[39] The Sudanese government's decision in October 2006 to expel outspoken UN envoy in Khartoum Jan Pronk demonstrated once again how a government with a degree of regional support (in this instance, notably, from the Arab League) could withstand international humanitarian and human rights pressure.

[40] On El Salvador, see in particular Michael W. Doyle, Ian Johnstone, and Robert C. Orr, eds., *Keeping the Peace: Multidimensional UN Operations in Cambodia and El Salvador* (Cambridge: Cambridge University Press, 1997).

[41] See the Special Court's useful Web site at www.sc-sl.org.

political management missions, as in Nepal in 2007. Thus, although the connection between human rights and the Council's agenda on its face would not seem to have evolved much in recent years, in fact human rights continue to play a meaningful and evolving role in its strategies.[42]

Democratization

The Council also appeared to be increasingly engaged in the promotion of democracy, *inter alia*, by mandating the organization and monitoring of elections, a trend as unlikely during the Cold War as would have been the prominence of humanitarian considerations in the Council's work after 1990.[43] But the Council favored the electoral process not so much as an end in itself but as a means of effecting a "new deal" in countries emerging from civil war in which power could, in some cases, be shared with former combatants in rough proportion to electoral results. Such elections proved an unreliable indicator of the extent to which genuinely democratic cultures would take root. The stilted, power-driven, and unstable coalition arrangements resulting from Cambodia's UN-monitored elections of 1993 and 1998 contrasted with the more natural, relaxed electoral rhythms apparently achieved in El Salvador, where an alternation of power between rival parties seems more likely in the long run.[44]

The case of East Timor, where the outcome of a UN-implemented referendum over independence led to a murderous rampage by militias in 1999, also illustrated that the UN needs to be careful not to promote elections in the absence of adequate measures that help protect the civilian population against the wrath of those who lose.[45] And that this country's politics proved sufficiently unstable as to require a second deployment of multilateral troops in 2006 points to the often excessively hasty and overoptimistic scenarios for UN withdrawal after elections.

Similarly, the ebb and flow of domestic Nepali politics, in the wake of the country's historic agreement on a "peace process" as between several internal political movements and parties in November 2006, subsequently supported by a Security-Council-authorized UN political management mission (eight hundred-strong in September 2007), point not only to the Council's increasing inclination to support

---

[42] See UN Documents S/2007/7, January 9, 2007; S/2007/235, April 26, 2007; and S/2007/442, July 18, 2007. Also see a valuable series of reports from the International Crisis Group: "Nepal's Peace Agreement: Making It Work," ICG Asia Report no. 126, December 15, 2006; "Nepal's Institutional Process," ICG Asia Report no. 128, February 26, 2007; "Nepal's Maoists: Purists or Pragmatists?", ICG Asia Report no. 132, May 18, 2006; and "Nepal's Troubled Terai Region," ICG Asia Report no. 136, July 9, 2007. See also Kanak Mani Dixit, "A Tryst with Nepali Destiny," *Himal Southasian*, August 2007.

[43] Ratner, *The New UN Peacekeeping: Building Peace in Lands of Conflict after the Cold War.*

[44] For an excellent work dealing with elections in postconflict situations, see Krishna Kumar, ed., *Postconflict Elections, Democratization and International Assistance* (Boulder, CO: Lynne Rienner Publishers, 1998).

[45] Ian Martin, *Self-Determination in East Timor: The United Nations, the Ballot, and International Intervention* (Boulder, CO: Lynne Rienner Publishers, 2001).

70 David M. Malone

such processes but also to the sensitivity and difficulty for the UN in helping to underpin productive political management by parties not always fully committed to goals to which they formally subscribe.[46]

NEW FIELDS OF COUNCIL ENDEAVOR, NEW APPROACHES, AND CONCERNS RELATING THERETO

If new drivers of decision making on managing internal conflict characterized much of the 1990s (and continues to the present), an important second feature of the Council's evolution since the end of the Cold War – and in particular since 9/11 – has been the movement into new fields of endeavor and the adoption of new, more regulatory approaches – courting new controversies.

A More Legal and Regulatory Approach

A first example lies in fact finding. As pointed out by law scholar James Cockayne, the Security Council is increasingly turning to legal techniques and expertise to underpin its fact-finding activities, because legal frameworks help build legitimacy.[47] Often, these frameworks are drawn from or build on the foundations of international criminal law. The Council has been creative in the ways it has done this: by referring matters to the International Criminal Court for further investigation (e.g., on Darfur), by developing ad hoc commissions of inquiry to assess the evidence of crimes, and by calling on member states to provide policing expertise to assess the adequacy of national investigation efforts and complement them where necessary (e.g., for the investigation into the assassination of former Prime Minister Rafiq Hariri in Lebanon in 2005–2006).[48]

Indeed, the Hariri investigation and the tribunal likely to ensue from it are significant in a number of ways – they represent an expansion of the Council's willingness to use judicial techniques to influence the behavior of member states and may prove that international courts can help elucidate state involvement in terrorism.[49]

Additionally, the Council is steadily entrenching its supervisory role by creating subsidiary committees that oversee member state compliance not only with specific sanctions regimes but also with more general standards it sets (e.g., on child soldiers)

---

[46] In September 2007, Nepal's Maoists withdrew from the transitional government in order to press, through "street agitation," their demand for abolition of the monarchy and the establishment of a republic, prior to elections for a constituent assembly.

[47] James Cockayne, *Evolving Challenges to Human and International Security: Global Organized Crime,* Coping with Crisis Working Paper Series, International Peace Academy, New York, 2007.

[48] Following the Hariri assassination in Beirut on February 14, 2005, the Security Council, in SCR 1595 of April 7, 2005, established an Independent Investigation Commission (UNIIC), initially for a period of three months. See also SCR 1664 of March 29, 2006.

[49] The notion sometimes entertained that such tribunals could prosecute "state terrorism" would likely prove contentious, not least as the term itself has been applied to date in a highly politicized fashion mainly to Israeli practices by its opponents.

An Evolving UN Security Council

and mandatory guidelines it issues, notably in the fight against terrorism, on which I focus next, and in the struggle to prevent nuclear proliferation to nonstate actors.

The results of this approach, as on Iraq, have sometimes been decidedly mixed, especially when the Council's attention span wanders or when the P5 fall out over implementation of Council decisions. Indeed, the Iraq case is cautionary on the Council's, and the UN's, ability to pull off complex legal and regulatory regimes over extended periods of time – as suggested by the International Inquiry Committee (aka Volcker Committee) report on the Oil for Food scandal of 2005–2006.[50]

The Fight against Terrorism

More regulatory and ambitious approaches have also characterized the Council's approach to terrorism after 9/11. It is worth noting, though, that the Council has been more active in addressing terrorism for longer than is widely believed.[51]

Indeed, terrorism was the subject of the Council's first-ever heads of state level summit, on January 31, 1992, at the end of which Security Council leaders "expressed their deep concern over acts of international terrorism and emphasized the need for the international community to deal effectively with all such acts."[52] Soon thereafter, the Council adopted sanctions against Libya over its noncooperation with the investigation of two airline-bombing incidents, a course of action that ultimately brought about a trial of the Libyan suspects by a Scottish tribunal in the Netherlands.[53] The Council's decisions on this case were contested early on by Libya, which claimed that the Convention on International Civil Aviation of December 7, 1944, and its implementing machinery were the appropriate framework within which to discuss the Lockerbie case, but the International Court of Justice sidestepped the merits of this argument.[54]

Council actions against terrorism have produced somewhat varied results. The Council's sanctions against Sudan, following an assassination attempt against Egypt's President Mubarak, were only of a diplomatic type but seem to have been somewhat effective in persuading the Khartoum regime to expel a number of foreigners and

---

[50] For the IIC's reports, see www.iic-offp.org.

[51] See Chantal de Jonge Oudraat, "The UN and Terrorism: The Role of the UN Security Council," in Jane Boulden and Thomas G. Weiss, eds., *Terrorism and the UN: Before and after September 11th* (Bloomington, IN: Indiana University Press, 2004).

[52] See UN Document S/23500 of January 31, 1992.

[53] In January 2001, the court found one suspect guilty and acquitted the other. For some of the Council's decisions, see SCR 758 of March 31, 1992; SCR 883 of November 11, 1993; and SCR 1192 of August 27, 1998, suspending sanctions on the arrival of the two suspects in the Netherlands.

[54] The Council's expanding role in the early 1990s, and both the number and sweeping scope of its resolutions, gave rise to growing calls for judicial review of its decisions by the ICJ. See Dapo Akande, "The International Court of Justice and the Security Council: Is There Room for Judicial Control of Decisions of the Political Organs of the United Nations?", *The International and Comparative Law Quarterly* 46, No. 2 (1997), p. 309; and Mohammed Bedjaoui, *Nouvel order mondial et contrôle de la légalité des actes du Conseil de sécurité* (Brussels: Bruylant, 1994).

to impose more stringent visa requirements.[55] However, the Council-imposed sanctions against the Taliban regime, in the wake of devastating bombings at U.S. embassies in Kenya and Tanzania in 1999, proved ineffective against a regime almost completely isolated from the international community, even after the sanctions measures were strengthened in 2000.[56]

The attacks against U.S. targets on September 11, 2001, brought home to the Council as a whole how serious terrorist threats could be and sparked more expansive efforts. The Council's move into a new phase of actively combating the financial networks supporting terrorism and safe havens for terrorists under the terms of its resolution 1373 of September 18, 2001, was unusual, indeed unprecedented, in imposing as mandatory on member states the provisions of the draft convention on the suppression of terrorism financing, thus initiating a potentially habit-forming process of the Council "legislating" for all member states, a very controversial move.[57] It created a much ballyhooed Counter-Terrorism Committee (CTC) to monitor compliance of all states with its terms, a body that, after an initial period of self-levitation and credibility induced by its energetic first chair, Sir Jeremy Greenstock, seems to have lapsed mostly into paper-pushing while key states (notably the United States) drive the fight against terrorism bilaterally.

However, even with the establishment in 2001 of the CTC and later that of the Counter-Terrorism Executive Directorate (CTED) underpinning it, the UN lacks both a single forum with a sustained attention span and a mandate to address terrorism and draw together the disparate capacities and initiatives around the UN system seeking to contribute to the global struggle against terrorism. As Rosand and von Einsiedel document in Chapter 8 of this volume, the Council's membership, currently limited to fifteen, gives little voice to the concerns and priorities of the bulk of the UN member states, and the Council has no Charter-based authority for developing coordination mechanisms among the agencies, programs, and funds of the system.[58] Edward C. Luck commented in late 2006: "The core goal of pulling together a coherent and integrated UN approach to counterterrorism remains as elusive as ever."[59]

The issue of how to promote international humanitarian law while also pursuing the fight against terrorism has been the subject of growing concern (and

---

[55] For the Council's decisions on Sudan, see SCRs 1054 of April 26, 2006, and 1070 of August 16, 1996. The sanctions were ultimately lifted in 2001.

[56] Sanctions were originally imposed in SCR 1267 of October 15, 1999. They were strengthened in SCR 1333 of December 7, 2000.

[57] See Axel Marschik, "The Security Council as World Legislator?: Theory, Practice and Consequences of an Expanding World Power." IILJ Working Paper No. 2005–18, http://ssrn.com/abstract=871758.

[58] The UN's Office on Drugs and Crime (UNODC) in Vienna, at the CTC's request, plays an important role in providing guidance to states in legislating and implementing antiterrorism measures. In addition, the International Maritime Organization, International Atomic Energy Agency, and International Civil Aviation Organization are mandated to oversee relevant antiterrorist conventions and assist countries to comply with requirements of those conventions. The IMF and the World Bank provide legislative assistance to countries on prevention of terrorist financing.

[59] Correspondence with the author, October 30, 2006.

An Evolving UN Security Council 73

research).[60] Fears that the fight against terrorism might overwhelm respect for humanitarian law, such as that enshrined in the Geneva Conventions, were exacerbated by practices in Afghanistan, Iraq, Guantanamo Bay, and elsewhere following the events of 9/11. The debate remains a lively one, not least in the domestic politics of the UK and the United States. Suffice it here to note that the Security Council needs to seek a balanced approach to these two objectives and that it has not always succeeded in this delicate task in the eyes of all observers.

A Warning Siren: The Imperial Security Council

Several recent developments have been no less controversial. SCR 1540 of April 28, 2004, again legislated for member states, this time on the prevention of nuclear proliferation to nonstate actors that might use nuclear technology and products for terrorist purposes. Member states, on the whole, disliked this intensely. SCR 1566 of October 8, 2004, in its operative paragraphs 2 and 3 appeared to be attempting to impose a definition of terrorism on the membership as a whole, having been adopted explicitly under Chapter VII of the Charter, a move that was roundly denounced by a number of delegations in the UN General Assembly's Sixth Committee. Moreover, states – particularly small and poor states – have been experiencing significant "reporting fatigue" in attempting to meet the stringent reporting requirements created for them under SCRs 1267, 1373, and 1540, the Council having proved remarkably insensitive to what their constituency's traffic could bear.[61] In a report of April 2006, Kofi Annan was uncharacteristically sharp in his comments on the Council's performance in pursuing its antiterrorism agenda and provided a number of detailed recommendations relating to these and other matters that the Council has been slow to come to terms with.[62]

Discussing the shift to an "Imperial Security Council," Simon Chesterman writes,

> The scope of the Council's expanding powers...is likely to be determined by the tension between end-driven demands of responding to perceived threats to peace and security, and the means-focused requirements of legitimacy. This tension...is most graphically displayed in the passage of quasi-legislative resolutions. The temptations of legislation by Council fiat must be balanced, however, by a recognition that implementation depends on compliance by member states.[63]

---

[60] See Hans-Peter Gasser, "Acts of Terror, 'Terrorism' and International Humanitarian Law," *International Review of the Red Cross* 84 No. 847 (2002), pp. 547–70.

[61] http://www.securitycouncilreport.org/site/c.glKWLeMTIsG/b.1203337/k.9D7F/December_2005brCounterTerrorism_Committee_Issues.htm provides a sense of these and other resentments among member states.

[62] See UN Document A/60/825 of April 27, 2006.

[63] Simon Chesterman, "The Security Council as World Legislator? Theoretical and Practical Aspects of Law-Making by the Security Council," May 26, 2006, Institute for International Law and Justice Discussion Paper, drawn from http://www.iilj.org/research/UNSecurityCouncil.html.

74 David M. Malone

Defection from implementation of Council decisions, which could result from over-reach in legislating for member states, would decisively undermine the Council's authority. It is thus clear that the Council needs to tread carefully in this area, whatever the demands of expediency would argue in capitals of the P5.[64]

Concerns about "the imperial Council" are relevant *inter alia* to the Council's very mixed track record when reacting (often overreacting) to immediate stimuli without much thought to "process integrity," wider consultation, and the perceptions of others whose cooperation is vital to the successful implementation of their decisions.[65] A consequential example: the Iraq sanctions regime fell apart largely because of a stubborn refusal to heed the opinion of experts and public alike, double standards applied by the P5 relative to sanctions-busting neighbors of Iraq, and the Council's inability to oversee with any degree of consistency and authority the activities of the Oil for Food Program it had created.[66]

One issue that has bedeviled the Council in extending its regulatory reach, notably through sanctions regimes, has been that of due process, particularly relating to the listing of individuals and entities targeted.[67] This topic deserves much fuller treatment than can be accommodated in this chapter. It has been the source of considerable research and policy development activity, particularly since the adoption of SCR 1267 in 1999 relating to sanctions against the Taliban regime in Afghanistan.[68] There has been some improvement in procedures within Security Council subsidiary bodies such as sanctions committees, but it is not yet either consistent or convincing.[69]

The Security Council and Transnational Crime

A further area of burgeoning Council activity in the post–9/11 period lay in transnational crime. The Council's scope for dealing with questions of transnational crime is substantial. Sanctions committees have the capacity to play a key role in mapping particular organized crime groups, which could allow the Security Council to

---

[64] Thomas M. Franck has argued usefully that the Council should develop rules of procedure to require consultation with the broader membership when the Council purports to adopt resolutions that are general rather than particular in their effects.

[65] Council decisions based on intelligence asserted or supplied by its members in confidence pose particular challenges from this perspective. See Simon Chesterman, "The Spy Who Came in from the Cold War: Intelligence and International Law," IILJ Working Paper 2006/9, pp. 39–50, at www.iilj.org.

[66] See James Cockayne and David M. Malone, "The UN Security Council: 10 Lessons from Iraq on Regulation and Accountability," *Journal of International Law and International Relations* 2, No. 2 (Fall 2006), pp. 1–24.

[67] One interesting recent article touching on this topic can be strongly recommended: Nicolas Angelet, "Criminal Liability for the Violation of UN Economic Sanctions," *European Journal of Crime, Criminal Law, and Criminal Justice* 7, No. 2 (1999), pp. 89–102.

[68] See Bardo Fassbender, "Targeted Sanctions and Due Process," Study Commissioned by the UN Office of Legal Affairs, March 20, 2006. See also the High-level Panel's concerns in UN Document A1/59/656, para. 153, December 4, 2004, echoed by the UN Summit of 2005 comments in UN General Assembly Resolution 60/1, para. 109.

[69] See "Strengthening Targeted Sanctions through Fair and Clear Procedures" at www.watsoninstitute .org.

implement more aggressive countermeasures to their activities.[70] Generically, the Council has "strongly" urged states to implement the Financial Action Task Force Money-Laundering and Terrorist Financing Recommendations, and more recently the Council has taken steps to broaden cooperation between sanctions committees and Interpol.[71]

However, this has not yet generated synergies between sanctions bodies and other elements of the UN system, not least UN-sponsored international investigations and tribunals. Moreover, despite its recognition that terror and crime are intimately related, the Council has taken few steps to integrate countercrime and counterterror strategies.[72] Nevertheless, the UN system has developed a sophisticated international investigative capacity in relation to criminal tribunals and special courts and to commissions of inquiry in Darfur, Cote d'Ivoire, and Lebanon and also into aspects of UN peacekeeping.

Relatedly, policing components have played an increasingly prominent role in UN peace operations. However, policing functions within UN PKOs are focused more on the provision of public order than on operations against organized crime groups. Exceptions have included the Special Trafficking Operations Program (STOP) established by the UN International Police Task Force within United Nations Mission in Bosnia-Herzegovina (UNMIBH) in 2001 to deal with human trafficking and, most recently, a revised mandate for the UN Stabilization Mission in Haiti (MINUSTAH), which aims to upgrade its crime prevention capacities, particularly its ability to deal with gangs, drugs, and arms trafficking.[73] It remains to be seen, however, whether such units will have the intelligence-gathering and analytic capacity necessary to generate effective organized crime-fighting strategies.[74]

THE SECURITY COUNCIL AND THE DEVELOPMENT OF INTERNATIONAL CRIMINAL LAW

Notwithstanding some differences in focus and most importantly in methods between the early post–Cold War years and the more recent, particularly post–9/11,

---

[70] The relationship between sanctions and organized crime is often interactive: by restricting access to sought-after goods, the Council raises the premium and thus the rewards for sanctions-busters, whose control of black markets can be exceptionally lucrative. And in some cases, neighboring states may be inclined to ally themselves with such criminal networks, as recent events surrounding Iraq and the Balkans suggest. See Phil Williams and John T. Picarelli, "Combating Organized Crime in Armed Conflict," in Karen Ballentine and Heiko Nitzschke, eds., *Profiting from Peace: Managing the Resource Dimensions of Civil War* (Boulder, CO: Lynne Rienner, 2005), pp. 123–52.

[71] See SCR 1617 of July 29, 2005, Operative Paragraph 7; and SCR 1699 of August 8, 2006, respectively. See also Nick Wadhams, "US Introduces Council Resolution to Boost Cooperation with Interpol," Associated Press Newswires, August 3, 2006.

[72] On this link, see, for example, SCR 1373 (2001), Operative Paragraph 4.

[73] See SCR 1702 of August 15, 2006. See also Sebastian von Einsiedel and David M. Malone, "Peace and Democracy for Haiti: A UN Mission Impossible?", *International Relations* 20, No. 2 (Spring 2006), pp. 153–74.

[74] On intelligence and the UN, see Simon Chesterman's interesting monograph *Shared Secrets: Intelligence and Collective Security* (Sydney, Australia: Lowy Institute for International Policy, 2006).

Council activity, there has been an extremely important cross-cutting theme in the Council's engagement and at times radical innovation on questions of international criminal law. It is here, perhaps, that the Council's impact on the framework of international relations has been most pronounced.

The Council in the 1990s may be remembered in part for its contribution to radical innovation in international criminal law, notably through its creation of ad hoc International Criminal Tribunals for the former Yugoslavia (ICTFY) in 1993 and Rwanda (ICTR) in 1994 to bring to justice those responsible for war crimes, crimes against humanity, and genocide.[75] The foremost champion of these tribunals was the United States.[76]

Nothing in the UN Charter foresaw or authorized the Council's creation of such judicial bodies, but nothing in the Charter precluded it. In an era of unprecedented Council activism, the establishment of these tribunals signaled just how expansive the Council's interpretation of its own powers had become. And because the P5 either actively supported or consented to the creation of the tribunals, the Council decisions can be regarded as both broadly consensual and precedential. And the Council has, since then, encouraged the creation of a variety of special courts involving international participation to address serious crimes in Sierra Leone, Cambodia, and elsewhere.[77] Nevertheless, assessments of the track record of the Special Tribunal for Sierra Leone are mixed, particularly with respect to "value for money" and to local perceptions of the quality of justice rendered.[78]

The creation of the criminal tribunals greatly intensified pressures for a permanent International Criminal Court (ICC) with universal jurisdiction, a notion that had been promoted for some time but with little earlier success. After 1994, progress on negotiating a statute for such a court accelerated dramatically.[79] However, when the ICC statute was adopted in Rome in 1998, a number of states, including the United States, voted against the text, citing a variety of concerns.[80] China, like India, has kept the court at arm's length. Russia signed the statute, but, after much public soul-searching, has still not ratified. In the United States, the ICC became

---

[75] See Security Council Resolution 808 and 827 (1993) on the Former Yugoslav Tribunal, and Security Council Resolution 955 (1994) on Rwanda.

[76] In particular, Madeleine Albright championed the tribunals. See Madeleine Albright, *Madam Secretary* (New York: Miramax Books, 2003), particularly pp. 182–3.

[77] The Council continues to gnaw at the issue of impunity, most recently at Denmark's request, producing in June 2006 a Presidential Statement on the topic. See UN Document S/PRST/2006/28 of June 22, 2006.

[78] See John L. Hirsch, "Peace and Justice: Mozambique and Sierra Leone Compared," *Peace versus Justice? Truth Commissions and War Crimes Tribunals in Africa*, Chandra Sriram and Suren Pillay, eds. (Scottsville, South Africa: University of KwaZulu-Natal Press, 2007).

[79] See Mauro Politi and Giuseppe Nesi, eds., *The Rome Statute of the International Criminal Court: A Challenge to Impunity* (Aldershot, UK: Ashgate, 2001). The essay therein of Elizabeth Wilmshurst, "The International Criminal Court: The Role of the Security Council," is particularly instructive.

[80] See Marc Weller, "Undoing the Global Constitution: UN Security Council Action on the International Criminal Court," *International Affairs* [London], 78, No. 4 (October 2002), pp. 693–712.

An Evolving UN Security Council

a domestic political football in the dying days of the Clinton administration. The Clinton administration's Republican opponents portrayed the Court as potentially a major threat to U.S. troops deployed globally, and President Bush in 2001 repudiated the statute that Clinton had signed in his final hours in power.

David Wippman recently wrote with acuity on the challenges the Court faces and the opportunities it presents. He argues that the claims of both critics and supporters of the ICC have been exaggerated.[81] He notes that the staggering expense of ad hoc tribunals not only argues for an integrated approach but also suggests the ICC will be on a tight financial leash, precluding expansive interpretations of its remit.[82] He suggests that, at best, the ICC will be able to try only a few ringleaders in the man-made humanitarian or political disasters on its docket, with many perpetrators going free. But this was also the logic of the Tokyo and Nuremberg Trials. Seeing leaders dragged before courts can produce useful demonstration effects. (Deterrent effects are probably more dubious.)

There has been much debate over whether ICC prosecutions are compatible with the objective of national reconciliation, a debate touched on earlier with respect to Sierra Leone. Darryl Robinson reminds us that the Court has the discretion not to proceed with prosecutions where it views them as likely to be counterproductive to broader justice; that in the worst cases it almost always will be appropriate to prosecute a few of the worst perpetrators; that such proceedings are complementary with other forms of justice, mostly at the national level; and finally that national or international Truth Commissions aimed at promoting reconciliation need not be incompatible with a small number of well-targeted criminal prosecutions.[83]

The Court is now up and running (as of September 2007 with 105 states parties, Japan the most recent) and now has four cases on its docket. The most high-profile of these relates to Darfur, further to a decision in 2005 by both China and the United States to swallow their hostility to the Court and to allow referral to it by the Security Council of the findings of a UN expert panel on serious international crimes committed in relation to Darfur (including a sealed list of fifty-one suspects).[84] This development suggests that the ICC is likely to figure in a number of Council strategies in the future, while the Council itself may, on occasion, have to grapple with the fallout of ICC decisions that could affect peace and security.

A case referred by Uganda to the ICC, relating to a particularly violent and vicious rebel force, may be no less relevant to the Council in the future. Arrest

---

[81] David Wippman, "Exaggerating the ICC," in Joanna Harrington, Michael Milde, and Richard Vernon, eds., *Bringing Power to Justice? The Prospects of the International Criminal Court* (Montreal: McGill-Queens University Press, 2006), pp. 99–140.

[82] The ICTR and the ICTY together cost approximately $400 million in 2004.

[83] Darryl Robinson, "Serving the Interests of Justice: Amnesties, Truth Commissions and the International Criminal Court," *Bringing Power to Justice*, pp. 210–43.

[84] On March 31, 2005, the Security Council adopted SCR 1593, with 11 votes in favor, 0 against, and 4 abstentions, with the United States and China among the abstainers. In 2007, the U.S. government hinted at a more supportive view of the Court in this specific case. See http://www.amicc.org/docs/Darfur.

warrants for crimes against humanity and war crimes were made public by the ICC prosecutor against five senior commanders of the Lord's Resistance Army (LRA) rebel movement (including its leader Joseph Kony) on October 13, 2005. Execution of the arrest warrants remains outstanding. This case has been criticized by a number of Ugandans and nongovernmental organizations that believe that national reconciliation should trump criminal prosecution of Kony (and some of his confederates).[85] And it may come back to haunt both the ICC and Ugandan President Museveni if the latter settles his differences with the LRA politically, as seemed quite possible in late 2006.[86] Then, issues of amnesty and asylum may arise for the LRA leadership, and the Council might be tempted to request the ICC to suspend prosecutions.[87] At the same time, there is little doubt that the ICC's indictments were a significant factor in creating pressure on the LRA to cease its campaign of mayhem and terror in Northern Uganda.[88]

From the preceding paragraphs, it is clear that the Security Council's venture into the realm of international criminal law has been ground-breaking and, for good or ill, more decisive than have been to date its decisions on terrorism or transnational crime.

CONCLUSIONS: COUNCIL DECISIONS AND CONCEPTIONS OF SOVEREIGNTY

Arguably the most important, although one of the least noticed, of the consequences of Council decisions in the post–Cold War era, taken as a whole, shaped and driven by the factors discussed previously, has been to erode and shift at the international level the understanding of national sovereignty. The development in the nature and scope of Council decisions, many setting precedents even where the Council asserted that they did not, arose from evolving interpretations of the Charter and deeply affected understanding of sovereignty at the international level, both shaped by, and influencing, the Council. These shifts are accounted for by the new drivers of Council decision making, including terrorism, and by the P5's ability to work together more often than not, although the dynamics of their interaction are complex and ever shifting.

[85] For a relevant informed blog commentary see http://lawofnations.blogspot.com/2005/04/icc-watch-prosecutor-northern-ugandan.html. For a fuller analysis, see http://www.globalsecurity.org/military/library/news/2005/10/mil-051010-irino2.htm.

[86] Museveni and the LRA leadership met in southern Sudan in October 2006, and although that meeting did not resolve outstanding differences, it may have helped create a dynamic that could. For an update on the situation in northern Uganda, see a September 2006 report from the International Crisis Group at: http://www.crisisgroup.org/home/index.cfm?id=4374&l=1.

[87] For further speculation along these lines, see an October 2006 brief by Security Council Watch at: http://www.securitycouncilreport.org/site/c.glKWLeMTIsG/b.2087351/k.E8B6/October_2006BRUganda.htm.

[88] See Nick Grono, "What Comes First, Peace or Justice? Uganda's Dilemma," *International Herald Tribune*, 27, October 2006.

It is now widely (although not universally) accepted that tyrants can no longer seek refuge behind the walls of sovereignty to shield themselves from international concern and even action over massive human rights violations and humanitarian catastrophes. The Council, by intervening repeatedly to address the humanitarian consequences of mostly civil wars, often authorizing coercive measures, and by designing increasingly complex and intrusive mandates for international actors within member countries, sometimes without their consent, has not so much overridden article 2(7) of the Charter (which exempts Chapter VII decisions from its nonintervention provisions) but sharply redefined in practice conceptions of what can constitute a threat to international peace and security and a proper topic for international intervention.

The degree of intrusiveness the Council has been prepared to mandate since the end of the Cold War is striking. And the Council's willingness in several instances documented earlier to "legislate" for member states by imposing on them complex regulatory requirements suggests not only a sense of urgency (e.g., with respect to terrorism) but also a risky willingness to override the treaty-making prerogatives of sovereign countries that have been one of the hallmarks of international relations in recent centuries.

Whether these recent developments evolve into meaningful trends should provide an interesting field for academic study and for policy research and analysis in decades to come.

5

Too Many Institutions? European Security Cooperation after the Cold War

Richard Gowan and Sara Batmanglich

INTRODUCTION: A WAR OF INSTITUTIONS

In July 2008, the Russian ambassador to the North Atlantic Treaty Organization (NATO) set out proposals to consolidate – or supplant – Europe's patchwork of post–Cold War security institutions.[1] These included a new forum to bring together NATO, the European Union (EU), and the Organization for Security and Cooperation in Europe (OSCE) with Russia's own institutional networks in the former Soviet Union. Although NATO's initial reaction was noncommittal, the initiative played on Western concerns about the incoherence of Europe's security architecture. Russia found a starker way to show the strains affecting that architecture less than a fortnight after its approach to NATO: going to war with Georgia.

Moscow claimed a rapid victory. But this was also a war of institutions. The fighting was the culmination of the erosion of the security framework put in place in Georgia in the early 1990s to freeze its post-Soviet civil wars. This framework included not only Russian and Georgian peacekeepers, co-deployed under the aegis of the Commonwealth of Independent States (CIS) in the separatist enclaves of South Ossetia and Abkhazia, but also monitors from the OSCE in the former and the United Nations (UN) in the latter. This was one of the most convoluted collective security arrangements outside the former Yugoslavia. Its collapse was stimulated by new institutional dynamics – and in turn stimulated a vast amount of institutional activity. Russia's willingness to go to war in the summer of 2008 was partly attributable to its concern that NATO might offer Georgia a path toward membership in the latter half of the year. If Russia was motivated by a desire to preempt this, which international organizations could credibly mediate a ceasefire? With the UN Security Council paralyzed, the EU (through its French presidency) took the lead, backed by the OSCE (through its Finnish Chairman-in-Office). Once

---

[1] Judy Dempsey, "Russian Proposal Calls for Broader Security Pact," *International Herald Tribune*, July 28, 2008.

European Security Cooperation after the Cold War

the war was over, the UN, EU, and OSCE co-chaired the Russo–Georgian talks in Geneva. This did not prevent Russia from vetoing first the OSCE and then the UN missions within the next nine months. But European leaders searched for an institutional *modus vivendi* with Russia: French President Nicolas Sarkozy endorsed consideration of Moscow's proposals "to lay the foundations of what could possibly be a future pan-European security system."[2]

Reviewing this narrative, it is obvious that Europe's security institutions failed in many regards over Georgia, yet they also demonstrated a significant ability to absorb and mitigate the conflict. They rapidly built a diplomatic process around the ground war that offered both sides a way out before dissipating some of the tensions involved by shifting focus to institutional issues. This chapter argues that this followed a recurrent pattern in Europe's post–Cold War history, and (more controversially) that *European governments can often maximize their influence by working through multiple institutions* – an argument that, building on the work of Stanley Hoffmann, we call "institutional pluralism."

This leaves us in a small minority among European security analysts. For most, the fragmented response to the Georgian war seemed to be a sad verdict on the outcome of nearly two decades of initiatives to turn Europe (and specifically the EU) into a unified foreign policy actor. The crisis inspired a small host of papers arguing that it proved the need for the EU to speak with a single voice.[3] It might thus seem odd to argue that the sheer complexity of Europe's security institutions can play to its advantage in international affairs, even if only inconsistently. Other challenges for Europe have been compounded by inter-institutional frictions. These include Kosovo, where Russian obduracy prevented a smooth transition from UN administration to EU-led supervision in 2007–2008, and Afghanistan, where Europe and the United States have attempted to align NATO, UN, and EU missions to limited avail.

Nonetheless, the form of pluralism we identify is not *necessarily* incompatible with European governments following unified and effective policies. Institutional pluralism is able to succeed where leading governments apply coherent strategies across incoherent institutions. This chapter underlines that Europe's record is a mix of success and failure in this regard. First, we offer a brief explanation of why European leaders initially accepted institutional pluralism as a response to the Yugoslav conflict in early 1990s, setting a precedent for later crises. Second, we look at how Europe and the United States tried to use a web of institutions to

---

[2] Ian Traynor, "Sarkozy Backs Russian Call for Pan-European Security Pact," *The Guardian*, November 15, 2008.

[3] See, for example, Nicu Popescu, Mark Leonard, and Andrew Wilson, *Can the EU Win the Peace in Georgia?* (European Council on Foreign Relations, August 2008); and Tomas Valasek, *What Does the War in Georgia Mean for EU Foreign Policy?* (Center on European Reform, August 2008). The debate was all the more sensitive as Irish voters had just rejected the Lisbon Treaty, a reform package intended, *inter alia*, to consolidate the EU's foreign policy mechanisms.

mollify Russia during NATO enlargement. Third, we summarize how the divided European powers used institutional pluralism in their efforts to shape American decisions before and after the war in Iraq – as well as rebuild trust within Europe after the invasion. The Russian and Iraqi cases demonstrate the limits of institutional pluralism as a strategy. In the fourth part of the chapter we turn to cases in which it *has* maximized European leverage: Lebanon, Africa, and Iran.

We cannot conclude that there is a guaranteed correlation between the increases in European leverage and the successful resolution of the challenges we cite – the crises cited in our final section are still ongoing. So why do we identify these as relative successes? The simple answer is that in these cases European governments have taken leadership roles, in spite of limits to what they can achieve without external assistance. We broadly agree with Robert Kagan's prognosis that an essential factor in explaining European foreign policies is the continent's relative weakness, which causes its leaders and intellectuals to invest their trust in international institutions.[4] Where we differ from Kagan is over his supposition that building, maintaining, and expanding international security institutions is an essentially utopian enterprise detached from power politics. He saw the Georgian war as the "official return of history," demonstrating the futility of institutionalism:

> Yes, we will continue to have globalization, economic interdependence, the European Union and other efforts to build a more perfect international order. But these will compete with and at times be overwhelmed by the harsh realities of international life that have endured since time immemorial.[5]

We believe this equation of institutionalism and the pursuit of perfectibility is misleading. A recurrent motive for much European policy has been to preserve the existing international order – consisting of multiple, overlapping, and imperfect institutions – rather than to conjure up a better one. Kagan overlooks this deliberately limited case for international institutions. The essentially conservative approach to multilateralism that we identify derives from both the legacy of Cold War institutions and the threat posed to regional stability by chaos in the former Yugoslavia in the early 1990s. This combination of factors established institutional pluralism as an ordering principle in European affairs – a principle complicated by pressure for the expansion of NATO from the mid-1990s.

Before turning to these topics, it is worth identifying a theoretical basis for institutional pluralism. The best available basis may be Stanley Hoffmann's work on world order and pluralism, published in the late 1970s.[6] It may seem a counterintuitive choice insofar as this work focused on American policy choices, whereas much of

---

[4] See Robert Kagan, *Of Paradise and Power* (New York: Knopf, 2003).
[5] Robert Kagan, "Putin Makes His Move," *The Washington Post*, August 11, 2008.
[6] See Stanley Hoffmann, *Primacy or World Order: American Foreign Policy since the Cold War* (New York: McGraw-Hill, 1978); and "The Uses of American Power," *Foreign Affairs* 56, No. 1 (1977).

European Security Cooperation after the Cold War 83

Hoffmann's earlier and later writings concentrated on European affairs.[7] But in the aftermath of Vietnam, he believed that the United States had much to learn from the "messy" and "à la carte" process of cooperation that had emerged in Western Europe in the period since World War II.[8] That messiness contrasted with an American desire to define precisely how it should engage with the world. This privilege might no longer be available: "the United States has had difficulty shaping the movements and outcomes of world affairs," so "the problem for American policy consists in maximizing our opportunities for influence."[9]

Hoffmann set out three guidelines for how to act. The first was conservative: "protect and support the elements of order that exist already."[10] The last was radical. The United States must replace the confrontational logic of the Cold War with "relationships that are only partially adversary and allow for sufficient cooperation to make order possible."[11] Between these two guidelines (conceptually as well as numerically) was the principle of pluralism, by which other countries should be encouraged to develop a stake in managing and preserving order.[12] This demanded flexibility and a willingness to accept second-best options that would allow for "ulterior progress, rather than perpetual competition."[13]

Hoffmann's advice for the United States was superseded by the Reagan revolution in a matter of years. But read today it provides a remarkably useful summary to the types of goals European states often pursue. If we review our account of the Georgian war, we see the Europeans struggling to protect existing "elements of order" (the OSCE and UN presences in Georgia), attempting to maintain a cooperative relationship with Russia during and after the conflict – and searching for progress with Moscow on institutional issues within months of the crisis, presumably to increase Russia's stake in maintaining order in the future. Throughout the sections that follow, we will perceive a European desire to increase leverage that matches Hoffmann's interest in "maximizing our opportunities for influence." If Hoffmann's estimate of America's waning power was mistaken in the 1970s, his recommendations fit very well with the priorities of a relatively weak Europe.

The starting point for the rest of the chapter is this: given the constraints on Europe's power, and its preferences for order, how has it performed relative to Hoffmann's guidelines? We must look not for progress toward a "better world," but

---

7 A more recent point of reference is the work of Daniel W. Drezner. See "The Power and Peril of International Regime Complexity," *Perspectives on Politics*, No. 7 (2009), pp. 65–70. Drezner emphasizes that major powers may prefer to work through multiple institutions – by contrast, we are concerned with why European countries facing a relative decline in their power would choose to do so.

8 Hoffmann, "The Uses of American Power," p. 35.

9 Ibid., pp. 28–29.

10 Ibid., p. 29.

11 Ibid., p. 35.

12 Ibid., p. 34.

13 Ibid., p. 35.

for evidence of a capacity to protect and sustain various forms of order. But this raises another problem central to our argument. What forms of order are European governments required to defend?

INSTITUTIONAL PLURALISM ASCENDANT: THE POST–COLD WAR SETTLEMENT AND BALKAN WARS

When Stanley Hoffmann wrote about pluralism, he imagined that one implication of allowing other countries a greater say in international affairs would be "a world of many coalitions."[14] He was skeptical that the United States could play a predominant role in shaping international institutions. Indeed, he was disappointed that the European Community (EC) had not matured sufficiently to display substantial autonomy from Washington. Yet at the end of the Cold War, European governments were entangled in a variety of international institutions including NATO, the EC, and the OSCE's precursor, the Conference on Security and Cooperation in Europe (CSCE). Forty years of confrontation had proved an unexpectedly fecund period for institutional innovation – it should not be forgotten that the Soviet system had also institutionalized its power through the Warsaw Pact and Council for Mutual Economic Assistance (Comecon). Additionally, the Balkan wars were soon to bring the UN into continental Europe, from which it had previously been operationally absent. If anyone had reminded a European leader of Hoffmann's injunction to "protect and support the elements of order that exist already," they would have been asked precisely which elements of which order they were referring to.

Whereas Hoffmann had perceived pluralism as allowing a wide variety of states to participate in managing international order, the problem in Europe after the Cold War was twofold: not only to decide which *states* had influence but also to define which *institutions* this influence should be applied through. This dual challenge was further complicated by the fact that the main security institutions embodied different distributions of authority among the major regional and global powers. Whereas the UN formalized the power of the Permanent Five members of the Security Council, NATO's command structures gave the United States a privileged position in Western European security. The EC represented an emerging political entity, but one with an as yet no hard security dimension (its military counterpart, the Western European Union [WEU] being largely soporific), whereas the CSCE reflected the bipolar balance of power that had crumbled in the 1980s.

If this collection of organizations appeared ripe for rationalization, any significant political reforms would require a new consensus on a concept of order for Europe – which would in turn mean altering the balance of power within and between organizations. This did not prevent a bout of institutional reforms. NATO

[14] Ibid., p. 45.

adopted a series of new strategic concepts, and NATO members and their erstwhile adversaries accepted arms limitations under the 1990 Conventional Forces in Europe Treaty.[15] The EC was converted into the EU by means of the 1991 Maastricht Treaty, which paved the way for its later absorption of the WEU and development of a defense identity. The CSCE became the OSCE in 1995, having taken on significant operational obligations in the Balkans and former Soviet Union. On paper, all three organizations (NATO, EU, and OSCE) recognized a new security environment characterized by opportunities for cooperation.

Important as these changes were, there was much less progress in redefining the political bases of European order. Although ready to rethink the role of institutions, states were typically wary of losing influence over high-level decision making within them. Russia pursued concentrating decision-making powers in the OSCE, but the United States blocked it, not wishing to grant authority to a body that did not fully reflect its increased power.[16] Within the EU, foreign policy decisions required (and still require) consensus, unlike other significant areas subject to a system of qualified majority voting. There has been no alteration to NATO's political decision-making structures. European countries, like the United States and Russia, have also benefited from the lack of Security Council reform at the UN – around a third of the Council consists of EU members at any time.

So, although Europe's security architecture underwent major changes in the 1990s, its political underpinnings remained surprisingly consistent. In 1996, the British security analyst Paul Cornish summarized Europe's failure to address core questions of order. Noting a surplus of architectural metaphors in international relations, he joked, "A good deal of the discussion to date has indeed taken place on a conceptual building site":

> Evidence of design and construction has, however, been well concealed for several years, [and] the architectural competition to design a new (or rebuilt) structure of European security has proved to be a long-running event. Even the most professionally prepared and aesthetically pleasing blueprint failed to eliminate the competition, simply because the clients had not really decided (or been compelled to decide) exactly what they wanted to build.[17]

But if political inertia was one major obstacle to rationalizing Europe's institutions, two dynamic factors also militated against doing so. The first was the extent to which the architectural debate was caught up with urgent operational and political concerns during the Balkan wars. The second was the Clinton administration's

---

[15] On the importance of the Conventional Forces in Europe Treaty, see Robert Cooper, *The Breaking of Nations* (Atlantic Monthly Press, 2003), pp. 27–29.
[16] Fraser Cameron, "The European Union and the OSCE: Future Roles and Challenges," *Helsinki Monitor*, 6, No. 2, (1995), p. 25.
[17] Paul Cornish, "The End of Architecture and the New NATO," *International Affairs*, 72, No. 4, p. 752.

decision to promote NATO enlargement, discussed in the next section. Both upset institutional relationships, causing European states to balance commitments in some forums against those in others – and associate order and their own influence with greater pluralism rather than less.

The precise impact of the collapse of Yugoslavia on Europe's institutional evolution remains difficult to quantify. It is tempting to speculate that had it been avoided, Europe might have settled on a less complicated security structure – but this cannot be proven. An absence of war might have created even greater inertia. What can be described with some certainty (and which Cornish's description of generalized stasis may have missed) is the extent to which responding to the Balkan crisis pushed European states to address the roles and relationships of regional organizations and the UN. Susan Woodward has best summarized this process, and the ensuing paragraphs are based on her account.[18] Woodward's critique of Western policy is that European governments reduced the UN Security Council to a "handmaiden of European security," exploiting rather than respecting its unique legal status.[19] By contrast, we are more concerned with the ad hoc process in which European governments drew on elements of a range of international organizations to create a highly complex response that spread responsibility very widely.

This approach resulted from the fact that although there was undoubted desire among some European governments, most notably France and Germany, to engage in the conflict, they lacked the institutional mechanisms to do so. In political terms, the EC had no inherent locus in Yugoslavia, and so turned to the CSCE in 1991 to legitimize EC-led mediation efforts over Croatia and Slovenia – CSCE negotiators worked alongside the EC in some talks. The WEU drew up plans for a military intervention in Croatia. But the United States objected to this as undermining NATO, causing the French to turn to the UN to authorize a peacekeeping force. The EC and UN merged their negotiating efforts (without much success), and the UN, CSCE, and EC/EU maintained separate monitoring missions in the region. Having invested in this multiplicity of deployments, European governments managed to keep NATO in a secondary role until the end of 1995.

As Woodward notes, this institutional complexity concealed the fact that the majority of personnel and political direction came from Western Europe. Moreover, such a brief rendering of the events involved cannot capture significant differences among the leading Western European states on how to utilize institutions. Germany, for example, was wary of France's interest in the UN route, whereas Britain was instrumental in supporting the American position that NATO's prerogatives should not be challenged. When, in 1995, the French and British governments used force against the Bosnian Serbs, their ground commanders did so independently of the

[18] Susan Woodward, "The Security Council and the Wars in the Former Yugoslavia," in Vaughan Lowe, Adam Roberts, Jennifer Welsh, and Dominik Zaum, eds., *The United Nations Security Council and War* (Oxford University Press, 2008), pp. 406–41.

[19] Ibid., p. 407.

Security Council.[20] European analysts skeptical of institutional pluralism believe that it was tried in Bosnia and failed.

Nonetheless, the decisions to turn to the CSCE and UN for political cover for mediation and peacekeeping at the start of the war established pluralism as a norm in managing the Balkans. Although the 1995 Dayton agreement that ended the Bosnian war approved a NATO deployment to replace the UN's military force, the latter continued to have a police and civilian presence, while the OSCE launched a parallel mission. The UN and OSCE shared duties in Croatia. Demonstrating the degree to which European policy blurred institutional boundaries, the EU negotiated the Stability Pact for South-East Europe, a subregional arrangement based on OSCE principles with its legal instruments deposited at the OSCE in Vienna. When the West confronted Serbia over Kosovo in 1998 and 1999, European governments led by France insisted that the UN and OSCE must be involved, rather than accept the American position that NATO alone should handle the crisis. What began as an ad hoc search for diplomatic legitimacy morphed into an ordering principle – of simultaneous and overlapping engagement in crises by multiple organizations – that we have seen repeated in the response to the Georgian war.

Institutional pluralism has not gone unchallenged in the Balkans. Replacing the web of institutional arrangements left behind after Dayton became a test for the EU in Bosnia, as it gradually took over policing and military duties from NATO and the UN from 2003 onwards. But this process was unsteady – complicated by both American skepticism and European errors – and when UN envoy Martti Ahtisaari published proposals for "supervised independence" in Kosovo in 2006, he argued that the EU, NATO, and OSCE should continue to play roles in the province.[21] It was widely understood that this plan was meant to balance EU and NATO support for Kosovo's independence with OSCE assistance to its Serb and other minorities. In reality, the international community's failure to agree on the province's future resulted in an even more complex institutional hybrid by which a residual UN presence has helped legitimize the EU's role. Ahtisaari's plan showed how institutional pluralism evolved from improvisation to political design. Ensuing events showed that improvisation is still necessary – and still favors pluralism.

However, two qualifications must be made about the form of pluralism that emerged from European engagement with the Balkans. The first is that, because of its ad hoc roots and crisis-driven nature, it often is as short-sighted and inefficient as its critics claim. The second is that it has reflected but never resolved the inherent political differences embedded in the institutions involved. European assertions of leverage inside the UN and OSCE have sometimes reduced other powers' faith

---

[20] See also Rupert Smith, "The Security Council and the Bosnian Conflict: A Practitioner's View," in Lowe et al., op. cit., p. 450.

[21] See Center on International Cooperation, *Annual Review of Global Peace Operations 2008* (Lynne Rienner, 2008), pp. 50–51.

in those institutions. At the UN, France and Britain's defense of peacekeeping in Bosnia in the Security Council in the early 1990s alienated both the United States (which thought the strategy fundamentally flawed) and Russia, which acquiesced but felt wounded by a lack of respect for its interests.

Russia was also conscious that, if the CSCE/OSCE generally served European (and later U.S.) interests in the Balkans, Moscow did not have the same degree of influence over the institution's activities in the former Soviet Union. In the first half of the decade, Boris Yeltsin's government not only accepted CSCE monitoring of CIS troops in South Ossetia but also encouraged the organization to engage in the Nagorny-Karabakh region of Azerbaijan and even Chechnya (OSCE missions also deployed to former Soviet republics in Central Asia). It was increasingly disappointed that these gestures failed to win it leverage comparable to that of the Europeans in Croatia and Bosnia, and by 1996 it was increasingly "grudging" toward the OSCE, looking for other mediation mechanisms.[22]

Although European powers were able to utilize a wide range of institutions in their search for order in the Balkans in the 1990s, they risked systemic tensions. These tensions reemerged in the following decade as Russia regained strength. Moscow's complaint was that, although there had been no formal reform of political decision making in the leading security institutions, Western Europe and the United States had informally coopted the OSCE in a way that devalued its autonomy. Senior Russian officials complained that the OSCE "was turning into an instrument for serving the interests of other organizations," meaning that "NATO deals with security issues, the EU with economic issues, while the OSCE will only monitor the adoption of these organizations' values by countries that have remained outside the EU and NATO."[23] This is similar to Woodward's depiction of the Security Council as "handmaiden of European security."

The Europeans had arguably failed to follow Hoffmann's guideline that pluralism should mean accepting greater freedom of action for other countries – they had spread responsibilities across institutions, yet reduced Russia's sense of ownership over them. This points to what may be an ineluctable tension in institutional pluralism: it is almost impossible to implement "joined-up" strategies through multiple organizations without creating tensions within each forum. A recent example outside the Balkans is Afghanistan, where efforts to advance a joint strategy through the NATO, UN, and EU missions in the country – perhaps by appointing a "superenvoy" to oversee all three, proposed in late 2006 – have encountered substantial resistance in each organization.

Returning to the case of Russia in the 1990s, criticism of European policy should be mitigated by two considerations. First, Russia was in such a parlous state in the

---

[22] Michael Mihalka, "A Marriage of Convenience: The OSCE in Nagorny-Karabakh and Chechnya," *Helsinki Monitor*, 7 No. 2 (1996), p. 13.

[23] Pál Dunay, *The OSCE in Crisis* (EU Institute for Security Studies, Chaillot Paper No. 88, 2006), p. 70.

early 1990s that diplomats feared for its internal cohesion rather than for its systemic interests. Second, Russia saw the overwhelming threat to those interests as coming not from European actions in the OSCE and UN, but from U.S. commitment to NATO expansion.

NATO expansion is also essential to explaining the evolution of institutional pluralism in Europe after its initial appearance during the Balkan Wars. In the next section we discuss efforts to reconcile Russia to the growth of NATO by offering it enhanced influence in other regional and international structures. This is institutional pluralism as grand strategy rather than as crisis management – and notable because it was a strategy advocated not in the face of U.S. skepticism (as over Yugoslavia) but as a function of U.S. policy.

INSTITUTIONAL PLURALISM FAILS: NATO EXPANSION

If the collapse of Yugoslavia instigated a pluralist response within Europe, it convinced the Clinton administration of the need to rationalize the continent's security situation through expanding NATO. The European failure to stabilize the Balkans caused American policymakers to lower their (in many cases, already very low) opinion of both the UN and Western European capabilities. By contrast, they encountered a strong desire for NATO's protection among new democracies in Eastern Europe. The Clinton administration bought into this – and in turn cajoled and coerced often-skeptical existing NATO members to do likewise.[24] This is the major exception to the case, made by Bruce Jones and Shepard Forman in Chapter 1, that the United States largely absented itself from international institutional reform in the Clinton era. This was not pure chance. The decision to concentrate on NATO was a counterpart to American suspicion of alternative security institutions, informed by events in Somalia and Yugoslavia. NATO enlargement, combined with Washington's insistence on deploying through the Alliance in Bosnia after Dayton, could be read as a rejection of institutional pluralism. Yet it initiated U.S. and European interest in how Russia might be induced to accept NATO's growth through engagement in other international and regional forums.

This secondary process is our focus here – the main narrative of NATO enlargement has received much attention elsewhere, and need not be recounted here. It is worth noting that, in expanding its membership and operational responsibilities, NATO has become a far more flexible organization than in the Cold War, creating openings and obstacles described by Mats Berdal and David Ucko in Chapter 6. One outcome of the organization's evolution has been to make it more open to institutional pluralism itself, learning to work with the UN and (uneasily) the EU. But this has not made Russia any more open to its growth.

---

[24] See Ronald D. Asmus, *Opening NATO's Door: How the Alliance Remade Itself for a New Era* (Columbia University Press, 2002).

The 1990s debate over how to handle Russia was captured in an exchange published in *International Affairs* in 1998. On one side was a British expert on Russia, Jonathan Haslam, who demanded to know if and when Russia would be allowed a new "seat at the table" in international affairs.[25] On the other was an American general, William E. Odom, who noted that Russia had its permanent place in the Security Council (which "it probably no longer deserves in light of its diminished power") and many other seats to boast of:

> Russia has participated in all of the groups concerned with the war in Bosnia and the crisis in Kosovo. US-Russian summits have continued in the tradition of US-Soviet summits, although without substantive justification. Russia has been invited to the windows of all international financial institutions: the IMF, the World Bank... and numerous commercial banks, particularly in Britain, Germany and the United States. Russia issues its paper on Western private capital and bond markets. Can Moscow credibly claim that Russia is being excluded?[26]

Odom's argument echoed another of the principles of pluralism laid down by Hoffmann in the 1970s: that interaction between states must take place on multiple tracks, which although interconnected should not be held hostage by problems over any one topic. Russia's position on relations in Europe could not be defined in terms of NATO alone. Although many of the "seats" identified by Odom had not been deliberately devised by the United States and its allies to compensate Russia for NATO expansion, he also noted two that had.

One of these was directly related to the security issue. This was the May 1997 "Founding Act" on NATO–Russian relations that promised "consultation, cooperation, joint decision-making, and joint action"; committed both sides to strengthen the OSCE; and paid homage to Chapter VIII of the UN Charter, which authorizes regional security arrangements.[27] Rhetorically at least, there was a sizeable dose of institutional pluralism in this document. More concretely, it instituted a NATO–Russia Permanent Joint Council and a Russian diplomatic mission to NATO – precisely the mechanisms through which Moscow would propose a new security pact in 2008.

The second deliberate compensatory mechanism for Russia was its invitation to join the G7/G8 (also in 1997), which Moscow had genuinely treated as a priority. This offer accorded with the view of Strobe Talbott, the Deputy Secretary of State and initial opponent of NATO expansion, that Russia's integration into the international system was tied to "its ability and willingness to participate in, contribute to and benefit from the process of globalization."[28] Talbott was also sensitive to Russia's

---

[25] Jonathan Haslam, "Russia's Seat at the Table: A Place Denied or a Place Delayed?", *International Affairs*, 74, No. 1, pp. 119–30.

[26] William E. Odom, "Russia's Several Seats at the Table," *International Affairs*, 74, No. 4, p. 815.

[27] *Founding Act on Mutual Relations, Cooperation and Security Between NATO and the Russian Federation* (May 27, 1997), http://www.nato.int/docu/basictxt/fndact-a.htm (accessed November 10, 2008).

[28] Haslam, op. cit., p. 130.

European Security Cooperation after the Cold War 91

regional concerns, arguing that any extension of NATO to embrace Estonia, Latvia, and Lithuania must be balanced by a framework that respected Moscow's interests in the Baltic. He and his subordinates likened the resulting "Northern European Initiative" to the medieval Hanseatic League.[29]

Although internally divided over the need to mollify Russia, the Clinton administration thus attempted to balance NATO's growth with institutional openings from the global to the subregional levels. There was an additional and specifically European initiative. The EU was also moving toward expanding into Eastern Europe – an enlargement carried through in 2004 – so its members had compound reasons to restructure relations with Russia. This involved institutionalizing EU–Russian relations, begun with the signing of a Partnership and Cooperation Agreement in 1994. This provided for regular summits and coordination meetings. It was followed in 1999 by an EU "common strategy" toward Moscow that attempted to compensate for the fresh diplomatic wounds of the Kosovo crisis with language on "maintaining European stability, promoting global security and responding to the common challenges of the continent through intensified co-operation with Russia."[30] Although Russian politicians and officials appeared ignorant of how the EU worked, here was one more institutional framework for cooperation.

But the Kosovo war had effectively undercut U.S. or European institutional initiatives. Neither Russia's presence in the G8 nor the existence of the Joint Permanent Council had allowed it to halt NATO's decision for war – and nor had its veto on action in the Security Council. Whereas the collapse of Yugoslavia had led Western European states to spread their response across institutions, the United States and its allies now acted through NATO when other institutional roads were closed. Russia's "seats" outside NATO had given it less influence than it supposed.

Russia responded to the EU's 1999 Common Strategy with a declaration on the need to end "NATO-centrism" in Europe.[31] Moscow showed that it too understood the value of institutional tradeoffs, conditioning its outreach to the EU on support for entry into the World Trade Organization – and an implicit assertion of enduring authority of members over the CIS. Nonetheless, Moscow has continued to bridle at the complexity of its links to the EU, and the regular EU–Russia summits produce a flood of declarations with little substance.[32] Russia's behavior in the G8 is often counterproductive. Even some positive initiatives have negative side effects: the NATO-Russia Council has compounded Moscow's loss of interest in the OSCE.[33]

Whatever the balance of tactical successes and failures with Russia, it is clear that institutional pluralism has failed *as a strategy* in this case. Russia's handling of Kosovo

---

[29] Asmus, op. cit., pp. 230–1.
[30] David Gowan, *How the EU Can Help Russia* (Center for European Reform, 2000), p. 10.
[31] Ibid., p. 11.
[32] Laetitia Spetchinshsky, "Russia and the EU: The Challenge Ahead," *Studia Diplomatica*, LX, No. 1 (2007), p. 157.
[33] Dunay, op. cit., p. 70.

and Georgia has shown that it is not satisfied with the uncertain status provided by multiple seats at multiple tables. Its call for a new European pact indicates that it would prefer cohesive terms of its own making. Its assertive attitude toward the West reflects political contingencies – such as the obvious rifts within NATO over issues from Afghanistan to missile defense – and energy economics. But a more general lesson may be that although institutional pluralism can persist in a context of small and fractured states as in the Balkans – especially if the main concern is to sustain international order in the face of localized chaos – it may be unsustainable in relations with major powers. To test this, we turn to European efforts to "manage" the United States over Iraq by institutional means.

IRAQ: FAILURE OR PRELUDE TO GREATER PLURALISM?

The institutional ramifications of the Iraq war are a recurrent motif in this volume. Our concern here is not the overall impact of the U.S.-led invasion on multilateralism; rather it is how European states (both in favor of action and against it) used a variety of institutional mechanisms during the crisis. Like Georgia, Iraq was a war of institutions: the relatively brief initial ground war was preceded by prolonged wrangling within not only the UN but also NATO – although its aftermath saw considerable institutional activity aimed at affecting events in Iraq and reducing the damage to international organizations.

European governments were instrumental to both phases of activity. Although the American decision to invade was a very public rejection of an institutional approach, both its supporters and its opponents in Europe grounded their reaction in institutional politics. The United Kingdom predicated its military support on efforts to get Security Council approval – and France and Germany used the Council as their primary platform to object.

The impact of these maneuvers at the UN is described in David Malone's chapter. Here we can see an effort to "protect and support the elements of order that exist already," however complicated by competing national interests. But the diplomacy of the crisis was not confined to the UN. It played out in NATO, where Germany, France, and Belgium used the principle of unanimity to delay planning for the defense of Turkey against any attack from Iraq. Transatlantic relations were still mediated through institutions.[34] If Europe and the United States had wanted to entangle Russia in organizations in the 1990s, their own mutual entanglement created numerous institutional pressure points.

This was underlined when France, Germany, and the caucus of other states opposed to the invasion held a mini-summit to call for new initiatives on EU defense cooperation – implicitly at the expense of NATO, and thus American influence in

---

[34] See Elizabeth Pond, *Friendly Fire: The Near-Death of the Transatlantic Alliance* (Washington, DC: Brookings Institution Press, 2003).

Europe. The United States proved that it too could play institutional games by slowing the transfer of military responsibility in Bosnia from NATO to the EU until the end of 2004. European security cooperation was temporarily turned into a proxy for disputes over war in the Middle East.

Reviewing these clashes in late 2003, Stanley Hoffmann concluded that the institutionalized rivalry before the war was less surprising than what came after it – a refusal by the United States to return to the "institutional game."[35] Pro- and antiwar European governments alike assumed that Washington would turn to the UN and NATO to handle the fallout of the invasion. Some, like France, appeared to believe that this would allow them to reduce American influence over Baghdad.[36] Even the OSCE's Secretariat offered its services.[37] In short, the European expectations of a postconflict mission looked very Balkan, showing how deeply ingrained the precedent of institutional pluralism in the 1990s had become. Although the United States did accept a UN assistance mission (largely evacuated after its headquarters were bombed), it otherwise rejected this approach.

It is a truism that Iraq was a setback for European visions of order: efforts to contain or guide Washington before and after the conflict foundered on the Bush administration's distaste for institutionalism, pluralist or otherwise. But the aftermath of the war also saw European governments attempt rapprochement toward one another through institutional means – as in the UK's decision to support a French-led EU operation to the Democratic Republic of Congo (*Operation Artemis*) to reinforce UN troops in the east of the country. *Artemis* reaffirmed the possibility of European defense and a shared European commitment to the UN. If the run-up to Iraq had seen diplomatic debacles across institutions, EU members now attempted to restore faith in institutionalism as a whole.

This was an important element of the first *European Security Strategy*, agreed by the EU's members in December 2003. Although making a much-quoted call for a "more coherent" EU, the *Strategy* gives considerable weight to other organizations: "the development of a stronger international society, well functioning international institutions and a rule-based international order is our objective."[38] In this context, it contains repeated references to the UN, NATO, and World Trade Organization – and more limited nods to the OSCE and non-European organizations including the African Union and the Association of South East Asian Nations (ASEAN). A respect for institutional pluralism is identifiable in this EU-centric document.

---

[35] Stanley Hoffman, "US-European Relations: Past and Future," *International Affairs*, 79, No. 5, p. 1036.

[36] On European positions on Iraq in the immediate aftermath of the war, see Richard Youngs, *Europe and Iraq: From Stand-off to Engagement?* (London: Foreign Policy Centre, 2004).

[37] "OSCE Chairperson encourages UN Security Council to seek OSCE support in Iraq, Afghanistan," OSCE Press Release, May 7, 2004, http://www.osce.org/item/8275.html (accessed November 10, 2008).

[38] *A Secure Europe in a Better World* (adopted by European Council, Brussels, December 12, 2003), p. 9.

94   *Richard Gowan and Sara Batmanglich*

This trait would be even more prominent in a report on the implementation of the *Strategy* delivered to EU governments by the European Council Secretariat in December 2008. This argued both that "we have deepened our relationship with the OSCE" and that "the EU and NATO must deepen their strategic partnership," whereas "everything the EU has done in the field of security has been linked to UN objectives."[39] For a paper emanating from the staff of an international institution, this was remarkably generous to the efforts of other organizations. As frequent references to the Georgian war implied, this was partially motivated by a desire to show that Europe's complex, pluralistic form of order remained viable. Had this been validated in other crises since the Iraq debacle?

PLURALISM AT WORK: AFRICA, LEBANON, AND IRAN

In searching for cases where European governments have made effective use of institutional pluralism, our focus moves away from security within Europe to crisis management outside it. We begin with peace operations in Africa and Lebanon, before turning to efforts to counter Iran's nuclear ambitions. In the first two cases, there is an obvious thematic link to the Balkan crises of the 1990s in spite of the geographical shift: if Europeans' own experience of peacekeeping involved a high degree of institutional pluralism, we would expect them to apply this model to other regions – which they do.

In Africa, European policy since the later 1990s has been driven by two principles familiar to Hoffmann: a desire for order and an urge to let others lead in maintaining it. These are not entirely altruistic preferences – they stem from a lack of political and military support in Europe for long-term engagements in Africa – and continue to be complicated by colonial legacies such as the French role in Chad and Côte d'Ivoire. But Africa has been seen as an environment in which the EU can prove its worth as a security actor through both direct limited military missions and indirect support to other organizations. The success of *Operation Artemis* in 2003, stabilizing the eastern Congo and relieving the UN, is often held up as a model for European action – perhaps overstating its virtues.

At the strategic level, European support for order in Africa has involved financial and occasional operational support to UN operations on the continent, combined with assistance to the nascent African Union (AU) from 2002 onward. The EU has also developed formalized relationships with subregional organizations such as ECOWAS, implemented through a predictable panoply of needs assessments, ministerial summits, and joint strategies.[40] The European Commission has won particular praise for its African Peace Facility, a fund that proved essential to the

---

[39] European Council Secretariat, *Report on the Implementation of the European Security Strategy: Providing Security in a Changing World* (Brussels, December 11, 2008), p. 11.

[40] See Bastien Nivet, *Security by Proxy? The EU and (Sub-)Regional Organizations: The Case of ECOWAS* (EU Institute for Security Studies, Occasional Paper No. 63).

AU peace operation in Darfur. The development of Africa's security institutions is described by Bah in Chapter 14, but it is clear that European funding has been essential to this process – and that this funding has fostered pluralism by supporting institution-building at all levels.

This support for the UN, AU, and subregional organizations has also allowed the EU to make tactical interventions in the Congo (in 2003 and 2006) and Chad and the Central African Republic (2008–2009) without being dragged into long-term obligations in the region. These operations have worked alongside or laid the groundwork for UN missions – as, in Darfur, the EU and NATO provided logistical support to AU peacekeepers. These limited interventions have given the EU considerable leverage over other organizations' decision making: the deployment of European troops to Chad acted as the trigger for a UN police mission and promise of a UN follow-on force, for example. Through promoting (and paying for) institutional pluralism in this way, European governments have remained influential in African security without taking excessive risks.

This approach – nicely described by one analyst as "security by proxy" – has clear limits. African governments have been riled by the complexity of European funding rules, and opposed European policies at the UN on Zimbabwe and Sudan. The UN's efforts to stabilize the Congo were shaken when the EU chose not to send troops to reinforce it during the major crisis of late 2008. In the medium to long term, Europe is almost certainly declining as a force in African affairs – but a strategy of institutional pluralism has allowed the EU to limit the rate of that decline and protect its interests in Africa.

European engagement in the Middle East may also be a case of decline management. But in both Lebanon and Iran, European governments have engaged with the UN in a way that has maximized their leverage (this may be contrasted with the Quartet on the Middle East Peace Process, in which the EU participates but has much less leverage). In the case of Lebanon, European governments managed to assert themselves in the resolution of the 2006 war between Israel and Hezbollah despite limited influence over the combatants. They did so by offering peacekeepers to the UN, but avoided normal UN troop pledging and deployment mechanisms, instead holding a special session of the European Council with Kofi Annan to discuss their contributions.[41] They also demanded a special cell be formed in New York to oversee the mission outside normal UN structures: by working through the UN and EU simultaneously, the European contributors (especially the lead nations, Italy and France) secured a privileged status for the mission.

This was a relatively simple maneuver when compared to the EU's relationship with the UN Security Council and the International Atomic Energy Agency (IAEA) over Iran. Wing describes the IAEA's handling of the Iranian crisis in Chapter 7.

---

[41] Center on International Cooperation, *Annual Review of Global Peace Operations* 2007 (Lynne Rienner, 2007), p. 9.

But the IAEA's room for maneuver has been in considerable part defined by its level of support from the governments of Britain, France, and Germany (the "E3"), which have spoken for the EU (if not always harmoniously) during the crisis and been involved in direct negotiations with Tehran. The E3's strategy has been to tie support for the monitoring work of the IAEA to a range of trade incentives to Iran from the EU – including peripheral offers such as assistance with pesticides.[42] At times, the primary role of the E3/EU has been to defend IAEA's Director-General Mohamed ElBaradei's approach to Iran's obligations against heavy U.S. criticism. Insofar as ElBaradei reports to the IAEA Board, on which the E3 and a number of other EU members sit, the Europeans have addressed the Iranian case from across a range of multilateral platforms.

This has not always been easy. ElBaradei has not always aligned himself with European positions, shifting instead between the West and developing countries to defend his own position. Iran initially proved willing to play the game of tying its compliance with the IAEA to access to European markets, but as negotiations continued, Iran showed little inclination to make good on such proposed deals. Nonetheless, the EU's approach gradually gained purchase with the Bush administration. In June 2008, Secretary of State Condoleezza Rice added her signature to a new package of incentives that offered to "recognize Iran's right to develop research, production and use of nuclear energy for peaceful purposes" and also agreed to improve and encourage more direct dialogue and support Iran "in playing an important and constructive role in international affairs."[43]

The EU's institutional influence has always been conditioned on the implicit threat of U.S. action against Iran – when, in December 2007, Washington published a National Intelligence Estimate that played down the Iranian threat, EU diplomats privately lamented that their leverage had been significantly curtailed. Nonetheless, the EU engagement with Iran does show some of the benefits of institutional pluralism. The European defense of the IAEA countered radical elements in the United States that might have preferred to employ force early in the crisis. This prevented a wider loss of faith in the Security Council and IAEA as effective mechanisms for countering proliferation – it sustained order. Through this, the EU has maintained a voice in shaping international decisions, which it could not have sustained through rhetorical support for the IAEA alone – or through economic incentives detached from a framework for monitoring Iranian behavior. A strategy of institutional pluralism combining the EU and IAEA's assets thus succeeded in amplifying Europe's combined ability to influence the evolution of the Iranian crisis.

---

[42] This paragraph and the next follow Richard Gowan, "The European Security Strategy's Global Objective: Effective Multilateralism," in Sven Biscop and Jan Joel Andersson, *The EU and the European Security Strategy: Forging a Global Europe* (Routledge, 2008), pp. 55–57.

[43] "P5+1 Updated Incentives Package" (June 17, 2008), http://2001–2009.state.gov/r/pa/prs/ps/2008/jun/105992.htm (accessed November 12, 2008).

CONCLUSION

This chapter has moved rapidly across a series of major and complex challenges to Europe – and largely omitted others discussed elsewhere in this volume, most obviously Afghanistan – to prove three potentially unpopular points noted in the introduction. The first is that there has been a pattern of institutional pluralism in Europe's post–Cold War history that runs counter to many analysts' preference for integration and rationalization. The second is that this form of pluralism can work, although only in specific circumstances. The third is that it is a guiding principle rooted in European politics by a triad of factors. These are the Cold War legacy of institutions, which has never been fully discarded; the Balkan wars, which created lasting precedents for pluralistic responses to crises; and Europe's relative decline, which inclines it toward conservative definitions of success. The utility of institutional pluralism in Africa or Lebanon cannot offset its failure to change the strategic calculations of either Russia over NATO or the United States over Iraq.

But this returns us to Hoffmann's warning that it is sometimes necessary to accept "messy" pluralism rather than hanker after perfect, but perfectly unachievable, versions of order. In periods of global change – such as that which followed the end of the Cold War and that we are now entering – second-best options and mitigation strategies may often be all that is available to policymakers. Institutional pluralism is in many ways intellectually unsatisfying and operationally ineffective – but it is resilient, and sometimes even useful.

6

Whither NATO[1]

Mats Berdal and David Ucko

NATO IN AFGHANISTAN: THE BEGINNING OF THE END OR THE END
OF THE BEGINNING?

In October 2006 the International Security Assistance Force (ISAF) in Afghanistan –
under North Atlantic Treaty Organization (NATO) command since August 2003 –
assumed operational control of the whole of the country. With nearly forty thousand
troops drawn from more than thirty-five countries, the Alliance was now charged
with providing security and bringing stability to a deeply fractured country *outside* its treaty-defined area of operations. The range of tasks given to NATO forces in
Afghanistan is broad and complex, from combat operations at one end to the rebuilding of roads, bridges, and schools at the other. On the face of it, the assumption of
such extensive responsibilities is testimony to an extraordinary transformation on the
part of the Alliance, evidence of just how far it has come from its early and initially
timid forays into peacekeeping on the European continent in the early 1990s.

And yet, NATO's first operation outside the Euro-Atlantic area has proved a
far greater challenge than initial planning assumptions, some of them simplistically
lifted from its experiences in the Balkans, appeared to suggest. By early 2009, progress
made in extending the authority of the Afghan government outside Kabul remains,
at best, patchy. Critically, military operations have failed to reverse the resurgence of
Taliban influence since 2002, which now extends beyond the movement's traditional
strongholds in the southern provinces of Helmand, Uruzgan, and Kandahar.[2] Not
only has the insurgency spread further into Afghanistan but it has also gained a firmer
foothold in the border regions with Pakistan and, crucially, within Pakistan itself,

---

[1] Research for this paper was enabled by the generous support of the Rockefeller Foundation.
[2] International Council on Security and Development, *Struggle for Kabul: The Taliban Advance*
(London: MF Publishing Ltd, December 2008), pp. 5–6. For a detailed account of the Taliban
resurgence since 2002, see Antonio Giustozzi, *Koran, Kalashnikov and Laptop – The Neo-Taliban
Insurgency in Afghanistan* (London: Hurst, 2007).

which presents NATO with a particularly difficult dilemma.[3] Within Afghanistan itself, holding on to territory recaptured from Taliban forces is hampered by NATO's limited troop strength, the use of "national caveats" by allied governments, and, not least, by the slow pace at which Afghan security forces are being turned out.[4] The resulting insecurity has stifled reconstruction and development activities, especially in southern ethnic Pashtun provinces, and has added to the already difficult job of raising troops for the mission. Continued instability has also frustrated NATO's cooperation with key civilian players on the ground, including the Afghan authorities and the myriad of outside agencies, international organizations, and nongovernmental organizations (NGOs) involved in rebuilding the country. All of this has in turn exacerbated differences, a long time there beneath the surface, among key NATO allies about the balance of strategic priorities for Western engagement in Afghanistan.[5]

To many observers, NATO's faltering mission in Afghanistan represents a microcosm of a wider malaise within the Western Alliance. On this view, the growing disjunction between certain underlying political realities and the high-sounding ambitions of NATO communiqués can no longer plausibly be denied or easily papered over. Those realities include a complex of domestic political constraints on the actions and commitments by individual Alliance members to current operations. More worryingly, they also include increasingly sharp divisions among Allies – most critically between the United States and other NATO members – about the wider strategic purposes of the Alliance.

The suggestion that NATO's involvement in Afghanistan presents the Alliance with a make-or-break moment is, unsurprisingly, not a view publicly embraced by NATO governments or alliance officials. While acknowledging that "getting it right in Afghanistan" has become the Alliance's most urgent priority, they have instead stressed that concern with Alliance cohesion and credibility is hardly new.[6] In fact, throughout the Cold War, the state of the Alliance was discussed largely in terms of the need to overcome periods of "disarray," "trouble," and "crisis."[7] This tendency continued into the post–Cold War period, though the discourse was then of the need to demonstrate "relevance" in a world no longer divided along bipolar lines. Against such a history of institutional survival, the obvious temptation has been to conclude that there is nothing *qualitatively* new about NATO's current predicament and that, as in the past, acceptable compromises, if not solutions, will be found.

---

3 Dekter Filkins, "Pakistan Says 1.3 Million Flee Fight with Taliban," *New York Times*, 12 May 2009.

4 Private interviews, NATO Brussels, June 2007. See also "Afghanistan Conflict – Military Challenges," *Strategic Comments* 13, Issue 8, October 2007.

5 For this and for the contradictions between the different objectives pursued by the Western powers in Afghanistan, see Anatol Lieven, "Afghanistan: An Unsuitable Candidate for State Building," *Conflict, Security and Development* 7, No. 3 (2007), pp. 483–9.

6 Jamie Shea, "A NATO for the 21st Century: Toward a New Strategic Concept," *The Fletcher Forum of World Affairs* 31, no. 2 (Summer 2007), p. 49.

7 See relevant chapters in Gustav Schmidt, ed., *A History of NATO: The First Fifty Years, Vols. 1–3* (Basingstoke: Palgrave, 2001).

There is clearly some truth to all of this. The history of the Alliance is notable for the ability of allies to live with intramural tensions, and it may fairly be assumed that its involvement in Afghanistan, whatever the outcome, will not result in its formal liquidation. That said, NATO's mission in Afghanistan has raised key questions about the *possibilities* as well as the *limitations* of NATO's contribution to international peace and security outside the Euro-Atlantic area, and it is with these questions that this chapter is concerned. They include, on the one hand, familiar difficulties relating to the problems of burden sharing, the absence of political consultations among allies, the generation of forces, and maintenance of defense expenditure to match new ambitions. More profoundly, though clearly related, they include questions about the unity of political purpose and the clarity of strategic direction required for global engagement to be sustained in an environment bereft of Cold War certainties. Central to this is the question of U.S. attitudes toward the Alliance and its purpose in a post–9/11 world. Finally, though often neglected in debates about NATO's post–Cold War evolution, there is the issue of how the wider world – a category ranging from major powers outside the Alliance, notably Russia, China, and India, to international organizations and looser groupings of states – is likely to view a Western Alliance committed, in the words of its Secretary General, "to address security challenges at their source, whenever and wherever they arise."[8]

OUTLINE AND ARGUMENT IN BRIEF

This chapter does not seek to provide an account of the Alliance's post–Cold War operational history. The chief concern here is with the manner in which the Alliance has responded to changing strategic circumstances; the constraints, internal and external, that have impinged on its activities and are likely to continue to do so; and, finally, given these, the kind of contribution to international peace and security that can and cannot be expected of NATO, especially beyond its core Euro-Atlantic area. To this end the chapter is divided into three parts.

The first explores the distinctive characteristics of the Alliance, its workings and its politics, pointing to elements both of *continuity* and of *break* in its long history. It highlights some basic, though oft-forgotten, features that govern the way NATO operates, including its intergovernmental character, consensus-oriented approach to decision making, and limited common assets. These features – which the United States, especially since 9/11, has tended to view as burdensome and stultifying – provide for the element of continuity in Alliance history. At the same time, the removal of baseline certainties regarding the central purpose of the Alliance following the

---

[8] Jaap de Hoop Scheffer, "Managing Global Security and Risk," address given at IISS Annual Conference, September 7, 2007 (www.nato.int/docu/speech/2007/s070907a.html).

end of the Cold War provides a sharp break in that history and, in turn, has altered the context within which to understand both the politics and the workings of the Alliance.

Against this backdrop, the second part of the chapter examines the attempt to "modernize" or "transform" the Alliance, the need for which was deemed to have been highlighted by NATO's Kosovo campaign in 1999 but which only got underway in earnest in 2002. It surveys the achievements and limitations of NATO's "transformation" relating this process to the change in strategic context brought on by the September 11, 2001, attacks and the far-reaching reorientation of U.S. priorities that these events provoked. Central to the narrative is NATO's inability to garner the political unity necessary for transformation to occur and for the related capabilities to be used. In the absence of an agreed-upon blueprint for NATO as an actor, transformation has done little to bestow the Alliance with the type of "relevance" initially sought through this process. Mired in this very same divisiveness, even one of the more impressive outcomes of transformation on paper, NATO's Response Force (NRF), lacks a clear purpose and has, for a variety of political reasons and strategic factors, yet to be used for its intended function.

By way of conclusion, the final section looks at the kinds of contributions that NATO, given its strengths and weaknesses, can most usefully be expected to make to international peace and security. An overall assessment of its post–Cold War record suggests that it may be more realistic and valuable for NATO to concentrate its efforts on the development of what are still demanding stabilization and wider peacekeeping tasks, rather than pursue an unlikely role in major combat operations. At the same time, NATO's Afghanistan campaign has brought home the difficulties and constraints of assuming a "global role" in complex stability operations. These difficulties are not insurmountable, but call for a more honest appraisal of what it takes to project stability beyond the NATO homestead. To be effective, NATO's engagement in these endeavors will more often than not require it to operate and use its distinctive assets as a "service agency" for the international community, aiming to *complement* not *supplant* the efforts of other bodies and organizations.

I. THE NATURE OF NATO AS AN ALLIANCE: SOURCES OF CONTINUITY AND CHANGE

The longevity of NATO as a standing military alliance is unprecedented in the history of alliances. It has proved remarkably resilient in the face of changing strategic circumstances and has, at least until now, challenged one of the basic (if unexceptional) findings of alliance theorists, namely, that alliances are likely to disintegrate once the unifying threat that brought them into being disappears. Yet NATO was always more than *just* an aggregation of brute military power. As the preamble to the North Atlantic treaty makes clear, it has also been held by its members to enshrine a set of common beliefs and values rooted in the "principles of democracy, individual liberty and the rule of law." Crucially, since its inception NATO has also, both in political and in military terms, served as "the dominant forum for relations between the United States and Western Europe."[9]

Although NATO still performs these functions, much has changed with the end of the Cold War. To capture the sources of continuity and discontinuity and to understand better its peculiarities and current challenges, it is helpful to view NATO's post–Cold War evolution by reference to three distinctive features of the organization as an alliance: its intergovernmental and political character, its role as the military and political framework for U.S.-European relations, and the juxtaposition of its aggregate resources with its limited common and easily deployable assets.

NATO as an Alliance of Equals

NATO has tended (and to a surprising degree continues) to be viewed as an actor in its own right, not as an intergovernmental organization whose decisions in all key bodies are reached by consensus. This tendency – clearly not found to the same degree in discussions either of the UN or other regional organizations – is partly a legacy of the Cold War. Not only was the membership then smaller but also, crucially, the unity of purpose provided by a common strategic threat contributed powerfully to alliance cohesion. The fact that it has always been composed (on the whole) of liberal democracies and disposed of formidable economic and military resources has also reinforced the sense that it constituted a unitary actor. Yet NATO is not and never was a supranational organization; it proceeds by consensus, and its members possess distinct, at times competing, interests and perspectives on the world around them, while also facing different domestic political pressures on their alliance policies.

With the disappearance of a central overarching threat in the early 1990s and the subsequent growth in membership from sixteen to twenty-six countries, reaching consensus has become that much harder. Put differently, although NATO has always been an intensely political alliance, its intergovernmental character has become more salient to an understanding of its workings. The ensuing frustration, especially in the United States, with the consensus-driven approach to decision making has led some to suggest that new "business practices" need to be introduced into the running of the Alliance, for example by exploring the use, as in the EU, of qualified majority voting.[10] This does not, of course, address the issue of underlying political differences and, unsurprisingly, little progress has been made in this area. In terms

---

[9] Philip Windsor, *Strategic Thinking: An Introduction and Farewell* (Boulder, CO: Lynne Rienner, 2002), p. 95.

[10] Lt General Karl Eikenberry, then the Deputy Chairman of NATO's Military Committee, speaking at the Military Leaders Forum, IISS, September 28, 2007.

of decision-making structure, therefore, and in its ways of doing business, NATO has not changed much from its Cold War days.

At first glance, the 1990s provide evidence of an Alliance eminently able to withstand the expansion of its membership and the removal of its *raison d'être*. Less than a year after the dissolution of the Soviet Union, NATO was already engaged in several parallel missions in support of UN forces in the former Yugoslavia.[11] In late 1995, having earlier in the year played a key role in bringing the war in Bosnia to an end, NATO assumed the chief burden of implementing the Dayton Peace Accord, deploying a stabilization force (SFOR) to the country, and committing itself to a major peace-support operation.[12] Finally, in March 1999, without explicit authorization from the UN Security Council and for the first time in its history, NATO launched major combat operations against a sovereign state, the Federal Republic of Yugoslavia (FRY). This campaign was justified as a response to an "overwhelming humanitarian necessity" and was followed by the deployment of NATO ground forces into the province of Kosovo to conduct another major peace operation in the region.[13] To many, this marked the final stage in the transformation of an alliance originally created for the purpose of collective defense, abjuring the use of force "except in self-defense" at the London Summit of 1990, into one embracing peace enforcement and assuming quasicollective security functions.[14]

How to account for this quick adaptation in the absence of a central, identity-furnishing threat? NATO's engagement in southeastern Europe, like the process of eastward enlargement, was ultimately about resolving unfinished Cold War business and the consolidation of security in Europe. As such, the element of common interest on the part of Alliance members was still considerable and explains why collective action was possible. Even so, a closer look at NATO's activities in the 1990s, particularly its operations in the Balkans, reveals that alliance relations were often strained and marked by profound tensions over appropriate policy toward the region, as well as by highly uneven levels of commitment and exposure to risk. This was most clearly the case in 1992–1995 when transatlantic tensions ran deep over

---

[11] These missions included the enforcement of a maritime embargo in the Adriatic and a "no-fly-zone" over Bosnia-Herzegovina, as well as the provision of "protective airpower" for the United Nations Protection Force (UNPROFOR) in Bosnia. For an account of the evolution of NATO-UN relations in the 1990s see Mats Berdal, "From Operation 'Maritime Monitor' to 'Allied Force': Reflections on Relations between NATO and UN in the 1990s," in Gustav Schmidt, ed., *A History of NATO: The First Fifty Years* 1 (Basingstoke: Palgrave, 2001), pp. 57–71.

[12] SFOR was eventually replaced by a EU-led force in December 2004. NATO continues to maintain a small HQ element in Sarajevo.

[13] This formulation first appeared in a Foreign Office note circulated to NATO allies in late 1998 setting out "the UK view on the question of the international legal basis for a possible use of force by NATO in Kosovo." "FRY/Kosovo: The Way Ahead; UK View on Legal Base for Use of Force," FCO, October 7, 1998.

[14] Nicola Butler, "NATO: From Collective Defence to Peace Enforcement," in Schnabel and Thakur, eds. *Kosovo and the Challenge of Collective Intervention* (Tokyo: UNU Press, 2000), pp. 273–90.

Bosnia, with French and British views of the conflict differing sharply from those of the United States and other allies, notably Germany.[15] This was also the case during NATO's Kosovo operation, which, in spite of the common front displayed at the Washington summit in April 1999, revealed divisions among allies. The discord stemmed in part from disagreements about how to conduct operations. At a deeper level, however, such disagreements were a reflection of wider political tensions over the purposes of the Alliance in the absence of a common unifying threat. It was hardly surprising therefore that once the Alliance began to think more explicitly in global terms, considering operations truly "out-of-area," tensions would become more acute.

An Unequal Alliance: America and NATO

Although NATO's intergovernmental character and rules of decision making make it an alliance of equals, it is also – and always has been – a deeply unequal alliance, with the United States by far its most powerful member. Given this reality, how to maintain the American commitment to Europe has been a constant theme of alliance relations and the chief source of the many "crises" to have filled the textbooks about its history. As indicated previously, the Alliance's ability to weather these crises owed much to the fact that NATO was more than simply a military alliance in the traditional sense, and the strength of the U.S. commitment did not, mercifully, rest merely on the abstruse workings of deterrence theory. Its roots lay in a set of common values that contrasted sharply with those of its principal Cold War antagonist and that provided the "determining framework for America's vital interests."[16] As one of the most astute observers of the Alliance noted on the occasion of its twenty-fifth anniversary,

> NATO was always held to represent a set of values and beliefs which themselves did much, in the internal decision of American governments and in internal debates of the United States to define the *American* role in the world. NATO was the paradigm of the American alliance system in the era of containment; NATO was the touchstone of continuing American commitments in the period of limited withdrawal; NATO gave (some) substance to the legend of the free world which provided a sense of emotional cohesion in the earlier period of the Cold War; NATO continued (in part) to enshrine appreciable political and moral values when the experience of Vietnam, Santo Domingo, and the rest had brought the concept of the free world into disrepute and ridicule.[17]

[15] The low point may well have been late 1994. See, for example, Herman von Richthofen, German ambassador to NATO, writing in the *Financial Times*, "Cracks are appearing in the Alliance's cohesion," December 2, 1994.

[16] Philip Windsor, "NATO's Twenty-Five Years," in Mats Berdal, ed., *Studies in International Relations – Essays by Philip Windsor* (Brighton: Sussex Academic Press, 2004), p. 94.

[17] Ibid.

Although NATO's ministerial and Summit meetings have continued to stress the importance of preserving the "transatlantic compact," its foundations are now much shakier.

In the immediate aftermath of the terrorist attacks on the United States in 2001, NATO appeared to have been given a new lease on life. The Alliance invoked Article V, declaring the attack on the United States to be an attack on the whole of the Alliance, and endorsed a series of measures in support of the U.S. response to the attacks. Initial efforts to develop new political guidance for the Alliance also appeared to accept U.S. views on the need for NATO to deploy "as and where required," in conformity with the emerging doctrine of preemption.[18] Yet, in spite of this, the United States clearly did not view NATO – nor has it since come to view it – as the principal vehicle through which to fight its "war on terror." As Senator Richard Lugar, an influential and respected Atlanticist, observed only a few months after the attacks, although "the US did have confidence in a select group of individual allies... it did not have confidence in the institution that is NATO."[19] In the ensuing years, as Renée de Nevers has persuasively shown, NATO played only a "limited role in the US war on terror."[20] In part, this was because NATO's "deeply institutionalised consensus-based model [was] not the U.S. preferred approach for multilateral cooperation in the war on terror,"[21] which instead favored looser coalitions of the willing or, as the 2006 U.S. *National Security Strategy* put it, "partnerships... oriented towards action and results rather than legislation or rule-making."[22] As a result, in the view of many, NATO came to be treated by the United States as little more than a military contractor of first resort.

NATO's modest role is, however, also a function of the divisions, once the initial shock of the attack had subsided, that soon emerged between the United States and many European allies (with the partial exception of the UK) about the nature and gravity of the threat posed by terrorism. While the George W. Bush administration wanted to see NATO as the "cornerstone" of the U.S.-led coalition against terror, European capitals differed on how to prosecute this war on terror, or whether this is even an appropriate conceptualization of the security challenges facing NATO member states today.[23] Under the Obama administration, the language and tone of the debate have changed, a shift much welcomed by most European nations.

---

[18] John R. Deni, *Alliance Management and Maintenance: Restructuring NATO for the 21st Century* (Aldershot: Ashgate, 2007), p. 86.

[19] Senator Richard Lugar, "NATO'S Role in the War on Terrorism," US-NATO Missions Annual Conference, Brussels, Belgium, January 18, 2002.

[20] Renée de Nevers, "NATO's International Security Role in the Terrorist Era," *International Security*, 31, No. 4, (Spring 2007), p. 57. See also, Deni, *Alliance Management and Maintenance*, chapter 7.

[21] Nevers, "NATO's International Security Role," p. 39.

[22] See White House, *The National Security Strategy of the US of America* (Washington, DC: White House, 2006), p. 46.

[23] "Remarks by the President and NATO Secretary General," October 10, 2001, www.whitehouse.gov/news/releases/2001/10/20011010-6.html.

Nonetheless, the muted response among NATO's European members to calls from the new U.S. administration in early 2009 for an increased effort in Afghanistan shows that the issue is not simply one of European disagreements with the deeply unpopular administration and policies of George W. Bush.[24] Indeed, sharp divisions still surround the specific role of NATO in addressing the security threats of the post–9/11 era, however they may be understood.[25] Added to this, newer members, often those in Eastern Europe, are concerned that the focus on global terrorism obscures the continued need to deter and defend against security threats stemming from Russia, be they the type of cyber-attacks that affected Estonia in April 2007, threats over energy security, or more traditional reassertions of military power and influence. Indeed, over the past three years in particular, Russia's determined effort to reassert, often in a crude and provocative manner, its claim to Great Power status has not only deteriorated its relations with the West but has also exposed growing divisions within the Alliance over how best to respond to the resurgence of Russian power and over the priority that ought to be placed on this effort alongside what is now a broad and varied NATO agenda.

For all these reasons, the "transatlantic compact" that held the Alliance together has been badly frayed. This assertion may appear at odds with the declaratory statements that typically accompany the Alliance's high-level meetings. It is, however, plainly borne out by a closer look at the diversity of views and the competing domestic political pressures within NATO countries that are shaping operations in Afghanistan and are complicating the attempt to develop a "global Alliance.'"

The lack of consensus also explains why NATO's Strategic Concept has not been updated since 1999, despite a sea change in strategic environment. The endorsement of the Comprehensive Political Guidance (CPG) by NATO at Riga in 2006 – a kind of stopgap measure in the absence of a fuller agreement – was clearly a compromise solution masking conflicting perspectives among allies. Indeed, the CPG is widely seen as having avoided all the difficult questions by offering something to everyone. As others have noted, "for traditionalists, the CPG reaffirms NATO's core mission of collective defense and stresses the continuing relevance and importance of Article V. For expansionists or globalists, the CPG also stresses that NATO needs to be prepared for a wide range of missions including those that are asymmetric or fall out of the Euro-Atlantic area."[26] When NATO turned sixty in April 2009, a second precursor document – the "Declaration of Alliance Security" – was drafted, but it, too, is an interim measure pending an unlikely grand bargain on transatlantic priorities and political preferences.

---

[24] See Craig Whitlock, "Afghanistan Appeal May Temper European Allies' Ardor for Obama," *Washington Post*, February 6, 2009.

[25] These divisions are examined in Martin Butcher, "NATO, Riga and Beyond," *Disarmament Diplomacy*, no. 84 (Spring 2007).

[26] Julianne Smith, et al., *Transforming NATO (. . . again): A Primer for the NATO Summit in Riga 2006* (Washington DC: Center for Strategic International Studies, 2006), p. 16.

Limited Common and Deployable Assets

A further factor limiting NATO's ability to act is the fact that it has few capabilities on its own or ones that it can call on quickly and without complications. There is a temptation in discussions about the Alliance to mistake the military power of (some of) NATO's member states with that of the Alliance itself, forgetting in the process that the troops and equipment made available to NATO are often only a portion of total resources and are often also double- or triple-hatted. In terms of troop numbers, an aim set in Riga in 2006 – to work toward making 40 percent of the armed forces of each member state available for NATO deployment – illustrates that the whole is indeed less than the sum of the parts. Added to this, each nation can refuse to commit its troops to missions that it feels are too dangerous or demanding. And if they do commit, nations can still impose "caveats" on when exactly their troops may be used. The result, as the mission in Afghanistan has illustrated, has been a shortage of troops and a lack of operational flexibility, undermining the Alliance's ability to meet its objectives.

There is also a need to understand what NATO has at its disposal in terms of equipment. When George Robertson took his post as NATO Secretary General in 1999, he famously listed his three top priorities as "capabilities, capabilities, capabilities."[27] This referred not only to the underinvestment in defense on the part of NATO Europe but also to the lack of common assets under NATO's control. In the words of one analyst, NATO capabilities then included "an air defense system; some command, control and communications assets (mostly fixed, and therefore not very useful for interventions); oil pipelines, and about three dozen Airborne Warning and Control Systems (AWACS)."[28] Steps have since been taken to place more assets in the hands of NATO, rather than those of its member-states. The Alliance is acquiring an Alliance Ground Surveillance (AGS) system for aerial reconnaissance, pursuing various missile-defense systems for troops and populations, and, in June 2004, a multinational CBRN (chemical, biological, radiological, nuclear) battalion was declared operational. Nonetheless, the point remains that for action to be taken, NATO needs to borrow the bulk of its military assets from its member-states, which complicates its ability to act as a global security actor – particularly when, as seen, there is little consensus among these member-states as to when and how the Alliance should engage.

II. NATO'S POST–COLD WAR TRANSFORMATION: ACHIEVEMENTS AND LIMITATIONS

The strategic backdrop to NATO's evolution has changed dramatically, first with the end of the Cold War, then with the expansion of NATO operations throughout the

---

[27] As cited in Aisha Labi, "Have Skills, Will Travel," *Time Magazine*, January 27, 2003.

[28] Philip Gordon, "Europeanization of NATO: A Convenient Myth," *International Herald Tribune*, June 7, 1996.

1990s, and finally with the September 11, 2001, attacks and the ensuing reorientation of U.S. strategic priorities. Struggling with an ever-growing membership, widening divisions among said members – particularly between the United States and its European allies – and the limited common assets available to the Alliance itself, the effort to retain NATO's relevance across these different strategic settings would always be problematic. The most concerted effort to ensure such relevance came in the form of "transformation" – a U.S.-driven attempt to modernize the Alliance's Cold War structures and don it with the type of capabilities and assets thought to guarantee its continued centrality into the twenty-first century.

The Roots and Course of Transformation

The ever-expanding scope of NATO operations in the 1990s revealed a growing mismatch in defense capabilities between the United States and its European allies. By the time of the Kosovo operation, only the United States possessed the advanced capabilities needed to conduct the campaign as desired.[29] The campaign therefore sat badly with the U.S. military, which felt politically constrained by Alliance members who were at the same time unable to bring much to the table in terms of capability.

The weakness of NATO Europe was ascribed to its disinvestment in the defense sector in the 1990s. Throughout this decade, Alliance members, including the United States, had sought to cash in on the presumed "peace dividend" to flow from the collapse of the Soviet Union.[30] The drop in defense spending was shared across the Alliance, but its effect was felt in Europe rather than the United States, whose budget, even in 2000, eclipsed that of NATO Europe combined by $295bn to $163bn, and whose 1,483,000-strong armed forces outnumbered the largest military in NATO Europe, that of Turkey, by 690,000 troops. Related to NATO Europe's military weakness was its configuration for territorial defense rather than global power projection. With few exceptions, the general lack of strategic air- and sealift capabilities within NATO Europe meant that Alliance operations conducted further afield would rely heavily on U.S. assets. This limitation posed a serious problem for the United States, which more than other Alliance members saw NATO's future as a global security actor not as one restricted to contingencies within or on the periphery of its treaty-defined area of interest.

---

[29] That is, a campaign of aerial bombardment and not a ground invasion, which in strictly military terms would have been far more effective in achieving the central aim of halting "ethnic cleansing" operations by FRY security forces. Over the skies of Kosovo and Belgrade, the U.S. military delivered "90 per cent of the precision-guided munitions," provided "100 per cent of NATO's jamming capability, 90 per cent of the air-to-ground surveillance, and 80 per cent of the air refuelling tankers." See Robert Bell, "Transformation Scorecard," *NATO Review*, no. 1 (Spring 2005), p. 22.

[30] From the mid-1980s to 2000, the average allocation made by NATO countries to the defense sector decreased from 3.18% to 1.99% of GNP. See Data Analysis Section, NATO-Russia Compendium of Financial and Economic Data Relating to Defence (Force Planning Directorate, Brussels, December 18, 2006), www.nato.int/docu/pr/2006/p06-159.pdf and *SIPRI Yearbook 2002* (Oxford: OUP), chapter 7.

In the aftermath of the Kosovo intervention, questions began to surface regarding the viability of this lopsided Alliance: to the United States, NATO's future was tied to the ability of its European partners to counteract their declining defense budgets and fill the "capability gaps" exposed in Kosovo. This backdrop informed the subsequent effort at NATO modernization: the Defense Capabilities Initiative (DCI). Endorsed at the Washington Summit in April 1999, the DCI laid out fifty-nine targets to be met, spread across five areas: mobility and deployability; sustainability; effective engagement (meaning, roughly, technology and defense equipment); survivability; and interoperable communications.[31] Spearheaded by then U.S. Secretary of Defense William Cohen, the DCI clearly reflected the U.S. government's interest in NATO developing capabilities for major combat operations and its conviction, not shared across the Alliance at this point, that NATO had either to "go out of area or go out of business."[32]

The DCI did not get far; it suffered from a lack of enforcement mechanisms, and its effects, already limited, were also scattered across the entire European armed forces, including stationary forces.[33] Many of the deficiencies of the DCI were corrected with NATO's second effort at modernization: the Prague Capability Commitments (PCC). Rolled out during NATO's Prague Summit in 2002, the PCC focused on similar types of capabilities as vied for in the DCI, but the commitments were this time tailored and country specific, and issued with time frames for their implementation.[34]

The Prague Summit saw the introduction of a second – also U.S.-driven – transformation initiative: the NATO Response Force (NRF). A brainchild of then Secretary of Defense Donald Rumsfeld, the NRF was designed to be a 25,000-strong, European-dominated combined force, deployable worldwide in a minimum of five days, either as a spearhead or a stand-alone force, and sustainable for a period of thirty days.[35] Beyond constituting a technologically enabled force, the NRF would also provide a "catalyst" for transformation and a focal point for the PCC: troops committed would train together and gain familiarity with advanced capabilities, and as troops rotated through the force, such experience would be spread across the European force structure.[36]

---

[31] Frank Boland, "NATO's Defence Capabilities Initiative: Preparing for Future Challenges," *NATO Review*, no. 2 (Summer 1999), pp. 26–28.

[32] Richard Lugar, "NATO: Out of Area or Out of Business: A Call for US Leadership to Revive and Redefine the Alliance." Presentation to the Open Forum of the US Department of State, August 2, 1993.

[33] Hans Binnendijk and Richard Kugler, "Transforming European Forces," *Survival*, 44, no. 3 (January 2002), p. 126.

[34] For details of these objectives see "Prague Capabilities Commitment (PCC)" at www.nato.int/issues/prague_capabilities_commitment/index.html.

[35] See Public Information Office, "Fact Sheet: NATO Response Force," March 2005, www.1gnc.de/history/history2005/nrf/LoRes%20NRF%20Mar05%20GBR.pdf.

[36] This function is laid out by NATO Secretary General, Jaap de Hoop Scheffer in a joint press conference on the NRF) with General James L. Jones, SACEUR, on October 13, 2004. See http://www.nato.int/docu/speech/2004/s041013b.htm. See also Jeffrey P. Bialos and Stuart L. Koehl,

NATO Europe has since Prague experienced some success in developing new defense capabilities. In broad terms, different European NATO countries have taken the lead in specific areas – airlift, sealift, anti-CBRN capabilities – and achieved much by pooling their resources in intergovernmental consortia.[37] The momentum behind the implementation of the PCC was such that a 2006 NATO press kit was able to claim that "by the end of 2008, over 70 per cent of the 460 or so commitments made by Allies will have been fulfilled" and that "most of the remainder will be completed by 2009 and beyond."[38] The veracity of this statement is difficult to corroborate as most PCC progress reports are classified, yet while the available evidence is mixed, important headway has certainly been made. The most evident sign of progress was the November 2006 declaration that the NRF had reached full operational capability. At the Riga Summit, the NRF was presented as comprising a "brigade-size land component with forced-entry capability; a naval task force including a carrier battle group, an amphibious task group and a surface action group; and an air component capable of 200 combat sorties a day."[39]

Enduring Challenges

Despite these accomplishments, NATO has not escaped the talk of irrelevance and of crisis – the very language that prompted the transformation process. To a degree, such talk is misinformed about the progress made since 1999 and the time required for what is after all an intergovernmental alliance to commit itself to and carry through on reforms. But while acknowledging the strides made, a closer look at NATO's transformation reveals several underlying problems.

Most fundamentally, NATO's transformation was never grounded in an Alliance-wide agreement on its future roles and missions. The absence of a clear and shared vision of the Alliance's purpose has resulted in capability development being disconnected from the requirements of current and likely future operations, in the cart being put in front of the horse. And, as might be expected, the development of capabilities in this manner has done little to displace the underlying political

---

The NATO Response Force: Coalition Warfare through Technology Transfer and Information Sharing (Washington DC: Center for Technology and National Security Policy, NDU, 2005), p. v.

[37] The progress includes Norway and Denmark's efforts to augment European strategic sealift capabilities; the commitment of seven European NATO partners to acquire Airbus A400M for European strategic airlift; the acquisition and pooling of three to four C-17 aircraft by another consortium of fourteen NATO states (and Sweden); the finalization of another group of fifteen NATO countries of a charter arrangement for *Antonov* 124–100 aircraft from Ukraine; and the leasing of tanker aircraft by a consortium of nations led by Spain. See Carl Ek, "NATO's Prague Capabilities Commitment," *CRS Report for Congress*, RS21659 (Washington DC: CRS, July 22, 2008), p.3. See also NATO Press Release, "Riga Summit Declaration," November 29, 2006, www.nato.int/docu/pr/2006/p06-150e.htm and NATO Parliamentary Assembly, *Progress on the Prague Capabilities Commitment*, November 2005.

[38] See NATO Riga Press-kit document, November 2006, pp. 5–6.

[39] NATO Updates, "NATO Response Force declared fully operational," November 29, 2006, www.nato.int/docu/update/2006/11-november/e1129c.htm.

differences plaguing the Alliance – problems accentuated in the aftermath of the 9/11 attacks.

The political vacuum in which transformation has occurred helps explain the limited progress of both the DCI and the PCC. Certainly, the latter initiative has enjoyed more success in pushing NATO Europe to develop new capabilities, but the transformation process as a whole remains hamstrung by critical unanswered questions: what missions is the Alliance prepared to undertake and where? By skirting these existential questions, the Alliance never arrived at a convincing blueprint for transformation so that while European allies signed off on the relevant initiatives, they did not provide the buy-in necessary for their success. Some European nations failed to see why they should invest limited resources in "generation-after-next" combat capabilities; others wanted NATO to remain focused on its treaty-defined area and therefore resisted the push toward expeditionary capabilities.[40] The enduring divisiveness explains in part why the combined European defense spending actually decreased from 2.17% of GDP in 1996 to 1.77% in 2006 and why, of 1.8 million personnel in the combined armed forces of the EU, only 10% are "deployable," in the widest sense of the term.[41]

In itself, transformation could neither provide NATO with a new raison d'etre nor render the Alliance more "usable" for future war-fighting. In short, capability development has not, and will not, displace the political constraints that come with fighting as an Alliance. First, the political process involved in approving a NATO combat operation is still likely to be considered prohibitively time consuming, as illustrated by a NATO war-game held in October 2003.[42] And, as Michael Mihalka notes, "Even for those countries that do not need parliamentary approval for short-term deployments, such as France, there remain questions as to whether UN authorization is required" – an authorization that "may be slow in coming, if it comes at all."[43] To the U.S. government, the notion of the UN Security Council carrying a potential veto over NATO combat operations is pure anathema, but in Europe – particularly after the Iraq War – coercive action without UN authority will be a hard sell.

In this sense, NATO is simply not geared toward the type of engagements envisioned through its own modernization process. This is the main reason why, when NATO countries have engaged in major combat operations in recent years, it has

---

[40] Marco Overhaus, "Transatlantic Co-Operation and the Future of NATO," *Foreign Policy in Dialogue*, vol. 8, no. 25 (2008), pp. 22–23.

[41] For the respective statistics, see *European Military Capabilities: Building Armed Forces for Modern Operations* (London, IISS, June 2008), p. 93; and Tim Bird, "The European Union and Counter-Insurgency: Capability, Credibility, and Political Will," *Contemporary Security Policy*, vol. 28, no. 1 (2007), p. 192.

[42] Peter Spiegel, "War game at NATO talks highlights the need for quick deployment," *Financial Times*, October 10, 2003.

[43] Michael Mihalka, "NATO Response Force: Rapid? Responsive? A Force?," *Connections: The Quarterly Journal*, vol. 4, no. 2 (2005), p. 79.

been outside the Alliance, often through a U.S.-led "coalition of the willing." This is a trend that is likely to continue, as even when the need for action is agreed upon, the constant search for consensus among 26 member states is sure to undermine military and strategic effectiveness while in operation. Already during the Kosovo intervention in 1999, the U.S. government and military derided the air campaign as "war by committee," where the political reservations of each member-state had to be allowed for before action could be taken. In the immediate aftermath of the September 11, 2001 attacks, Washington was therefore glad to accept NATO's help in patrolling U.S. airspace, a largely symbolic gesture, but when it came to the planning and conduct of more serious combat operations in Afghanistan, it declined the offers of assistance made by its NATO allies.[44] For the United States, the first priority in Afghanistan, as in Iraq, was to achieve its stated objectives, not to provide NATO with an opportunity to prove its relevance, particularly as the latter objective was seen as compromising the former. And, as illustrated in both of these campaigns, the U.S. military really needed no help from NATO in conducting what were, notwithstanding subsequent developments, successful combat victories.

Pushing in the Wrong Direction

Whether transformed or not, it seems clear that NATO's future role in major combat operations may be limited. A quick glance at NATO's current and recent operations corroborates this finding: continued peacekeeping in the Balkans; a military training mission in Iraq; a naval patrol mission in the Mediterranean; logistical support to the African Union force in Darfur; humanitarian assistance in the aftermath of the Katrina hurricane and the 2006 Pakistan earthquake; and, of course, a large-scale stabilization effort in Afghanistan. This recital of activities and operations points to the third problem with the transformation process. Even against a backdrop of various humanitarian endeavors and stability operations, NATO's transformation process has remained firmly focused on major combat operations, revealing a lack of appreciation for the political and military requirements of NATO's recent, ongoing and, in all likelihood, future operations. This too helps explain the limited success of transformation in bestowing relevance to the Alliance and in modernizing the European armed forces.

The conventional slant to the transformation process was a natural product of its American origins, as it – the militarily superior force – sought to shape the European armed forces in its own image. Although technologically advanced and deployable,

---

[44] As argued by U.S. Senator Lugar in a speech given only months after 9/11, "Rightly or wrongly, the legacy of Kosovo has reinforced the concern [within the U.S.] that NATO is not up to the job of fighting a modern war." See Senator Richard G. Lugar, "NATO'S Role in the War on Terrorism," U.S.-NATO Missions Annual Conference, Brussels, Belgium January 18, 2002. See also John R. Schmidt, "Last Alliance Standing? NATO after 9/11," *The Washington Quarterly*, vol. 30, no. 1 (Winter 2007), pp. 97–98, 103–104.

the U.S. military has historically focused predominantly on achieving and maintaining *conventional* primacy, that is, domination against adversaries shaped and operating like itself. Conversely, and as a result, it has struggled with irregular or nonstate adversaries and in operations requiring more than the destruction of military targets.[45] By grounding NATO's transformation in its own strategic culture, the U.S. military was always likely to replicate this narrow specialization across the Alliance.

It might have been expected that NATO's virtually uninterrupted institutional experience with peacekeeping during the 1990s, in Bosnia, Kosovo, and then Macedonia, would also have made a mark on the DCI and PCC. However, although official NATO documentation typically acknowledged the importance of these types of campaigns, their complexity was often downplayed.[46] Much like the U.S. military of the time, the Alliance read too much into the consensual nature of the peacekeeping operations of the 1990s and failed to consider the possibility that future stability operations would present altogether more serious challenges.[47]

It did not help that NATO transformation was conceived during the U.S. military's own "transformation era," in which it was swayed by its apparent ability to defeat almost any adversary through precision-guided munitions and other high-technological capabilities. When the DCI were endorsed in 1999, the requirements for military effectiveness were informed by the major military operations of the preceding decade – in Iraq, Bosnia, and Kosovo. Particularly within the United States, these campaigns were seen as vindicating its investment in the emerging technology of the Revolution in Military Affairs (RMA): precision-guided munitions, primarily, but also advanced communications technology and various surveillance and reconnaissance systems. By the time the PCC were endorsed in 2002, the U.S. military was one year into the Afghanistan campaign, then interpreted within the senior echelons of the U.S. military as a resounding validation of its own transformation program. In Washington, D.C., the initial routing of the Taliban by horse-mounted U.S. special operations forces and combat air controllers calling in precision air strikes from bombers overhead was taken to epitomize the promise of transformation – these advanced conventional capabilities, it was reasoned, could defeat not only traditional adversaries but also "shape and then dominate in an unconventional conflict" fought against insurgents and terrorists.[48]

The U.S. intellectual foundation for NATO's process of transformation was evident also in the reforms made to NATO's command structure. At the Prague Summit,

---

[45] Frederick W. Kagan, *Finding the Target: The Transformation of American Military Policy* (New York: Encounter Books, 2006).

[46] See Henning-A. Frantzen, *NATO and Peace Support Operations, 1991–1999: Policies and Doctrines* (New York: Routledge, 2005), pp. 2–3, 5, 78–81.

[47] David Ucko, *The New Counterinsurgency Era: Transforming the U.S. Military for Modern Wars* (Washington DC: Georgetown University Press, 2009), ch. 3.

[48] "President Speaks on War Effort to Citadel Cadets," South Carolina, December 11, 2001.

NATO officially replaced the Allied Command Atlantic with the Allied Command Transformation (ACT), which was to guide the Alliance's modernization. Tellingly, the new command was co-located with the U.S. Joint Forces Command (JFCOM), stood up in 1999 to drive the U.S. military's own transformation. The ACT commander was also to double-hat as the commander of JFCOM, indicating strong congruence between the United States and NATO modernization processes. Gradually, the terminology of U.S. force transformation was exported and adopted in NATO circles: "network-centric operations," "effect-based" strikes, and, of course, "transformation" itself.

Particularly since the invasion of Iraq, much scorn has been poured on the U.S. military's faith in transformation and the way in which it blinded Pentagon planners from considering the need to "win the peace" as well as the war. As the U.S. military itself has learned, wars are today more ill-defined and "irregular" affairs, involving adversaries employing concealment among civilian populations, hit-and-run attacks, and dispersion to avoid becoming a likely target of precision-guided munitions. In those places where NATO has already been (and is currently) involved, the very distinction between war and peace has become blurred, a defining feature, many say, of contemporary conflict. Accordingly, the types of operations that NATO will have to conduct, assuming it maintains an active operational role, will require different capabilities and a different understanding of war from what has been advanced through NATO transformation to date.

While the U.S. military is taking onboard important lessons from its campaigns in Iraq and Afghanistan, the course of NATO transformation remains fundamentally unchanged since 2002 and continues to focus narrowly on major combat operations.[49] This is worrying; even if Afghanistan proves to be the only large-scale NATO attempt at "statebuilding" in such a contested environment, future land-based campaigns will call for similar skill sets and combinations of forces: military police, linguists, engineers, civil affairs specialists, medics, and construction teams, all of whom will require specific training.

Given the increased frequency of stability operations since the end of the Cold War and the global trend toward urbanization, not to mention NATO's comparative superiority in conventional combat and the attractiveness and effectiveness of

---

[49] No major transformation initiative has been issued since the PCC in 2002, which therefore continue to inform the course of transformation. Nor have NATO Summit communiqués since Prague recognized any need to broaden transformation or build capabilities for a wider range of missions. The one exception to this trend is a sentence in the Riga Summit communiqué of 2006, which alluded to an "initiative . . . ensuring the ability to bring military support to stabilisation operations and reconstruction efforts in all phases of a crisis" (see NATO, "Riga Summit Declaration," November 29, 2006, www.nato.int/docu/pr/2006/p06-150e.htm, para. 24). The CPG, issued at Riga, also made a few valuable mentions of the need to focus on stabilization activities and postconflict reconstruction, but the impact of this document on NATO capability-development has so far been minimal. See NATO, "Comprehensive Political Guidance," Endorsed by NATO Heads of State and Government on November 29, 2006, Riga, Latvia.

asymmetric tactics to potential adversaries, when NATO ground troops are again deployed, they will most likely face challenges not too far removed from those encountered in Afghanistan: how to operate among a civilian population, how to train indigenous forces, and how to build government capacity.

Some European countries do foresee a larger role in stability operations and have adapted their militaries accordingly. As part of its conversion to an all-volunteer force, the Italian Army has designed its brigades for use both in combat support and stability operations.[50] Germany has also assigned 70,000 of its troops to stability operations, creating a sustainable force of 14,000, though these units would probably not be available for missions conducted in nonpermissive environments. These initiatives are furthermore exceptions to a norm: "virtually all European forces now assigned to NATO as readily available formations are configured for major combat operations."[51] NATO militaries will thus need to re-role or refit their troops for stability operations as and when necessary, a practice that unnecessarily complicates their employment and that is often insufficient.

The above analysis suggests that NATO should acknowledge stability operations as a profitable and, some might say, Alliance-saving niche for NATO Europe, or for NATO as a whole. This does not mean a simple or wholesale trade-off between combat capabilities versus those designed for traditional peacekeeping tasks. It is rather to acknowledge that it is highly unlikely that NATO will conduct, as an Alliance, the types of major combat operations prioritized through its transformation program. If engagements in stability operations and wider peacekeeping are more likely, as seems to be the case, there is a clear imbalance in NATO's orientation and capabilities that can be and should be rectified.

The proposed realignment is not without difficulties and is likely to run into resistance. Just as with major combat operations, there is no consensus whether and when the Alliance should undertake stabilization and wider peacekeeping operations. Although developing capabilities to conduct stability operations would be less challenging than for major combat operations, and although these capabilities would also have a greater likelihood of being used, these operations also suffer from an undeserved reputation of somehow being less glamorous than climactic war fighting. Many within Europe would view a concentration on stability operations as an admission of military weakness, whereas in the United States, such a specialization would likely be perceived as free-riding – contributing on the margins yet demanding the rights of full Alliance membership. For all this, the relevance sought through transformation would be better ensured if NATO embraced and prepared for the types of operations it currently struggles to conduct, rather than the unlikely conventional wars for which there is both insufficient will and capacity.

---

[50] Hans Binnendijk and Richard Kugler, "Needed – A NATO Stabilization and Reconstruction Force," *Defense Horizons*, no. 45 (September 2004), p. 3. "S&R" refers to "stability and reconstruction."

[51] Ibid.

The NRF: A Symptom of Malaise

Nothing illustrates the confusion surrounding the direction and purpose of NATO transformation better than the NATO Response Force. Paradoxically, the NRF is in some ways a remarkable achievement of NATO transformation: proposed in 2002 and declared operational in 2006, its evolution demonstrates NATO's ability to adapt swiftly to new demands. It provides NATO with a focal point for its modernization, a standing sizeable force and a capability to respond forcefully and on short notice (in theory deployable within five days) to emerging crises worldwide. At the same time, the NRF is also victim to the unquestioned assumptions regarding the types of capabilities most needed in today's strategic environment. As a result, although NATO documentation claims that the NRF is "capable of carrying out the full range of Alliance missions," a cursory look at its structure reveals its clear optimization for short-notice combat operations – a mission that it is unlikely to perform.[52]

First, conventional combat operations are, as noted, exceedingly rare for the Alliance. More importantly, the lengthy political process necessary for the North Atlantic Council (NAC) to authorize the use of force (partly a function of the bureaucratic and structural factors discussed earlier) undermines the ability of the NRF to deploy quickly – one of its chief selling points. Clearly, the deployment of AWACS in the immediate aftermath of 9/11 was both rapid and largely unproblematic, but a forcible intervention, involving ground troops, into a non-NATO country could not be launched as quickly or as seamlessly. The issue is not only one of political differences of opinion; a number of NATO members still resist the very idea of out-of-area engagements, a split that would further limit the scenarios in which the NRF might be used.

Should a need for an intervention arise, there are also strong arguments not to send the NRF. Beyond the difficulties of achieving agreement to deploy, it is doubtful whether NATO Europe will have the capabilities required to get the job done. So far, the NRF's development has been "hampered by the continuing inability of European allies to devote the resources required to acquire key logistical capabilities, such as strategic lift, or to train and equip sufficient numbers of combat troops to U.S. standards."[53] The continued lack of strategic sea- and airlift capabilities is particularly critical, as it undercuts the NRF's ability to mobilize without significant U.S. support within the vied-for time frame. It is also uncertain whether this shortfall will be addressed in the near future, given the at best uneven investment in the defense sector within NATO Europe.

If the NRF is unlikely and perhaps also unable to fulfill its intended purpose, what could be its fallback uses? The discussion is ongoing and reveals the lack of unity among NATO members. So far, the NRF has been used twice, both in humanitarian

---

[52] NATO, *NATO Transformed* (Brussels: NATO, June 2004), p. 10.
[53] Schmidt, pp. 98–99.

endeavors. It first deployed in September 2005 to the U.S. Gulf Coast to deliver assistance to the victims of Hurricane Katrina and then, the following month, to Pakistan to provide relief to the survivors of the October 8, 2005, earthquake there. Larger in scale than the Katrina operation, the deployment to Pakistan involved the use of tactical airlift, command and control, engineering units, and field hospitals, and was critical in saving many lives and in enabling a more effective relief effort. At the same time, even such a benign and plainly well-intentioned deployment sparked tensions within NATO, with some members arguing that humanitarian operations were not the intended function of the NRF – that it should not become "an arm of the International Red Cross."[54]

A second possible function of the NRF is to act merely as a "catalyst" for transformation, to develop a heightened combat capability within NATO Europe. Although this is an important aim, there are underlying problems. First, to what extent would this function not simply reinforce the problematic leaning of transformation described earlier? Second, the transformation of troops in the NRF relies on them having already acquired sufficiently advanced capabilities – seldom the case among the armed forces of NATO Europe.[55] Third, with NATO struggling to find enough troops to conduct operations in Afghanistan, it appears illogical to keep those associated with NRF in training simply to help them "transform," to the degree possible. An alternative, suggested by Jamie Shea, is to consider the NRF "not only as a tool for experimentation but also as a real fighting force that can be used when NATO is under pressure – for instance, as a reserve in Afghanistan."[56] This and similar proposals have elicited little or no support from major European allies.[57] Until such a course of action is taken, nations reluctant to contribute to ongoing operations, particularly in Afghanistan, have been accused, off the record, by senior NATO officials of seeking to "hide out" in the NRF so as to avoid deployment.[58] Clearly this was not the outcome intended by Donald Rumsfeld when he first proposed establishing the reaction force at the Prague Summit of 2002.

III. NATO'S ROLE IN INTERNATIONAL PEACE AND SECURITY

Two closely related conclusions emerge from the ongoing process of transformation and from NATO's post–Cold War operational experience, as surveyed in this chapter. First, NATO's transformation has clearly not displaced the continued uncertainty and divisions within the Alliance over its role in the post–Cold War world. Hopes

---

[54] Statement of a member of the French mission to NATO, as quoted in Smith et al., p. 30. See also "NATO Summit Talks End on a Sour Note," *New York Times*, June 30, 2004.

[55] Smith et al., p. 59.

[56] Shea, p. 51.

[57] David Brunnstrom and David Morgan, "NATO Allies Offer Limp Response to U.S. Afghan Call," *Reuters*, February 19, 2009.

[58] Interview with senior NATO officials, Brussels (summer 2007).

that more sophisticated capabilities, changed command structures, and new rapid reaction forces would, in themselves, bestow the Alliance with a clear function and new relevance were ill founded, in part because the pursuit of these "transformational" initiatives was conducted with little consideration of whether, when, and where they were to be used. Most fundamentally, the transformation process never reconciled the divergences in opinion across the Alliance as to whether it remains a collective defense organization, concerned about Russia or other "neighborhood" threats, or a global-security actor, conducting operations far from its traditional North Atlantic homestead.

While innovating in line with missions it will only rarely see, NATO has paid insufficient attention to the requirements of the operations it has increasingly undertaken, namely, stability operations and wider peacekeeping. As NATO's experiences in the Balkans in the 1990s have showed, the Alliance already holds many assets that would be valuable in such operations, ranging from its logistics and strategic-lift capabilities to its headquarters functions and intelligence assets. Yet the demands of stability operations conducted in complex environments where other actors may be reluctant or unable to operate will typically be more arduous. Although reconstruction activities, the provision of basic services, and the establishment of governance are tasks that, ideally, are best conducted by civilian agencies, the frequent inability of the latter to operate in insecure conditions has and may well force NATO troops to assume responsibility for these areas as well, alongside the provision of security.

To meet the demands of modern-day operations, the way forward for NATO may be to embrace stabilization and wider peacekeeping tasks more openly as a *core business*. This would involve developing its own capacity to conduct such missions.[59] As important, it would involve exploring, in concrete ways, how the Alliance can assist other multilateral bodies in mitigating some of the more persistent weaknesses and vulnerabilities of large-scale peace operations, most of them now under UN auspices. In this respect, NATO's post–Cold War record and its distinctive characteristics suggest five areas where the Alliance has already made some but could be making a much greater difference:

- *Providing and/or assisting with the organization, management, and running of headquarters in the field.* An example of this function is the use of elements of the mobile core of Northern Army Group (NORTHAG) headquarters in support of UN forces in Bosnia in the early 1990s.[60] Since then, following the reform of its force structure, NATO has six High Readiness Forces Headquarters

---

[59] One proposal for doing so is outlined in C. Richard Nelson, *How Should NATO Handle Stabilisation Operations and Reconstruction Efforts?* Policy Paper (Washington DC: Atlantic Council, September 2006). A successful (and perhaps therefore rarely mentioned) operation in which NATO operated closely and effectively alongside the EU and the OSCE was *Operation Essential Harvest* in the Former Yugoslav Republic of Macedonia in 2001 in which the Alliance undertook support to local disarmament and weapons collection.

[60] At the time, NATO offered a much larger contingent than the UN was prepared to accept.

at its disposal that, in theory, might form the nucleus around which larger multinational operations can be based.

- *Providing and/or coordinating strategic lift capacity to facilitate more rapid deployment.* This may include the coordination of lift through established movement-control structures such as NATO's new Movement Coordination Centre for strategic lift established in July 2007, or it may involve more direct involvement, as in the assistance given to AU peacekeepers rotated in and out of Darfur since 2005.
- *Providing and/or assisting with logistics support, tactical mobility, and other specialized units.* In July 2005 the International Crisis Group explored the option of deploying a NATO "bridging force" to Darfur, drawing on the NRF and NATO's obvious strengths in "planning, command and control and logistic support."[61] Although the proposal was, for political reasons, unlikely ever to go very far, it did provide an interesting example of how NATO can, political circumstances permitting, play a supportive role for other organizations, in this case the AU.
- *Training, mentoring, and assistance with Security Sector Reform (SSR).*[62] The collapse of Yugoslavia into violence in the early 1990s clearly showed that the passing of the Cold War would not itself translate into an era of continent-wide order and stability. Systems of communist control may have crumbled with surprising and welcome speed, but the transition to stable, pluralistic, and market-oriented regimes would have to be actively assisted. NATO's contribution to this transition, which involved SSR broadly conceived, was clearly not insignificant and has probably been underestimated. One aspect of its work was the development of partnership programs, which, although sometimes ridiculed for their lack of substance, did nonetheless assist the delicate process of transition within the militaries of former Warsaw Pact countries. NATO has continued its security sector reform and capacity-building role in the Balkans, is providing training in Afghanistan and Iraq, and is exploring similar roles for other organizations outside Europe. The need to build credible, accountable, and effective indigenous capacity in war-torn countries through training, mentoring, and assistance requires more systematic attention than it has received in Afghanistan or other peace and stability operations. It has even been suggested that NATO should consider the creation of a dedicated "Military Advisory Force."[63]
- *Providing quick reaction forces to assist peace operations in force protection, meeting direct challenges to a mandate or, if required, for extraction purposes.*

---

[61] See "The AU's Mission in Darfur: Bridging the Gaps," ICG, Policy Briefing No. 28, July 6, 2005, p. 12.

[62] This role is also highlighted by Jamie Shea, "A NATO for the 21st Century", pp. 52–53.

[63] Daniel Korski and Michael Williams, "Creating a NATO Military Advisory Force," *World Defence Systems*, no. 17, November 2008, pp. 148–151.

These could be deployed "'over-the-horizon" or at a certain stage, notably early, of a mission. The role of such a force would, in principle, be similar to that played by the French-led European Union (EU) force, Operation Artemis, deployed in eastern Congo in 2003 in order to prepare the ground for an expanded UN force (MONUC). In early 2000, a robust British force deployed to Sierra Leone (Operation Palliser) and helped prevent the collapse of the fledgling UN mission in that country. The absence of more robust forces of this kind has often proved an Achilles heel in major peace operations, making them vulnerable to sudden deteriorations in the operational environment.

To emphasize NATO's possible role in support of other organizations and bodies is also to highlight the second, and arguably more fundamental, conclusion to emerge from this analysis: on its own the Alliance cannot provide *solutions* to specific security challenges, though it may, if political circumstances permit, form an important and valuable part of international attempts to do so. There are two major reasons for this.

In the first instance, NATO is a military alliance, and although the threat of and use of force may be appropriate in certain circumstances, military force, for it to be effective, must serve wider political purposes and be employed alongside other instruments. As a military alliance, NATO possesses certain unique assets discussed earlier, and many of these have already proved useful in peace operations. These can and should be developed further. Yet as Secretary General Jaap de Hoop Scheffer has noted, "transforming for stabilisation operations is not 'just' a new capability initiative . . . it is about developing a 'new mission model' that successfully integrates the Alliance's actions with those by international actors."[64]

The second reason why NATO should prioritize its role *alongside* and in *support* of other actors relates to the issue of legitimacy, or more precisely NATO's lack of widespread international legitimacy of the kind commanded by the UN, however flawed the world body's ability to deliver may be in other respects. It is true that the North Atlantic Committee bypassed the Security Council over Kosovo in 1999, but this is generally seen as a matter of regret and an exception to be avoided, particularly among NATO's European members. The fact is that outside the North Atlantic area, NATO continues to be viewed as serving a distinctive Western agenda. Indeed, in many quarters – witness statements from groupings such as the G-77 and the NAM – the Alliance is essentially seen as an instrument of U.S. "hegemonic policies." This view has only been reinforced since 9/11, so that while NATO emphasizes its role in bringing "reconstruction and development" to Afghanistan, the vast majority of UN member-states see it merely as an extension of the U.S. "war on terror." Whether one accepts the validity of this view – and it may seem paradoxical in light of this chapter's emphasis on the diversity of interests and intergovernmental character of the Alliance – it is undeniably a widespread perception and has formed

---

[64] As cited in Nelson, p. v.

the backdrop to all discussions about a possible role for NATO outside its core area, whether in Lebanon in 2006 or in Darfur in 2004–2006. As Jacques Chirac, whatever his other motives, rightly observed in the summer of 2006 when the Alliance was contemplating a peacekeeping role in southern Lebanon, "NATO is perceived, whether we like it or not, as the armed wing of the West in these regions, and consequently, in terms of its image, NATO is not the right organisation here."[65] At times, NATO's own rhetoric and public diplomacy have done little to counter the blanket association of NATO with U.S. policies. Thus, when NATO's Secretary General spoke of the readiness to meet "security challenges at their source, whenever and wherever they arise," the obvious connection made outside NATO was with the U.S. "doctrine of preemption" and the notion of preventive wars.

The Alliance needs not only to be more honest and realistic about its comparative advantages and limitations but also to develop more meaningful relationships with other multinational organizations. In many places, NATO is already working alongside other actors, but the scope for deepening ties is, judging from Afghanistan, considerable. This includes relations with the EU, which remain fraught with tension.[66] This is not just a challenge for NATO. Many bodies, not least the UN, are deeply and instinctively distrustful of the Alliance, wishing to keep it at arm's length while hoping to tap into its assets and resources. It was the UN Secretariat, not NATO, which held out against a more substantive and meaningful agreement on practical cooperation than the anodyne and vague Joint Declaration on UN-NATO Secretariat Cooperation signed in September 2008.[67] As long as this tendency persists, there will always be obstacles to the development of the Alliance as a service agency for the international community.

[65] Interview with Jacques Chirac, President of the French Republic, for "Le Monde" newspaper, July 26, 2006, see www.elysee.fr/elysee/elysee.fr/anglais_archives/speeches_and_documents/2006/.

[66] See Judy Dempsey, "German General Giving up on Afghan Mission," *International Herald Tribune*, 12 September 2007.

[67] "Joint Declaration on UN–NATO Secretariat Cooperation," Annex to DSG (2008) 0714 (INV), September 23, 2008.

7

The Evolution of Nuclear Nonproliferation Institutions*

Christine Wing

The end of the Cold War represented the first real opportunity to extricate the world from the nuclear dilemma. But what seemed possible in the early 1990s – that states might finally eliminate nuclear weapons from their military postures – seemed, by 2006, to be a distant hope at best, an opportunity lost.

This is not to downplay the importance of what did happen following the Cold War's demise. Between 1990 and 2006, the United States and Russia reduced their nuclear arsenals from nearly 58,000 warheads (more than 95% of the world's total) to 26,000, with promises to continue reductions.[1] As these reductions occurred, the United States and Russia cooperated to secure dismantled nuclear materials in Russia, an action that would have been unimaginable a few years before. And more generally, nuclear rivalry among the major powers abated as the potential for all-out nuclear war receded.

But there is another side to the story. Existing nuclear powers had continued to upgrade their arsenals. It became clear that four additional states had acquired nuclear weapons, all in politically sensitive areas where there were few agreements to manage the threat of their potential use. The United States withdrew from the Anti-Ballistic Missile Treaty and moved to deploy missile defense systems. The risk of further proliferation, and the desire of nuclear weapon states to preserve the military advantage that these weapons confer, continued to drive much of international political relations.

Multilateral arrangements to reduce nuclear dangers have existed since the 1960s, particularly in relationship to the potential for nuclear proliferation. This chapter explores how these arrangements changed in the years following 1990. To make the discussion manageable and to bound the question, we focus specifically on the treaty-based parts of the nuclear nonproliferation regime and the relation among them.

---

* The author thanks Tristan Dreisbach and Fiona Simpson for their assistance in preparing this chapter.
[1] Figures are from Robert S. Norris and Hans M. Kristensen, "Global Nuclear Stockpiles, 1945–2006," *Bulletin of Atomic Scientists* (July/August 2006), 64–66.

Evolution of Nuclear Nonproliferation Institutions 123

We begin with an overview of the nonproliferation regime, as it will be discussed here, and describe the system-level changes that took place between the end of the Cold War and 2006. In the following two sections, we explore the specific developments that contributed to those overall changes, and in the final section we discuss their implications for two key institutions, as well as the system more broadly.

THE NUCLEAR NONPROLIFERATION REGIME: AN OVERVIEW

Because of their tremendous destructive power, nuclear weapons pose a fundamental risk to all states. States try to limit that risk in three ways: deterrence of nuclear attack – largely attempted through activities at the national level (developing weapons programs and forming alliances); defense against nuclear attack, for example, ballistic missile defense, also largely national; and/or active efforts to prevent the spread of the weapons themselves. It is in the third of these – nonproliferation – where most multilateral approaches have occurred.[2]

Existing multilateral nonproliferation arrangements are sufficiently extensive and complementary that they are typically considered to constitute a "regime." This regime has several core elements whose number and relative importance may shift over time, but generally are structured to assure that no states have nuclear weapon programs, other than the five that are acknowledged by the Non-Proliferation Treaty (China, France, Russia, the United Kingdom, and the United States); that nonnuclear weapon states are able to develop and operate nuclear power programs, or otherwise make use of civilian nuclear technologies; that states with nuclear weapons eventually disarm those weapons; and most recently, that nonstate actors are prevented from acquiring or using weapons or weapons-relevant materials. As will be discussed, the nonproliferation regime includes both treaty-based agreements with many members, and several smaller, more informal arrangements that are important for containing trade in proliferation-sensitive materials and that do not aspire to universality.

The NPT, the IAEA, and the Security Council

This chapter focuses on key multilateral mechanisms that are widely subscribed and are anchored in three broadly based interrelated entities: the Non-Proliferation Treaty (NPT) itself, the International Atomic Energy Agency (IAEA), and the UN

---

[2] The discussion in this section draws on Christine Wing, *Nuclear Weapons: The Challenges Ahead* (New York: International Peace Academy, 2008), pp. 2–4. More generally, the information in this chapter is drawn from the websites of, or material produced by, numerous research institutes, including the Acronym Institute; the Federation of American Scientists; globalsecurity.org; the James Martin Center for Nonproliferation Studies at the Monterey Institute of International Studies; the Nuclear Threat Initiative; and the Project on Defense Alternatives, among others. Treaty texts, additional data, and organizational information can be found at the websites of the International Atomic Energy Agency, the Office of Disarmament Affairs at the United Nations, the Comprehensive Test Ban Organization, and various U.S. government sites.

Security Council. Although these three are emphasized here, it is important to note that they are supplemented by a related set of more organizations and agreements that help to operationalize the NPT. These include the Nuclear Suppliers Group (NSG), which plays an important role in regulating the export of nuclear and nuclear-related materials.[3]

The NPT was opened for signature in 1968 and came into force in 1970. The NPT creates two categories of states: the nuclear weapons states (NWS), that is, those that had manufactured and exploded a nuclear weapon or device before 1967; and nonnuclear weapons states (NNWS), that is, all others that join the NPT.

The treaty is built on a set of bargains between the NWS and the NNWS. Essentially, NNWS agree to forego the development of nuclear weapons, but can receive active assistance from NWS, and others, for the development of civilian nuclear energy applications. As noted previously, NWS also agree to make good faith efforts to disarm their nuclear weapon holdings – a condition that was sought by the NNWS when the treaty was negotiated, and has remained contentious over time.

The treaty does not directly include compliance measures, but it requires that NNWS negotiate Safeguards Agreements with the IAEA, whose statute does address compliance. The NPT is reviewed every five years in a conference of all states parties; several preparatory committees precede these conferences. This means that the NPT is under nearly constant discussion (but not necessarily action) by member states.

As of this writing, nearly all states are party to the NPT. India, Israel, and Pakistan all have nuclear weapon programs; none has ever joined the NPT. The Democratic People's Republic of Korea (DPRK) was party to the treaty but withdrew in 2003, although some contest the legitimacy of that withdrawal.

The IAEA was formed in 1957. Currently 144 states are members. A Board of Governors of thirty-five states, including the five nuclear weapon states, governs the agency.[4] The IAEA assists states in their efforts to develop peaceful nuclear technologies, including nuclear power. The agency also concludes and monitors Safeguards Agreements with NNWS in order to assure that no nuclear material is diverted from civilian nuclear energy programs to military use. NWS are not required to have Safeguards Agreements, although they can make some limited voluntary agreements that would not result in IAEA access to military programs. The IAEA also may conclude Safeguards Agreements with non-NPT states that have civilian nuclear programs.

---

[3] The NSG includes approximately forty-five states. Other nonproliferation instruments are the Zangger Committee, which helps states identify what materials should be safeguarded if they are supplied to NNWS; and the Missile Technology Control Regime, which controls transfers of missiles and related materials that might be used for nuclear (or other WMD) delivery systems. Finally, the regime contains negotiated restraints on nuclear testing, such as the Limited and Partial Test Ban Treaties, and in recent years, the unilateral moratorium on testing that is maintained by the NWS. All these agreements create both direct and normative value for the regime.

[4] Membership on the Board of Governors is established to ensure that it includes the states with advanced nuclear technology as well as other states selected on a regional basis, for limited terms.

In all cases, the agreements are bilateral, between the IAEA and the safeguarded country. At the time that the Safeguard Agreement is signed, a state declares all of its nuclear material holdings and related activities. This creates the baseline to which the IAEA compares results of its in-country inspections of declared nuclear facilities and materials.

When IAEA inspectors detect instances of possible noncompliance, these are reviewed through a substantial internal process and reported to the Director General (DG) as appropriate. The DG can then report this noncompliance to the Board of Governors. The Board calls on the state to remedy its noncompliance; if it fails to do so, the Board may report the noncompliance to member states, the Security Council, and the General Assembly. The practice has been that the Board of Governors has the authority to decide if and when to refer a state's noncompliance to the Security Council, although some states dispute the extent to which that discretion should be exercised.

The Security Council has three possible roles related to questions of proliferation and nonproliferation. Under the Charter itself, the Security Council is responsible for determining and acting on threats to international peace and security. The Council therefore carries authority to address instances of proliferation that constitute such a threat; that proliferation does represent such a threat was specifically articulated in a 1992 statement by the heads of state of Security Council members.[5] Second, as noted, the IAEA may refer instances of NPT noncompliance to the Security Council; the NPT does not further define the Council's role in enforcing compliance. Finally, Article X of the NPT requires that states that withdraw from the treaty notify the Security Council (and other states parties) three months in advance of the withdrawal. Again, the NPT does not stipulate how the Council should address such notification.

Although we discuss these three institutions as closely related elements of a treaty-based "NPT system," we also, at points in the discussion, distinguish between the "NPT itself" (or "the NPT and its associated review processes"), on the one hand, and the IAEA and the Security Council, on the other. Whereas both the IAEA and the Security Council carry critical responsibilities for nonproliferation, both were also created independently of the NPT and have functions in addition to their NPT-related role. They are part of the NPT-based regime, but they also may take positions that are different from, and sometimes at odds with, the concerns of the NPT as defined by states parties at any given moment; hence, the need to treat these three interconnected elements as having some autonomous identity.

Big Picture Changes

Given current proliferation challenges, it can be easy to forget the extent of change that occurred in the nuclear nonproliferation regime after 1990. Table 7.1 highlights

---

[5] "Note by the President of the Security Council," S/23500, January 31 1992. Available at http://www.stimson.org/cnp/pdf/S23500_UNSC.pdf.

126   *Christine Wing*

TABLE 7.1. *Three aspects of the NPT-based nonproliferation regime*

	1990	2006
Coverage	Total members: 141 of 159 states	Total members: 188 of 192 states
	Declared NWS that have joined the NPT: 3 (UK, U.S., USSR)	Declared NWS that have joined the NPT: 5 (China, France, UK, U.S., USSR)
	Declared NWS that are NPT eligible but have not joined: 2 (China, France)	0
	Suspected or known NWS that are outside the NPT and not NPT eligible (as a nuclear weapon state): 4 (India, Israel, Pakistan, South Africa)	3 (India, Israel, Pakistan)
	Nuclear "threshold" states that have not joined the NPT: 2 (Argentina, Brazil)	0
	States to emerge from dissolution of Soviet Union, states with nuclear weapons on their soil: 3 (Belarus, Kazakhstan, Ukraine)	
Compliance	Official: Public record indicates full compliance with NPT nonproliferation commitments by all NPT member states. Actual: National intelligence suggests several NPT member states may be attempting to develop nuclear weapons program (DPRK, Iran, Iraq, Libya); later revelations demonstrate this is the case	Three NPT member states have been found to be significantly out of treaty compliance, attempting to develop nuclear weapon programs: Iraq, DPRK, Libya. Initial findings are not made by IAEA in any of the three cases. Iraq and Libya in compliance by 2006. DPRK withdrew from NPT in 2003, status unresolved
		Serious questions about Iran's nuclear program; many believe Iran to be developing a weapons program
Enforcement Capability	Not tested	Security Council has overseen successful disarmament in Iraq but in a contested and lengthy process
		Security Council has condemned nuclear activity in DPRK, but is not involved in ongoing negotiations
		No established way to address withdrawal from NPT
		Not yet effective in addressing Iranian case

some of these, as they pertain to the treaty-based parts of this regime. The table identifies three key attributes of binding multilateral arrangements: coverage – the degree to which these arrangements, in this case the NPT, capture all relevant parties; compliance – the extent to which states parties adhere to agreed commitments; and enforcement capabilities – the ability of the regime's constituent institutions to detect treaty violations and to assure that states move back into treaty compliance.

On the question of treaty coverage, this table shows that in 1990 there were 141 members of the NPT, with 18 states not having joined. By 2006, 188 of 192 states were NPT members. However, this growth in numbers does not fully communicate the importance of the growth in membership. In 2006, when only four states remained outside the NPT, the treaty was very close to universality – a condition that clearly had not obtained in 1990. Equally important, of the states that did become NPT members after 1990, eight either had nuclear weapon programs or were thought to be capable of such programs. The way in which this occurred – and the importance of the exceptions – will be discussed more fully in the following two sections.

The compliance picture is murkier. Officially, in 1990 there were not – and had not yet been – any major questions or charges of noncompliance with the IAEA Safeguards Agreement. However, some observers strongly suspected that four NPT members were secretly developing nuclear weapons,[6] even though these states had not been found in noncompliance by the IAEA itself; this proved true in at least three cases. Thus NPT compliance has not been universal since before 1990. But the end of the Cold War, and ensuing political transformations, made it easier to detect and publicize that noncompliance.

Finally, beyond compliance is the question of enforcement capabilities. With no formal IAEA findings of safeguards noncompliance, the Security Council's enforcement capabilities were still untested in 1990. This soon changed, as the international community confronted publicly revealed proliferation attempts in Iraq and the DPRK and later in Libya and possibly Iran. The Council's ability (and sometimes its authority) to address these cases was highly contested and problematic, remaining so to this day.

Thus, in broad terms we can say that treaty coverage improved after the Cold War, whereas compliance and enforcement, largely untested in 1990, proved to be difficult beginning in the early 1990s, and lasting up until 2006. The following section explores how and why this was the case.

1990–2001: THE DEFINING DECADE

As implied previously, the 1990s brought contradictory developments for the treaty-based nonproliferation system and its constituent institutions. Formal elements of

---

[6] Dramatic evidence of such suspicion was seen in Israel's 1981 attack on the Osirak research reactor in Iraq.

128   *Christine Wing*

the NPT itself were more fully realized, as the "old" nonproliferation agenda moved forward in ways not possible during the Cold War. At the same time, the structural weaknesses of the Cold War regime began to appear, placing new demands on the regime's constituent institutions and drawing both the IAEA and the Security Council into much more active engagement in efforts to deal with actual proliferation.

These two processes – consolidation of the formal NPT agenda, on the one hand; challenge and change, on the other – were obviously intertwined, although, as we shall see, they took place within somewhat different periods.

New Progress on the Old Agenda: NPT Consolidation

Table 7.1 shows that the net gain in post–Cold War NPT membership was forty-seven states. In part this reflects the addition of more than thirty states to the international system. But more importantly, as noted previously, this includes several states whose decisions were particularly important for the NPT system as a whole: France and China, the two states that were eligible to accede to the NPT as nuclear weapon states, did so in 1992, which meant that all five nuclear weapon states that were acknowledged by the NPT were treaty members. And six states, with actual or potential nuclear weapons, decided to abandon the nuclear weapon path:

- South Africa, which had stopped its nuclear weapon program in the late 1980s (having produced six weapons), joined the NPT in 1991.
- Belarus, Kazakhstan, and Ukraine, which "inherited" nuclear weapons from the former Soviet Union, agreed to turn the weapons over to Russia and to join the NPT. Belarus and Kazakhstan acceded to the NPT in 1993; Ukraine, in 1994.
- Argentina and Brazil, which were thought to have the ability and possible intention to develop nuclear weapon programs, formally abandoned the weapons path, and agreed in the early 1990s to inspections of each other's nuclear holdings. Argentina became party to the NPT in 1995; Brazil, in 1998.

These changes had several implications. The likelihood of proliferation beyond the five NWS was significantly reduced; the authority and legitimacy of the NPT system itself were strengthened; and those states that had nuclear weapons programs, but were not in the NPT, were increasingly outside the norm of nonproliferation as officially agreed by all other states.

A second aspect of "NPT consolidation" was the decision by states parties to extend the treaty indefinitely. According to Article X (2) of the treaty, states would decide, twenty-five years after entry into force, whether to extend the treaty – either indefinitely or for "fixed periods." With the NPT having come into force in 1970, this meant that the extension decision would come up in 1995.

After an often-contentious meeting – a central issue was how willing the NWS were to commit themselves to serious disarmament steps – the conference decided to

Evolution of Nuclear Nonproliferation Institutions 129

extend the treaty indefinitely, doing so without a vote. Measures accepted included a set of Principles and Objectives containing certain specific steps seen as contributing to disarmament. These included the completion of negotiations for a Comprehensive Test Ban Treaty (CTBT) by 1996 and the early negotiation of a treaty to ban the production of fissile materials. Although the PrepComs leading to the 2000 Review Conference were also characterized by substantial disagreement, the 2000 conference itself produced consensus, including a set of thirteen "practical steps" toward nuclear disarmament. These reinforced and made more specific the 1995 Principles and Objectives.

Following the 1995 NPT extension, the negotiation of the CTBT– under discussion since the 1950s – was agreed and opened for signature in 1996. The treaty stipulated that, to enter into force, forty-four states that had either nuclear power or research reactors must ratify the treaty. (As we shall see, this proved to be a stumbling block to the treaty's entry into force.) The treaty established a Comprehensive Test Ban Treaty Organization, whose Preparatory Commission was to work toward ratification of the Treaty. Its Secretariat was established in 1997.[7]

Challenges: The Roots of Change

The first challenge to the NPT came from nuclear weapon programs in NPT states, initially in the form of evidence emerging from Iraq. Through the inspections mandated by the Security Council and carried out by the IAEA, it was clear by the summer of 1991 that Iraq, a long-standing party to the NPT, had been developing a covert nuclear weapon program for many years. During that time, the IAEA had inspected declared sites in Iraq, but those safeguard inspections were not sufficient to detect the large clandestine program.

Within a year, the information about Iraq was followed by evidence that the DPRK may have also engaged in activities that violated the terms of the NPT. IAEA inspections revealed important discrepancies with the DPRK's initial declarations about its nuclear holdings. Invoking its right to conduct "special inspections," at the end of 1992 the IAEA requested to see two facilities. The DPRK refused access. Thus began a difficult process in which the DPRK at various times curtailed inspections, withdrew from the NPT, and subsequently "suspended" that withdrawal. This lasted until the negotiation, in the summer of 1994, of an "Agreed Framework" between the United States and the DPRK. This agreement offered the DPRK energy assistance and the eventual provision of light water reactors, in exchange for its agreement to verifiably freeze and eventually dismantle its weapons program. The United States

---

[7] Lawrence Scheinman, "Issue Brief: Comprehensive Test Ban Treaty," website of the *Nuclear Threat Initiative*, April 2003, http://www.nti.org/e_research/e3_9a.html; "Comprehensive Test Ban Treaty," *Acronym Institute*, http://www.acronym.org.uk/ctbt/index.125htm; CTBTO Preparatory Commission. http://www.ctbto.org/.

130 Christine Wing

also agreed to provide the DPRK with "formal assurances against the threat or use of nuclear weapons by the U.S."[8]

Equally problematic has been the issue of nuclear weapon programs in non-NPT states. As the IAEA and the Security Council worked to adapt to their new role in restricting active proliferation, the NPT faced growing difficulties that neither multilateral institutions nor individual states were able to address effectively, exemplified during this period by the Indian and Pakistani nuclear tests conducted in 1998. It was not a surprise that these states had nuclear weapon programs, but it was no longer possible to act as though there were only five NWS. The question this posed was stark: how meaningful is a nonproliferation treaty if major states can legally develop and deploy nuclear weapons? The answer was obscure at best. Both states and the Security Council issued denunciations of the tests, but their inability to take effective, lasting action was the more telling.[9]

With the evolution of technologies, a mounting challenge to the NPT has been the risk of nuclear acquisition by nonstate actors or states that illegally trade in nuclear materials. Concerns about the risks of proliferation to terrorists and "states of concern" continued to grow in the United States and elsewhere. These concerns were not wholly new, but they were intensifying as evidence mounted about presumed illicit trade in nuclear-related materials among China, Pakistan, North Korea, and perhaps other actors. Bilaterally, the United States initiated the Cooperative Threat Reduction program, which assisted Russia in securing its weapons complex, and preventing proliferation of dismantled nuclear materials. However, at the multilateral level, concerns over nuclear terrorism did not yet rise to the level of the implementation of new institutional approaches.

As the decade closed, the earlier movement toward a strengthened regime began to erode. By 2001, the CTBT had not yet entered into force. More than one hundred states had ratified the CTBT, but of the forty-four states that were required to ratify the treaty before entry into force, thirteen had not done so. This included China, the DPRK, Egypt, India, Iran, Israel, Pakistan, and the United States.[10] Indeed, despite the United States' previous enthusiasm for the CTBT, the U.S. Senate rejected ratification in 1999. Nor were any of these "non-ratifying" states expected to join the CTBT in the near future.

Still, the five NWS did eventually stop testing within this decade, and none has resumed as of this writing. Similarly, although deadlocked on a Fissile Material Cutoff Treaty (FMCT), four NPT weapon states nonetheless have said publicly that they have stopped fissile material production (for weapons purposes); China, the state that has not made such a declaration, is thought also to have ceased such production.

---

[8] "Agreed Framework between the United States of America and the Democratic People's Republic of Korea. Geneva, October 21, 1994." http://www.kedo.org/pdfs/AgreedFramework.pdf.

[9] Resolution 1172 (1998); June 6, 1998. http://www.un.org/News/Press/docs/1998/sc6528.doc.htm.

[10] The last underground test by the United States was in 1992, the Soviet Union in 1990, the United Kingdom in 1991. Both France and China continued testing until 1996.

Evolution of Nuclear Nonproliferation Institutions

Although not satisfying the standard of irreversible and binding adherence to a negotiated treaty, this restraint did accomplish the practical objectives of no testing and no fissile material production, at least by NWS.

Finally, the ultimate meaning of the agreements reached at the 1995 NPT conference seemed increasingly ambiguous. PrepComs leading up to the 2000 Review Conference were contentious, largely around questions of NWS pursuit of the Principles and Objectives agreed to in 1995, though other issues were important as well: the question of universality in the wake of the tests by India and Pakistan; safeguards; and worries about the Anti Ballistic Missile (ABM) Treaty as the United States moved to allow the development of missile defenses. Yet the conference successfully negotiated a final document that reaffirmed the 1995 agreement and, as noted earlier, was adopted by consensus.

The U.S. Role, 1990–2001

In the period after the Cold War, the United States was the single most important actor in both consolidating the NPT regime and in determining the way in which the international community responded to emergent challenges. But that role was quite different in each case.

Each of the NPT changes that took place in the first half of the decade – strengthened NPT membership, treaty extension, CTBT negotiation – was in accord with U.S. interests as perceived by both the George H. W. Bush (Bush I) and the Clinton administrations. Indeed, the United States nurtured, and sometimes led, these developments. The United States worked aggressively with the former Soviet states and Russia to assure that all Soviet nuclear weapons were returned to Russia. NPT extension was actively sought, and the U.S. government negotiated seriously to achieve this goal. It was a major actor in the negotiation and completion of the CTBT, and the first country to sign that treaty. To the extent that the multilateral activity around these issues was controversial, it was often precisely because of the strong U.S. interests in outcomes: if less important, the United States could have walked away.

In the 1996 National Security Strategy, there is a particularly clear articulation of how the Clinton administration understood its leadership role, at least as it was expressed publicly. One might dispute the degree to which the administration claimed credit for all that happened – or that the effect of U.S. engagement was altogether benign – but the document is nonetheless telling about U.S. interests and the pursuit thereof:

> The President launched a comprehensive policy to combat the proliferation of weapons of mass destruction and the missiles that deliver them. The United States has secured landmark commitments to eliminate all nuclear weapons from Ukraine, Belarus, and Kazakhstan, ... The United States led the successful international

effort to extend the NPT indefinitely and without conditions by consensus of Treaty parties at the 1995 Review and Extension Conference. The President's August 1995 initiative to support a true zero yield [CTBT] provided a significant boost to the CTBT negotiations and has opened the door to completing and signing a CTBT in 1996.[11]

The U.S. role in these cases was to strengthen *existing* multilateral approaches to nonproliferation, not to create new approaches. In a sense, the United States was moving on tracks already laid by decades of multilateral activity: the problems had been largely defined over the last thirty years, and possible solutions had been largely identified. Except for the question of nuclear weapons in former Soviet republics, the formal nonproliferation agenda seemed almost untouched by the profound shifts in the underlying dynamics of global political relations.

When it came to other, *newer* challenges, however, the United States was more likely to define both the problem and the solution, taking approaches that were innovative at times, and substantially outside the NPT system. For example, the Cooperative Threat Reduction (CTR) program, an extraordinary development for two recent military rivals, addressed the newly emerging security threat of "loose nukes." CTR was a bilateral effort throughout its early years. It was also during the first Clinton administration that the United States began to articulate a strategy of counterproliferation, with the intention of using military force to stop proliferation, either state or nonstate – a distinctly unilateral (or potentially coalitional) response.

In the case of Iraq, it was the United States that defined the problem (initially, the Iraqi invasion of Kuwait) and the solution (eventually, Security Council-imposed embargoes backed by the authority to use force if Iraq did not withdraw from Kuwait; later, proof of weapons of mass destruction (WMD) disarmament before the lifting of sanctions). This is not to say that other states were irrelevant: U.S. planning took place in close consultation with the UK and, in this case, the Soviet Union. But the initiative was in U.S. hands, and the United States was instrumental in determining the degree to which the Iraq case was in the Security Council's hands.

Initially, this worked well from a U.S. perspective. The United States successfully shepherded Security Council resolutions, which, at least to the United States, ultimately provided Council authorization for military action against Iraq if it did not meet the Council's demands for Iraqi withdrawal from Kuwait. Once that attack had taken place, under U.S. leadership but with coalition partners, and the war was over, the United States and the UK together drafted Resolution 687; this resolution set the terms of the postwar settlement with Iraq, including its disarmament of all WMD.

The problem for the United States came when the Council splintered over the question of lifting sanctions. The United States wanted those sanctions continued

---

[11] The White House, "A National Security Strategy of Engagement and Enlargement," February 1996. Text is from Section I. Accessed at http://www.fas.org/spp/military/docops/national/1996stra.htm.

Evolution of Nuclear Nonproliferation Institutions   133

until they were convinced that all WMD, including nuclear, were gone from Iraq. Not all of the five permanent members (P5) agreed, and Council action to end sanctions remained impossible into the next decade. Still, U.S. interests were effectively blocked, but not overridden.

The approach to the DPRK was very different. Here, the intensity of Council engagement was much less, despite the IAEA's ongoing frustrations and occasional referrals to the Council. Unlike Iraq, where the incontrovertible discovery of WMD programs awaited the outcome of a war fought on other grounds, the United States was already actively working the DPRK case on a bilateral basis while working with allies in northeast Asia and eventually also building up military forces in the region. The threat of referral to the Council was an important part of the U.S. strategy, but not a commitment to have the problem of DPRK's weapons program decided there. Although the Council did issue statements about the desirability that the DPRK and the IAEA find solutions to their disputes over inspections, the question never came to the Security Council for actual resolution. And it was the United States that was ultimately responsible for decisions about the shape and nature of the Agreed Framework.[12]

SEPTEMBER 2001 TO THE END OF 2006

From 9/11 to the Invasion of Iraq

In the wake of 9/11, two familiar issues began to dominate the multilateral nonproliferation agenda: the growing fear that terrorists could acquire nuclear weapons and continuing revelations about actual state-level proliferation – revelations that were worrisome in their own right and that also fostered uncertainty about the viability of the NPT's fundamental bargains. Tying these concerns together were unfolding discoveries about the A.Q. Khan network, discussed in the next section, and what they suggested about the possibilities for illicit trade in nuclear materials.

The danger that terrorists would use nuclear weapons was difficult to approach through an NPT lens. The NPT is a treaty among states; it stipulates if and how states parties can transfer or receive nuclear-related material. With a few exceptions, the treaty does not address potential proliferation to or by nonstate actors – either nonstate suppliers or nonstate recipients.[13] At a minimum, meaningful multilateral action would need some base beyond the NPT.

---

[12] Based on Leon V. Sigal, *Disarming Strangers: Nuclear Diplomacy with North Korea* (Princeton, NJ: Princeton University Press, 1998); Joel Wit, *Going Critical: The First North Korean Nuclear Crisis* (Washington, DC: Brookings Institution Press, 2004).

[13] For example, the NPT says in Article I, "Each nuclear-weapon State Party to the Treaty undertakes not to transfer to *any recipient* whatsoever nuclear weapons or other nuclear explosive devices . . . "; and in Article II "Each non-nuclear-weapon State Party to the Treaty undertakes not to receive the transfer from *any transfer or* whatsoever of nuclear weapons or other nuclear explosive devices . . . " [emphasis added] Although the Zangger Committee and the NSG help states to assure that exports

The groundwork for that multilateral action was laid in this period. Shortly after 9/11, the Security Council passed a wide-ranging counterterrorism resolution. It required that states prevent, suppress, and criminalize the financing of any terrorist activity. Resolution 1373 was passed under Chapter VII of the UN Charter, meaning that it applied to all states. This was the first time in the UN's history that the Council had "legislated" for all states; although not yet addressing WMD proliferation to nonstate actors, Resolution 1373 paved the way for such action within a few years.

Concerns about existing proliferation were succinctly summarized in George W. Bush's 2002 State of the Union address, where he identified Iraq, the DPRK, and Iran as an "axis of evil." The danger was not only state-to-state but also state-to-terrorist: that "state sponsors of terrorism" would transfer WMD capability to nonstate actors as well as use these capabilities in their own interests.

Shortly after the initial phase of the war in Afghanistan, the United States began pressing for international action to address what it said were continuing WMD efforts in Iraq. In September 2002, the Council adopted Resolution 1441, also under Chapter VII, finding that Iraq "remains in material breach of its obligations," requiring that country to provide a full accounting of, and fully disarm, its WMD and delivery systems, and demanding access for the IAEA and the newly organized UNMOVIC.[14]

The fact that the resolution was passed under Chapter VII created the possibility that military force could be used if Iraq did not comply. Despite indications from the IAEA and UNMOVIC that no WMD programs had yet been identified, a U.S.-led coalition invaded Iraq in March 2003, without formally returning the issue to the Security Council. This was a highly contested action that would further complicate the Council's ability to address proliferation issues in the future.

Second, the DPRK's nuclear-related activities came back on the multilateral agenda. In 2002, assertions about a North Korean uranium enrichment program initiated a series of events that resulted in the DPRK's eventual withdrawal from the NPT. With the IAEA's continued exclusion from the country, there was relatively little information – but much concern – about the status of the DPRK's program. In 2002, an Iranian exile group made public allegations of undeclared nuclear activity by Iran. Over the next few months and into 2003, the IAEA began to pursue these reports. The DPRK and Iran would continue to demand sustained Council attention going forward.

From the Invasion of Iraq to the End of 2006

The U.S. decision to invade Iraq in early 2003 was highly divisive, and the resulting acrimony colored efforts to address continuing proliferation challenges. But

do not contribute to proliferation, these concern the actions of supplier states, and participation in these arrangements is not mandatory for NPT members.

[14] United Nations Monitoring Verification and Inspection Commission, created by the Security Council in 1999.

Evolution of Nuclear Nonproliferation Institutions   135

eventually – and somewhat paradoxically – this was also the period in which more "structural" changes began to emerge, often led, and always supported by, the United States.

Continuing Proliferation. Given that the Iraqi government had been overthrown and that the country was occupied by the United States, the focus of proliferation concern shifted to other states. But both the DPRK and the Iranian issues seemed intractable, with substantial disagreement among the P5 about how to proceed. Shortly after the DPRK's withdrawal from the NPT, the Board of Governors found the country in "further" noncompliance with its safeguards obligations, and referred the DPRK to the Security Council. The Security Council expressed its "concern" but did not take further action. In 2005, the Six-Party Talks were again underway and again broke off. The DPRK tested a ballistic missile in July 2006 and a nuclear explosive in October. The missile test led to condemnation by the Security Council, the nuclear test to sanctions. Six-Party Talks would again resume and again break off, with no resolution as of this writing.

In 2003, when the IAEA began inspections for a potential Iranian program, it discovered that Iran did have several undeclared enrichment and reprocessing activities, as well as a prohibited import of nuclear materials. For nearly three years, the IAEA attempted to collect more information about, and to clarify, these possible violations of Iran's Safeguard Agreement. Progress was slow. A diplomatic process, initiated by three EU states, also yielded no lasting results. In the fall of 2005, and under increasing pressure from the United States, the IAEA Board of Governors found Iran in noncompliance with its safeguards obligations; the question was referred to the Security Council early in 2006. After Iran ignored several Council demands that it suspend its enrichment activities, the Security Council imposed limited sanctions on Iran in December 2006. Questions about Iran's nuclear program also remain unresolved as of this writing.

More successful, however, was the process leading to Libya's 2003 announcement that it would dismantle its WMD programs, including nuclear. The Libyan announcement grew out of secret talks among Libya, the United States, and the United Kingdom. Although these conversations were well underway by the fall of 2002, some analysts believe that they were given additional momentum by the U.S. invasion of Iraq in March 2003 and by the October seizure of enrichment equipment from a ship headed for Tripoli. For the remainder of the year, the three states conducted closely held negotiations that led to Libya's December announcement. Once the agreement was in place, the IAEA was invited to verify dismantlement of the nuclear program.[15]

---

[15] Discussion in this paragraph is drawn from Bruce W. Jentleson and Christopher A. Whytock, "Who 'Won' Libya?: The Force-Diplomacy Debate and Its Implications for Theory and Policy," *International Security* 30, No. 3 (Winter 2005/06), pp. 47–86.

Although many interpreted the Libya case as hopeful, the ongoing revelations about the A.Q. Khan network were increasingly worrisome. In 2004 the world was learning that Dr. Abdul Qadeer Khan, previously head of the Khan Research Laboratory in Pakistan, had for many years organized widespread, illegal trade in components for the development of nuclear weapons. These involved trade with a variety of both state entities and businesses, underscoring and heightening worries about nuclear proliferation to terrorists and certain states.[16]

What about the NPT? The 2005 NPT Review Conference produced much heated debate but no forward movement – if anything, it contributed to a growing sense among many states that disagreements about NPT implementation were intractable and that the viability of the regime itself was thrown into question. The September Summit of Heads of State did not help: it was unable to agree on any language concerning nuclear policy, and therefore left this important subject unaddressed in the final document.

Structural change: innovation begins. As noted earlier, several new initiatives, not necessarily reactive to specific events, also began in this period. The Proliferation Security Initiative (PSI) was established by the United States in May 2003, initially with eleven "core" states, all from the global North. The goal of this informal grouping was to cooperate to interdict shipments of WMD-related material and equipment. An early success was said by the United States to be capture of enrichment equipment on its way to Libya, although there is dispute about whether this actually represented a PSI activity. The precise form and membership of PSI are vague – it is a process, not an organization, according to the Bush administration.[17] At PSI's inception, some states expressed reservations about the legality of these interdictions, though these appear to have lessened over time.

Nearly a year later, in April 2004, the Security Council adopted Resolution 1540, which prohibits states from supporting nonstate actors in acquiring WMD-related material and requires them to adopt legislation to criminalize such an acquisition, and to put in place export controls to detect illegal activity. Like UNSCR 1373 before it – and despite vigorous opposition from some Council members – Resolution 1540 was passed under Chapter VII authority, again applying to all states.

Third, the proliferation cases that surfaced after 1990 put an old issue squarely on the emergent multilateral agenda. From the inception of the nuclear age, there has been a good understanding of the proliferation risk associated with civilian nuclear power. Various studies have taken place over the last thirty years to determine the viability of establishing a multilaterally controlled supply of nuclear fuel. In

---

[16] Much has been written about the Khan network. A useful overview is the Carnegie Endowment for International Peace, "A.Q. Khan Nuclear Chronology," *Issue Brief, Non-proliferation VIII. No. 8* (September 7, 2005). http://www.carnegieendowment.org/static/npp/Khan_Chronology .pdf.

[17] The U.S. Department of State described PSI as "a set of activities" rather than as "a formal, treaty-based organization." http://usinfo.state.gov/is/img/assets/4756/brochure1.pdf.

theory, this would eliminate the need for states to develop their own sensitive fuel cycle activities, notably uranium enrichment and plutonium reprocessing – the difficult and expensive technologies that could also feed a weapons program. In 2004, Director General Mohammed ElBaradei appointed an internationally diverse set of experts to revisit this question for the current context. Its 2005 report did not resolve the question, but it did mark the beginning of a substantial international debate about guaranteed fuel supplies. Numerous countries proposed specific plans, which remain under active consideration.

In July 2005, with potentially large implications for the NPT regime, the United States and India announced an agreement to expand cooperation in civil nuclear commerce. If approved by their respective countries (and with appropriate exceptions made by the NSG), the United States could export nuclear-related materials and technology to India, as well as fresh fuel. India would put its civilian nuclear program under IAEA safeguards, permit the IAEA to inspect elements of its civilian program, and sign an Additional Protocol, among other steps.

The proposed deal was contested in both countries, for a variety of reasons. One important implication for the nonproliferation regime was that this agreement, if implemented, would provide the first structured way of integrating a non-NPT nuclear weapon state into the NPT system. For this reason, some nonproliferation advocates favored this measure. Others said that, although not supporting India's military nuclear program directly, it could provide indirect support by allowing India, with imported fuel in hand, to transfer indigenously produced fuel to its military program – and, in this sense, raise questions about the NPT obligation of NWS not to support the development of nuclear weapons by other states.

The U.S. Role

As suggested previously, in this period the United States became much more active in shaping new multilateral approaches to WMD dangers. The United States (as well as some allies) put their concerns about proliferation to terrorists at the heart of nonproliferation. This included concerns about "state sponsors of terrorism," so addressing the existing issues of Iraq, the DPRK, and Iran acquired an additional motivation: to prevent these state sponsors of terrorism from passing along nuclear technology and/or materials.

Both PSI and UNSCR 1540 are clear examples of U.S. leadership in building multilateral capacity for preventing nuclear terrorism. Both measures represented significant innovation in the nonproliferation system. Unlike the agreements of the Cold War nonproliferation regime – the NPT and the NSG – PSI is "a set of activities," employing policing or military functions, whose rules are more informal and do not require approval by legally binding multilateral institutions. UNSCR 1540 innovates in a very different way: it creates universal obligations, not by the decisions of individual states, but through decision by the Security Council.

In this period, we also see further U.S. efforts to use multilateral forums to provide legitimacy for unilateral objectives – or at least objectives not held by the majority of states. This appears true (though not wholly successful) in the U.S. invasion of Iraq. And of course, the invasion was argued and justified in terms of WMD threats, and, in this sense, represented the completion of the long Security Council stalemate about sanctions and inspections.

In a different way, this is also the case in relation to Iran. The EU is clearly an important player in resolving the Iranian nuclear issue – but one would not mistake this for the ability to make the ultimate determination of that issue. This is not to argue that the United States can or will want to effect such a resolution unilaterally, nor that it will be successful in shaping IAEA or Security Council action. But it is to say that there will be no resolution to which the United States does not agree (i.e., if the United States does not agree, it is not a resolution of the issue).

Third, the U.S. interest and willingness to engage the NPT process declined substantially in this period. That willingness was at its peak in the first half of the 1990s. It fell off in the second Clinton administration, suggesting that the post–9/11 direction was already in process before the George W. Bush (Bush II) administration came into power. After 9/11, the United States became even less interested and less willing to pursue solutions through the NPT – at times seeming actively hostile to it.

CONCLUSIONS

Periodization

The editors of this volume suggest that the post–Cold War evolution of multilateral security institutions, and the role of the United States in that evolution, can usefully be understood in three periods: roughly 1990 to 9/11/2001, 9/11/2001 to March 2003, and March 2003 to the present. One question they pose is whether these periods make sense for the topics on which we are writing.

This chapter suggests that, concerning questions of nonproliferation, one might more usefully think in terms of pre–9/11 and post–9/11 (although we also note that the period up to the mid-1990s could be considered on its own). The dynamics of the nonproliferation regime were most dramatically affected by 9/11, as that event both motivated and created space for a different U.S. approach. This approach heightened the importance of preventing proliferation to nonstate actors, but devalued multilateral activity except when it could be achieved without extended negotiation among states.

Still, a complete analysis of the determinants of change in nonproliferation institutions would need also to look at the effects of shifting domestic politics in the United States. One might argue, for example, that the evolution of nonproliferation institutions could be equally, or perhaps better, considered in terms of the differences between the Clinton administration and the Bush II administration, or in shifts in congressional power. To the extent that U.S. policy sought to strengthen the non-proliferation regime as it stood in the early 1990s, this was most effectively pursued in the first Clinton administration. As congressional power shifted to the Republican Party, congressional support for nonproliferation eroded. This is not to argue that other factors were unimportant in the declining role of the United States in the formal regime – the difficulties of NPT compliance were important as well – but that a full understanding of the evolution of international institutions also requires analysis at the domestic level.

Institutional Implications

By the end of the 1990s, both states and multilateral institutions had confronted the major challenges that would beset the nonproliferation regime in the next decade: the potential for exploiting civilian nuclear programs to develop military programs, the fact that non-NPT members could legally develop nuclear weapon programs, and inadequate mechanisms for controlling nuclear-related commerce and the nuclear black market. Our earlier discussion reviewed the contours of changes in the NPT itself. This section turns to how its two supporting institutions, the IAEA and the Security Council, evolved in this period.

Implications for the IAEA. The discovery of Iraq's covert program in 1991, and revelations about the DPRK's program in 1992, raised serious questions about the IAEA's ability to detect nuclear weapon programs when materials or activities have not previously been declared. In light of this, the IAEA intensified its efforts to strengthen the safeguard system, including more aggressive use of its legal authority to conduct ad hoc inspections and environmental sampling; putting forward to states the 1997 model "Additional Protocol" (AP), which would give the IAEA additional access for detecting nondeclared materials and activities; and enhancing its own information collections and analysis. Though less discussed, another important consequence of the IAEA's role in Iraq and DPRK was that it seemingly expanded the agency's mandate in effect if not in statute. Although previously the agency had carried out inspections to determine compliance with Safeguards Agreements, in Iraq it was asked also to inspect the dismantlement and disarmament of formerly covert nuclear weapon programs. This task required additional or different skills, both technical and political. Concerning Iraq, the line of authority ran to the Security Council, not to the Board of Governors.

Despite a decade of negative press about the alleged ineffectiveness of inspections, and despite the many obstacles created by Iraq and dissension in the Security Council, the IAEA's experience in Iraq actually confirmed the effectiveness of onsite inspections and verification and monitoring, at least in coercive situations such as

140   *Christine Wing*

the postwar settlement in Iraq. On the other hand, the experience with the DPRK demonstrated the constraints on the IAEA's role when a state refuses to cooperate with treaty-required inspections.

The Security Council. Other chapters in this book explore structural changes that took place in the Security Council following the end of the Cold War. The discussion here focuses on the Council's role in relationship to proliferation issues in the context of the NPT.

The Security Council's formal NPT-related responsibilities remained the same after the Cold War, but the process of addressing those responsibilities ultimately led to a different role in the nonproliferation regime. As we have seen, the Council's responsibility for handling referrals from the IAEA was untested in 1990. Simply taking up these referrals, then, activated the Council's role.

The situation that may have been most defining for the Council, that is, the long engagement with Iraq, was actually the one case that fell outside the regular arrangements of the NPT-based system. The question of Iraqi WMD did not arrive at the Council via the IAEA; rather it arrived as the result of decisions to use military force to reverse Iraq's invasion of Kuwait. As often noted, if Iraq had not invaded Kuwait, its weapon programs might have gone undetected.

Nonetheless, the Council's experience with Iraq colored subsequent action that it might take on noncompliance. The long, tortuous process in the Council did not actually derive from the difficulty of conducting inspections, as much as from disagreement within the Council about how to end the war – whether to link the lifting of sanctions to the results of inspections, and judgments about the quality of those inspections. In retrospect we see that accurate findings from inspections of Iraq's nuclear program were available quite early, but for various reasons those findings were unacceptable at the time. Indeed, the difficulty of resolving the Iraq case was an example of how politicized even the collection of information can be. Furthermore, the Council had oversight responsibility for war termination and disarmament in Iraq, in a way it had never done before. This was difficult, demanding of the Council's resources, and complex. It is not, however, likely to be a condition in future Council action.

The U.S. Role

What stands out most markedly from this review of the post–Cold War years is how the United States increasingly treated the NPT system in an instrumental way. While in the early 1990s one might argue that the United States functioned with a concern for the system as a whole, its interest in strengthening the treaty-based part of the system declined over time. By 2005, at the NPT review, it was difficult to discern much U.S. concern for the regime as whole. Essentially, the United States came to use the NPT system when it could advance national interests narrowly defined, but

Evolution of Nuclear Nonproliferation Institutions   141

went outside the multilateral framework, or prioritized national military power, in most other cases.

An underlying question of this book is whether, and to what extent, the United States brought "strategic leadership" to the proliferation problem in the sixteen years since the Cold War ended. The simple answer is no, with a partial exception for the early 1990s. In the period right before and after the Soviet collapse, the Bush I administration did bring larger strategic considerations to its interaction with the Soviet Union, its decision to unilaterally withdraw tactical nuclear weapons from overseas deployments, its support for negotiation of the Chemical Weapons Treaty, and its approach to Iraq's invasion of Kuwait. None of these actions concerned nuclear proliferation questions directly, but they gave significant shape to the environment in which this proliferation was addressed.

But the answer is somewhat more complex, in that the United States did, by default, bring leadership to global decisions about proliferation. This leadership was not necessarily "strategic" or clearly articulated, but it did exist. Given its disproportionate military and economic power, whatever the United States did affected the international system. We have argued throughout that the changes taking place within the nonproliferation regime generally tended in the direction of U.S. interests. In this process, the United States did not get everything it sought – but neither were there lasting, structural changes to which the United States was strongly opposed.

Systemwide

The lack of strategic leadership on the part of the United States (or any other state) does not mean that there was no order in the way in which the NPT system evolved, however. If we look at the NPT system as a whole – the NPT itself, the IAEA, and the Security Council – we see two discernible shifts from 1990 to 2006.

First, within this system, the locus of initiative and responsibility was shifting from the NPT and its associated review processes to the IAEA and the Security Council. In part this reflected the consequences of unfolding events: as we have seen, during the 1990s, and for the first time, both the IAEA and the Security Council had to address specific cases of proliferation, matters that were not in the purview of the NPT review processes. Simultaneously, however, the discussion and review processes themselves were increasingly politicized and unproductive. By 2005, it had apparently become impossible, within the NPT context, to reach any major agreement on how to handle proliferation risks in the post–Cold War world.

Second, although the NPT was still the central element in the nonproliferation regime, there emerged a strong incentive to create other mechanisms as well. It has been, and will continue to be, supplemented by new multilateral initiatives. PSI and UNSCR 1540 are two such measures; doubtless more are on the way. The addition of other multilateral arrangements meant, by definition, that the relative weight of the NPT has declined within the larger nonproliferation regime.

Together, these two developments – a shift of power to the IAEA and the Security Council, coupled with the addition of new nonproliferation measures not anchored in the NPT – meant that the locus of power was shifting to a smaller set of states. The NPT is nearly universal. Although it has built-in inequalities – most obviously that five states are allowed to possess nuclear weapons, whereas 183 are not – its review processes nonetheless give equal weight to each state. The IAEA also has many member states, but its decisions are taken by a thirty-five member Board of Governors. The Security Council – where the most power lies – is the smallest: fifteen states, five of which are veto-carrying NWS.

Thus, at a system-wide level, the net effect of the efforts to address the proliferation problem was to shift multilateral debate and decisions from a broader to a narrower base. Whether these trends will continue is a different story. The way in which existing proliferation concerns (the DPRK and Iranian nuclear program) are resolved – or not resolved – will be important in shaping the evolving nonproliferation framework. More broadly, the NPT review process has relentlessly highlighted that NNWS are unlikely to accept forever the conditions of the global nuclear debate, and indeed, several key nuclear weapon states have begun to talk more seriously about the importance of nuclear disarmament. The next decade, as always, will be critical.

8

9/11, the War on Terror, and the Evolution of Multilateral Institutions

Eric Rosand and Sebastian von Einsiedel

According to conventional wisdom, U.S. counterterrorism policy during the administration of George W. Bush was marked by a high degree of unilateralism. And indeed, the Bush administration's policy revealed a strong ideological predisposition against international rules and standing multilateral institutions, which was exacerbated by the terrorist attacks of 9/11. The "black book" of cases, in which the United States effectively circumvented, abrogated, unsigned from, downgraded, opposed, or undermined standing multilateral treaties and arrangements, is long: from the Conventional Test Ban Treaty to the Anti-Ballistic Missiles Treaty, from the Kyoto Protocol to the Rome Statute on the International Criminal Court, from the United Nations (UN) to the North Atlantic Treaty Organization (NATO). For many observers, the U.S. decision to go to war against Iraq in March 2003 in the absence of an explicit Security Council mandate served as evidence that Washington had nothing but contempt for international rules and norms and multilateral institutions.

Reviewing the Bush administration's approach to multilateral counterterrorism and the evolution of the international institutional architecture in the counterterrorism field during its tenure, this chapter paints a more nuanced picture.[1]

The 2006 U.S. National Strategy for Countering Terrorism ambitiously but misleadingly states: "During the Cold War we created an array of domestic and international institutions and enduring partnerships to defeat the threat of communism. Today, we require similar transformational structures to carry forward the fight against terror."[2] Of course, 9/11 did not spark anything like a "Dean Acheson

---

[1] This is by no means the first attempt to counter caricatures of U.S. counterterrorism policy during the Bush years. We follow here and elaborate on a general line of argument that has been offered elsewhere by Prof. Edward Luck. See Edward C. Luck, "The US, Counter-terrorism, and the Prospects for a Multilateral Alternative," in J. Boulden and T. Weiss, eds., *Terrorism and the UN* (Bloomington: Indiana University Press, 2004), pp. 74–101.

[2] The White House, "US National Strategy for Combating Terrorism," Washington DC, The White House (September 2006).

moment." The proclamation of the "global war on terror" (GWOT) as new grand strategy was not followed by the creation of new and ambitious international organizations, alliances, and regimes that characterized the early years of the Cold War. Indeed, overall, one remarkable aspect of multilateral counterterrorism cooperation is its low degree of institutionalization. And terrorism scholar Daniel Benjamin laments the "large lacuna in the world of international organizations," namely, the fact that "there is no international agency devoted to exclusively dealing with issues of counterterrorism."[3]

It is often suggested that this is mainly because the leaders in charge during the time of 9/11 were less visionary, creative, and multilaterally minded than were Dean Acheson and his compatriots. Although this may be true, a number of other factors may have been more determining. First, terrorism arguably posed less of an existential threat than the Soviet Union ever did, thus requiring less ambitious responses. Second, the U.S.-led GWOT, unlike the fight against communism, was not seen as the pivotal struggle of our times in many other parts of the world. Third, some have convincingly argued that the nature of the threat of terrorism, emanating from a shadowy network of nonstate actors, was less amenable to formal multilateral responses than the state-centered Cold War threat.[4] At the same time, the multilateral institutional framework we inherited from the Cold War has proven more resilient and adaptable to new security challenges such as terrorism than it is often given credit for.

And indeed, progressive and significant adaptation rather than creation of new institutions was the key feature of institutional innovation in the international counterterrorism architecture during the administration of George W. Bush. Some seventy multilateral bodies now feature counterterrorism-related activities and programs. In this process, the United States was often a key actor and a shaping force (albeit not the only one). U.S. leadership in this process was generally episodic and took place in the absence of a discernible guiding strategy. Adaptive steps, especially at the UN, were generally initiated in the aftermath of significant terrorist attacks, first and foremost 9/11, but also the attacks in Madrid, Beslan, London, and elsewhere.

In this chapter we argue that whether the United States seriously engaged or led in these institutional adaptation efforts was driven by the following factors in order of declining importance: (1) by inherent limitations of the respective institutions and bodies themselves, relating to their political cohesiveness, their ability to make a practical contribution to U.S. counterterrorism efforts, and the robustness of their enforcement mechanism; (2) by the extent to which a certain policy area lent itself to be dealt with in multilateral fora: one was thus likely to see a high degree of multilateral engagement and institutional adaptation in the areas of countering terrorist financing, norm setting, and standard setting; a medium degree

---

[3] Daniel Benjamin, "Terrorism and International Organisations." Unpublished paper presented at International Peace Academy workshop on The UN and Terrorism (New York, January 2005).

[4] Edward C. Luck, "The US, Counter-terrorism, and the Prospects of a Multilateral Alternative."

of engagement and adaptation in the field of law enforcement cooperation; and a low degree of engagement and adaptation in intelligence sharing, military cooperation, and international justice; (3) by ideological predisposition of individual policymakers in key positions; and (4) last, by ideological predisposition of the Bush administration.

THE UN SECURITY COUNCIL

The attacks of 9/11 highlighted the increasingly transnational nature of the threat, which was no longer confined to a handful of state sponsors. The Bush administration immediately realized that it would need partners, both bilateral and multilateral, to help trace bank accounts, share information, secure borders, bring terrorists to justice, and build the capacity of all states to combat terrorism. Building on the wave of sympathy engendered by 9/11, the United States sought to make counterterrorism a priority for multilateral bodies and began to push for the adaptation of Cold War institutions.

Both its proximity to Ground Zero and its being the only universally representative global body empowered to address issues of international peace and security made the UN the logical place for the United States to turn its attention the day after the attacks. Although the UN's pre-9/11 effort was ambivalent, the new focus on al Qaeda allowed UN members to unite to condemn a specific terrorist group and thus enable the United States to move terrorism near the top of the UN's agenda.

The Security Council – with its unique ability under the UN Charter to impose binding obligations on all member states – offered the United States the quickest route for globalizing the fight against terrorism. On September 12, 2001, the United States prevailed on the Council not only to condemn global terror but also to recognize the U.S. right to self-defense under the UN Charter in responding forcefully to the unprecedented attacks.[5] Around two weeks later, the United States introduced another draft resolution designed to encourage member states to cut off the various sources of international terrorism and enlist the operational counterterrorism cooperation of all states. The next day, the Council adopted what still remains perhaps its most ground-breaking resolution ever – Resolution 1373 – which imposed significant obligations on all states to, *inter alia*, enhance legislation, strengthen border controls, coordinate executive machinery, and increase international cooperation in combating terrorism. The resolution included provisions from a variety of international treaties related to terrorism that did not have universal support, in particular the Terrorism Financing Convention (which had only a handful of states parties at the time). Circumventing the traditional treaty-making process was a bold and controversial step but with the UN community itself feeling victimized by the 9/11 attacks and wanting to show solidarity with the United States, the text was adopted with no debate or discussion.

[5] UN Security Council Resolution 1368 (September 12, 2001).

Although the United States was leading the charge to turn the Council into a norm-setting body in the field of counterterrorism, thus usurping the General Assembly's traditional leadership role in this area, it was at first indifferent to the idea of creating a UN mechanism to oversee state implementation of the norms. Although Resolution 1373 did establish a monitoring body, the Counter-Terrorism Committee (CTC), it was the result of a French proposal, which the United States acquiesced to in the interest of getting the text adopted as quickly as possible.

Early on, two key appointments ensured strong U.S. support for the new mechanism. The first was the selection of Sir Jeremy Greenstock, the UK Permanent Representative to the UN, as the CTC's first chair. Having its closest ally in the Council sitting in the chair allowed the United States to work quietly behind the scenes to chart the proper course for the CTC. The second was the appointment of Ambassador Thomas McNamara to serve in the office of Deputy Secretary of State Richard Armitage as the special coordinator for UN counterterrorism matters. Securing and maintaining the interest of someone with Armitage's stature were crucial to building support for the CTC in Washington.

From its inception, the CTC was hampered in carrying out its broad mandate by a lack of resources and manpower, relying on only a handful of consultants (many former UN diplomats with little relevant experience) hired by the UN Secretariat on short-term contracts. By 2003, the United States and the UK were working quietly on the design of a larger, more professional expert body to support the CTC's work. After months of contentious negotiations among Council members and between the Council and the Secretariat, the Council in March 2004 adopted Resolution 1535 establishing the Counter-Terrorism Executive Directorate (CTED), which was expected to provide new momentum to monitoring and promoting implementation of Resolution 1373, including through field visits.

Resolution 1535 marked the high point of U.S. engagement on CTC issues. After that, U.S. engagement on the CTC seriously waned. The United States became increasingly disappointed that the Council proved incapable of naming and shaming countries that openly defied the provisions of Resolution 1373. Instead, the CTC became largely a process-oriented, paper-producing body unable to deliver quality analysis on country needs and priorities or to serve as an effective clearinghouse for technical assistance requests. Other Council ambassadors too lost interest in the CTC's work, which was seen as increasingly technical and routine, leading to a leadership vacuum.

Increasing U.S. disenchantment with the CTC contrasted with its continued leadership in shaping the course of the Council's "Al-Qaida/Taliban Sanctions Committee" (or "1267 Committee"). Following the 9/11 attacks, the United States convinced the Council to extend what had been a set of sanctions (asset freeze, arms embargo, and travel ban) focused on Afghanistan to all parts of the globe. The United States energetically promoted their implementation against those individuals and entities associated with al Qaeda, the Taliban, or Osama bin Laden included on the committee's consolidated list, which now counts well over four hundred names. Although the travel ban and arms embargo have produced few tangible results, the financial sanctions led to the freezing of some $100 million, most of it in the months following 9/11.[6] In an atmosphere of goodwill, in which the committee trusted almost any name the United States put forward, the committee added more than two hundred names to the list in the weeks after 9/11.

U.S. support for the 1267 Committee was temporarily undermined by open disagreements with its Monitoring Group, the expert group that was to assist the committee in monitoring states' implementation of the sanctions. Washington, already irked by the group's independence, lost its patience when in the runup to the Iraq War the Monitoring Group gratuitously injected itself into the debate over the existence of a direct connection between al Qaeda and Saddam Hussein, telling the press that it has "never had information presented to [it] – even though [it has] asked questions – which would indicate that there is a direct link."[7] This episode led the United States to spearhead successful Council efforts in January 2004 to replace the Monitoring Group by a new mechanism that would be more responsive to U.S. sensitivities. The mandate of the new group, the Monitoring Team, has since been renewed three times, each time in the context of efforts to strengthen and improve the effectiveness of the sanctions themselves.

Although the United States played the leading role in adapting both the CTC and the Al-Qaida/Taliban Sanctions Committee, it adopted a radically different position on the question of a monitoring mechanism during the negotiations leading up to Resolution 1540. Against the background of the discovery of the A. Q. Khan nuclear proliferation network in April 2004, the resolution, similar in scope and ambition to SCR 1373, would require all UN member states to take legislative and regulatory steps to prevent terrorists and other nonstate actors from getting their hands on weapons of mass destruction (WMD) and their means of delivery.

Even though President George W. Bush had originally introduced the proposal for such a resolution in his speech to the General Assembly in September 2003,[8] the United States actively (but ultimately unsuccessfully) opposed efforts to establish a UN mechanism to oversee implementation of such a resolution, preferring to see individual member states, first and foremost itself, assuming a monitoring role. The

---

[6] According to information provided to the Al-Qaeda/Taliban Sanctions Committee by member states, as of late July 2006, $91.4 million, mainly in the form of bank accounts, had been frozen by thirty-five states under this sanctions regime. UN Security Council Al-Qaeda/Taliban Sanctions Committee, Fifth Report of the Al-Qaeda/Taliban Sanctions Monitoring Team, S/2006/750 (New York, September 20, 2006), p. 21.

[7] "Washington Insistent Links Exist between Al-Qaeda, Iraq," *Agence France-Presse*, June 27, 2003; see also Timothy O'Brien, "Threats and Responses; U.N. Group Finds No Hussein-Al-Qaeda Link," *New York Times*, June 27, 2003; "UN Probe Finds No Al-Qaida Links to Iraq," *Gazette* (Montreal, June 27, 2003).

[8] The White House, "President Bush Addresses United Nations General Assembly," Office of the Press Secretary, 23 September 2003, http://www.whitehouse.gov/news/releases/2003/09/20030923-4.html.

U.S. strategy was to instrumentalize the Council's norm-setting power while limiting its operational role.

U.S. opposition to the creation of a Council committee to oversee implementation came at the same time as it was leading the charge on efforts to strengthen the CTC via the creation of the CTED. The apparent contradiction in the U.S. position was largely the result of the ideological makeup of the different U.S. government officials involved in the two issues. U.S. policy toward the CTC was shaped by career State Department officials (such as Ambassador McNamara), who were generally less suspicious of multilateral institutions than their political-appointee counterparts. By contrast, U.S policy toward Resolution 1540, was directed by John Bolton, then serving as Under Secretary of State for Arms Control and International Security, whose disdain for multilateral institutions was well known even before he served as U.S. ambassador to the UN.

However, in the end, the United States found itself isolated in the Security Council. For a majority of Council members, a committee modeled on the CTC, which could help states find the assistance they would need to implement the resolution's onerous obligations, was a *sine qua non* for supporting the draft. Thus, when it came to adopt Resolution 1540, the United States was forced to compromise, and it did agree to the establishment of a committee and the appointment of eight independent experts for an initial two-year period ending in April 2006. During this period both the U.S. Vice President's office and the Under Secretary of State for Arms Control and International Security's office followed the committee's work closely, ensuring that the U.S. delegation missed few opportunities to remind fellow committee members of the temporary nature of the body and the limits of its mandate. At the same time, because of this high-level interest in Washington in the resolution itself, the United States continued to use it as an important tool to further U.S. nonproliferation policies.[9]

The U.S. tendency to see the UN in instrumental terms rather than attempt to generate broader, longer term benefits by pursuing a more principled multilateral approach impeded the United States from promoting a coherent role for the UN, and more specifically for the Security Council, on counterterrorism. Some eight years after 9/11, the Council features four subsidiary bodies and three expert groups dealing with some aspects of terrorism, often hastily established in response to specific crises. This proliferation of Council counterterrorism programs and initiatives has produced overlapping mandates, turf battles between and among committees and expert groups, duplication of work, multiple and sometimes confusing reporting requirements for states, and tension between the Council and the UN Secretariat that has only recently been eased. The Council itself has recognized many of these shortcomings since 2004 and has repeatedly called for improvements in numerous

---

[9] Despite the initially cautious approach that the United States took toward the committee, it quickly realized that it was helpful in building support among the UN membership for implementing the resolution and thus supported a two-year extension of its mandate until April 2008.

resolutions and presidential statements but has yet to take the steps needed to improve the situation.[10]

The bipartisan 2005 Gingrich/Mitchell Task Force on UN Reform recommended that the United States take the lead in the Council "to rationalize the work of the ... Security Council committees ... " and to explore the option of "combining their staffs, and combining the committees themselves."[11] Yet, the Bush administration ignored this recommendation. Instead, U.S. policies toward the various Council committees continued to be driven by different senior officials in different agencies who were generally more concerned about using the UN to further their narrow interests than improving the UN's overall performance on counterterrorism. With the most influential Council member showing little interest in getting that body to focus on creating a more coherent and effective Council counterterrorism program, it should come as little surprise that the Council's focus was allowed to drift away from terrorism and that the high level of attention previously devoted to terrorism was redirected to other priorities.

THE UN SECRETARIAT, THE GENERAL ASSEMBLY, AND THE PROSPECTS OF TRANSFORMATION

During much of the post–9/11 period, the UN Secretariat was at best a bystander in the institutional innovation and adaptation that took place in and under the Security Council. At worst, it was a nuisance and an impediment – at least in the eyes of some of the Council's permanent members. In the immediate aftermath of 9/11 UN Secretary-General Kofi Annan forcefully spoke up against terrorism on various occasions. He also made a good-willed but ill-fated attempt to prod UN member states to reach a breakthrough in the General Assembly on the definition of terrorism. But with the approaching Iraq war and growing controversy around the U.S. counterterrorism agenda, the Secretary-General eventually preferred to assume a much lower profile on this issue, fearing a backlash from nonaligned countries. The Secretariat's Department for Political Affairs, nominally the UN's "focal point" on counterterrorism, never dedicated any full-time staff to the issue, and senior Secretariat aides were openly critical of the U.S. counterterrorism agenda.

Against this background, it was maybe unsurprising that the United States and other permanent members insisted that any support structure of the CTC (first the expert group and later CTED) should be set up under the direct authority of the Security Council rather than in the Secretariat. The Secretariat in turn strongly opposed CTED's creation and pushed back against any attempt to dilute

---

[10] See, for example, UN Security Council Resolutions 1735 (December 22, 2006); 1617 (July 29, 2005); 1566 (October 8, 2005); and 1535 (March 26, 2004); see also UN Security Council Presidential Statements S/PRST/2006/56 (20 December 2006); S/PRST/2005/3 (January 18, 2005).

[11] *American Interests on UN Reform: Report of the Task Force on the United Nations* (Washington, DC: United States Institute for Peace, 2005), p. 76.

its influence. As part of its strategy, the Secretariat enlisted some of the elected members of the Council to fight its battles, which it characterized in terms of preventing the Permanent Five (P5) efforts to further expand the Council's role. The disagreements with the Secretariat left scars and mutual suspicions that were slow to heal.

With counterterrorism ghettoized in the Security Council and the Secretariat largely marginalized, it was up to the latter to regain the initiative. The opportunity to do so came when the UN High-level Panel on Threats, Challenges and Change, a blue ribbon commission established by Kofi Annan in the fall of 2003 to review the UN's role in peace and security, urged the Secretary-General in its December 2004 report to take a lead role and promote a comprehensive global counterterrorism strategy. On March 10, 2005, acting on the panel's recommendation, the Secretary-General announced such a strategy, centering around what he termed the "five Ds": (1) to dissuade disaffected groups from choosing terrorism as a tactic to achieve their goals, (2) to deny terrorists the means to carry out their attacks, (3) to deter states from supporting terrorists, (4) to develop state capacity to prevent terrorism, and (5) to defend human rights in the struggle against terrorism. These initial five Ds were further elaborated a year later in a 2006 report entitled "Uniting against Terrorism."[12]

The strategy tried to fulfill multiple and not easily reconcilable goals. On the one hand, the Secretary-General hoped that a UN-promulgated strategy could bridge international divisions by providing a comprehensive vision of a global counter-terrorism effort that all states could comfortably sign up to without joining the GWOT. On the other hand, the strategy was an effort to get skeptics among the nonaligned countries to acknowledge that terrorism is indeed a serious threat to international peace and security requiring a global concerted response and, indirectly, to prove to the United States that the Secretariat was now an actor worth engaging on counterterrorism.

To ensure that the strategy would be more than mere rhetoric, the Secretary-General, in the summer of 2005, created an interdepartmental Counter-Terrorism Implementation Task Force. The Task Force for the first time brought together twenty-three representatives from all departments and organizations of the larger – and confusingly fragmented – UN system that were in some way involved in the UN's overall counterterrorism effort, including the Council's expert bodies, key Secretariat departments, technical-assistance-providing agencies, as well as the World Bank and the IMF.[13] Following in the footsteps of the defunct Policy Working Group on terrorism, the Task Force was chaired by a key policy advisor of the

---

[12] UN Secretary-General, Uniting against Terrorism: recommendations for a global counter-terrorism strategy, A/60/825, 27 April 2006, http://www.un.org/unitingagainstterrorism/.
[13] The Task Force includes one non-UN entity, the International Criminal Police Organization. For more information on the Task Force see http://www.un.org/terrorism/cttaskforce.html.

Secretary-General until the May 2009 appointment of a full-time, lower level chair, and meets periodically at the level of experts who deal with terrorism in their day-to-day work.

It is too early to tell whether the creation of the Task Force will lead to a more coherent UN response to terrorism. Supported by only minimal staff and few resources, and without the authority to take and enforce decisions (the Secretary-General has no directive authority over many task force members, who have separate and independent governing bodies), the creation of the Task Force only constitutes institutional adaptation "lite."

Nevertheless, some Council members, in particular the United States, eyed the developments in the Secretariat with deep suspicion. The United States and others among the P5 were of course keen to keep the issue of counterterrorism exclusively confined to the Security Council where they could control the agenda. There was also a general attitude from the U.S. side, particularly pronounced during the ambassadorship of John Bolton, which rejected the notion that the UN Secretariat was imbued with any institutional autonomy and instinctively opposed any policy initiatives emerging from the Secretariat.

But the United States was by no means alone in that attitude, in particular vis-à-vis the Secretary-General's strategy. Although European countries and some Latin American and African countries seemed to wholeheartedly support the subsequent counterterrorism strategies generated by the Secretariat, many member countries from the Organization of Islamic Conference (OIC) and from the nonaligned movement were skeptical. Complaining that the issues of "root causes" and "foreign occupation" were not sufficiently emphasized, they declared that a strategy pronounced by the Secretary-General had no standing and insisted that the General Assembly would have to elaborate its own intergovernmentally agreed strategy.

Yet, with a history of divisive debates on the definition of terrorism that pitted the OIC and most other nonaligned countries against the global North – often in the context of the intractable Israeli–Palestinian conflict – many observers were surprised that the General Assembly responded to the call in the 2005 World Summit Outcome Document and adopted the first-ever global counterterrorism strategy,[14] albeit after a year of sometimes difficult negotiations.[15] It was a significant validation of Secretary-General Kofi Annan's initiative eighteen months earlier.

Although in many ways a typical UN consensus product carefully avoiding a stance on sensitive topics (such as the question of definition or the role of radical Islam) and resembling a laundry list more than a strategy, the General Assembly

---

[14] UN General Assembly, United Nations General Assembly Resolution 60/288, A/RES/60/288, New York, September 8, 2006.

[15] See, for example, Associated Press, "U.N. General Assembly adopts counter-terrorism strategy," *International Herald Tribune*, September 9, 2006. Available online at: www.iht.com/articles/ap/2006/09/08/news/UN_GEN_UN_Counter_Terrorism.php (accessed August 10, 2007).

document is nevertheless remarkable. Although it neither proposes any new initiative nor allocates new resources to fight the threat, the fact that the General Assembly was able to adopt a document outlining the breadth of the challenge and spelling out, in relative detail, the multifaceted approach needed to address the threat is unprecedented. The General Assembly Strategy calls for a holistic, inclusive, and nonmilitary-focused approach to counterterrorism. It gives priority attention to addressing the socioeconomic and political conditions conducive to the spread of terrorism such as poverty, political exclusion, corruption, and festering conflicts, which are exploited by extremists. Among the Strategy's more significant aspects are that it provides General Assembly imprimatur to and urges cooperation with the entire Security Council counterterrorism program, calls on a range of existing technical assistance efforts to be stepped up, and endorses the Secretary-General's call for a biosecurity initiative to counter the misuse of biotechnology. The fact that this document was adopted in the face of initially significant misgivings from many nonaligned countries was in no small part due to the tactical skills of the then-General Assembly president who convincingly argued that this was the General Assembly's once in a lifetime opportunity to regain some of the space and relevance on counterterrorism issues it had lost to the Security Council in the course of the previous decade.

Disappointingly, the United States showed little interest in building on this achievement by trying to use the Strategy as a vehicle for strengthening the overall UN counterterrorism program. Even though the UN document reinforced the Bush administration's own September 2006 updated counterterrorism strategy, which emphasized nonmilitary tools, international cooperation, and multilateral institutions,[16] the U.S. approach was dominated by concerns about a diminution of the Council's role.

This begs the question as to whether there is room for a qualitative transformation of the UN's counterterrorism program beyond the adoption of the Strategy. The two areas where the UN has a comparative advantage in the global counterterrorism campaign are in the fields of norm-setting and capacity-building.

The UN has made considerable contributions in the norm-setting arena. Over the past three and a half decades, the General Assembly and UN agencies such as the International Civil Aviation Organization (ICAO) and the International Maritime Organization (IMO) have adopted sixteen international conventions and protocols related to terrorism, covering nearly every conceivable discrete act of terrorism, and the Security Council has established its own global counterterrorism legal framework. The one gap in this area concerns the lack of an agreed definition of terrorism (or, more precisely, agreement on the exceptions to that definition), which continues to confound the UN membership. Yet, although the UN is the central

---

[16] The White House, U.S. National Strategy for Combating Terrorism, September 2006, http://www.whitehouse.gov/nsc/nsct/2006/.

forum for debates on this issue, it is largely powerless to resolve it. Instead, it will likely need to await a peaceful resolution of the Israeli–Palestinian conflict, which is the underlying issue preventing agreement.

In the capacity-building field, however, the UN could be doing much more. Strengthening the counterterrorism capabilities of all states has been near the top of the international counterterrorism agenda of countries both in the global North and South. It is one of the few counterterrorism issues at the UN that has generally not been affected by the divisions within the UN membership on the conflicts in the Middle East. Instead, there is a broad consensus among all UN member states on the important role the UN should be playing in this area.

The Council's CTC was supposed to assume a leading role in identifying capacity needs of all member states, helping states prioritize needs, and reaching out to donor states and organizations to provide the necessary assistance to fill the gaps. Some eight years since its establishment in October 2001, the CTC has yet to adequately fulfill its mandate, lacking the resources, expertise, and broad political support from both donor and recipient states to do so. Given the Council's diminishing legitimacy in this area, we are unlikely to see the CTC transform itself into an effective body, although the Fall 2007 appointment of the former Australian counterterrorism ambassador, Mike Smith, to head the CTC's Counter-Terrorism Executive Directorate, has led to considerable improvements. In 2003, dissatisfied with the lack of concrete results from the CTC, the United States pushed the G8 to create the Counter-Terrorism Action Group (CTAG) to coordinate the delivery of global counterterrorism assistance of the major donors. Yet the CTAG, like the G8 itself, is an ad hoc political mechanism with no permanent secretariat. Like the CTC, it lacks the legitimacy in the global South to enable it to assume a role in coordinating global, multilateral, nonmilitary counterterrorism efforts. It has yet to deliver the results G8 leaders hoped for.

A more effective UN mechanism would help shoulder the capacity-building and training burdens, spread among many countries and organizations that currently are undertaken and subsidized by the United States and a handful of other states. It could focus on identifying and correcting vulnerabilities in countries that are not priority countries for the United States, its G8 partners, or the European Union (EU), which without prompt attention might risk becoming safe havens or breeding grounds for terrorists. In addition, it could work with those priority countries with which the United States may lack access or leverage.

A 2007 survey in *Foreign Policy* of 100 top foreign policy and terrorism experts in the United States revealed that more give higher priority to strengthening the UN than strengthening the Department of Homeland Security, killing terrorist leaders, or increasing the military response to terrorism.[17] Yet, doing so will likely require the

---

[17] "The Terrorism Index," *Foreign Policy*, July/Aug 2006, http://www.foreignpolicy.com/issue_julyaug_2006/TI-index/index.html.

redistribution of the counterterrorism work within the UN system: the transformation from the improvisational and temporary Security Council-led effort into a more broadly representative one where the United States would have less control.

Terrorist Financing

In the absence of a coherent and consistent counterterrorism policy toward the UN, the Bush administration focused its attention on using the different component parts of the UN, including within the Security Council, to help further U.S. interests in discrete terrorism-related fields, particularly counterterrorist financing. The U.S. interest in pursuing this agenda extended beyond the UN to other multilateral bodies. In fact, a number of international organizations, including those that had been built on a base of anti-money-laundering work that began as part of the fight against drug trafficking in the 1980s, evolved after 9/11 to include counterterrorism financing within their mandates. The United States was the key driver for serious adaptation of a range of formal and informal multilateral bodies, including the Financial Action Task Force (FATF) and the IFIs. Other countries and multilateral bodies willfully went along with the U.S.-led efforts, and somewhat surprisingly, support for these multilateral initiatives did not wane, despite the controversy of the GWOT.

The Bush administration recognized early on that in order to address terrorist financing comprehensively, global standards needed to be set and effective technical assistance programs – complemented by political pressure – put in place to ensure that all countries could meet these standards.

The United States led a push to refocus the FATF's mission shortly after 9/11, capitalizing on its expertise on money laundering to combat terrorist financing.[18] Shortly thereafter, all of the then twenty-nine member jurisdictions agreed to adopt eight (now nine) special recommendations on terrorist financing. Since then, the United States has spent considerable efforts to put these new standards into place all over the world. One of FATF's key innovations – again the result of U.S. leadership – was the use of "peer-review" and blacklisting mechanisms, which "combined international legitimacy with effective sanctions mechanisms to ratchet up international banking [and other terrorist financing-related] standards."[19]

Recognizing the difficulties that FATF with its limited membership would have in gaining support from non-FATF members for implementing the FATF standards, many of which are broad in nature and require significant resources to implement, the United States pushed for the establishment of "FATF-style regional bodies" (FSRBs) in all regions, including Africa and the Middle East. These regional bodies succeeded in placing the FATF standards in the appropriate regional and cultural

---

[18] FATF was created by the then-G7 in 1989 to focus on money laundering issues.
[19] James Cockayne, "Transnational Organized Crime: Multilateral Responses to a Rising Threat," Coping with Crisis Working Paper, International Peace Academy, New York, April 2007.

context and have helped enhance the more than 150 states' or territories' support for these standards.[20]

As for the IFIs, the President of the World Bank and the Managing Director of the IMF immediately following 9/11 issued strong statements supporting the work of the international coalition against terrorism. U.S. leadership was central to overcoming the longstanding opposition of the governing boards of both IFIs to include counterterrorist financing within their respective mandates. Moving beyond hortatory statements, the IFIs began working together in 2002 to assess country compliance with the FATF anti-money-laundering and counterterrorist financing (AML/CFT) standards and provide technical assistance to members to improve their legal and regulatory frameworks in this area.[21]

The United States also worked with its G8 partners and FATF to coordinate bilateral and international technical assistance efforts to priority countries in the terrorist financing campaign. Further, the United States played a leading role in involving the Egmont Group, whose membership is composed of national financial intelligence units (FIUs), in global efforts to increase the international sharing of terrorist financing information and promote financial transparency more broadly. In addition to getting the Egmont Group to expand its mandate beyond organized crime and money laundering to include terrorist financing, it has made the establishment of national FIUs in all countries a priority. Partly as a result of these efforts, there are now more than 100 FIUs worldwide, up from a few dozen prior to 9/11.[22]

A number of factors explain the intense and sustained Bush administration engagement with a range of multilateral bodies on terrorist financing issues. First, there were a number of existing bodies whose work in related areas, including antimoney laundering, allowed for easy adaptation. Second, there was the need to develop global standards to combat terrorist financing and related issues and build national capacities to meet these standards, both areas where multilateral institutions often have a comparative advantage. Perhaps equally significant, however, was the heightened attention terrorist financing-related issues received (and continue to receive) from a number of U.S. agencies and the creation of various interagency counterterrorist financing mechanisms that regularly consider U.S. policies

[20] For a detailed description of FATF's current mandate, see www.fatf-gafi.org/dataoecd/14/60/36309648.pdf.

[21] They subsequently began collaborating with FATF and in March 2004 the governing boards agreed to make the AML/CFT assessments a regular part of the Financial Sector Assessment Program and Offshore Financial Center assessments, which offer comprehensive review of financial sector strengths and vulnerabilities in key economic and financial areas. See Juan Carlos Zarate, Assistant Secretary, Terrorist Financing and Financial Crimes, U.S. Department of the Treasury, "Testimony before the House Financial Services Subcommittees on Domestic and International Monetary Policy, Trade and Technology and Oversight and Investigations," September 30, 2004, http://www.treas.gov/press/releases/js1971.htm.

[22] Ibid.; see also, "The Egmont Group: Financial Intelligence Units (FIUs)," http://www.egmontgroup.org/about_egmont.pdf.

toward the various international bodies in this field.[23] Although the plethora of such mechanisms led to interagency turf battles and coordination challenges, their mere existence has helped ensure continued U.S. engagement with multilateral institutions in this field.[24]

In 2002, a Council on Foreign Relations Independent Task Force on Terrorist Financing recommended the creation of a new international organization specializing in terrorist financing issues, arguing that no existing institution was in the position to effectively address this issue. Reflecting the success the United States had in adapting the existing multilateral mechanisms, including those within the UN, to combat terrorism financing, the Task Force concluded in a follow-up report two years later that the need for a new body had diminished[25] (although that proposal had never been seriously considered by the policy community in any case). Yet, the CFR Task Force added, "The need for proper coordination and clearer mandates [of the different organizations involved in counterterrorist financing activity] has increased for the same reason. Duplicative efforts should be minimized and resources reallocated to the most logical lead organization."[26] This, however, has yet to occur.[27] Such an organization has not been identified, and each separate body continues to pursue its own mandate, with little regard for trying to reduce duplication and/or maximize synergies with other bodies with sometimes overlapping mandates. Given the difficulties the United States had in getting its own house in order during the Bush years, despite the numerous coordinating mechanisms, it was unlikely to make rationalizing the international effort a priority in the near term.

INTELLIGENCE AND LAW ENFORCEMENT COOPERATION

Most intelligence cooperation takes place and will likely continue to take place bilaterally, with countries still reluctant to share intelligence on a multilateral

[23] For example, the president established a Policy Coordination Committee under the auspices of the NSC to ensure proper coordination of U.S. counterterrorism financing activities and information sharing among all relevant U.S. agencies, including Defense, State, Homeland Security, Treasury, and other law enforcement and intelligence agencies. In addition, an interagency process was established to coordinate designating terrorists (both domestically and at the UN) and blocking their assets. Finally, the NSC established the State Department-led interagency Terrorist Financing Working Group (TFWG) to coordinate the delivery of training and technical assistance to the countries most vulnerable to terrorist financing. See United States Government Accountability Office, "Terrorist Financing: Better Strategic Planning Needed to Coordinate U.S. Efforts to Deliver Counter-Terrorism Finance Training and Technical Assistance Abroad," Report GAO-06–19, October 2005, http://www.gao.gov/new.items/do619.pdf.

[24] Ibid.

[25] Maurice R. Greenberg et al., "Update on the Global Campaign against Terrorist Financing," Second Report of the Independent Task Force on Terrorist Financing, Council on Foreign Relations, New York, June 15, 2004, http://www.cfr.org/content/publications/attachments/Revised_Terrorist_Financing.pdf.

[26] Ibid.

[27] See, for example, Anne C. Richard, "Fighting Terrorist Financing: Transatlantic Cooperation and International Institutions," Center for Transatlantic Relations (2005), p. 53.

9/11, the War on Terror, and the Evolution of Multilateral Institutions   157

basis, let alone with a multilateral institution. Especially in the United States, most intelligence officials still prefer to work bilaterally with contacts they trust in foreign governments. In the United States, for instance, policymakers and analysts seem to have concluded that multilateral cooperation in the intelligence field with its allies should not be pursued as NATO is "unwilling" and the EU "incapable" of being a useful partner in this endeavor.[28]

Even within the highly integrated EU, sensitive intelligence tends to be shared on a bilateral basis or among countries with shared interests rather than in a centralized framework because of fears of leaks.[29] With the EU now counting twenty-seven member states this is unlikely to change any time soon. And the appointment in 2004 of a EU counterterrorism "tsar" in the wake of the Madrid train bombings to, inter alia, coordinate intelligence sharing, has done little to overcome member states' tendency to keep sensitive intelligence close to their chest.[30] Proposals to turn NATO's North Atlantic Council into an intelligence sharing body have gone nowhere for the same reasons.

Many states have found it easier to cooperate multilaterally in the field of law enforcement. There, with the Bush administration being the key driver, the trend was one of deepening multilateralism and gradual institutionalization, in many cases starting with the G8, and slow institutionalization in Interpol and elsewhere but in particular with respect to the EU.

The G8's Lyon-Roma Anti-Crime and Terrorism Group (LRACTG), established before 9/11, has been at the center of post–9/11 U.S. multilateral law enforcement cooperation efforts, with Washington continuing to see it as a valuable forum for deepening counterterrorism cooperation with its allies.[31] With multiple U.S. agencies and dozens of officials engaged in a well-organized process geared toward concrete outputs, the LRACTG likely received more attention from the Bush White House than any other mechanism in the field of multilateral counterterrorism cooperation.

---

[28] Nora Bensahel, "The Counterterror Coalitions: Cooperation with Europe, NATO, and the European Union," RAND Research Paper (Santa Monica: RAND, 2003), p. 46.

[29] See, for instance, Peter Grier and Mark Rice Oxley, "Five Years after 9/11: A Shifted View of the World," *The Christian Science Monitor*, September 11, 2006; See also Philip Shishkin, "Europol's Antiterror Role Muted by Limited Powers," *The Wall Street Journal*, April 7, 2004.

[30] Frustrated by a lack of resources and mandate from EU members, the first and only EU counterterrorism coordinator, Gijs de Vries, resigned in the spring of 2007; see Sarah Laitner, "Counter-terrorism Post Still Vacant," *Financial Times*, May 8, 2007. He was replaced in September 2007 by Gilles de Kerchove.

[31] Counterterrorism practitioners from a range of U.S. government agencies, including Homeland Security, Justice, Treasury, State, and the CIA, meet several times a year with their G8 counterparts in a series of different working groups. Since 9/11, these groups have developed counterterrorism standards and best practices on a wide variety of law enforcement and border security topics. For example, at the June 2004 G8 summit, G8 leaders committed to strengthen international counterterrorism cooperation by launching the Secure and Facilitated International Travel Initiative (SAFTI). Designed by the United States, this initiative, which sought to maximize effective information exchange among G8 states as a key element of strengthening international border security, included a twenty-eight point action plan committing members to implement security-enhancing projects in a variety of transportation security fields.

In addition to the G8 process, Washington devoted considerable resources to strengthening U.S.–EU law enforcement cooperation during the Bush years. Primarily as a result of a new degree of seriousness and growing integration at the EU level, itself actively promoted by the United States, there was an increasingly institutionalized cooperation between the United States and EU in matters of police, judicial, and border control issues. Contacts between U.S. and EU officials – from the cabinet to the working level – increased substantially during the Bush administration and helped strengthen the broader U.S.–EU relationship.[32]

Because both the United States and Europe recognize that law enforcement cooperation and information sharing are essential to fighting global terrorism, day-to-day cooperation between the United States and EU (and its members) will continue. However, with generally limited European-level coordination, with most European counterterrorism mandates vested in the individual states and with a number of powerful EU members remaining opposed to giving the EU's supranational bodies more competency in this area, the limits of EU–U.S. institutional cooperation seem to be reached.[33] In addition, some Bush administration officials reportedly expressed doubt as to the utility of cooperating with EU institutions given the often strong existing bilateral relations between U.S. law enforcement agencies and national police and intelligence services in individual EU member states.[34] Further, as has been pointed out, counterterrorism cooperation between U.S. and European law enforcement agencies suffered during the Bush years from corrosion at the political level, brought about by the Iraq war and the "war on terror" more broadly.[35]

The increasing multilateralism in U.S. law enforcement cooperation extended beyond Europe and its non-European G8 partners. Examples include the "3+1 Group on Triborder Area Security," a U.S. initiative that included Paraguay, Argentina, and Brazil. It was created in 2002 to enhance the capacities of the "Three"

---

[32] Kristin Archik, "U.S.–EU Cooperation against Terrorism," Congressional Research Service, October 16, 2006, p. 2, http://www.fas.org/sgp/crs/terror/RS22030.pdf. Apart from the U.S.–EU counterterrorism working group, which includes many of the same U.S. officials who are involved in the LRACTG, the Secretary of State, Attorney General, and Secretary of Homeland Security meet at the ministerial level with their respective EU counterparts at least once a year to discuss police and judicial cooperation against terrorism. Among the fruits of this cooperation are a 2004 U.S.–EU Summit Declaration on Combating Terrorism, U.S.–EU Extradition/Mutual Legal Assistance Agreements, joint biometric standards to enhance the security of travel documents and closely consulted to ensure the future interoperability of border control systems, an agreement that allows airlines to provide EU-origin passenger data for flights to the United States, cargo screening, and inspection procedures under the Container Security Initiative. In addition, two U.S.–Europol agreements were concluded in 2001 and 2002 to allow U.S. law enforcement authorities and Europol to share both strategic and personal information. Further, Europol has posted two liaison officers in Washington, and the FBI has stationed a U.S. liaison officer in The Hague to work with the EU's Counter-Terrorism Task Force, housed in Europol. Id.

[33] Sarah Laitner, "EU Plan to Fight Terror in Tatters," *Financial Times*, September 23, 2006.

[34] Ibid., p. 5.

[35] Daniel Benjamin and Steven Simon, *The Next Attack: The Failure of the War on Terror and a Strategy for Getting It Right* (New York: Times Books, 2005).

to fight cross-border crime and combat money-laundering and potential terrorist financing activities in that region. It has served as a forum to allow technical experts from the participating countries to share information and identify ways to strengthen law enforcement and other forms of counterterrorism cooperation.[36] In addition, the United States established a network of regional law enforcement academies to improve international cooperation in fighting transnational crime and terrorism, with U.S. law enforcement officials providing much of the training.[37]

Although, overall, during the Bush years the United States showed a preference for small, informal bodies composed of like-minded states over formal international institutions, the trend toward increased U.S. multilateral cooperation in law enforcement is likely to continue. The FBI's global presence and activities have increased since 9/11. FBI Director Mueller, for instance, envisioned an "official international antiterrorism alliance in the law enforcement arena with a structure similar to NATO, united partners joined against common enemies" building on a growing network of FBI liaison offices abroad.[38] Although such a structure is unlikely to materialize any time soon, the significant challenge would be to design a light structure (read: small and efficient secretariat) that allows for the sharing of often-sensitive law enforcement information in a secure and timely manner among a broad enough group of states and yet allows for efficient decision making.

NATO AND MILITARY COOPERATION

During the Cold War, multilateral military cooperation and the establishment of regional defense alliances – with NATO as the crown jewel – were the linchpins in the U.S. strategy to contain the Soviet Union. In the years following the Soviet Union's disintegration, the United States invested great energy to have NATO expand eastward and to adapt its mission to include military crisis management in the Balkans and elsewhere outside of the traditional NATO orbit.

Against this background, one may well have expected that NATO would figure prominently in the "war on terror." And indeed, just a day after 9/11, NATO, on the initiative of its Secretary General, George Robertson, for the first time invoked

---

[36] For more on the Triborder Area, see Arlene Tickner, "Latin America and the Caribbean: Domestic and Transnational Insecurity," Coping with Crisis Working Paper No. 6, International Peace Academy, New York, 2007.

[37] Speaking before the United Nations General Assembly at its fiftieth anniversary on October 22, 1995, then-President Clinton called for the establishment of a network of International Law Enforcement Academies (ILEAs) throughout the world to combat international drug trafficking, criminality, and terrorism through strengthened international cooperation. Twelve years later, the U.S. and participating nations have moved ahead with the establishment of ILEAs to serve three regions: Europe, Asia, Africa; and a graduate facility in Roswell, NM. http://www.state.gov/p/inl/crime/ilea/.

[38] Robert Mueller, "Tomorrow's FBI: A Vision for Meeting Future Challenges," June 22, 2004, http://www.cfr.org/publication/7140/tomorrows_fbi.html?breadcrumb=%2Fpublication%2Fpublication_list%3Fgroupby%3D1%26type%3Dtranscript%26page%3D4.

the North Atlantic Treaty's Article V, which proclaimed that an attack on one of the Alliance's members should be considered an attack against all.[39] However, at a NATO meeting in Brussels two weeks after the attack, Deputy Secretary of Defense Paul Wolfowitz poured cold water on the hope of many NATO members that invocation of Article V would lead the United States to carry out any military response within a NATO framework.[40] Although the United States accepted military contributions from some European allies on a bilateral basis, the United States was in fact not inclined to carry out the subsequent Operation Enduring Freedom in Afghanistan in an Alliance framework.

This reflected a key lesson the Bush administration seems to have drawn from the Kosovo war, where U.S. policymakers and commanders resented the constraints of "warmaking by committee" imposed by the Alliance structure. And, according to a RAND report, "NATO was unable to provide a command structure – or even substantial capabilities – that would override U.S. concerns about using the NATO machinery."[41] Of course, the United States' right to defend itself after the attacks of 9/11 was so widely acknowledged (including by the UN Security Council) that unlike in the case of the Kosovo War the United States did not need NATO to legitimize its military action.

Washington's rejection of NATO caused great concern in many European capitals about the undermining effect this may have on the Alliance. Criticism of the U.S. go-it-alone attitude could not disguise continuing if decreasing differences over whether counterterrorism should become one of NATO's core missions. Indeed, led by France, many Europeans even in the aftermath of 9/11 continued to oppose turning NATO into a global counterterror force as pushed for by the United States.[42] This attitude was only reinforced by transatlantic disagreements over the Iraq War.

Yet this did not stop the United States from continuing to push for adaptation of NATO to increase its footprint in counterterrorism activities and take some steps to improve its long-term counterterror capabilities. Emphasizing the global terrorist threat, at the 2002 NATO Summit in Prague the United States successfully pressed for agreement on the so-called Prague Capability Commitments (PCC), which build on earlier NATO efforts to improve members' operational capabilities to address evolving defense needs, including in counterterrorism.[43] The Prague Summit also decided on the creation of a by now fully operational NATO Response Force, which should be able to take on a broad range of missions worldwide on short notice.

---

[39] ANZUS and the OAS invoked similar articles in the Eastern and Western Hemisphere, respectively.

[40] See Louise Richardson, *What Terrorists Want: Understanding the Enemy, Containing the Threat* (New York: Random House, 2006).

[41] Nora Bensahel, "The Counterterror Coalitions," p. 16.

[42] Nora Bensahel, "The Counterterror Coalitions," pp. 23–25.

[43] Robert Axelrod and Silvia Borzutzky, "NATO and the War on Terror: The Organizational Challenges of the Post–9/11 World," *The Review of International Organizations* 1, No. 3 (September 2006), pp. 293–307; see also Carl Ek, "NATO's Prague Capabilities Commitment," CRS Report, January 24, 2007, at http://www.fas.org/sgp/crs/row/RS21659.pdf.

In addition, the United States successfully prodded a reluctant NATO to take on an increasing role in the ground war in Afghanistan, where the Alliance is now in command of the International Security Assistance Force (ISAF). And in 2004, NATO was strong-armed by Washington into establishing a training program for Iraqi security forces.[44] However, contrary to Washington, most Europeans would characterize the Alliance's engagement in Afghanistan and Iraq as an effort in postconflict reconstruction rather than in counterterrorism. Also, the main thrust of U.S. adaptation initiatives during the Bush administration was to push a military burden-sharing agenda, which goes back to the 1990s and is only indirectly related to terrorism.

At the Riga Summit in November 2006, NATO adopted a new strategic concept last updated in 1999. It states at the outset that terrorism and WMD "are likely to be the principal threats to the Alliance over the next 15–20 years."[45] In that sense, the Alliance has moved a long way since the 1999 strategic concept, in which the only reference to terrorism was a cautious acknowledgment that "Alliance security interests can be affected by other risks of a wider nature, including acts of terrorism . . ."[46]

This breakthrough in rhetoric barely constitutes transformation of NATO into an organization capable of fighting terrorism. In the field of Special Military Operations, arguably the area most relevant to military counterterrorism, Alliance capabilities and interoperability remained rudimentary, with most member states preferring to keep those forces as purely national assets.[47] Also in the area of consequence management of terrorist WMD attacks, NATO has failed to make much progress – mainly because of France's insistence that such capabilities be established within an EU framework.[48] And, as pointed out by a recent CSIS report, homeland defenses also "remain[ed] strangely absent from the Alliance's transformational agenda."[49] True adaptation to the terrorism challenge thus remains elusive at NATO.

INTERNATIONAL CRIMINAL TRIBUNALS

With large-scale international terrorist attacks on the rise over the past few years, questions as to where and how to try terrorist suspects have become more prevalent. Jealously guarding their judicial sovereignty, most states continue to prefer to use

---

[44] Nicholas Burns, "The War on Terror Is NATO's New Focus," *International Herald Tribune*, October 6, 2004.

[45] NATO, "Comprehensive Political Guidance," Endorsed by NATO Heads of State and Government on November 29, 2006, at http://www.nato.int/docu/basictxt/b061129e.htm.

[46] NATO, The Alliance's Strategic Concept, Approved by the Heads of State and Government participating in the meeting of the North Atlantic Council in Washington, DC, on April 23 and 24, 1999, at http://www.nato.int/docu/pr/1999/p99-065e.htm.

[47] Julianne Smith et al., "Transforming NATO (again . . .): A Primer for the NATO Summit in Riga 2006," CSIS Study, Washington, DC, November 2006, pp. 36–39.

[48] Bensahel, "The Counterterror Coalitions."

[49] Julianne Smith et al., "Transforming NATO (again . . .)," p. 62.

their own domestic courts in cases where they have jurisdiction, that is, if the terrorist offense was carried out in their territory or against their nationals.[50] Throughout the 1990s, many high-profile terrorist cases were successfully tried in national courts. These included trials related to the first World Trade Center bombing case in 1996–1998, the "La Belle" bombing case in Germany in 1997, the African Embassy bombings, tried in the United States in 2001, and the Lockerbie case tried in the Netherlands in 2001.[51] None of these cases gave rise to significant calls for creating new or using existing international tribunals to try the perpetrators.[52]

However, in the aftermath of the 9/11 attacks, discussion on the use of international tribunals to try terrorist suspects gained significant prominence. Increasingly, representatives of governments and international organizations as well as legal scholars advocated the creation of such tribunals, arguing that they would "symbolize global justice for global crimes" and carry greater legitimacy than national verdicts.[53] For many, this line of argument gained further credence against the background of the internationally much criticized military order by the U.S. president in November 2001 authorizing secret trials of terrorist suspects before U.S. military commissions, raising concerns regarding human rights, due process, and judicial impartiality.[54] Some also argued that international tribunals would offer a way out of the dilemma for countries that faced legal barriers with respect to extraditing terrorist suspects to the United States because of its continued application of the death penalty.

In "op-eds" and in legal circles, several options were discussed on what type of international tribunal would be most appropriate to try terrorists. A number of commentators suggested the use of the International Criminal Court (ICC) – once established – for this purpose.[55] Indeed, this question had come up during the

---

[50] Suspects of acts of terrorism that amount to crimes against humanity may also be tried in courts of countries whose domestic laws confer universal jurisdiction with respect to such crimes.

[51] In the Lockerbie case of those alleged to have committed the bombing of Pan American Flight 103 over Lockerbie, Scotland, on December 21, 1988, the trial was held by a Scottish court sitting in the Netherlands. See Richard J. Goldstone and Janine Simpson, "Evaluating the Role of the International Criminal Court as a Legal Response to Terrorism," in *Harvard Human Rights Journal* 16 (Spring 2003).

[52] Goldstone and Simpson, "Evaluating the Role of the International Criminal Court."

[53] Richard Goldstone cited in Ed Vulliamy, "US Dilemmas over Trials of Bin Laden," *The Guardian*, November 4, 2001. Carla del Ponte, Chief Prosecutor of the ICTY cited in Nicole Winfield, "UN Urges International Trial for Bin Laden," *The Record*, December 20, 2001. Anne-Marie Slaughter, "Luncheon Address: Rogue Regimes and the Individualization of International Law," *New England Law Review*, No. 36, p. 820. See also Anne-Marie Slaughter, "Use Courts, Not Combat, to Get the Bad Guys: Pre-emptive Justice," *International Herald Tribune* November 20, 2003.

[54] The White House, "Detention, Treatment and Trial of Certain Non-Citizens in the War against Terrorism," Military Order of 13 November 2001, at § 1(e), 66 Fed. Reg. 57,833, 57,834 (2001). See also Slaughter, "Use Courts, Not Combat."

[55] Goldstone and Simpson argue that the "ICC could be a very effective forum for the prosecution of acts of terrorism" and it has the potential to "have a significant deterrent effect on future acts of terrorism." See Goldstone and Simpson, "Evaluating the Role of the International Criminal Court."

negotiation of the Rome Statute establishing the Court. But negotiators were unable to define the crime of terrorism, thus preventing it from falling under the Court's jurisdiction.[56] Yet, the Rome Statute, which eventually entered into force in July 2002, gave the Court jurisdiction, *inter alia*, over crimes against humanity,[57] and a number of prominent observers argued that large-scale attacks constituted exactly that.[58] Nevertheless, at least in the foreseeable future, it is unlikely that the ICC will take on any terrorist cases. The Court can only become active when countries that have primary jurisdiction are "unwilling or unable" to prosecute. It is difficult to imagine that any government will defer its own jurisdiction in favor of the ICC for any terrorist act amounting to a crime against humanity. The Bush administration's intense efforts to undermine the court in its early years of existence have recently given way to a more pragmatic approach illustrated by the Security Council's referral of Darfur war crime cases to the ICC in March 2005.[59] However, not surprisingly, the Bush administration showed no interest in helping to broaden the Court's scope of activity by agreeing to Council referrals of terrorism cases.

A more likely scenario than the ICC has always been the possibility of the Security Council establishing ad hoc terrorism tribunals under its Chapter VII authority, building on the precedents of the International Criminal Tribunals for the Former Yugoslavia (1993) and Rwanda (1994).[60] However, given that the United States does not even trust its own federal courts to try suspected al Qaeda members currently in U.S. custody, it is not surprising that the Bush administration has never considered having the Security Council establish a court to try them. Moreover, at the time of 9/11, the Security Council had already developed a certain "tribunal fatigue" with the Rwanda and Yugoslavia tribunals being increasingly criticized as ineffective and overly costly. Instead, the trend pointed toward the creation of hybrid arrangements, in which special domestic courts were established with the support of the UN, as

[56] Goldstone and Simpson recount that the 1994 Draft Statute for the ICC proposed the inclusion of so-called treaty crimes that are offenses criminalized under various treaty regimes, including terrorism, drug trafficking, apartheid, and grave breaches of the four 1949 Geneva conventions. The Rome Statute's Preparatory Committee, however, felt strongly that the Court's statute should define the crimes within its jurisdiction, rather than simply list them as the International Law Commission's Draft had done. However, no consensus could be reached on the definition of these treaty crimes. See Goldstone and Simpson, "Evaluating the Role of the International Criminal Court."

[57] Article 7 of the Rome Statute states, "Crime against humanity means murder when committed as part of a widespread or systematic attack directed against any civilian population." See Rome Statute of the International Criminal Court, UN Doc. A/CONF.183/9 (1998).

[58] For instance, the then United Nations High Commissioner for Human Rights, Mary Robinson, expressed the opinion that the attacks of September 11 constituted a crime against humanity while speaking at the U.S. Institute of Peace in Washington on October 17, 2001.

[59] Security Council Resolution 1593, March 31, 2005.

[60] See, for instance, UN Secretary-General Kofi Annan, press encounter after meeting with the Norwegian Prime Minister Kjell Bondevik, December 11, 2001, at www.un.org/apps/sg/offthecuff.asp?nid=282. Paul Williams and Michael Scharf, "Prosecute Terrorists on a World Stage," *Los Angeles Times*, November 18, 2001. The Security Council resolutions establishing the courts were 808; 827, for the ICTY; and 955, for Rwanda.

was the case with the tribunals set up to try war crimes committed in Cambodia during the Pol Pot regime and in Sierra Leone during its civil war in the late 1990s.

A hybrid court was also what the Security Council had in mind when it came to establish a tribunal to try potential suspects in the terrorist attack that killed former Lebanese Prime Minister Rafik Hariri in February 2005. In late 2006 and early 2007, the Western permanent members of the Security Council exerted great pressure on Lebanon to establish a special domestic court, and the UN's Department of Legal Affairs engaged in preparatory work with the Lebanese government. However, political opposition within Lebanon prevented the creation of the court from moving forward. In late May 2007, after months of fruitless efforts, the Security Council lost its patience and adopted a resolution establishing a court under Chapter VII.[61] Reflecting the controversial nature of the unprecedented Security Council action, five Council members, including China and Russia, abstained on the vote on the resolution.

The Hariri episode suggests that the creation of ad hoc tribunals to try terrorism cases remains a possibility in exceptional circumstances in which key powers of the Security Council, in particular the United States, have important interests. The creation of a permanent international tribunal to take on terrorism cases, however, will remain highly unlikely for many years to come, particularly so long as there remains no agreed international definition of what constitutes a terrorist act.

PROSPECTS FOR A NEW COUNTERTERRORISM ORGANIZATION

Despite the global threat that terrorism continues to pose and the increase in counterterrorist activity worldwide, this issue remains one of the few global, let alone security issues that does not have a dedicated international body. The need to fill this lacuna has become more apparent with the continuation of terrorist attacks around the globe; the proliferation of counterterrorism programs and initiatives at the global, regional, and subregional levels and in different substantive areas since 9/11; and the UN's uneven performance in this field.

Yet, in spite of its focus on counterterrorism, the Bush administration seemed to favor the use of existing (now adapted) institutions to help further U.S. counterterrorism objectives. Similarly, despite drafting the G8 2006 heads of state statement that called for a more coherent UN counterterrorism program and response to the threat, the United States appears to lack any interest in spending the necessary time, energy, and political capital to actually transform the UN effort.

Juxtaposed against this seeming U.S. complacency is the growing dissatisfaction among many countries with the current UN-led arrangement, in which the Security Council continues to assume such a central role. The lack of effective coordination and cooperation has almost come to define the UN's post–9/11 response, leading

---

[61] Security Council Resolution 1757, May 30, 2007.

countries such as Costa Rica and Switzerland to call, as early as in 2004, for the establishment of a UN high commissioner for terrorism to coordinate all of these initiatives. The fourteen-country Group of Friends of UN Reform echoed these calls in 2005.[62] Pakistan and Saudi Arabia have also put forward proposals on how to improve the UN's performance in this area and the global multilateral counter-terrorism effort more generally. Although some of these proposals are motivated by a desire to undermine what some countries see as the Council's usurpation and abuse of power, the Council's ineffectiveness is widely acknowledged, including among the P5.

If the United States took a lead role in reshaping the institutional counterterrorism architecture, it would go a long way to reassuring other countries that its September 2006 strategy has substance rather than just slogans. Terrorism is a truly global problem, and the United States should demonstrate it is committed, wherever possible, to tackle the challenges through peaceful, multilateral cooperation. Supporting a new global counterterrorism body either within or outside of the UN would clearly show such resolve.

Even with a policy change from the United States, the prospects for which increased with the election of Barack Obama in November 2008, getting a wide range of states from the global North and South on the same page as to the mandate of a new body will be a challenge, as different countries want different things from such an institution. Among the possible purposes a body could serve are facilitating the exchange of intelligence and other information and expertise, coordinating and delivering capacity-building assistance, overseeing states' implementation of UN counterterrorism obligations, grading states' performance, and naming and shaming underperformers. From a U.S. perspective, a new body would provide a forum for it to show its commitment to multilateral approaches to combating terrorism and enable it to work better with traditional and nontraditional allies in this area. This would lend greater legitimacy to its own counterterrorism efforts. Support from the global South will diminish the less the body focuses on capacity-building and the more it focuses on setting standards and grading performance and identifying nonperformers. Meanwhile, the United States and some partners, although perhaps eager to see a more effective mechanism to coordinate not only capacity-building efforts but also the work of the more than seventy multilateral bodies involved in counterterrorism, may be less inclined to support a new body that lacks these capabilities.

---

[62] The Group of Friends consists of Algeria, Australia, Canada, Chile, Colombia, Germany, Japan, Kenya, New Zealand, Netherlands, Pakistan, Spain, Singapore, and Sweden. See Group of Friends Non-Paper, "The Role of the United Nations in the Fight against Terrorism," 2005, available at www.un.int/mexico/2005/Terrorism.pdf.

9

Evolution and Innovation: Biological and Chemical Weapons

Fiona Simpson

Three international agreements attempt to contain the risks posed by weapons of mass destruction (WMD). These are the Nuclear Nonproliferation Treaty (NPT), which was agreed to in 1968 and entered into force in 1970; the Biological Weapons Convention (BWC), opened for signature in 1972 and entering into force in 1975; and the Chemical Weapons Convention (CWC), agreed to in 1992 and entering into force in 1997. Each agreement reflects the technical and political challenges of the weapon system that it addresses, and in this sense, each is self-evidently distinct. Yet the treaties all have their origins in the Cold War era; grapple with the issues of weapon definition, verification, and compliance; and are widely subscribed – most states belong to each. Moreover, it is possible to see some "learning" from one treaty to another, seen in the considerably more detailed terms of the BWC and CWC, which reflect a desire for greater specificity than can be found in the NPT. Together the three treaties constitute a strong international norm against the proliferation, further acquisition, or use of these indiscriminate weapons capable of causing great death and destruction.

This chapter explores how the two more recent agreements, the BWC and CWC, have unfolded in the years before and especially since the end of the Cold War (the NPT regime is discussed in Chapter 7). As will be discussed, although the BWC has entered into force, the continued failure to negotiate verification and compliance conditions has meant that the treaty's role is still primarily normative; nonetheless, changing political dynamics shaped its prospects in various ways between 1990 and 2006. Conversely, the CWC is in effect: member states are destroying their chemical stockpiles (albeit slowly); the agreement has explicit verification and compliance terms; and a substantial implementing agency, the Organization for the Prohibition of Chemical Weapons (OPCW), has been in place since 1997.

THE BIOLOGICAL WEAPONS CONVENTION

Overview and Early History

The Convention on the Prohibition of the Development, Production and Stockpiling of Bacteriological (Biological) and Toxin Weapons and on their Destruction was opened for signature in 1972. It built on the 1925 Geneva Protocol prohibiting the use of asphyxiating, poisonous or other gases, and of bacteriological methods of warfare.[1] The prohibition of the use, rather than the existence, per se, of these weapons was understood to be a limitation of the Geneva Protocol, and by the end of the 1960s, the international community began to move toward the negotiation of a treaty banning biological weapons.

Whereas biological and chemical weapons had heretofore been addressed together, in July 1969, the United Kingdom (UK) submitted a draft convention to what was then the Eighteen-Nation Committee on Disarmament (ENDC), which proposed banning the development, production, and stockpiling of biological weapons (the ban on their use already having been addressed by the Geneva Protocol). The new separation between biological weapons and chemical weapons was initially opposed by the Warsaw Pact countries, which countered the UK's draft with one of its own, under which chemical and biological weapons continued to be linked.[2] The UK's draft convention did not include provisions for routine inspections, as it was considered that "a ban on biological weapons did not require intrusive verification and could therefore be concluded quickly."[3] It did, however, contain procedures for the investigation of suspected treaty violations under UN auspices. In an internal U.S. government document (1969), this lack of on-site verification was identified as a cause for concern, and it was asserted that the proposed Convention

> does not provide assurance of compliance because there is no provision for on-site verification and violations could not be detected by unilateral means alone. Acceptance of an unverifiable treaty provision would weaken our ability to resist similar obligations in other arms control contexts.[4]

[1] The Geneva Protocol had its genesis in the use of poisonous gases during World War I and was originally a protocol to the 1925 Convention for the Supervision of the International Trade in Arms and Ammunition and in the Implements of War. This Convention, in turn, built on the 1899 Hague Declaration and 1907 Hague Conventions, which similarly prohibited the use of poison and poisonous weapons.

[2] The BWC ultimately contained a compromise in the form of a reference to chemical weapons in its Article IX, in which each State Party affirmed "the recognized objective of effective prohibition of chemical weapons and, to this end, undertakes to negotiate in good faith with a view to reaching early agreement on effective measures for [a Chemical Weapons Convention]."

[3] Jozef. Goldblat, *Arms Control: A Guide to Negotiations and Agreements.* (Oslo: PRIO, 1996), p. 93.

[4] "U.S. Policies on Chemical and Biological Warfare and Agents." Report to the National Security Council. Submitted by the Interdepartmental Political-Military Group in response to NSSM 59, November 10, 1969, in *Foreign Relations*, Documents on Arms Control, 1969–1972, released by the Office of the Historian.

Shortly thereafter, and partially in response to the growing consensus regarding the need for a total ban on such weapons, the United States formally renounced biological weapons and associated itself with the UK proposal.[5] The BWC was negotiated and then opened for signature within three years, entering into force in 1975.[6]

The Convention comprises fifteen articles and prohibits the development, production, or stockpiling of biological agents, toxins, or weapons (as well as related equipment or means of delivery).[7] As envisaged in the original draft proposed by the UK, the Convention (Article VI) allows for investigations in the event of a breach of obligations, providing for any state party to lodge a complaint with the UN Security Council against another. In addition, Article X of the Convention required that States Parties undertake to facilitate and participate in "the fullest possible exchange of equipment, materials and scientific and technological information for the use of bacteriological (biological) agents for peaceful purposes" and stated that the Convention should be implemented "in a manner designed to avoid hampering the economic or technological development of States Parties." Conversely, Article III of the Convention prohibits the transfer of, or assistance in acquiring, prohibited items.

The Cold War Years: 1976–1990

The two Review Conferences that took place during these years, in 1980 and 1986, were characterized by Cold War suspicions regarding compliance with the Convention (particularly U.S. suspicions regarding the Soviet Union) and thus relatively modest expansions in the remit of the Convention. At the first Review Conference, and in the continuing absence of a verification mechanism, voluntary confidence-building measures were introduced, aimed at increasing transparency and trust between the states parties. These measures were accompanied by the elaboration of Article X to include specific kinds of state-to-state cooperation, such as information exchanges and training of personnel.[8]

---

[5] The announcement by the United States was made in November 1969. For a useful and comprehensive overview of the history of the U.S. decision, see Jonathan Tucker, "A Farewell to Germs: The U.S. Renunciation of Biological and Toxin Warfare, 1969–70," in *International Security* 27, no. 1 (2002), pp. 107–48. Also see "U.S. Policies on Chemical and Biological Warfare and Agents." Report to the National Security Council. Submitted by the Interdepartmental Political-Military Group in response to NSSM 59, November 10, 1969, in *Foreign Relations*, Documents on Arms Control, 1969–1972, released by the Office of the Historian, accessible at: http://www.state.gov/r/pa/ho/frus/nixon/e2/83586.htm.

[6] In addition to the UK's draft convention, Canada and Sweden had also put forward position papers on the subject of such a convention, and at the request of the General Assembly, a report by the UN Secretary-General had been issued on the effects of chemical and bacteriological (biological) weapons and calling for their elimination from military arsenals.

[7] In prohibiting biological agents and toxins, Article I of the BWC made an exception for their application to "prophylactic, protective or other peaceful purposes."

[8] Final Declaration of the First Review Conference of the Parties to the Convention on the Prohibition of the Development, Production and Stockpiling of Bacteriological (Biological) and Toxin Weapons and on their Destruction. BWC/CONF.I/10 (Part II).

Biological and Chemical Weapons 169

The tenor of the debate had changed by the time of the Second Review Conference, which involved more candid expressions of mistrust, in the form of accusations of noncompliance with the Convention. During this conference, the United States accused the Soviet Union of having violated the terms of the BWC through the possession of an active biological weapons program and also declared that scientific advances had made it easier to manufacture agents in increasingly smaller facilities – a development, it argued, that "further complicated verification of compliance with the Convention."[9] Nonetheless, the confidence-building measures (CBMs) identified during the First Review Conference were successfully expanded in scope, and the manner of investigations of alleged noncompliance (Article V) and of technology assistance (Article X) was elaborated.[10]

The Cold War years, then, saw discussion in the context of the BWC concentrating on issues of compliance and confidence building but, given the mistrust that existed between the United States and USSR, not on efforts to bring about a verification mechanism. Even the modest progress attainable during these years met with mixed success, with 1987 seeing as few as thirteen states submitting the requested list of CBMs called for only a year earlier.

The Post–Cold War Regime: a Study in Contradiction *(1991–2000)*

Held in 1991, the Third Review Conference came at a time when the question of the proliferation of WMD was very much a topic for discussion in the international community, not only because of the end the Cold War, and fears regarding the possible "brain-drain" of weapons expertise from the Soviet Union, but also because of the revelations of WMD development that had emerged from Iraq following the Gulf War and the inspections being carried out by the UN Special Commission on Iraq. As a consequence, this Review Conference was distinguished from those of the past by moving forward on the question of establishing a verification protocol, although accusations regarding noncompliance with the Convention by others were again raised, including by the United States and again in reference to the Soviet Union.[11]

The creation of the expert group on verification, VEREX, was a significant departure, however, as it constituted the first formal multilateral attempt to identify measures that could resolve the question of whether a state had violated its obligations

---

9 Second Review Conference of the Parties to the Convention on the Prohibition of the Development, Production and Stockpiling of Bacteriological (Biological) and Toxin Weapons and on their Destruction. Summary Record of the Third Meeting. September 18, 1986, BWC/CONF.II/SR.3.

10 Final Declaration of the Second Review Conference of the Parties to the Convention on the Prohibition of the Development, Production and Stockpiling of Bacteriological (Biological) and Toxin Weapons and on their Destruction. BWC/CONF.II/13/II.

11 "Conference Can Strengthen Biological Weapons Regime." Remarks of Arms Control and Disarmament Agency (ACDA) Director Ronald Lehman to the Third Review Conference of the Biological and Toxin Weapons Convention. September 10, 1991. Accessed at: http://www.fas.org/nuke/control/bwc/news/910910–196372.htm.

under the Convention. In addition, the number of confidence-building measures that had been identified at past Conferences was increased, and a new form was created in order to facilitate their submission, in the hopes of improving the somewhat dismal rate of return.

Nonetheless, the creation of VEREX did not mean that U.S. concerns over verification of the BWC had abated. Rather, the end of the Cold War allowed the United States to make its position clear, declaring,

> [I]t is our view that the BW Convention is not effectively verifiable.... The United States would be interested in studying potential measures that would assist in verification of the convention, but we do not currently know of any way to make it effectively verifiable.[12]

The statement went on to assert that "so far, no persuasive case has been made for the effectiveness of either routine or challenge inspections of biological facilities."[13] Although this position was held by the soon-to-be outgoing administration of George H. W. Bush, the incoming Clinton administration, as will be discussed later, would ultimately only reverse this position with regard to the acceptability of challenge inspections.

Notwithstanding U.S. skepticism, VEREX went to work, meeting four times between 1992 and 1993, during which time it became clear that the American skepticism was not shared by many of its traditional allies. The author of the very first draft convention, the UK, again proved an active participant in the work of the group (and, later, on the issue of BWC verification more generally), taking the position from the outset of VEREX's work that "a verification regime aimed at detecting evasion which performs only moderately well is likely to have a significant deterrent effect on potential evaders."[14]

By the time the work of VEREX had concluded, culminating in a 1994 "Special Conference" to consider its final report, the Clinton administration had settled into office in the United States and had begun a reevaluation of the U.S. position on the prospects for, and role of, verification under the BWC.[15] The decision by the Special Conference to establish another Ad Hoc Group to negotiate a legally binding instrument that might include verification measures was supported by the States Parties to the Convention, including, in an apparent departure from its traditional standpoint, the United States.

---

[12] Ibid.

[13] Ibid. The United States also consistently expressed concern that Article X of the Convention, calling for the provision of assistance in biotechnology for peaceful purposes, should not end up contributing to weapons proliferation.

[14] "Verification of the BWC: Possible Directions." Working Paper submitted by the United Kingdom to the Ad Hoc Group of Governmental Experts to Identify and Examine Potential Verification Measures from a Scientific and Technical Standpoint. March 30, 1992. BWC/CONF.III/VEREX/WP.1. Other states that worked actively to support the establishment of a verification protocol included, but were not limited to, Canada, Germany, South Africa, and Sweden.

[15] The final report of VEREX comprised the identification of twenty-one possible measures aimed at strengthening the Convention.

Biological and Chemical Weapons 171

However, the United States was at pains to point out that its understanding of the word "verification" referred to those measures designed objectively to verify compliance with a treaty with enough confidence that they would detect a militarily significant violation in a timely manner; it differed from the more expansive understanding of "verification" adopted by VEREX. Rather than focus on compliance and detection of violations, VEREX identified "verification measures" as being measures that would strengthen the effectiveness and implementation of the Convention, with a significant part of their role being more qualitative in nature. Despite highlighting this distinction, the United States nevertheless expressed a growing awareness of the need for some sort of legally binding verification. Still, and no doubt influenced by the experience of the abortive confidence-building trilateral inspections that had recently been undertaken alongside the UK and Russia in 1993 and 1994,[16] in supporting the work of VEREX, the United States cautioned states parties that any protocol should "reflect what is technically and politically feasible."[17]

The Ad Hoc Group then began its negotiations on the text of the protocol in 1995, slightly more than a year before the Fourth Review Conference of the BWC was to be held. The American reevaluation regarding a verification protocol had concluded with the United States backing a July 1996 G7 statement in which states undertook to "work hard to implement the [BWC], including the establishment of an effective verification mechanism."[18] In keeping with this, at the Fourth Review Conference, the U.S. statement spoke favorably of the prospects for the Ad Hoc Group to "bring the Convention into the 1990s, through a legally binding compliance protocol that provides for new off-site and on-site activities."[19]

When describing the desired remit of the Protocol, however, the United States specified the need for mandatory declarations, the expansion of CBMs, the inclusion of, "at a minimum,"[20] field and facility investigation of cases of concern over compliance, and a target date of 1998 for the completion of the protocol. The statement did

[16] In April 1992 shortly after the Third Review Conference, Russian President Boris Yeltsin admitted that the former Soviet Union had operated an offensive biological weapons program until early 1992, in spite of its accession to the Convention. The result was a UK–U.S.–Russian Joint Statement on Biological Weapons, which aimed to initiate trilateral data exchanges and site visits at military and private sector biological facilities. In October 1993 and January 1994, visits to several Russian nonmilitary facilities were carried out by UK and U.S. officials, with reciprocal visits by Russian officials taking place in 1994. Russia was unwilling to provide access to military facilities, however, and the trilateral process soon foundered, with no inspections taking place after 1994.

[17] "Statement of U.S. Representative Donald A. Mahley to the Committee of the Whole." Special Conference of the States Parties to the Convention on the Prohibition of the Development, Production and Stockpiling of Bacteriological (Biological) and Toxin Weapons and on their Destruction. September 22, 1994. BWC/SPCONF/WP.16.

[18] "Towards Greater Security and Stability in a More Cooperative World." G-7 Chairman's Statement. June 29, 1996. Accessed at: http://www.g7.utoronto.ca/summit/1996lyon/chair.html#global.

[19] Statement by John Holum, Director of the Arms Control and Disarmament Agency (ACDA), to the Fourth Review Conference of the Parties to the Convention on the Prohibition of the Development, Production and Stockpiling of Bacteriological (Biological) and Toxin Weapons and on their Destruction. November 26, 1996. Accessed at: http://www.acronym.org.uk/dd/dd10/10bwc.htm.

[20] Ibid.

not make any mention of routine inspections in its protocol wish list. Nonetheless, the U.S. acceptance of the word "verification" as activities aimed at strengthening the Convention, as opposed to ensuring compliance or verifying declarations, allowed it, for the time being, to work with those states that also favored the negotiation of a legally binding protocol. The fact that, as other commentators have noted, "the objective and purpose of the Protocol to the U.S. was not verification"[21] in the conventional sense, meant that references within the Ad Hoc Group to "verification" tended to elicit a restatement by the United States of its position that the BWC was unverifiable according to the traditional understanding of the term; thus the word itself fell from favor (among its allies) during the work of the Group.[22]

By the time of the introduction of a rolling text of the protocol in July 1997, divisions within the Ad Hoc Group were becoming clear, with some desiring a two-pillar regime of declarations and investigations (akin to "challenge" inspections), and others – including the UK, the European Union (EU), Canada, and South Africa – desiring a three-pillar verification regime of declarations, investigations, and "visits" (routine, albeit randomly selected, inspections). The rolling text reflected this controversy with the proposed annex on nonchallenge "visits" lacking any content, in contrast to the proposed annex on investigations.[23] A year later, the cracks were starting to show more clearly, as the United States made it clear that it opposed routine inspections to verify states' declarations, although the draft protocol continued to incorporate provisions for such visits. In May 1999, an exchange of letters between U.S. Secretary of State Madeleine Albright and U.S. Secretary of Commerce William Daley made U.S. opposition to these visits clear. In outlining this stance, the United States referred to industry concerns, particularly by the Pharmaceutical and Research Manufacturers of America (PhRMA).[24] In the same month, the EU Common Position on the protocol was presented, which called for, among other things,

> effective follow-up to declarations in the form of visits, on the basis of appropriate mechanisms of random selection, so as to ensure transparency of declared facilities and activities, promote accuracy of declarations, and ensure fulfillment of declaration obligations in order to ensure further compliance with the Protocol.[25]

---

[21] See Jez Littlewood, *The Biological Weapons Convention: A Failed Revolution* (Aldershot: Ashgate Publishing, Ltd., 2005), p. 56.

[22] Ibid., p. 90.

[23] See Malcolm Dando, "Strengthening the Biological Weapons Convention: Moving Towards the Endgame." *Disarmament Diplomacy*, no. 21 (December 1997). Accessed at: http://www.acronym.org.uk/dd/dd21/21bwc.htm.

[24] See Marie Isabelle Chevrier, "Preventing Biological Proliferation: Strengthening the Biological Weapons Convention – An American Perspective." Paper presented at Biosecurity and Bioterrorism Focus Group and Roundtable. Instituto Diplomatico Mario Toscano, Villa Madama, Rome, Italy. September 18–19, 2000. Accessed at: http://www.mi.infn.it/~landnet/Biosec/chevrier2.pdf Also see Henrietta Wilson, "The BTWC Protocol: The Debate about Visits." *Disarmament Diplomacy*, issue no. 40 (September–October 1999). Accessed at: http://www.acronym.org.uk/dd/dd40/40btwc.htm.

[25] Common Position of 17 May 1999. Article 3. (1999/346/CFSP) Accessed at: http://www.sussex.ac.uk/Units/spru/hsp/1999-0517%20AHG%20CP.pdf.

The acceptance of the relaxed definition of "verification," which had facilitated U.S. participation in the negotiations alongside the UK, EU, and other like-minded states, therefore appeared to be at a breaking point, with the EU now explicitly calling for verification practices as being intended to ensure compliance and prevent violations – a verification goal that the United States opposed as being both undesirable and unworkable. By the end of 1999, one commentator attending the sessions of the Ad Hoc Group wrote of a "growing impatience with the United States" and "an increasing view among some delegations . . . that they will have to choose between having a regime that accommodates the United States' reluctance for intrusive verification but that is weak, or proceeding with an effective mechanism in the knowledge that the United States may pull away and refuse to participate."[26] Attempts to bridge this divide by the EU and the UK via a series of working papers proved unsuccessful.

The End of the Road: The Failure of the Protocol and Post–9/11

With the election of George W. Bush in 2000, the traditional unwillingness of the United States to countenance random visits was compounded by the new administration's return to an intensified version of the pre-1992 skepticism-in-principle of the whole enterprise. In March 2001, in an attempt to reach agreement on the text of the protocol in time for the Fifth Review Conference, the chair of the Ad Hoc Group issued a composite text, which attempted to resolve the outstanding issues, and which included provisions for a standing body to monitor the implementation of the Convention and protocol (an Organization for the Prohibition of Biological Weapons, OPBW) as well as provisions for the two types of inspections that had been the subject of discussion: visits and investigations.

As the new U.S. administration worked out its formal position on the subject, the United States itself stayed silent during the discussions of the text. By May 2001, however, rumors were growing that it would reject the protocol.[27] The EU, on the other hand, continued to express public support for the protocol and its adoption. Finally, in July, during the final session of the Ad Hoc Group, the United States announced that not only was the text unacceptable, being unable to increase confidence or prevent violations but also, with its inclusion of routine visits, being likely to put national security and commercial proprietary information at risk. This skepticism regarding the protocol and the compromise text was not, however, unique to the United States but was also shared by several countries of the Non-Aligned Movement of States (NAM), who now stayed quiet in the face of the more vocal

---

[26] See Henrietta Wilson, "The BTWC Protocol." Accessed at: http://www.acronym.org.uk/dd/dd40/40btwc.htm.

[27] Jenni Rissanen, "U.S. Jeopardises BWC Protocol," in *Disarmament Diplomacy* issue no. 57 (May 2001). Accessed at: http://www.acronym.org.uk/dd/dd57/57bwc.htm.

174   *Fiona Simpson*

opposition to the protocol by the United States. In November 2001, at the Fifth Review Conference, Under-Secretary of State John Bolton asserted that, "the arms control approaches of the past will not resolve our current problems. This is why we reject the flawed mechanisms of the draft Protocol previously under consideration by the Ad Hoc Group."[28] Bolton outlined U.S. support for efforts related to strengthened national (legal) implementation of the Convention's provisions, as well as an increased focus on biosecurity and an investigation mechanism for suspicious outbreaks or alleged incidents, before adding that the time for "'better than nothing protocols" and "Maginot [treaties]" was over.[29]

The Conference was ultimately suspended following a U.S. proposal to terminate the mandate of the Ad Hoc Group altogether, but was reconvened a year later, in 2002. During this meeting, states parties were able to agree to hold annual one-week meetings each year prior to the Sixth Review Conference. Those meetings were to be preceded by a meeting of experts with an agenda for each year agreed on at the Fifth Review Conference – a program of work that was seen by many at the time as representing a bare minimum of effort.[30]

In the years since, the United States has turned its attention to selected and informal coalitions of like-minded states, bilateral agreements, and other focused measures to deal with the question of biological weapons possession and proliferation. It had always been supportive of undertakings like the Australia Group, established in 1985 with the goal of harmonizing export controls among participating States in order to prevent the development of chemical and biological weapons. Following 9/11, the United States has also created and espoused the Proliferation Security Initiative (PSI) and UN Security Council Resolution 1540 as more effective means than the Convention, or the proposed protocol, through which to prevent the spread of biological weapons (as well as nuclear and chemical weapons and their means of delivery), not only to states but also to nonstate actors – a gap in coverage that the United States cited as a particular limitation of traditional arms control instruments. In addition, the United States supported the successful efforts, initiated by the UN's Office for Disarmament Affairs, to update the guidelines for the Secretary-General's mechanism to investigate alleged uses of biological and chemical weapons.

The Convention itself has labored on, with the intersessional series of meetings being held and their agreed agendas strictly adhered to by the United States, which expected others to do the same and, in particular, to avoid even the appearance of holding negotiations. The Sixth Review Conference in 2006 saw Canada and the UK

---

[28] Statement of the Honorable John R. Bolton, Under-Secretary of State for Arms Control and International Security, to the Fifth Review Conference of the Biological Weapons Convention. Accessed at: http://www.us-mission.ch/press2001/1911bolton.htm.

[29] Ibid.

[30] In 2003, the meetings were to focus on national implementation measures and biosecurity; in 2004, on capabilities for responding to investigations of outbreaks and alleged use; and in 2005, on the role of scientists and the adoption of codes of conduct.

Biological and Chemical Weapons

(which at the time held the presidency of the EU) once again playing an active role in attempting to maintain what momentum remained. Two new subregional groupings of states emerged and produced several working papers,[31] and the Conference itself emerged with agreement on another intersessional process, on an action plan to promote universality, and, perhaps most surprisingly given U.S. opposition to even the overtones of a BWC secretariat, on the establishment of an Implementation Support Unit (ISU) within the UN's Office for Disarmament Affairs.

Conclusions

Zero-Sum Innovation. The evolution of the BWC in the years immediately following the Cold War was characterized by an attempted reform of the way the Convention was implemented. A verification protocol that was legally binding and that would have led to the creation both of inspections and of an inspectorate was an ambitious undertaking, particularly in light of the historic ambivalence of the United States. With the end of the Cold War, an opportunity appeared to present itself for addressing what had long been viewed as a shortcoming in the Convention: the lack of a verification mechanism. Had it succeeded, the creation of a verification protocol would have constituted a major innovation in the regime.

However, the flipside of this intense focus on a BWC protocol was the lingering potential for the entire momentum of the regime to be thwarted by its failure. With the drive toward the protocol as the focus of BWC-related efforts during the 1990s, it followed that a failure to negotiate and approve the protocol relegated the 1990s to being a "lost decade" in the history of the BWC itself. This sense that a failure of the protocol was ipso facto a failure of the regime was exacerbated by the manner of its rejection by the United States, which rebuffed not only the protocol but also what it perceived to be the outmoded approaches to traditional arms control more generally.

U.S. Policy toward the BWC: The Persistence of Memory. In spite of its occasionally tempestuous relationship with the BWC, the emphasis that the United States has always placed on the overarching question of preventing the proliferation of WMD cannot be overlooked. The result is a complicated, even contradictory posture: the persistent importance placed on the principle of nonproliferation versus the varying degrees of skepticism that have marked the U.S. approach to traditional, multilateral nonproliferation instruments, particularly the BWC. The goal and importance of the nonproliferation of WMD are consistent, whereas U.S. faith in how effectively arms control treaties and conventions can realize that goal has often fluctuated.

---

[31] These two new groupings consisted of (1) Japan, Australia, Canada, South Korea, Switzerland, Norway, and New Zealand (known as JACKSNNZ); and (2) the Central, Latin, and South American states of Argentina, Brazil, Chile, Colombia, Costa Rica, Ecuador, Guatemala, Mexico, Peru, and Uruguay.

In the context of the BWC, however, these fluctuations are less significant than might be assumed, in spite of the unprecedented rejection of the protocol in 2001. Prior to 2001, attempts at innovation in the regime, most obviously following the end of the Cold War, have been led and most actively supported by other states. Although the United States, particularly during the Clinton administration, spoke favorably of and involved itself in such activities, it was by no means a crusader for such change in practice.

Instead, U.S. doubts over the verifiability of the BWC appear to be a continuing theme including throughout the post–Cold War negotiation efforts. As discussed earlier, even in the wake of the revelations in Iraq and the end of the Cold War, the U.S. position in 1991 maintained that the BWC was not verifiable. With the election of the Clinton administration, this position changed in large part because the United States showed itself willing, for the sake of continuing the discussion, to modify its understanding of the term "verification," whereas the EU and others who favored a verification protocol were equally willing to accept this definition. With the traditional gap thus plastered over, negotiations for a legally binding protocol were able to proceed.

The plaster, however, had already begun to show cracks by 1998, when the long-standing unwillingness of the United States (and U.S. industry) to accept intrusive routine inspections, or "visits," and the determination of the EU states that the protocol should consist of three pillars, not two (i.e., declarations, investigations, and visits) became clearer. The prospects for an agreed-on protocol were already growing dim by the end of the 1990s. The election of a new administration in the United States – one that was hostile not only to routine visits but also to the whole architecture of the BWC regime – meant that the edifice of cooperation finally crumbled. In terms of the outcome, however, the new administration may have changed only the "when" and the "how," rather than the "what."

Prospects: The Seventh Review Conference and Beyond. The intersessional process, renewed during the Sixth Review Conference, will again proceed according to the agenda agreed on in advance.[32] Whether the discussions will be as strictly managed as between 2003 and 2005 remains to be seen. Regardless, it remains unclear whether a change in U.S. policy or in the U.S. administration would necessarily lead to a resuscitation of the protocol, given that certain consistent "deal-breakers" appear

---

[32] In 2007, the meetings discussed ways and means to enhance national implementation, as well as regional and subregional cooperation on implementation. In 2008, the meetings discussed national, regional, and international measures to improve biosafety and biosecurity, and education, awareness-raising, and the adoption of codes of conduct. In 2009, the meetings will focus on enhancing international cooperation, assistance, and common understandings and effective actions on promoting capacity building in the fields of disease surveillance, detection, diagnosis, and containment of infectious diseases.

Biological and Chemical Weapons 177

to have a history that is older than the current administration. Even in a scenario in which the United States dropped its opposition in principle to a legally binding protocol, agreement on such a protocol would also require the United States to accept the possible verifiability of the BWC (something that states such as the UK have explored and sought to address); drop its objections to an "OPBW"; and, in what appears to be a perpetual stumbling block, drop its objections to any form of routine visits. Alternatively, those states seeking a three-pillar system of declarations, investigations, and visits would be required to do away with the third pillar. Because neither set of circumstances appears likely, the current status quo in the BWC seems set to continue through to the Seventh Review Conference and beyond.

THE CHEMICAL WEAPONS CONVENTION

Of the three main institutional components that make up the regimes surrounding WMD, the Chemical Weapons Convention (CWC) is arguably the most comprehensive. In providing for routine verification measures and challenge inspections, it surpassed the BWC; by imposing the same rights and obligations on all states parties, it avoided the two-tier system (or, in the eyes of some, the double standard) that has proved so problematic for the NPT. In addition, it created an organization (the Organization for the Prohibition of Chemical Weapons, OPCW) designed specifically and solely to implement the provisions of the Convention, as opposed to making use of an existing organization to do so, as the NPT did with the IAEA.

Nonetheless, the CWC – like the BWC – has also been characterized by a complicated relationship with the United States, one that has run the gamut from constructive to ambivalent to thorny. And, again like the BWC, as U.S. leadership in the creation and success of a CWC (and OPCW) has waxed and waned, other states have stepped in, in an attempt to take over the reins of leadership and guide the convention and organization toward success. The conflicted relationship between the United States and the CWC continues the theme of a broadly consistent skepticism on the question of "verifiability" and the capacity of international agreements (and, more specifically, international inspections) to prevent proliferation, particularly of biological and chemical weapons. However, and in contrast to the BWC, there appears to be a bigger "break" in U.S. policy during and post–Cold War, which moved, as noted previously, from constructive (until 1993) to ambivalent (from 1993 to 2000) to thorny (from 2000 to present).

The Chemical Weapons Convention: Overview and Early History

During the Cold War, international efforts to create a disarmament regime for chemical weapons had taken a back seat to those related to other WMD. As noted previously, although the 1925 Geneva Convention linked biological and chemical weapons, the two were delinked by the UK's draft BWC in 1969. With efforts then focused on the creation of a BWC (as well as an NPT), work on a Chemical Weapons Convention fell by the wayside, although Article IX of that treaty included the undertaking by states parties to negotiate "in good faith" toward the conclusion of such an agreement.[33]

In spite of this undertaking, actual progress toward a CWC was negligible for the next twenty years, caught up in Cold War politics and, specifically, the United States' steadfast insistence on intrusive verification and the Soviet Union's equally steadfast resistance thereto. In January 1984, however, a Warsaw Pact proposal calling for talks on chemical weapons showed the first signs of some flexibility on the verification issue.[34] Several months later, the United States countered with a proposal of its own, which contained "unprecedentedly stringent" provisions for verification and which was presented by then-Vice-President George H. W. Bush to the UN Conference on Disarmament, whose Ad Hoc Committee on Chemical Weapons was then tasked with negotiating the convention.[35] Although the Soviet Union rejected this draft as unworkable (calling, as it did, for an intrusive anytime-anywhere inspections regime), a dialogue had begun.

The dialogue, however, was short-lived. By February 1985, it became clear that no agreement was forthcoming, and later that year, a U.S. defense bill was put forward – and later approved – that would open the way for the United States to produce a new generation of chemical weapons after a sixteen-year moratorium.[36] Shortly thereafter – and, it has been suggested, possibly in response to this move by the United States – the Soviet Union again made an overture to the United States on chemical weapons abolition. The United States, however, rebuffed this overture. Then, in 1987, came the first signs of real movement when the Soviet Union accepted, in principle, the idea of challenge inspections – the need for which had been the focus of broader international efforts by the United States. In October 1987 the first of a series of confidence-building visits took place in the USSR, when the UK, the United States, and delegates from forty-three other states went to see a Soviet chemical weapons complex.[37] The following month, a return visit by Soviet delegates to the United States was carried out at a U.S. chemical weapons facility in Utah.

---

[33] In Article IX of the BWC, States Parties affirmed "the recognized objective of effective prohibition of chemical weapons and, to this end, undertakes to negotiate in good faith with a view to reaching early agreement on effective measures for [a Chemical Weapons Convention]."

[34] See Serge Schmemann, "Warsaw Pact Proposes Chemical Arms Talks," in *The New York Times*, January 11, 1984.

[35] See Robinson, J. P. Perry, "Origins of the Chemical Weapons Convention," In Benoit Morel and Kyle Olson, eds., *Shadow and Substance: The Chemical Weapons Convention* (Boulder: Westview Press, 1993), pp. 37–54.

[36] "Door Opened Again for U.S. Chemical Weapons," *The Times*, July 27, 1985. See also "Chemical Weapons: Editorial." *Christian Science Monitor*, June 21, 1985.

[37] Christopher Walker, "Russia Lifts Veil on Chemical Weapons Arsenal," *The Times*, October 5, 1987.

The End of the Cold War and Conclusion
of the Convention (1989–1993)

By the end of the decade, however, another state was taking on an active role as an interlocutor and advocate for the conclusion of a CWC. By 1989, Australia – always a supporter of a CWC and disarmament efforts more generally – was beginning to play a still more visible role on the world stage and was eventually able to exploit the post–Cold War international climate of security cooperation to advance an issue on which had already invested international political capital.[38]

Previously, Australia had formed the Australia Group, which established a system of export licensing and inspections in order to prevent the proliferation of dual-use goods associated with chemical and biological weapons, including precursor chemicals and associated technologies. In 1989, Australia initiated, and hosted, the first meeting involving not only future states parties to a Convention but also representatives from the chemical industry. This meeting was the first sign of Australia's growing role in the context of the future Convention – a role that one former Australian secretary of the Department of Foreign Affairs credited to a growing awareness within Australia that "for a small country to be heard, it must be diplomatically active."[39] This coincided with the precedence given to disarmament issues by the presiding government of Prime Minister Bob Hawke, as articulated in a series of speeches by Minister for Foreign Affairs, Gareth Evans, who argued for Australia's commitment to good international citizenship and the usefulness of Australia's role in promoting and facilitating, among other things, arms control and disarmament issues at the international level.[40]

The September 1989 meeting revealed both the progress that had been made as well as the gaps that remained. On a positive note, it appeared that the United States and the USSR were generally in agreement on the key elements of a bilateral approach, including with regard to a timetable for the destruction of their chemical weapons and the procedures for inspections. On the other hand, the United States was against the otherwise-popular idea of setting a deadline for the conclusion of negotiations on the Convention. Moreover, many of the developing states had called

---

[38] Marianne Hanson and Carl J. Ungerer, Promoting an Agenda for Nuclear Weapons Elimination: The Canberra Commission and Dilemmas of Disarmament. *Australian Journal of Politics & History* 44, Issue 4 (December 1998), pp. 533–51.

[39] See David Clark Scott, "Australia Creates New Mediating Role on International Stage," in *The Christian Science Monitor* (December 12, 1989), p. 4 (quoting Stuart Harris).

[40] See Gareth Evans, "Making Australian Foreign Policy," in *Australian Fabian Society Pamphlet* 50 (Canberra, 1989), as referred to and discussed in Nicholas J. Wheeler and Tim Dunne, "Good International Citizenship: A Third Way for British Foreign Policy," in *International Affairs* 74, no. 4 (October 1998), pp. 847–70 (see especially pp. 854–6.) Also see "Australian Foreign Policy: Priorities in a Changing World." The Roy Milne Memorial Lecture 1989, delivered by Senator Gareth Evans, Minister for Foreign Affairs and Trade, to the Australian Institute of International Affairs, Melbourne, April 27, 1989. (IX/89) Accessed at http://www.crisisgroup.org/library/documents/speeches_ge/foreign_minister/1989/270489_fm_prioritiesinachanging.pdf.

for a Convention to involve an aid package for their own chemical industries – an initiative that was also opposed by the United States. Then, in October, the United States announced that it wished to retain some small stocks of chemical weapons for the first eight years of a Convention and its right to use them in retaliation against a chemical weapons attack.[41]

Within a year, however, a changing strategic environment brought about by the end of the Cold War, the threatened use of chemical weapons in the Gulf War, and subsequent discoveries about the Iraqi program accompanied progress on the CWC. In June 1990, the United States and USSR signed a bilateral agreement to destroy 98 percent of their chemical weapons, to stop CW production, and to cooperate in making every effort to conclude a multilateral convention.[42] However, the United States' international campaign in favor of challenge inspections slowed somewhat, as the United States itself modified its own position slightly in a policy review in August 1990, stating that "challenge inspections should be limited near certain installations for national security reasons" and that the challenged state and the inspection team would negotiate the extent of access inside the perimeter of an installation, with the challenged state having the final say.[43] Nonetheless, in May 1991, the United States decided not to retain the remaining 2 percent of its chemical weapons, as it had previously envisioned under the bilateral agreement with the USSR (which had also planned to retain a small capability). U.S. President Bush then renewed his support for the early conclusion of a Chemical Weapons Convention, setting a target date of May 1992 and calling for the negotiating body – the Conference of Disarmament's (CD's) Ad Hoc Committee on Chemical Weapons – to stay in continuous sessions if necessary.

The implementation of challenge inspections remained controversial throughout the negotiations, and not only within the United States.[44] So, too, did administrative questions regarding the implementing executive body for the Convention. In an attempt to resolve the lingering differences, Australia stepped in once again with a compromise draft proposal presented to the Conference on Disarmament by its Foreign Affairs Minister, Gareth Evans. Under this plan, the power of the executive body regarding oversight of challenge inspections and routine verification would be

---

[41] U.S. General Accounting Office (GAO), "U.S. and International Efforts to Ban Chemical Weapons." Report to the Chairman, Legislation and National Security Subcommittee, Committee on Government Operations, House of Representatives, September 30, 1991. GAO/NSIADSl-317. The United States also justified retaining chemical weapons for a limited period as being a way to provide an incentive for others to join the ban.

[42] *SIPRI Yearbook 1991: World Armaments and Disarmament.* (Oxford: Oxford University Press, 1991).

[43] U.S. General Accounting Office (GAO), "U.S. and International Efforts to Ban Chemical Weapons."

[44] China, for instance, expressed suspicion of challenge inspections, whereas many developing countries feared that challenge inspections could be abused by being invoked too readily and with too little evidence. (Peter Grier, "Anti-Chemical-Weapons Group Seeking a Home," in *Christian Science Monitor* (May 26, 1992), p. 7.

Biological and Chemical Weapons 181

increased in order to guard against abuse. In addition, the proposal limited challenge inspections to twelve per year per state and three per year for one site. Finally, states parties would be obliged only to declare factories making more than one hundred tons of possible chemical warfare agents per year.[45]

The draft text provided much of the basis for the final language of the Convention on these issues, and in late 1992, the draft CWC was presented for the approval of the CD in Geneva. The key aspects of the Convention focused on banning the development, production, acquisition, stockpiling, transfer, and use of chemical weapons. The Convention established three "Schedules" of chemical warfare agents and their precursor chemicals arranged in order of their importance to the production of chemical weapons and their range of legitimate peaceful uses. Its provisions were of indefinite duration and applied to all activities potentially related to chemical weapons. The 500-person OPCW, based in The Hague, would oversee the CWC's implementation and monitor and verify the inactivation, and later destruction or conversion, of all declared chemical weapons production facilities, as well as the destruction of declared chemical weapons stockpiles.[46] In addition, the OPCW was tasked with verifying the consistency of declarations and monitoring the nondiversion of chemicals for prohibited activities, as well as providing protection and assistance, through the OPCW, if chemical weapons were to be used (or their use threatened) against a State Party.[47]

The CWC's First Few Years: The Decline of U.S. Leadership

The CWC was opened for signature in 1993 and entered into force in 1997. At the time, the CWC was hailed as an unprecedented achievement in disarmament regimes. However, the four-year gap between the signature of the Convention by the United States (in January 1993) and its ratification by the U.S. Senate was indicative of the United States' move away from leadership on the issue, as well as a reassertion of a more traditional U.S. skepticism toward multilateral nonproliferation measures. These traditional doubts were heightened by the 1995 sarin attacks on the Tokyo subway system by the Aum Shinrikyo cult, which raised the specter of the dangers of chemical weapons in the hands of terrorists and, more importantly from the viewpoint of the skeptics, the inability of the Convention to address this possibility.

---

[45] "Evans Pushes Chemical Ban," *Herald Sun*, March 20, 1992.

[46] States Parties that have declared Chemical Weapons Production Facilities (CWPFs) include Bosnia and Herzegovina, China, France, India, the Islamic Republic of Iran, Japan, the Libyan Arab Jamahiriya, the Russian Federation, Serbia, the United Kingdom of Great Britain and Northern Ireland, the United States of America, and "another State Party." (See: http://www.opcw.org/factsandfigures/index.html#CWDestructionUnderWay). The unnamed State Party is apparently understood to be the Republic of Korea.

[47] See Web site of the OPCW: (http://www.opcw.org/factsandfigures/index.html).

Several future prominent members of the administration of President George W. Bush testified against the CWC in 1997, including future Secretary of Defense Donald Rumsfeld and then-former Secretary of Defense (and future Vice President) Dick Cheney, who called it "ineffective, unverifiable, [and] unenforceable."[48]

When that ratification finally occurred in April 1997, the resolution contained thirty-three conditions, twenty-eight of which were agreed to by the White House and within the Senate. Among these were certain conditions of particular concern to CWC supporters, including measures that granted the president the right to deny a request for inspection if it "may cause a threat to U.S. national security interests."[49] The CWC itself, on the other hand, contained no provisions for permitting denial of an inspection. A year later, in 1998, the implementing legislation for the CWC was caught up a bill regarding sanctions on Iran and was vetoed as a result, leaving the United States (along with quite a few other states parties) in technical violation of the Convention for failing to submit its declarations to the OPCW.

With the accession of the Bush administration in 2001, many of those hostile to the CWC returned to office. In 2002, a standoff took place between the United States and the Director-General of the OPCW, José Maurízio Bustani. The United States claimed mismanagement on the part of Bustani, and cited attempts on Bustani's part to circumvent the work of the UN Monitoring, Verification and Inspection Commission by promising Iraq a "way out" of its difficulties with the Security Council if it signed the CWC and submitted to OPCW inspections, charges that Bustani denied. Following a vote, Bustani was removed from office in April 2002.

However, outside the United States, the CWC appears to have slipped off the international radar as a whole. The Russian Federation was lagging behind on the disposal of its own chemical weapons, due to a lack of funds, and publicized its need for more money in order to carry out the work required. The slow pace of these disarmament efforts continued when the U.S. Congress froze funds supporting the work after Russia missed its April 2000 deadline for eliminating 1 percent of its stockpile. Finally, the OPCW's first few years were plagued by budgetary difficulties and a "constant budget shortfall."[50]

---

[48] "Chemical Weapons Convention" Hearings before the Committee on Foreign Relations, United States Senate, One Hundred and Fifth Congress, First Session, April 8, 9, 15, and 17, 1997. Accessed at: http://frwebgate.access.gpo.gov/cgi-bin/getdoc.cgi?dbname=105_senate_hearings&docid=f:39719.wais.

[49] See Steven R. Bowman, "Chemical Weapons Convention: Issues for Congress," *Report of the Congressional Research Service* (IB94029), Foreign Affairs, Defense and Trade Division.

[50] See Maurizio Barbeschi, "Organizational Culture of the OPCW Secretariat," in *Disarmament Forum*, (UNIDIR), no. 4 (2002). Barbeschi states, "... the largest share of the budget was staff costs. These costs included the salaries of inspectors verifying the destruction of CW. According to the CWC, inspection costs associated with verification of CW-related facilities are to be paid by the possessor state. The significant delays before reimbursement meant that the OPCW was operating on 'fictitious income' and constant budget shortfalls."

Conclusions

Drivers of Change. The decisions taken by the first Bush administration were of key importance in getting the successful CWC process underway. However, and as in the case of the BWC, the history of the CWC also reveals the importance of other state actors, in this case Australia. In the context of the BWC, efforts to negotiate a verification protocol to the Convention (rather than to negotiate the Convention itself) required leadership on the part of several other states to fill the vacuum left by the U.S. self-removal to the sidelines. By contrast, the negotiation of the CWC itself was characterized by U.S. leadership and activity.[51] The efforts of Australia were required, not to take a leadership position per se, but rather to bridge the gaps that existed between the United States (and its allies) and other states regarding the issues of challenge inspections and, later, administrative issues surrounding the structure of the OPCW. As noted previously, the eventual text of the CWC was very close to the compromise draft text put forward by Australia.

The U.S. leadership on the CWC that had characterized the years until 1993 came to an end very shortly thereafter. Senate ratification became uncertain, and when the ratification did occur in 1997, it was heavily conditioned. Unlike the BWC, however, the CWC had the backing of the industry in the United States, with the CEO and president of the Chemical Manufacturers Association (CMA) testifying in favor of the Convention at the Senate Hearings.[52] As discussed previously, the BWC protocol – and particularly the prospect of routine inspections – was opposed by PhRMA, which considered that "because the development of new medications is highly research intensive, pharmaceutical companies have far more valuable proprietary information at stake than makers of commodity chemicals."[53] Based on this assessment, PhRMA lent its support to the CWC, even while it continued to oppose the BWC protocol.

Prospects: Outstanding Issues and Lingering Questions. The Second Review Conference of the Convention was held in The Hague in April 2008, five years after the first. As always, questions surrounding disarmament deadlines are likely to be a topic of discussion, with neither the United States nor the Russian Federation likely to meet the 2012 deadline for destroying all their chemical weapons stocks. The United States has completed the destruction of 51 percent of its stocks, while

---

[51] Notably, the successful negotiation of the Convention was one of the 1989 presidential campaign pledges by George H. W. Bush.

[52] In this capacity, the testimony represented 193 chemical manufacturing companies, accounting for more than 90% of the nation's productive capacity for basic chemicals. (See: http://www.fas.org/cw/cwc_archive/1997_0415_WHworkinggroup_industry.html).

[53] See Jonathan Tucker, "Strengthening the BWC: Moving towards a Compliance Protocol." *Arms Control Today* (January/February 1998). Accessed at: http://www.armscontrol.org/act/1998_01–02/tucker.asp#PhRMA.

184   *Fiona Simpson*

the Russian Federation, having now received some of the requested aid from other states, has destroyed just over 20 percent of its stocks.[54]

In addition, questions regarding the universality of the Convention and national implementation by States Parties remain. As at the Second Review Conference, 183 states were members of the Convention. Those missing, however, included some states suspected of having a chemical weapons program, such as the Democratic People's Republic of Korea (DPRK) and Syria.[55]

Of growing concern are scientific advancements and the verification gaps that may result. As noted earlier, the CWC prohibitions focus on agents that have already been employed to manufacture chemical weapons, but there are new compounds that could be utilized in a military role. As science has developed, the threat of intangible technology transfer (i.e., chemical formulae) has increased accordingly, along with fears among some States Parties that the current inspection regime may not be able to take into account these new developments. As a result, the verification provisions of the CWC could lag behind the curve of scientific discovery.

Finally, and like other arms control treaties, the CWC applies to states and has yet to directly address the threat posed by nonstate actors. It was drafted and opened for signature prior to the 1995 sarin attacks by Aum Shinrikyo. Although these attacks increased concerns regarding the use of chemical weapons by terrorists, the years following 9/11 have raised them still further. As with the BWC, the emphasis placed on nonproliferation by the United States has remained at odds with the U.S. belief in the effectiveness of traditional multilateral arms control instruments to achieve it. Although such skepticism has been a long-running theme in U.S. policy, and predates the post-2000 Bush administration, that administration moved further than before in favor of pursuing ad hoc nonproliferation efforts, particularly to prevent proliferation to nonstate actors, such as those outlined under Security Council Resolution 1540 and as contained in the goals of the Proliferation Security Initiative.[56]

---

[54] For the U.S. figure, please see the Statement by Ambassador Eric M. Javits, United States Delegation to the Second Review Conference of the Chemical Weapons Convention. April 7, 2008. Accessed at: http://www.opcw.org/docs/csp/rc2/natl_statements/US.pdf. For the Russian figure, please see: http://www.nti.org/e_research/profiles/Russia/Chemical/index.html.

[55] The five other states that have yet to accede to the Convention, as of April 2008, are Angola, Egypt, Iraq, Lebanon, and Somalia.

[56] Notably the CWC contains provisions that would help to decrease the likelihood of diversion to nonstate actors or terrorist groups. The "general purpose criteria" under Article VII of the Convention were conceived to allow a more robust regulatory domestic framework within the chemical industry and would help prevent diversion to illicit uses. However, many CWC States Parties have not implemented all the obligations in Article VII of the Convention.

III

New Tools, New Mechanisms

10

Normative Evolution at the UN: Impact on Operational Activities

Ian Johnstone

The operational activities of international organizations do not occur in a normative vacuum. They are shaped by the normative climate in which they occur, and they in turn shape that climate. This chapter elucidates that proposition by tracing three especially important normative developments over the last fifteen years: the emerging "Responsibility to Protect (R2P)," the growing consensus on the value of democratic governance, and the centrality of counterterrorism to global security policy. I will test the impact of norms by reviewing operational activities that have been most deeply affected, primarily in the field of peace operations, but also humanitarian action, development assistance, and nonproliferation.

These developments have occurred through a dynamic process that involves influential member states, key figures within international institutions, and non-governmental entities. States are still the primary actors – especially the United States – but because the process has become more fluid, normative evolution at the United Nations (UN) is not driven entirely by the executive branches of government and their diplomatic representatives in New York and Geneva. The UN is both a venue for interaction among states and an "organizational platform" where actors other than states wield influence.

The chapter proceeds as follows. The next section presents a theoretical account of how and why norms matter in international politics and considers the role of the United States in promoting norms. I then address each of the three normative developments identified previously in turn, first by tracing the origins of the relevant norm, followed by an analysis of their impact on peace operations and then on other operational activities. The chapter concludes with questions about the durability of the norms, in light of difficulties encountered in carrying out the operational activities they underpin. Here again the central role of the United States is considered. I argue that the norms are likely to survive these difficulties, and indeed, their very resilience in the face of significant setbacks testifies to their continuing relevance.

188   *Ian Johnstone*

NORMS IN INTERNATIONAL RELATIONS THEORY[1]

Do Norms Matter?

In this chapter, norms are defined as "collective expectations for the proper behavior of actors with a given identity."[2] This definition is broad enough to cover the Responsibility to Protect and democratic governance. What makes counterterrorism a norm is less obvious, but it does capture a growing expectation in the post–9/11 climate that states must work collaboratively to address the threat of terrorism. The unanimous adoption of the United Nations Global Counter-Terrorism Strategy in September 2006 is a manifestation of this, the first time all 192 member states agreed on a common approach to fighting terrorism despite the lack of an agreement on a definition.[3]

Attention to the impact of norms on state behavior is associated with constructivist international relations theory. Social constructivists doubt that strategic calculations of interest based on fixed preferences provide a full account of what is going on in world politics. They argue that how states define their interests is determined in part by social structures; interests and even identities are affected by the interaction between states and other international actors. The preferences and therefore behavior of states are influenced by socially constructed norms. That behavior in turn affects the normative climate in which states interact. In other words, states and the international system are "mutually constitutive": the structure of the international system (including the normative structure) affects the identity and interests of states; states in turn "construct" the social world (including its normative underpinnings) in which they live.

When early social constructivists were criticized for focusing too much on the first half of that equation, how norms affect actors, they turned to the second half: explaining how states and other actors create norms.[4] Martha Finnemore and Katherine Sikkink describe a three-stage process.[5] Norms emerge in the first stage

[1] This section draws on Ian Johnstone, "The Secretary-General as Norm Entrepreneur," in Simon Chesterman, ed., *Secretary or General? The Role of the UN Secretary-General in World Politics* (2007); and Ian Johnstone, "US-UN Relations after Iraq: The End of the World (Order) as We Know It?" *European Journal of International Law* 15, No. 4 (2004), pp. 813–38.

[2] Peter Katzenstein, "Introduction: Alternative Perspectives on National Security," in Peter Katzenstein, ed., *The Culture of National Security* (New York: Columbia University Press, 1996), p. 5; Martha Finnemore and Kathryn Sikkink, "International Norm Dynamics and Political Change," *International Organization* 52 (1998), pp. 887–917; Audi Klotz, *Norms in International Relations: The Struggle against Apartheid* (Ithaca: Cornell University Press, 1995); Martha Finnemore, *National Interests in International Society* (Ithaca: Cornell University Press, 1996); Ann Florini, "The Evolution of International Norms," *International Studies Quarterly* 40 (1996), pp. 363–89.

[3] United Nations Global Counter-Terrorism Strategy, A/RES/60/288, September 8, 2006.

[4] Jeffrey Checkel, "The Constructivist Turn in International Relations Theory," *World Politics* 50 (1998), p. 340. See also Paul Kowert and Jeffery Legro, "Norms, Identity and Their Limits: A Theoretical Reprise," in *The Culture of National Security*, pp. 469–83.

[5] Finnemore and Sikkink, *supra* n. 2.

when individuals with strong ideas call attention to an issue and try to persuade state leaders to embrace a standard of appropriate behavior. These "norm entrepreneurs" usually need organizational platforms – like the UN – to induce government officials to endorse their cause. The second stage begins when a "tipping point" is reached and a critical mass of leaders has been persuaded to promote the norm. At that point, the norm spreads rapidly in what the authors call a "norm cascade." This process of international socialization tends to be led by states but also involves networks of individuals, nongovernmental organizations (NGOs), and international officials that pressure targeted actors to adopt new policies and laws. It is largely an exercise in persuasion, not in coercion, although the persuasion can be reinforced by sanctions and material incentives. In the final stage, the norms become internalized – they come to be taken for granted, not contested, but followed almost automatically. This internalization may happen in the minds of decision makers, but more importantly the norms structure the practices of national and international institutions. And they become embedded through "iterated behavior and habit."[6]

Finnemore and Sikkink were not referring only to legal norms, but the pattern they describe is not unlike Harold Koh's transnational legal process. His is a theory of how a sense of legal obligation affects the behavior of states and other actors. The central argument is that compliance with international law is due not only or even primarily to external enforcement but also to a process of "interaction," "interpretation," and "internalization" of the law.[7] The process is driven in part by calculation of interests: states obey the law even when it may not be in their short-term interest to do so because they perceive greater long-term benefits from the prospect of future cooperation with other states and from the stability and predictability provided by international legal regimes.

Compliance is also driven by gradual socialization to the values and norms embodied in legal rules: transnational interaction generates a felt sense of obligation that comes with membership and participation in a regime. Koh builds on both sets of insights – the instrumental calculation of interests and a constructivist sense of obligation – to explain more precisely how interests are altered and national identities affected by international law. Interaction with other governmental and nongovernmental actors creates an environment in which noncompliance generates friction. That friction can hinder ongoing interaction and harm a state's reputation. To avoid that, states internalize the law in domestic legal and political systems. In this way, the law acquires "stickiness": "as nations participate in a transnational legal process, through a complex combination of rational self-interest, transnational interaction, norm-internalization and identity-formation, international law becomes a factor driving their international relations."[8]

---

[6] Ibid., 905.
[7] Harold Koh, "Why Do Nations Obey International Law," *The Yale Law Journal* 106 (1997), p. 2659.
[8] Ibid.

190   *Ian Johnstone*

The U.S. Role in Promoting Norms

This normative process, as noted previously, starts with an individual who has a cause. These norm entrepreneurs are often the leaders of powerful states. A number of U.S. presidents fit the description, as John Ruggie has argued. At key moments in the twentieth century (specifically, 1919, 1945, and post-1947), the United States sought to reconstruct the international order "in terms of organizing principles that resonate with America's sense of self as a nation."[9] Pure appeals to national interest and great power politics have never been enough to sustain U.S. international engagement, given its relative ability to isolate itself from the rest of the world and long aversion to "entangling alliances." From Theodore Roosevelt on, U.S. leaders drew on principles to build a world order that would serve U.S. interests. Woodrow Wilson was the most explicit in enunciating a value-based approach to institution building and foreign policy. Franklin Delano Roosevelt, Harry Truman, and Dwight Eisenhower were much more comfortable with balance of power politics, but they all embraced "reformist aspirations for the international arena, linking U.S. engagement to a broader vision of world order which they felt would resonate with the American public."[10] That vision included security cooperation through international institutions, an open world economy, self-determination, and the promotion of democracy. Many of the same principles were at play at the founding of the United States: individual rights, antistatism, democracy, and the rule of law.[11] U.S. "nationalism" is rooted in those values, not in land or people. This defining feature of American "exceptionalism" has influenced the country's relationship to the rest of the world, situating the United States as the "city on the hill" for others to imitate.[12]

When rooted in an unexamined belief in the superiority of the country's founding principles and used to justify exemption from laws and institutions that bind others (the problem of double standards), then exceptionalism is a pejorative.[13] But

---

[9] John Ruggie, *Constructing the World Polity* (New York: Routledge, 1998), p. 201.

[10] Ibid, pp. 211–6. For a similar account of continuity in the multilateral thrust of the foreign policies of Wilson, FDR, Truman, and Eisenhower, see Ivo Daalder and James Lindsay, *America Unbound: The Bush Revolution in Foreign Policy* (Washington DC: The Brookings Institution Press, 2003), chapters 9–12.

[11] Ruggie, *Constructing the World Polity*, p. 218.

[12] Paul Kahn, "American Hegemony and International Law: Speaking Law to Power: Popular Sovereignty, Human Rights, and the New International Order," *Chicago Journal of International Law* 1, No. 1 (Spring 2000). See also, Stewart Patrick, "Multilateralism and its Discontents," in Stewart Patrick and Shepard Forman, eds., *Multilateralism and US Foreign Policy: Ambivalent Engagement* (Boulder, CO: Lynne Rienner, 2002), p. 7.

[13] Nico Krisch sees a pattern of the United States actively initiating the negotiation of and then exempting itself from their full application by not signing or ratifying them, or attaching far-reaching reservations. Nico Krisch, "Weak as Constraint, Strong as Tool: The Place of International Law in US Foreign Policy," in David Malone and Yuen Foong Khong, eds., *Multilateralism and US Foreign Policy: International Perspectives* (Boulder, CO: Lynne Rienner Publishers, 2003), pp. 45–53. See also, "Present at the Creation: A Survey of America's World Role," *The Economist*, June 29, 2002, Special Survey, p. 20.

Harold Koh reminds us that there is a positive face to American exceptionalism: leadership in promoting global order and global governance. As Koh argues, the United States is the only country capable, and at times willing, to commit resources and make sacrifices "to build, sustain and drive an international system committed to international law, democracy and the promotion of human rights."[14]

Of course U.S. engagement with international institutions has always been more ambivalent than the aforementioned account would suggest.[15] The ambivalence is tied in part to the fact that, having created institutions, norms, and a world order that regulate the behavior of other states, it is awkward for the United States itself to act without restraint – even if it has the material power to do so. John Ikenberry questions the simple hypothesis that the United States organizes and operates within institutions it can dominate and resists or opts out of those it discovers it cannot.[16] He argues that a more complex set of calculations is involved. In entering into institutional arrangements, leading states seek to "lock in" other states to the rules and policy orientations of the institutions, while at the same time trying to minimize limitations on their own autonomy and discretion.[17] Conversely, weaker states agree to be locked in because they expect the arrangement to impose some limits on the leading state, or at least make that state's behavior more predictable and less arbitrary. They also benefit from the greater bargaining power collective membership in an organization can provide, especially where decisions are taken on a one-state, one-vote basis. The bargain, therefore, entails *some* reduction in the policy autonomy of the leading state in exchange for a relatively stable order that suits its interests and works to the long-term benefit of all. It is driven largely by

---

[14] Harold Koh, "On American Exceptionalism," *Stanford Law Review* 55, No. 5 (2003), p. 1486. See also, Stewart Patrick, "Multilateralism and its Discontents," p. 7; Anne-Marie Burley, "Regulating the World: Multilateralism, International Law and the Projection of the New Deal Regulatory State," in John Ruggie, ed., *Multilateralism Matters: The Theory and Practice of an Institutional Form* (New York: Columbia University Press, 1993), pp. 125–6.

[15] Four recent collections of essays discuss this pattern of ambivalent engagement. Two mentioned previously, Stewart Patrick and Shepard Forman, *Multilateralism and U.S. Foreign Policy: Ambivalent Engagement* (2002); and David Malone and Yuen Foong Khong eds., *Multilateralism and US Foreign Policy: International Perspectives* (2003). Also, Rosemary Foot, S. Neil MacFarlane, and Michael Mastanduno, eds., *US Hegemony and International Organizations* (Oxford: Oxford University Press, 2003); and Michael Byers and George Nolte, eds., *United States Hegemony and the Foundations of International Law* (Cambridge: Cambridge University Press, 2003). Earlier collections include Charles William Maynes and Richard Williamson, eds., *US Foreign Policy and the United Nations System* (New York: Norton, 1996); and Margaret Karns and Karen Mingst, eds., *The United States and Multilateral Institutions: Patterns of Changing Instrumentality and Influence* (New York: Routledge, 1990). One of the best single-author studies on the U.S. policy toward international organizations is Edward Luck, *Mixed Messages: American Politics and International Organization, 1919–1999* (Washington DC: Brookings Institution Press, 1999).

[16] John Ikenberry, "State Power and the Institutional Bargain: America's Ambivalent Economic and Security Multilateralism," in Malone and Khong, eds., *Multilateralism and US Foreign Policy: International Perspectives*, p. 50. See generally, John Ikenberry, *After Victory: Institutions, Strategic Restraint and the Rebuilding of Order after Major War* (Princeton: Princeton University Press, 2001).

[17] Ibid., 53.

instrumental calculations of short- and long-term interests, and its efficacy depends on the extent to which both sides perceive an interest in institutionalizing the behavior of the other.

The institutional bargain is precarious, because it is subject to shifting power relations and calculations of interest. Powerful states may come to decide they can better achieve their interests unilaterally; weaker states may decide they can gain more by banding against the dominant state. The bargain becomes especially precarious when one state dominates the international system by every conceivable measure, as the United States has done for most of the post–Cold War era.[18] The United States has continued to play the role of norm entrepreneur during this period, but its commitment seems more tenuous than the role it played in creating the post–World War II institutional architecture – the UN, the Bretton Woods institutions, the North Atlantic Treaty Organization (NATO), the Organization of American States (OAS), and even the European Union (EU). Looking at the three normative developments that are the subject of this chapter, the United States had an important though indirect role in promoting the Responsibility to Protect, by taking the lead in the Security Council's authorization of a series of humanitarian interventions in the 1990s; it has long been at the forefront of the global democratization agenda, including by establishing a "community of democracies" some hoped would replace the UN as a legitimating body; and it has led in pushing international organizations to become more active in the field of counterterrorism. But when any of those agendas bumps up against short-term interests in particular cases, the United States is quick to back away from them, even at the risk of appearing hypocritical. Ikenberry's "institutional bargain" would suggest that the world's only remaining superpower can get away with this without paying much of a price. The institutions quickly lose their causal impact – they do not constrain the hegemon and sooner or later stop having any influence on the behavior of weaker states, which will see that the bargain is entirely one-sided. Of course whether the weaker states are in a position to redress the imbalance depends in part on the degree of cohesiveness among them. A unified G-77 can and has countered normative steps that undermine the principle of sovereignty by the sheer weight of its voting power in the General Assembly; a divided G-77 is less able to do that.

In any case, Ikenberry's conception of the bargain does not fully account for the causal impact of institutions. An instrumental calculation of interests does not account for the *normative* framework that the institutional bargain produces and reproduces. The bargain is not easily abandoned, especially when the rhetoric surrounding it is value-laden (e.g., expanding democracy and promoting liberty), because abandoning the bargain could be seen as rejecting those values. Put

---

[18] Stephen Brooks and William Wohlforth, "American Primacy in Perspective," *Foreign Affairs* 81, No. 4 (July/August 2002), p. 20. See also, "Present at the Creation: A Survey of America's World Role." *The Economist* (June 29, 2002, Special Survey), pp. 4, 8–9.

otherwise, participants become hoist on the petard of their professed commitment to the values and norms embodied in the bargain. They may be prepared to abandon or redefine those norms, but doing so requires a sustained political effort that entails more than a recalculation of fixed interests. Compliance with international law is far from automatic, but a country like the United States, which understands itself as "a nation under law,"[19] will not casually act outside the parameters of legal norms and institutions that it helped to create, regardless of the short-term instrumental benefits that may accrue from doing so.

RESPONSIBILITY TO PROTECT

Origins of the Norm

The Responsibility to Protect has its origins in the controversial doctrine of humanitarian intervention. Starting in the early 1990s, the Security Council began employing an expanding definition of what constitutes a threat to international peace and security, the threshold for action under Chapter VII of the UN Charter. The trend began with Iraq in the aftermath of the first Gulf War, when the Council declared in Resolution 688 the flow of refugees caused by Iraq's repression of its minority populations to be a threat to international peace. Though not expressly adopted under Chapter VII, the United States, the UK, and France claimed that it plus earlier resolutions were sufficient to build a "legal bridge" to Operation Provide Comfort in northern Iraq and no-fly zones in both the north and the south.

This ambivalent start was followed by Security Council-authorized interventions at least in part for humanitarian or human rights purposes in Bosnia, Somalia, Rwanda (though too late to stop the genocide), Haiti, and Sierra Leone. These developments occurred not as part of a systematic effort to rewrite the rules of international law, but rather as a case-by-case reaction to crises and as a function of the political dynamics within the Security Council. Although no single decision represented a radical departure from existing international law, they added up over the years to a significant evolution in the applicable norms.

This is where matters stood when the Kosovo crisis erupted in late 1998/early 1999. Unable to get Russian support for a Security Council resolution explicitly authorizing military action against Belgrade, NATO nevertheless launched an eleven-week bombing campaign on March 24, 1999. The weight of scholarly and official opinion at the time and to this day is that the action was illegal.[20] However, that finding does not mean NATO's intervention was widely deplored or condemned. The best way to characterize the reaction is that the illegality was "excused" on the grounds

---

[19] Kahn, "American Hegemony," p. 2.

[20] I review the arguments and literature in "Security Council Deliberations: The Power of the Better Argument," *European Journal of International Law* 14, No. 3 (2003), pp. 464–6.

of humanitarian necessity.[21] In other words, a "blind eye" was turned to the law's violation given the extreme circumstances, and those responsible (NATO countries) were in effect pardoned. Traces of this notion of humanitarian necessity as an excuse can be found in many of the official statements on Kosovo, as well as the failure of the draft resolution introduced by Russia to condemn the NATO action (by a vote of 12 to 3). The failure of the General Assembly either to condemn or support NATO is also indicative. It suggests a willingness to turn a blind eye matched by an unwillingness to announce that is what was going on.

These developments throughout the 1990s were driven largely by states, but non-state actors like the Secretary-General of the UN and nongovernmental activists were influential on the margins of deliberations in the Security Council. Indeed NATO's intervention in Kosovo was undertaken in the context of considerable pressure from an active citizenry in the United States and Europe, who after Rwanda were reluctant to see their governments stand by in the face of what many saw as attempted genocide.

These nonstate actors became even more active in the aftermath of Kosovo, driving the process that led to endorsement of the Responsibility to Protect in the World Summit 2005. The International Commission on Intervention and State Sovereignty (ICISS), an independent blue ribbon panel of eminent persons, coined the term. The establishment of the panel was the Canadian government's response to the challenge laid down by the Secretary-General in a speech he made in September 1999: "the core challenge to the Security Council and to the UN as a whole in the next century is to forge unity behind the principle that massive and systematic violations of human rights . . . cannot be allowed to stand."[22] The concept was affirmed by another independent commission – the High-level Panel on Threats, Challenges and Change (HLP) – and the Secretary-General in his report to the World Summit.[23] It was finally endorsed at the summit, though only after a rancorous and inconclusive debate about the scope of the responsibility and on precisely whom it fell. The HLP argued that, when governments were unable or unwilling to fulfill that Responsibility to Protect, it fell on the Security Council, and recommended the adoption of a set of criteria to be taken into account in deciding whether and how to exercise it. An early draft of the document that came out of the 2005 World Summit included a paragraph on the *responsibility* of the Security Council to act under Chapter VII when necessary. The United States objected on the grounds that this language implied a legal obligation. So the final outcome document simply

---

[21] This was the argument made by Belgium before the ICJ in a suit brought by Yugoslavia. For a fuller analysis of the concept of necessity, see Ian Johnstone. "The Plea of 'Necessity' in International Legal Discourse: Humanitarian Intervention and Counter-terrorism," *Columbia Journal of Transnational Law* 43, No. 2 (2005), pp. 337–88.

[22] SG/SM/136, GA 9596, September 1999. The cochairmen of the ICISS said in launching the report that it was a response to the Secretary-General's challenge. See Gareth Evans and Mohamed Sahnoun, "Intervention and State Sovereignty: Breaking New Ground," *Global Governance* 7, No. 2 (April/June 2001), pp. 119–25.

[23] Report of the Secretary-General to the General Assembly, "In Larger Freedom: Towards Development, Security and Human Rights for All," A/59/2005, March 21, 2005.

states that the international community is "prepared to take collective action, in a timely and decisive manner, through the Security Council, in accordance with the UN Charter, including Chapter VII, on a case by case basis" – implying the right but no obligation to act. There is no appeal to adopt guidelines or criteria for humanitarian intervention, out of fear that this could constrain Security Council members when they wanted to act, put unwelcome pressure on them when they did not want to, and might affect decisions about unilateral action. Despite the watered-down language, this was the first time a UN meeting had formally endorsed the concept, giving it the character of soft law. A "harder" version of the principle exists in the Constitutive Act of the African Union, but the World Summit marked the first time it was signed on to by every state in the world. Following up on the World Summit, the Secretary-General recently produced a report entitled "Implementing the Responsibility to Protect" in January 2009, which covers a range of activities from assistance to states, through noncoercive measures like human rights monitoring, to arms embargoes and military action.[24]

Impact of the Responsibility to Protect (R2P) on Peace Operations

Although the R2P norm now exists on paper, it has never been invoked as justification for full-scale coercive military intervention. Indeed the reluctance to act more force-fully in Darfur is seen as evidence that the norm is worth little more than the paper on which it is written. That judgment would be too hasty. Alongside development of the norm, the Security Council acquired the habit of granting peace operations (UN and non-UN) "protection of civilians" mandates.[25] The first time was in late 1999, in Sierra Leone, where the United Nations Mission in Sierra Leone (UNAMSIL) was given the mandate to "to protect civilians under the imminent threat of physical violence... within its capabilities and areas of deployment."[26] This resolution was adopted prior to the release of the ICISS report, but the Canadian government was instrumental in both the resolution and the report, suggesting that the connection between the protection of civilians mandate and the R2P norm is not coincidental. Indeed, the two developed in parallel. As the norm worked its way into international legal and political discourse – including its invocation in Security Council debates on Darfur[27] – the Council was busy giving eight more UN missions the mandate,

---

[24] Report of the Secretary-General, "Implementing the Responsibility to Protect," A/63/77, January 12, 2009.

[25] Ian Johnstone, "Dilemmas of Robust Peacekeeping," in *Annual Review of Global Peace Operations* (Boulder, CO: Lynne Rienner Publishers, 2006); Victoria Holt and Tobias Berkman, *The Impossible Mandate? Military Preparedness, the Responsibility to Protect and Modern Peace Operations* (Washington, DC: Henry L. Stimson Center, 2006).

[26] Security Council Resolution 1270, October 22, 1999, para. 14.

[27] See, for example, "The UN Security Council and the Darfur Crisis: A Country-by-Country Analysis," which looks at statements by Security Council members before, during, and after the adoption of Resolution 1706 on the establishment of UNAMID. Available at http://www.africaaction.org/resources/docs/SCAnalysis0610.pdf. On earlier debates in the Security Council on Darfur, see Alex

as well as several non-UN missions, including France's Operation Licorne in Côte d'Ivoire and the African Union mission in Darfur (AMIS).

Meanwhile, the Secretariat and Security Council have made halting efforts to better operationalize the protection of civilians mandate.[28] In 2002, the Office for the Coordination of Humanitarian Affairs (OCHA) prepared and the Security Council adopted an *Aide Memoire* as a tool to facilitate the consideration of protection issues in Security Council deliberations on the establishment, change, and close of peacekeeping operations. In the wake of the attacks of September 11, 2001, however, the *Aide Memoire* did not play a significant role in the design of peacekeeping mandates.[29] OCHA reviewed it in 2008, and on January 14, 2009, the Security Council adopted an updated version of the *Aide Memoire* as an annex to a Presidential Statement.[30] Meanwhile, in a key 2006 resolution, the Security Council expressed its intention to ensure that protection mandates "include clear guidelines as to what missions can and should do to achieve their mandate goals, and the protection of civilians is given priority in decisions about the use of available capacity and resources, including information and intelligence resources" (Resolution 1674, paragraph 16). This passage was interpreted by one government to require that "the UN Secretariat must – as an imperative – develop and implement a core doctrine on protection of civilians for those of its peacekeeping operations mandated to do so."[31] In addition, endorsement of robust military or police action to ensure security in or near refugee/IDP camps and to protect women and children from sexual violence could be inferred from the resolution.[32]

Despite these doctrinal advances, considerable discretion on how to implement the protection of civilians mandate is necessarily delegated to the peacekeepers. Thus, for example, in the Democratic Republic of the Congo (DRC), the United Nations Organization Mission in the Democratic Republic of the Congo (MONUC) has been engaging in robust action in eastern DRC, based largely on an expansive

---

Bellamy, "Responsibility to Protect or Trojan Horse? The Crisis in Darfur and Humanitarian Intervention after Iraq," *Ethics and International Affairs* 19, No. 2 (2005), pp. 31–54.

[28] For this review of Secretary-General reports and Security Council resolutions on the protection of civilians, I am grateful to Renata Capella-Soler who wrote a master's thesis entitled "From Discourse to Practice: Protection of Civilians in UN Peacekeeping Operations in Sudan," MA Thesis, Fletcher School of Law and Diplomacy (May 2009), unpublished manuscript on file with author.

[29] On the development of the POC agenda post–September 11, see Security Council Report, *Cross-Cutting Report No. 2, Protection of Civilians*, 14 October 2008, p. 6f.

[30] United Nations, *Statement by the President of the Security Council*, S/PRST/2009, 1*, January 14, 2009.

[31] Internal document commissioned by the Department of Foreign Affairs and International Trade, Government of Canada, *Protection of Civilians in UN Peacekeeping Operations: A Framework Document for Further Action and Study*, p. 6.

[32] In paragraph 19 of Resolution 1674, the Security Council "reaffirms the need to maintain the security and civilian character of refugee and internally displaced person camps...and encourages the Secretary-General where necessary and in the context of peacekeeping operations and their respective mandates, to take all feasible measures to ensure security in and around such camps and of their inhabitants...Condemns in the strongest terms all sexual and other forms of violence committed against civilians, in particular women and children, and undertakes to ensure that all peace support operations employ all feasible measures to prevent such violence and to address its impact where it takes place."

reading of the protection mandate, including preemptive action in certain circumstances.[33] The 2008 crisis precipitated by Laurent Nkunda tested the limits of MONUC's capacity, as well as the interpretation of its mandate. Pressure to act against Nkunda (who alledgedly was backed by Rwanda) on the one hand, and against the Forces Democratiques de Liberation du Rwanda (allegedly backed by the armed forces of the DRC) on the other, raised questions about the line between protection of civilians against minor spoilers and enforcement action against major parties to a conflict. The newly minted UN Capstone Doctrine states that the former is an appropriate function for peacekeepers; the latter is not.[34]

The same question has arisen in Darfur. AMIS had a protection of civilians mandate, though it lacked the capacity to fulfill it. The United Nations-African Union Mission in Darfur (UNAMID) also has a protection of civilians mandate, along with the authority to take forceful action to "prevent disruption of implementation of [the Darfur Peace Agreement] and armed attacks, without prejudice to the responsibilities of the government." This tortured language is the result of a compromise needed to get the Government of Sudan to agree to deployment of the mission. While doubts remain as to how effective UNAMID can be in the face of government intransigence and the absence of a viable political process, the mission has an authorized strength of some twenty thousand troops, with air assets that include attack helicopters, and more than six thousand police including nineteen formed police units. Whether and how effectively these assets can be used to protect civilians remains to be seen.

The protection function, moreover, has started to merge with a trend toward more proactive public order mandates for peace operations.[35] This is most apparent in Haiti, where the UN mission has both a protection of civilians mandate and Chapter VII authority to provide operational support to the Haitian police to maintain "the rule of law, public safety and public order."[36] The maintenance of public order in Haiti has meant taking on armed gangs in the shantytowns of Port-au-Prince that have been a perpetual threat to Haitian civilians, not least through kidnappings. This merger of the functions is the continuation of a trend that began in the Balkans and East Timor, where the peace operations missions had implicit protection of civilian mandates, even though the term was not used.[37]

---

[33] Major General Patrick C. Cammaert, "Learning to Use Force on the Hoof in Peacekeeping: Reflections on the Experience of MONUC's Eastern Division," ISS Situation Report, April 3, 2007; Jim Terrie, "The Use of Force in UN Peacekeeping: The Experience of MONUC," *African Security Review* 18, No. 1 (2008).

[34] *United Nations Peacekeeping Operations: Principles and Guidelines* (The "Capstone Doctrine"), 2008, p. 34. Available at http://pbpu.unlb.org/pbps/Library/Capstone_Doctrine_ENG.pdf.

[35] Richard Gowan and Ian Johnstone, "New Challenges for Peacekeeping: Protection, Peacebuilding and the 'War on Terror,'" Coping with Crisis Working Paper Series, International Peace Academy (2007), p. 6.

[36] Security Council Resolution 1529, February 29, 2004. This was reinforced by resolution 1608, which endorsed a more robust approach in Haiti by expanding the strength of the mission and deploying a rapid reaction force.

[37] For example, IFOR and SFOR in Bosnia (resolutions 1031 and 1088); KFOR in Kosovo (resolution 1244); INTERFET and then UNTAET in East Timor (resolutions 1264 and 1272).

Thus the Responsibility to Protect against massive and systematic human rights abuses is coming to be associated with more general law-and-order functions, where the peacekeepers exercise executive authority in violent postconflict societies. The connection between R2P and protection of civilian mandates provoked a reaction in the UN's peacekeeping committee (the C-34), precisely because many countries from the global South saw the mandate as the thin edge of the wedge toward unjustified interventions by the North against the South. This led to an acrimonious debate in the C-34 in 2009 that concluded with an appeal for the Secretariat to develop proposals on how to better fulfill the protection of civilian's mandate.[38] So although we do not yet have either the R2P principle or the protection capacity that its most enthusiastic proponents were advocating in the mid-1990s, evolving practice suggests a normative shift.

Impact of R2P on Other Operational Activities

Peacekeeping is not the only operational area affected by this normative shift. The notion of protection of civilians encompasses a good deal of the humanitarian work of UN agencies. The concept was introduced in 1998 in the Secretary-General's report on "The Causes of Conflict and the Promotion of Durable Peace and Sustainable Development in Africa."[39] The Secretary-General subsequently produced six major reports on the protection of civilians, most recently in June 2009. Between 1999 and 2007 the Security Council issued four thematic resolutions on the protection of civilians, the latest of which refers to the World Summit's endorsement of a Responsibility to Protect.[40] The Secretary-General described Security Council Resolution 1674 as "a watershed in the protection of civilians by providing a clear framework for action by the Council and the United Nations in this area."[41] Though it includes a good deal of language about peacekeeping, the resolution reflects an expansion of the protection of civilians agenda to peacemaking and peacebuilding activities as well, including the ending of impunity. In their totality, these reports and resolutions describe everything from humanitarian assistance and human rights monitoring to mediation, legal advocacy, and criminal prosecution as protection functions. Developing policy for the protection of civilians became a principal function of the Office for the Coordination of Humanitarian Affairs. And in November 2005, the Secretary-General called for a more "systematic partnership with regional and other intergovernmental organizations in the field of protection of civilians in armed conflict."[42]

---

[38] See Report of the Special Committee on Peacekeeping, June 2009.
[39] UN Document S/1998/318 or A/52/871, April 13, 1998.
[40] S/RES/1674, 28 April 2006.
[41] United Nations, Report of the Secretary-General on the Protection of Civilians in Armed Conflict, S/2007/643, 28 October 2001, para. 1.
[42] UN Document S/1998/318 or A/52/871.

Normative Evolution at the UN: Impact on Operational Activities 199

A significant area of humanitarian action where echoes of the R2P principle are heard concerns internally displaced persons (IDPs). Since a set of Guiding Principles was adopted in 1998, an increasingly rights-based approach has been taken to protection of IDPs. Those principles – and indeed the notion of the Responsibility to Protect – have their roots in the work of Francis Deng, the first Representative of the Secretary-General on the Human Rights of Internally Displaced Persons. Mr. Deng wrote of "sovereignty as responsibility" in the early 1990s and was instrumental in a campaign that led to adoption of the principles. They are explicitly nonbinding, but "reflect and are consistent with" international human rights and humanitarian law, while clarifying any gray areas and addressing gaps that may exist.[43]

The Guiding Principles were submitted to the Commission on Human Rights in 1998, where they have been "taken note of" and "welcomed" with increasing degrees of enthusiasm every year since. The UN General Assembly has also adopted yearly resolutions on the principles, culminating with the claim at the World Summit of 2005 that they provided "an important international framework for the protection of internally displaced persons."[44] The stated purposes of the principles are to provide guidance to the Representative in implementing his mandate, to states when confronted with situations of displacement, to all other authorities and groups in their relations with internally displaced persons, and to intergovernmental and nongovernmental organizations in carrying out their work.[45] Those purposes are being achieved: increasingly, the principles are being cited and used by UN agencies, regional organizations, NGOs, and governments.[46] They have been disseminated to the field staff of UN agencies and, through those agencies, to nongovernmental and governmental partners. They are included in training packages, invoked as advocacy tools, and used to design national programs of assistance for internally displaced persons (IDPs). Widely used and commented on, they are coming to provide the normative framework within which international protection and assistance activities on behalf of IDPs are conducted.[47]

---

[43] Report of the Representative of the Secretary-General submitted pursuant to Human Rights Commission resolution 1997/39, Addendum, Guiding Principles on Internal Displacement, E/CN.4/1998/53/Add.2, February 11, 1998, Introductory Note to the Guiding Principles, paras. 9 and 10. See also Walter Kalin, "The Guiding Principles on Internal Displacement as International Minimum Standard and Protection Tool," *Refugee Survey Quarterly* 24, No. 3 (2005), pp. 27–36; Roberta Cohen, "The Guiding Principles on Internal Displacement: An Innovation in International Standard Setting," *Global Governance* 10 (2004), pp. 459–80.

[44] GA Res 60/1, October 24, 2005.

[45] Guiding Principles, "Introduction: Scope and Purpose."

[46] Cohen, p. 467.

[47] Simon Bagshaw, *Developing a Normative Framework for the Protection of Internally Displaced Persons* (Washington, DC: Bridge Street Books, 2005), p. 12. See also, Patrick Schmidt, "The Process and Prospects for the Guiding Principles on Internal Displacement to Become Customary Law," *Georgetown Journal of International Law* 35 (Spring 2004); Ian Johnstone, "Law-making through the Operational Activities of International Organizations," *George Washington International Law Review* 40 (2008).

DEMOCRATIC GOVERNANCE

Democracy as an International Norm

At least prior to the U.S. invasion of Iraq, there was an emerging international consensus on the value of democratic governance and the legitimacy of democracy promotion by international organizations. According to Boutros-Ghali's *An Agenda for Democratization*, the legal foundation is the UN Charter itself. Although the word "democracy" does not appear in the document, it is written in the name of "we the peoples" and affirms the principles of self-determination, human rights and fundamental freedoms.[48] The Secretary-General cliams that the aforementioned language "roots the sovereign authority of states and therefore the legitimacy of the UN in the will of the people." This is reinforced by the Universal Declaration of Human Rights, which stipulates that the will of the people "shall be the basis of the authority of government,"[49] declares "all persons have the right to take part in the government of their country," and sets out a number of civil and political rights that relate to democratic governance. To these foundational documents Boutros-Ghali adds the Declaration on the Granting of Independence to Colonial Peoples (1960) – which reaffirms the right to self-determination and the right of all peoples to determine their political status – and, in a bit of creative interpretation, claims they provide a "clear and solid foundation" for a UN role in democratization.

This foundation was built on by Article 25 of the International Covenant on Civil and Political Rights (ICCPR), which guarantees a "right to political participation," including the right to take part in public affairs, to vote, and to be elected in "genuine periodic elections" by secret ballot. Various regional human rights documents set out the right in similar terms: the First Protocol to the European Convention on Human Rights, the American Convention on Human Rights, the African Charter of Human Rights, and the OSCE Charter of Paris. Some of the interpretative questions left open by these treaties, for example, whether "genuine" elections require party pluralism, have been answered by equivocal but nevertheless consistent findings of various judicial, quasijudicial, and nonjudicial bodies.[50] The Human Rights Committee, a body of eighteen independent experts set up to oversee implementation of the ICCPR, expressed skepticism that one-party elections would be "genuine," stating in a 1996 General Comment that the right to form and join political parties "is an essential adjunct to the rights protected by Article 25." Article 3 of the First Protocol to the European Convention on Human Rights uses language that is even narrower

---

[48] Boutros Boutros-Ghali, *An Agenda for Democratization* (New York: United Nations Department of Public Information, 1996), para. 28.

[49] Article 21 of the Universal Declaration of Human Rights.

[50] Gregory Fox, "The Right to Political Participation in International Law," in *Democratic Governance and International Law* (Cambridge: Cambridge University Press, 2000), pp. 48–90.

than Article 25, but has been interpreted by the European Court of Human Rights to prohibit the banning of political parties. The Inter-American Commission on Human Rights has determined that one-party elections are not "authentic" within the meaning of Article 23 of the American Convention. The Helsinki Final Act and other CSCE/OSCE documents – none of which are legally binding – include language that could be read as requiring party pluralism.

A substantial body of other evidence can be read as supporting an emerging entitlement to democratic governance.[51] This includes a series of International Conferences of New and Restored Democracies held since the early 1990s. In a parallel initiative, 107 countries met in Warsaw in the year 2000 for what was called the Community of Democracies conference, where they agreed to uphold "core democratic principles and practices" and declared "the will of the people as expressed through regular, free and fair elections shall be the basis for the authority of government. . . . "[52] Subsequent meetings were held in Seoul in 2002; Santiago in 2005; and in Bamako, Mali, in 2007. Not much concrete comes out of these conferences, but 100–120 countries meeting on a regular basis to declare their commitment to democratic principles has an impact on the global normative climate. Moreover, there is now a nongovernmental Council of the Community of Democracies to push the agenda, and in 2004, seventy governments organized themselves into a "democracy caucus" at the UN. In his 2008 presidential campaign, John McCain proposed the creation of a new international organization called a "concert of democracies," an idea that was greeted with some sympathy in academic circles.[53]

In April 1999, the Commission on Human Rights adopted a nonbinding resolution entitled "Promotion of the Right to Democracy."[54] The vote was 51 to 0 with only Cuba and China abstaining, following a debate not about the value of democracy, but about whether it is a "right." Six years later, in his report to the World Summit 2005, the Secretary-General declared, "Democracy does not belong to any country or region but is a universal right."[55] Meanwhile, quasi-nongovernmental organizations like the National Democratic Institute in Washington and the International Institute

---

[51] See generally the compilation of essays in, cited earlier, Gregory Fox and Brad Roth, eds., *Democratic Governance and International Law*. See also, Thomas Zweifel, *International Organizations and Democracy* (Boulder: Lynne Rienner Publishers, 2006); Daniele Archibugi, David Held, and Martin Kohler, eds., *Reimagining Political Community: Studies in Cosmopolitan Democracy* (Palo Alto: Stanford University Press, 1998); Richard Burchill, ed., *Democracy and International Law* (Aldershot: Ashgate Publishing, 2006); Thomas Carothers, *Critical Mission: Essays on Democracy Promotion* (Washington, DC: Carnegie Endowment for International Peace, 2004).

[52] Toward a Community of Democracy Ministerial Conference, "Final Warsaw Declaration: Toward a Community of Democracies," Warsaw, Poland, June 27, 2008. Available at: http://www.ccd21.org/articles/warsaw_declaration.htm.

[53] Ivo Daalder and James Lindsay, "Democracies of the World Unite," *The American Interest*, Vol. 2(3), Jan–Feb, 2007. Cf. Charles Kupchan, "Minor League, Major Problems: The Case against a League of Democracies," *Foreign Affairs*, Vol. 87(6), Nov–Dec, 2008.

[54] United Nations Commission on Human Rights Resolution, 1999/57.

[55] "In Larger Freedom," para. 149.

for Democracy and Electoral Assistance in Stockholm have become increasingly influential promoters of democracy around the world.

Further evidence includes the many regional organizations that list democracy promotion as one of their goals (the EU, AU, OAS, NATO, OSCE, ASEAN, Commonwealth, Mercosur, Andean Community, and ECOWAS), and it is a condition of membership for some (the Copenhagen criteria for accession to the EU require "stable institutions guaranteeing democracy"). The Commonwealth has suspended Nigeria, Pakistan, Fiji, Zimbabwe, and Pakistan again for persistent violations of the democratic principles set out in the Harare Declaration of 1991. The CSCE (now OSCE) 1991 Moscow Document directs member states not to recognize a regime that usurps power from a democratically elected government. In June 1991, the OAS adopted the Santiago Commitment to Democracy and Development, later given bite in the 1992 Protocol of Washington and the 2001 Inter-American Democratic Charter, which says that "unconstitutional interruption of the democratic order shall lead to suspension" from the organization (invoked in respect of Haiti, Guatemala, Peru, and Venezuela). In 1996, Mercosur added a "democracy clause" to its rules on membership in the organization, following an attempted coup against President Juan Carlos Wasmosy of Paraguay. The clause commits Brazil, Argentina, Uruguay, and now Venezuela to apply joint sanctions against any disruption in democratic institutions.[56] An Additional Protocol to the Andean Community's Cartagena Agreement (2000) stipulates that states can be suspended or sanctions imposed if there is a rupture in the democratic order.

Perhaps most strikingly, in July 1999, the OAU declared that any OAU member state whose government came to power by unconstitutional means after 1997 would be prohibited from participating in OAU meetings – reaffirmed in Article 30 of the Constitutive Act of the African Union. Comoros, Côte d'Ivoire, and Madagascar have all been suspended on the basis of that Article. The New Partnership for Africa's Development (NEPAD) has a peer-review system now under the auspices of the AU designed to promote "democracy, governance and peace and security" in Africa, as well as development. As of July 2008, twenty-nine countries had signed up for the process, including most of the countries that have been leading the democracy movement in South Africa. These regional instruments have not been applied consistently – as the inaction on Zimbabwe demonstrates – but they must be accounted for before dismissing "democratization" as a purely Western agenda.

Impact of the Democracy Norm on Peace Operations

An idea that runs through UN reports on peace operations is that strengthening democratic institutions has the effect not of doing away with all conflicts but of

---

[56] For a comprehensive review of democracy clauses in the charters of regional organizations, see Theodore Piccone, "International Mechanisms for Protecting Democracy," in Morton Halperin and Mirna Galic, eds., *Protecting Democracies: International Responses* (Lanham: Lexington Books, 2005).

ensuring that the natural conflicts of any society are resolved peacefully. A stated goal of peacebuilding is "participatory governance."[57] The transition period in a peace process is an opportunity to design institutions that foster nonviolent contestation and conciliatory politics.[58] They hold the promise of what Michael Doyle and Nicholas Sambanis call "participatory peace,"[59] which may but will not necessarily evolve into more robust forms of democratic governance.

Accordingly, the postconflict peacebuilding work of the UN includes measures like helping to convert rebel groups into political parties; institution building to create channels for political participation; support to civil society and marginalized groups; and assistance in the drafting and adoption of constitutions. Elections are the most common "democratic" feature of peace operations. The UN and regional organizations have conducted, certified, or helped with numerous elections in peace processes. They offer different forms of electoral assistance, ranging from organizing the entire election (as the UN did in Cambodia, Eastern Slavonia, and East Timor; and the OSCE has done in Bosnia and Kosovo), to supervision and verification (as the UN did in Namibia, El Salvador, Liberia, and the Democratic Republic of the Congo, and the OAS has done in Haiti), to coordination and support of international and national observers, to the provision of technical assistance by reviewing electoral laws and training electoral officials. When the UN or another organization certifies an election as free and fair, it is providing a stamp of international legitimacy that under a Westphalian concept of sovereignty would have been seen as unnecessary, even offensive. That many governments want – even need – this stamp of legitimacy says something important about the normative shift brought about by the democratization agenda.

The larger question in the context of peace operations is whether this reflects a purely Western, neoliberal agenda. Are peacekeeping and peacebuilding, to the extent that they aim to promote democracy, exercises in neocolonialism? If it is primarily Western and Northern countries – or organizations controlled by those countries – doing peacebuilding in the South, then it starts to look like what Roland Paris calls a modern version of the "mission civilatrice": the transformation of war-shattered societies into liberal democratic states with market-oriented economies – an ideological mission, in which the peacebuilders convey ideas of what a state should look like.[60] There does seem to be a "peacebuilding consensus" about the value of projecting a set of governance norms rooted in Western models, although the peace operations themselves (as opposed to international financial institutions

---

[57] Report of the Secretary-General to the Security Council "No Exit without Strategy," S/2001/394, April 20, 2001.

[58] Terrence Lyons, "Transforming the Institutions of War: Post-Conflict Elections and the Reconstruction of Failed States," in Robert Rotberg, ed., *When States Fail: Causes and Consequences* (Princeton: Princeton University Press, 2003).

[59] Michael Doyle and Nicholas Sambanis, *Making War and Building Peace* (Princeton: Princeton University Press, 2006), pp. 18–19.

[60] Roland Paris, *At War's End* (Cambridge: Cambridge University Press, 2004).

and bilateral donors) are less involved in inculcating economic liberalization.[61] But, to the extent that there is an emerging international consensus on the value of participatory governance, as argued previously, it is too simplistic to dismiss this as an entirely Western ideal.

Impact of the Democracy Norm on Other Operational Activities

Democratization is also part of the broader "good governance" agenda of the UN Development Program (UNDP), World Bank, EU, and other development agencies and donor governments. In *An Agenda for Democratization*, Boutros-Ghali analogizes democracy assistance to development assistance, allowing him to claim that the UN's work in this area is not interference in internal affairs in violation of Article II(VII) of the Charter.[62] The UN's role is not to offer a particular model or to impose a particular form of democracy – "each society must be able to choose the form, pace, and character of its democratization project" – but to respond to requests for assistance as best it can.

In 1997, there was a watershed in World Bank thinking about development. Articulated most forcefully in the 1997 World Development Report, it represents a shift away from the 1980s and early 1990s consensus in favor of a minimalist state, focusing instead on state effectiveness: in other words, not less government, but better government.[63] Improving state effectiveness requires reinvigorating public institutions and "bringing the state closer to the people." This meant giving people a voice, through the ballot box or by allowing those most directly affected by decisions greater participation in making those decisions.

This good governance agenda was taken a step further by the UNDP, culminating in its 2002 Human Development Report, "Deepening Democracy in a Fragmented World." Deeper democracy means stronger democratic institutions: political parties, an independent electoral system, separation of powers, vibrant civil society, free press, and civilian control over the military. Many of these activities are undertaken in the context of postconflict peacebuilding, but good governance has become a guiding principle for a broad range of UNDP programs.[64] What is most striking is the extent to which this conception goes beyond the early good governance agenda of the World Bank, whose roots were in structural adjustment and economic liberalization, and whose focus was on public sector management.[65] In the 1990s the UNDP

---

[61] Oliver Richmond, *The Transformation of Peace* (New York: Palgrave Macmillan, 2007).

[62] Boutros-Ghali, *An Agenda for Democratization*, para. 8.

[63] World Development Report 1997.

[64] Close to 40% of the UNDP's budget supports democratic governance in some way. The 2002 Human Development Report, "Deepening Democracy in a Fragmented World," makes the case for a connection between democracy and development, as well as peace.

[65] On the good governance agenda of the World Bank, see in particular the World Development Report of 1997, "The State in a Changing World." For a good comparison of the UNDP and World Bank approaches to good governance see Thomas Weiss, "Governance, Good Governance and Global Governance: Conceptual and Actual Challenges," *Third World Quarterly* 21, Issue 5 (2000), p. 795ff.

expanded the concept to include the strengthening of legislative and judicial institutions, empowering the poor through participation, promoting decentralization, strengthening local governance, and working with civil society organizations.[66] It goes beyond good economic management to include an emphasis on the political and civic dimensions of governance.

COUNTERTERRORISM

The Normative Framework for Counterterrorism

As noted in the introduction, despite the absence of an agreed definition of terrorism, the post–9/11 climate has generated a set of expectations about the need for collective action to counter terrorism, which – though not universal – suggests a degree of international consensus that was elusive prior to the attacks on the World Trade Center and the Pentagon. The United States led the charge, tapping into a normative process that had been underway for some years. Terrorism has been on the UN agenda since at least 1963, when the Convention on Offences and Certain Other Acts Committed on Board Aircraft was adopted. It was followed by twelve more treaties, the most recent of which are the 2002 International Convention for the Suppression of the Financing of Terrorism and the 2005 Convention on Nuclear Terrorism. Efforts to adopt a comprehensive convention against terrorism have foundered on the problem of a definition, most recently in the General Assembly session immediately after 9/11 and then again at the 2005 World Summit where the Secretary-General's attempt at a definition was rejected. Instead, the various conventions criminalize specific acts. The net effect is a normative framework that conceives terrorism as a global problem and requires or encourages states to adopt collaborative law enforcement measures to address the problem.

The normative framework has been stiffened by UN Security Council sanctions imposed in response to acts of terrorism – against Libya in 1992 following the Lockerbie incident, against Sudan in 1996, with respect to the assassination attempt on Egyptian President Mubarak, and against the Taliban in 1999, following the bombing of U.S. embassies in Kenya and Tanzania, for which Osama Bin Laden was held responsible. The sanctions resolutions have been accompanied by a long list of Security Council resolutions condemning specific acts of terrorism, like the hostage taking and death of numerous children in Beslan, Russia, and the bombings in Spain, as well as more generic statements on the need for collective action.[67] Indeed, in the resolution following Beslan, the Security Council achieved the elusive goal of agreement on a definition of terrorism.[68]

---

[66] For a statement of UNDP's work in this field, see Mark Malloch Brown, "Democratic Governance: toward a Framework for Sustainable Peace," *Global Governance* Vol. 9, No. 2 (April-June 2003), pp. 141–6.

[67] For the list of resolutions, see www.un.org/terrorism/SC-res.shtml.

[68] SC Resolution 1566 (October 8, 2004), para. 3.

Even more far-reaching, the Security Council adopted Resolution 1373 in the immediate aftermath of 9/11, obliging states to take a wide range of measures to prevent future terrorist acts. This unprecedented act of legislation by the Security Council imposes binding obligations on all states under Chapter VII of the UN Charter. It is not designed to resolve a specific dispute or bring about an end to a conflict, nor to compel a state to act or refrain from acting in a certain way. Instead, it imposes general obligations in a broad issue area for an indefinite period. This is qualitatively different from the Council's normal crisis management role. In adopting Resolution 1373, the Security Council was acting like a global legislature. The Security Council "legislated" again when it adopted Resolution 1540 in the year 2004, designed to stop weapons of mass destruction from falling into the hands of terrorists.

Meanwhile, the General Assembly has adopted a Global Counter-Terrorism Strategy, and the Secretary-General has established a Counter-Terrorism Task Force bringing together twenty-five entities from the UN system. Both of these initiatives originated with the Secretary-General. Moreover, the "collaborative law enforcement" policy is leading to the establishment of networks of governmental, intergovernmental, and private sector actors. For example, an international financial sector network is emerging, which includes the UN's Counter-Terrorism Committee, the UN Office for Drugs and Crime Prevention, INTERPOL, the OECD's Financial Action Task Force, the World Customs Organization, national regulatory agencies, financial intelligence units, banks, and other financial institutions.[69]

Impact of Counterterrorism Agenda on Peace Operations

Peacekeeping has not become a tool of counterterrorism, but peace operations are increasingly being deployed where terrorist threats are thought to exist.[70] The most obvious examples are Iraq and Afghanistan. In the first, coalition troops are engaged in direct combat against terrorists. Although the U.S.-led coalition in Iraq cannot properly be called a peace operation, the situation in Afghanistan illustrates how blurred the line between robust peacekeeping (where force is used for limited purposes) and war (where force is used to defeat an enemy) has become. From 2006, British, Canadian, Dutch, and other troops that are part of the International Security Assistance Force (ISAF) have moved to the south and east of the country, joining the United States in serious combat against the Taliban, effectively fusing its ongoing counterterrorism war with the peace operation led by NATO.

[69] See generally, Alistair Millar and Eric Rosand, *Allied against Terrorism* (Washington, DC: Brookings Institution Press, 2006); and Eric Rosand, Alistair Millar, and Jason Ipe, "The United Nations Security Council's Counterterrorism Program: What Lies Ahead?" International Peace Academy Paper, October 2007, available at: http://www.globalct.org/pdf/UN_Security_Council_Counter-Terrorism_Program.PDF.

[70] This section draws on Gowan and Johnstone, *supra* n. 35.

Moreover, the phenomenon may spread. Hezbollah is perceived as a terrorist threat by the United States and Israel, and there is a real fear that peacekeepers in southern Lebanon could become the target of terrorist action by al Qaeda. Following the Ethiopian-led, U.S.-backed intervention in Somalia against the Union of Islamic Courts, AU peacekeepers face an environment where the terrorist threat is real,[71] which is an unstated reason why the UN has been reluctant to replace the AU. There have also been threats of al Qaeda attacks against UN "non-African" peacekeepers if they ever deploy to Darfur.

Meanwhile, a number of UN peace operations have taken on aspects of counterinsurgency, raising dilemmas similar to those that arise in counterterrorism operations. In Sierra Leone, UNAMSIL was mandated to "deter and, where necessary, decisively counter the threat" posed by the Revolutionary United Front (RUF). In the Democratic Republic of Congo, MONUC has the authority "to use all necessary means" against militias in the east. The need to develop a capacity for peace enforcement against these sorts of threats has been on and off the UN agenda since Boutros Boutros-Ghali's *Agenda for Peace*.[72] But the central doctrinal issue has shifted since then. The failures in Somalia and Bosnia prompted reflection on the blurring of the line between peacekeeping and peace enforcement: are they "alternative techniques" or "adjacent points on a continuum, permitting easy transition from one to another"?[73] The Brahimi Report implicitly answered that they are on a continuum and the UN ought to be capable of engaging in both types of operation. Thus the Brahimi panel stated that the UN must be prepared to deal effectively with "spoilers" (groups who renege on their commitments or otherwise seek to undermine a peace accord by violence), and that peace operations must have bigger and better equipped forces "able to pose a credible deterrent threat in contrast to the non-threatening presence that characterizes traditional peacekeeping."[74] Similarly, the Capstone Doctrine states that UN peacekeeping operations "may use force at the tactical level, with the authorization of the Security Council, if acting in self-defense and defense of the mandate" and notes that the Council has given UN missions robust mandates authorizing them to "use all necessary means to deter forceful attempts to disrupt the political process, protect civilians under imminent threat of physical attack, and/or assist the national authorities in maintaining law and order. By *proactively* using force in defense of their mandates. . . . "[75] A distinction can and should be drawn between robust peacekeeping and war: the former contemplates the use of force for limited purposes, such as the protection of civilians or to defend

---

[71] See Report of Secretary-General to the Security Council, S/2007/204, April 20, 2007, paras. 24, 25.

[72] See Ian Johnstone, Benjamin Cary Tortolani, and Richard Gowan, "The Evolution of UN Peacekeeping: Unfinished Business," *Die Friedens-Warte* 80 (2006).

[73] Boutros Boutros-Ghali, Supplement to an *Agenda for Peace*, A/50/60 – S/1995/1, January 3, 1995, para. 36.

[74] Report of the Panel on UN Peace Operations, A/55/305-S/200/809, August 21, 2000, paras. 21, 61. Available at: http://www.un.org/peace/reports/peace_operations/.

[75] Capstone Doctrine, *supra* n. 34, pp. 33–34.

a peace process; the latter entails the use of force to defeat a designated enemy. The Capstone Doctrine is a step toward drawing that line, but detailed operational guidance has yet to be developed by the UN or any regional organization.

Impact on Other Operational Activities

The counterterrorism "norm" has also had an impact on efforts to stem the proliferation of weapons of mass destruction (WMD). Resolution 1540, the second truly legislative act of the Security Council, aims at preventing WMD from falling into the hands of terrorists. It demands that all states refrain from supporting efforts by nonstate actors to acquire such weapons and adopt appropriate legislation to prohibit that, as well as domestic enforcement measures to prevent WMD proliferation. It established for a period of two years – later extended for another two years, to April 2008 – a committee to oversee implementation.

Negotiation of Resolution 1540 was more contentious than 1373,[76] partly because it encroaches more deeply on existing nonproliferation treaties and the institutions established to monitor them. Ultimately, the resolution was adopted unanimously because those who had doubts about the propriety of this kind of Security Council action (such as Pakistan and India) could claim it temporarily filled a gap in the law to address an urgent threat, pending adoption of a multilateral treaty. They were also reassured by the explicit assurance in the resolution that it would "not conflict with or alter the rights and obligations" of parties to existing conventions. And the fact that it was explicitly connected to terrorism made the resolution more acceptable: as an antiterrorism rather than nonproliferation measure, it was easier to rationalize the minimal references in it to disarmament.[77]

Resolution 1540 has had some impact on the operational activities of the International Atomic Energy Agency (IAEA). The relationship between the 1540 committee and the IAEA is complementary. Operative paragraph 5 holds that "none of the obligations set forth in the resolution shall be interpreted so as to conflict with . . . or alter the responsibilities of the IAEA . . . " Many aspects of the IAEA's statutory mission are relevant to the objectives of the resolution, including legislative assistance, training to strengthen control over nuclear material, the development of standards for the

---

[76] The concerns expressed in the Security Council meetings of April 22 and April 28. S.PV.4950, April 22, 2004; S/PV.4956, April 28, 2004. They were also elaborated in my interviews with diplomats from the United States, Spain, Brazil, India, and Pakistan, between July 19 and July 21, all of whom were involved in the negotiations.

[77] Brazil in particular wanted to avoid the term "nonproliferation" in connection with SCR 1540, as that applied to states, and instead wanted to introduce new concepts like "non-access, non-transfer and non-availability" to nonstate actors. S/PV.4950, p. 4. On the connection between 1540 and the broader counterterrorism agenda of the Security Council, see Peter van Ham and Olivia Bosch, "Global Non-Proliferation and Counter-Terrorism: The Role of Resolution 1540 and Its Implications," in Olivia Bosch and Peter van Ham, eds., Global Non-Proliferation and Counter-Terrorism: The Impact of UNSCR 1540 (Washington, DC: Brookings Institution Press, 2007), pp. 7–9.

physical protection of nuclear material and facilities, and border control.[78] Resolution 1540 has similar implications for the Chemical Weapons Convention and the work of the Organization for the Prohibition of Chemical Weapons.[79] The effect on the biological weapons regime may be even more profound as there is no inspectorate for that treaty, meaning that 1540 establishes for the first time a rudimentary monitoring and verification system.[80] Thus although the resolution does not give a new mandate to the existing organizations, it may affect their priorities. More generally, the counterterrorism agenda has put pressure on the nonproliferation inspectorates to prove their value in stopping WMD from falling into the hands of terrorists, if for no other reason than the "doctrine of preemption" was put forward by the Bush administration as an alternative means of dealing with the problem.

HOW DURABLE ARE THE NORMS?

The norms that have driven UN operational activities in the three fields described earlier were all promoted and supported by the United States. The Security Council would not have acted as it did in Somalia, Bosnia, and Haiti in the early 1990s without U.S. leadership; nor would the Kosovo intervention have occurred. Although the second Bush administration did not lead the charge to endorse the Responsibility to Protect, it did not stand in the way, and the United States has been supportive of protection of civilians mandates in peace operations. The U.S. National Security Strategies (NSS) of 1994 and 1996 describe multilateral peace operations that "support democracy or conflict resolution" as a means of protecting U.S. national security, and referred to Bosnia, Cambodia, El Salvador, and elsewhere as places where the United States committed resources to achieve these ends.[81] The United States was the main sponsor of the Commission on Human Rights resolution promoting the right to democracy, and it has been supportive of the "good governance" agendas of the World Bank and UNDP. Resolutions 1373 and 1540 were both U.S. initiatives, the connection between counterterrorism and peace operations is explicitly drawn in the 2006 National Security Strategy,[82] and peace operations in places like Afghanistan and Somalia are seen by the United States as useful in the war on terrorism.

---

[78] Tariq Rauf and Jan Lodding, "UNSCR 1540 and the Role of the IAEA," in Bosch and van Ham, eds., *Global Non-Proliferation and Counter-Terrorism*, pp. 86–95.

[79] Ron Manley, "Restricting Non-state Actors Access to Chemical Weapons and Related Materials: Implications for UNSCR Resolution 1540," in Bosch and van Ham, eds., *Global Non-Proliferation and Counter-Terrorism*, pp. 73–85.

[80] Angela Woodward, "The Biological Weapons Convention and UNSCR 1540," in Bosch and van Ham, eds., *Global Non-Proliferation and Counter-Terrorism*, pp. 96–112.

[81] A *National Security Strategy of Engagement and Enlargement*, The White House, Washington DC, July 1994; A *National Security Strategy of Engagement and Enlargement*, The White House, Washington DC, February 1996.

[82] The *National Security Strategy of the United States of America*, The White House, Washington DC, March 2006, p. 16.

Yet none of the norms are deeply embedded in the discourse and operational activities of the UN. Indeed, recent developments, including actions by the United States, have raised questions about the depth of commitment to all three as well as possible conflicts among them. The watered-down language and reluctance to adopt criteria on R2P at the World Summit suggest continuing disagreement about the scope of the norm. The Secretary-General sought to find common ground in his January 2009 report on implementation by defining R2P broadly to encompass a wide array of functions the UN has always engaged in under different names (like conflict prevention and human rights monitoring). Yet the sharp end of the stick is coercive action and on that consensus has been elusive. The extended delay in sending a robust peacekeeping force to Darfur casts doubt on the will of the international community to carry through on the commitment, doubts that had not been laid to rest by the deployment of UNAMID in early 2008 given the many obstacles that remain in the path toward it becoming an effective operation. Moreover, John Prendergast and Colin Thomas-Jensen allege that the Bush administration's reluctance to push the government of Sudan harder on Darfur related to its continuing need for collaboration on terrorism – a conflict between humanitarian and counterterrorism norms that may play out elsewhere.[83]

Similarly, the invasion of Iraq set back the democratization agenda. How far that agenda had progressed is symbolized by the Arab Human Development Report of 2002, produced by a group of Arab scholars, which claimed that one of the principal barriers to better economic performance in the region was a lack of democratic freedoms and concluded that political pluralism should become a priority for Arab countries.[84] The controversial report was discussed in the Arab League for several years, and the organization even flirted with the idea of declaring a commitment to democratic reforms. This, however, became entangled with the U.S. "Broader Middle East Initiative," which linked the change of regime in Iraq to a strategy of promoting democracy in the Middle East and North Africa. Meanwhile, setbacks for U.S. policy in Iraq provided regimes in the Middle East a reprieve from the pressure to democratize.[85] Thomas Carothers claims autocratic regimes around the world have won public sympathy by arguing that opposition to Western democracy promotion is resistance not to democracy itself, but to American interventionism.[86] And the U.S. cooperation with Pakistan in the "global war on terror" came into sharp

---

[83] John Prendergast and Colin Thomas-Jensen, "Blowing the Horn," *Foreign Affairs* 86, No. 2 (2007), p. 60. For a good analysis of the U.S. conflicting agendas in Africa, see S. Sarjoh Bah and Kwesi Aning, "US Peace Operations Policy in Africa: From ACRI to AFRICOM," *International Peacekeeping* 15 No. 1 (2008).

[84] United Nations Development Programme, *Arab Human Development Report 2002*, pp. 2, 9.

[85] Marina Ottaway, "Who Wins in Iraq? Arab Dictators," *Foreign Policy* (March/April 2007), pp. 46–47.

[86] See also Thomas Carothers, "The Backlash against Democracy Promotion," *Foreign Affairs* 85, No. 2 (Mar/Apr 2007).

conflict with its democratization agenda, culminating in the rather tepid reaction to President Musharaff's suspension of the constitution and assumption of emergency powers in November 2007. The broader setback to democracy is highlighted by Freedom House, which saw reversals in political rights and civil liberties in 34 countries in the year 2008, although the number of electoral democracies only dropped by 2 to 91.[87]

Global counterterrorism efforts, meanwhile, have suffered from the formalization of the doctrine of preemption in the United States' National Security Strategy of 2002. Though not the official U.S. justification for military action in Iraq,[88] the Bush administration made the war look like the first test of this novel doctrine by referring to it often in the months before March 2003. Widespread international skepticism about the doctrine has sharpened divisions between those who see the struggle against terrorism as essentially a "war" to be fought through military means and those who would cast it as a matter of law enforcement and "battle of ideas."

Resistance to the three norms also seems to be building in centers of power other than the United States. Thus China is deeply reluctant to embrace the Responsibility to Protect, Russia and many post-Soviet states have dug in their heels against democracy promotion (and tellingly, Russia obstructed the deployment of OSCE observers for its parliamentary elections in 2007), and the Security Council's counterterrorism efforts have faced court challenges in the European Court of Justice and various national courts.[89]

Although these developments raise questions about the depth of commitment to the norms, they do not cast doubt on their durability. Indeed, some of the debates and difficulties encountered in operationalizing the norms may strengthen them. Consider, for example, the dilemmas associated with implementing protection of civilians mandates in peace operations. Probably the most serious dilemma is that, without adequate capacity, it can generate expectations that will not be fulfilled, despite the qualifying words "within the limits of the mission's capabilities and areas of operations." After Rwanda and Srebrenica, peacekeepers cannot simply stand by as civilians are massacred. But if peacekeepers were to be held responsible for every death they fail to prevent, the number of countries willing to contribute troops or police would decline dramatically. This and other dilemmas have prompted concern about the mandate – in the UN Secretariat and among troop contributors – and, as noted previously, prompted an acrimonious debate in the C-34. The

---

[87] *Freedom in the World 2009*, available at http://www.freedomhouse.org/template.cfm?page=70& release=756. This followed a similar decline in 2007, when 38 countries showed democratic setbacks. Available at: http://www.freedomhouse.org/template.cfm?page=395.

[88] See William Taft and Todd Buchwald, "Pre-emption, Iraq and International Law." *American Journal of International Law* 97 (July 2003), pp. 557ff.

[89] Ian Johnstone, "Legislation and Adjudication in the UN Security Council: Bringing down the Deliberative Deficit," *American Journal of International Law* 108 (2008).

debate nevertheless ended with an implicit appeal to develop doctrine (or in UN parlance "guidance") for the protection of civilians. Moreover, concerns about mandate implementation do not necessarily undermine the significance of the R2P norm; if anything, they will help it to develop in a viable way. Adopting expansive versions of a norm in intergovernmental conferences will not lead to behavior changes if they are impossible to implement. The case-by-case application by peacekeepers is a way of rendering an abstract concept like the Responsibility to Protect operational in an incremental way.

Similarly, *The Economist* argues that the democratic reversals of the last year (e.g., in Pakistan, Bangladesh, Kenya, and Russia), while worrying, do not signify a lasting trend: "Freedom House may well be right that democracy is on the back foot right now. In the longer run, its appeal is undiminished."[90] Peace operations, development agencies, and other international organizations have not abandoned democracy promotion, though good governance and participation are the more commonly used terms. It is unfortunate that democratization has come to be seen as an exclusively American endeavor, and that "democracy promotion" looks to many like a code word for "regime change."[91] The EU, OSCE, UNDP, and World Bank are still in business (as of this writing), and NEPAD and its peer review mechanism are still going concerns. Through experience, international organizations (including peace operations) have become more sophisticated about what democracy means and more sensitive about how to promote it. Indeed, those engaged in peacebuilding tend to be torn between the desire to play a proactive role in promoting international standards and the felt need to defer to "local ownership." Principles and methods drawn from the theory of deliberative democracy may be a way of reconciling these imperatives, while fostering the sort of participatory governance that sustainable peace requires.[92]

Cooperation on counterterrorism within international organizations remains a priority more than ever, in part because the alternative – unilateral, preemptive military action – is deeply problematic. Despite the reservations about Resolutions 1267, 1373, and 1540, the committees established to implement them are still functioning. In fact, the listing regime embodied in resolution 1267 and its progeny has been reformed, partly in response to the due process objections that have been raised and in order to preempt future court challenges. The UN General Assembly's global counterterrorism strategy, adopted in September 2006, reflects greater international agreement than many imagined was possible. Responsibility for carrying out that strategy lies with the Counter-Terrorism Implementation Task Force, a collection

---

[90] *The Economist*, "Democracy in Retreat: Freedom Marches Backward – Why the Setback Is Likely to Be Temporary" (January 19, 2008), p. 12.

[91] Carothers, *supra* n. 86.

[92] Johnstone, "Consolidating Peace: Priorities and Deliberative Processes," in *Annual Review of Global Peace Operations*; Michael Barnett, "Building a Republican Peace: Stabilizing States after War," *International Security* 30, No. 4 (2006), pp. 87–112.

Normative Evolution at the UN: Impact on Operational Activities   213

of more than twenty entities established in July 2005 to coordinate activities across the UN system.[93]

It is clear that the UN remains a conducive venue for the United States to project its soft power and promote norms.[94] Paradoxically, this is in part because other countries value the institution so highly. The permanent members of the Security Council certainly do, not least because the Council enables each to punch above its weight in global affairs.[95] This gives the United States considerable leverage over those countries, knowing the stock they place in keeping the United States engaged in the Council. The same logic applies, albeit with less force, to the rest of the UN membership. Precisely because weaker states value the UN as a venue for advancing their goals, the United States can use the organization to gain assent to its normative positions. The election of President Barack Obama creates an opportunity to recoup some of the normative leadership lost during the Bush years.

CONCLUSION

Thus the norms the United States helped to create and advance in the UN still have life. Having become institutionalized, they influence even the most powerful states. The U.S. government does not want to be seen as indifferent to the plight of civilians suffering atrocities, let alone back off from a commitment to democracy abroad or global cooperation on counterterrorism. These values do not always override other interests and they often conflict with one another; indeed, the extent to which any one of the norms is not respected in practice may have more to do with conflicts among them than a loss of relevance. Humanitarian and counterterrorism goals are not inherently incompatible – rebuilding weak states serves both – but reconciling them in particular cases, like Darfur and Somalia, is a political challenge. Democracy promotion can help in the fight against terrorism, but the two are not self-evidently mutually reinforcing.[96] Even the Responsibility to Protect and democratization, which would seem on the surface to be closely related, can create operational tensions. Protecting civilians in Darfur, for example, may require robust military action against government forces and their proxies, as well as the indictment of

[93] For a comprehensive review of progress made in implementing the global counterterrorism strategy, see Eric Rosand, "From Adoption to Action: the UN's Role in Implementing Its Global Counterterrorism Strategy," Center on Global Counterterrorism Cooperation, Policy Brief April 2009, http://globalct.org/images/content/pdf/policybriefs/rosand_policybrief_091.pdf.

[94] Joseph Nye argues that "soft power will help the US endure as the dominant state by turning its power into international consensus and U.S. principles into international norms," in *The Paradox of American Power* (Oxford: Oxford University Press, 2002), p. 69.

[95] Mats Berdal, "The UN Security Council: Ineffective but Indispensable," *Survival* 45, No. 2 (2003), pp. 10–14.

[96] On the conflict between counterterrorism and democracy promotion, see Audrey Ruth Cronin, "How Al-Qaida Ends: The Decline and Demise of Terrorist Groups," *International Security* 31, No. 1 (Summer 2006), pp. 7–48; Robert Art and Louise Richardson, *Democracy and Counter-terrorism: Lessons from the Past* (Washington DC: USIP, 2007).

war criminals. But the reaction of the ruling party in Sudan (the NCP) to forceful international action is likely to complicate achievement of the more long-term goal of creating a more pluralistic, democratic central government.

These tensions and contradictions are not resolved by sitting around a conference table, but through the rough and tumble of international practice. As this chapter has argued, a good deal of that practice occurs under UN auspices. States are still the principal actors but they are engaged in a fluid, pluralistic form of multilateralism. Alongside the executive branch and diplomatic arms of governments, legislatures and regulatory agencies are playing a more direct role in shaping what occurs in and around the UN. The Secretary-General and Secretariat have considerable autonomy, giving content to norms through the management of operational activities like peacekeeping, electoral assistance, and counterterrorism programs. NGOs and the private sector both advocate policies and partner with the UN and governments in implementing those policies. The process is dynamic and "sticky": as norms take root they influence practice; that practice in turn tends to embed the norms more deeply. And although the U.S. presidency has greater capacity than any other actor to drive this process, it cannot undo what it puts in motion by the stroke of a pen. The resilience of the norms described in this chapter, despite the hard knocks they have taken in recent years, testifies to their power.

11

Constructing Sovereignty for Security[1]

Barnett R. Rubin

The December 2004 report of the United Nations (UN) Secretary-General's High-level Panel on Threats, Challenges, and Change proposed the establishment of an intergovernmental Peacebuilding Commission to oversee UN operations to rebuild states after armed conflict. This commission would exercise budgetary authority over a Peacebuilding Fund, which would be kept fully replenished in advance of operations and would contain nonearmarked contributions. A Peacebuilding Support Office within the UN Secretariat would support the commission.[2]

In the aftermath of war, international actors often fret about the incoherence, tribalism, and division of war-torn countries. The High-level Panel's recommendations, however, recognize that the divisions, rivalries, and fragmentation of authority of the "international community" have constituted just as big an obstacle to what the UN calls "peacebuilding." The creation of a unified, multilateral decision-making body as a counterpart for the national government receiving the aid could finally make it possible to implement the Brahimi Report's recommendation for "integrated missions."[3]

Although political sensitivities prevented the panel from using the term "state-building," such operations have the paradoxical mission of helping others build sovereign states. They constitute the contemporary version of a long-standing security task – the stabilization of the periphery by Great Powers – which now must be carried out in a world governed by the universal juridical sovereignty of the nation-state. Even the administration of U.S. President George W. Bush, which adopted

---

[1] An earlier version of this article appeared in *Survival* 47, No. 4 (Winter 2005), pp. 93–106. The author and editors of this volume wish to thank the editor of *Survival* and Taylor and Francis for permission to reproduce it here.

[2] Report of the High-level Panel on Threats, Challenges and Change, *A More Secure World: Our Shared Responsibility*, A/59/565 (New York: United Nations, 2004); and "In Larger Freedom: Towards Development, Security and Human Rights for All," A/59/2005, available at: http://www.un.org/largerfreedom.

[3] Report of the Panel on United Nations Peace Operations (The Brahimi Report) (A/55/305-S/2000/809).

a doctrine of preventive war on the basis of unilateral judgment that governments might threaten U.S. security, was constrained to act within the same regime. Its inability to motivate Iraqis or international partners to collaborate with an occupation regime forced the administration to call on the UN to assist in the (initially unwanted) transfer of sovereignty to Iraqis.

This recourse to the UN, despite political differences between proponents of multilateral peacebuilding and prosecutors of unilateral preventive war, showed that these projects responded to a common security environment. The central fact of the environment in the past half-century has been the replacement of global juridical imperialism by global juridical national sovereignty. The UN incorporates this organizing principle in its charter. This structure has altered the options available to Great Powers for coping with security threats or challenges to their interests.

FROM IMPERIALISM TO PEACEBUILDING

The use by various states and organizations of specific terms for these operations such as "peacebuilding," "postconflict reconstruction," "nation building," or "stabilization" displaces these operations from their historical context. The use of different terms and the different types and degrees of political conflicts over the interventions in Afghanistan, Iraq, or Darfur show that such actions are not all manifestations of a common project. The U.S. pursuit of security from both terrorism and challenges to its strategic dominance has different implications than the pursuit of human security through processes of global governance. These doctrines, however, constitute different responses to a common problem: maintaining order and security, however defined, in an increasingly integrated global system juridically and politically organized around universal state sovereignty.

For centuries stronger powers have intervened along their peripheries to establish politically acceptable forms of order. Initially unlinked regional empires (China, Rome, Mayan) tried to stabilize relations with unruly peoples on their frontiers. With the construction of a more tightly linked system of mutually recognized and demarcated states in post-Westphalian Europe, the quest for security and profit on the periphery became an imperial – and ultimately global – extension of interstate competition among a single system of core states. European states tried to assure their interests by integrating new territories through conquest or royal marriages, imposing direct or indirect colonial rule, supporting subordinate buffer states, settling occupied territories with immigrants from Europe, and waging one kind of war against rebellious natives and another kind of war against each other. They tried to regulate their competition and make it more predictable through meetings such as the Berlin Conference, which tried to establish a stable division of colonial rule in Africa. For the first time, states cooperated to impose a common juridical framework over the entire globe, albeit one that institutionalized unequal political and legal status for different territories and peoples.

Constructing Sovereignty for Security 217

Creating such a common global framework was a precondition for transforming it. The contemporary global framework for security developed with the foundation of the UN system immediately after World War II. That war not only defeated fascism but also ended imperialism as a legitimate legal doctrine. The UN's first task was overseeing decolonization, extending the international regime of national sovereignty enshrined in the charter to the entire globe, a process that continued through the UN-supervised transition to independence of Timor Leste in 2002.

During the Cold War, the struggle over building postcolonial states largely took the form of competing foreign aid projects by the alliance systems led by the United States and the Soviet Union. Postcolonial states positioned themselves within the strategic relations of the Cold War. To extract aid, they sometimes adopted, or pretended to adopt, structures based on models supported by one or the other global contender.

The end of the Cold War freed the UN and some regional organizations to replace unilateral clientelism with multilateral statebuilding efforts, especially in the aftermath of conflict. Agreement by the Security Council to entrust such operations to the UN reflected both the end of zero-sum strategic competition and the lowering of the stakes in who controlled these states. Major powers had less interest in either undermining or supporting such efforts.

The terrorist attacks of September 11, 2001, showed that the United States could now be attacked from even the weakest state and hence reignited U.S. nationalists' strategic interest in the periphery. The regime of universal sovereignty, however, requires more powerful states and international organizations to work through the institutions of nation-states. Postwar operations attempt to transform states, rather than absorb them into other, more powerful, units.[4]

PEACEBUILDING AND STABILIZATION

Reduced to basics, state formation consists of the interdependent mobilization by a sovereign of three types of resources: coercion, capital, and legitimacy.[5] The sovereign wields coercion, in the form of what we hopefully call security institutions, to exercise a monopoly of (legitimate) force over a territory. He needs the accumulation of capital to produce income that can be extracted as revenues to fund state functions and services. Symbolic and cultural resources consecrate the use of force and public revenues as legitimate and link them into a meaningful whole to induce people to comply voluntarily as citizens. The state claims to exercise its power as the delegate of an imagined community – the nation.

---

[4] Robert Jackson and Carl G. Rosberg, "Why Africa's Weak States Persist: The Empirical and the Juridical in Statehood," *World Politics* 35, no. 1 (1982), pp. 1–24. For a recent interpretation, see Michael Barnett, "The New United Nations Politics of Peace: From Juridical Sovereignty to Empirical Sovereignty," *Global Governance* 1, no. 1 (winter 1995), pp. 79–97.

[5] Charles Tilly, *Coercion, Capital, and European States, AD 990–1992* (Oxford: Blackwell, 1992).

These resources have historically been mobilized in different combinations and contexts to build, destroy, or undermine states. Contrary to nationalist historiography, states do not form in isolation but in relation to one another, as part of an interstate system. Interstate borders need states on both sides – the Great Wall of China was not a border in the modern sense, as the Middle Kingdom did not recognize any equivalent entity on the other side. States' locations in the international strategic and market systems have largely determined the ways that they have formed. Some developed as trading (capital-intensive) states; others, as more militarized (coercion-intensive) ones. Some extracted resources from foreign conquests or investments and others from domestic economic development or external relations of dependence.

The generalization of the sovereign nation-state and the consecration of the territorial integrity of existing states by the UN system have altered the environment for latter-day state builders. During the formation of nation-states in Europe, rulers struggled and negotiated with subjects (who became citizens) to extract resources to wage war against external threats. In the postcolonial world, rulers struggled and negotiated with external powers to gain aid or capital to protect themselves from domestic threats. Citizens often became disenfranchised, as rulers looked to foreign patrons rather than to citizens for power resources. External powers were motivated not by concern for apolitical "stability," but by the strategic competition of the Cold War (and now the "global war on terror"), as well as by economic interests.

This process of extroverted state formation underlies many changes in the international system, including the shift from interstate to intrastate warfare and the crises of legitimacy and capacity of postcolonial states, leading to the violent contestation and collapse of many. Some states – Sierra Leone, Liberia – have collapsed due to a lack of strategic importance combined with access to resources that funded armed oppositions. Others – Afghanistan, Democratic Republic of the Congo – have collapsed due to competing political projects by global or regional powers that undermined the weak states. These crises have thus generated many of the apparently domestic armed conflicts that have confronted international actors in the past several decades.

Participants in peacebuilding or stabilization operations attempt to use foreign resources of the same types to build acceptable states in areas that pose a perceived threat to powerful actors. The threat may derive from the control of a state by an anti-status quo leader ("rogue" states – the main concern of the United States) or the breakdown of control under the impact of strategic or economic competition ("failed" or collapsing states – of greater concern to globalist humanitarians). These operations aim at building states, sometimes after a transitional stage of international administration or occupation. They aim to make such states more effective agents of control over their own territories and population. To what extent states exercise this control as sovereigns, in the service of nationally determined goals, and to what extent as agents of externally defined interests, whether hegemonic powers or international

Constructing Sovereignty for Security   219

standards, constitutes what Ghassan Salamé calls the "dual legitimacy" problem of global state formation.[6]

INTERNATIONALIZED STATEBUILDING

The doctrines of the states and organizations engaged in this effort often contradict the goal of statebuilding. Building a nation-state means creating a sovereign center of political accountability, which is not necessarily the same as building an ally in the war on terror. Multilateral operations often consist of juxtaposing existing capacities – humanitarian aid, war fighting, peacekeeping, economic guidance and assistance, civil society support, democracy assistance – without a coherent strategy. A strategic decision-maker would require command and budgetary authority over the entire operation, which was the rationale for the Brahimi Report's proposal for "integrated missions," but the main instruments of strategic planning often remain endless "coordination" meetings among rival organizations, and the stapler, which serves to assemble those organizations' programs into a single "plan."[7]

Such operations make use of the same types of resources as other processes of statebuilding: coercion, capital, and legitimacy. The core tasks of security provision are peacekeeping or other forms of international transitional security provision; dismantling irregular militias that compete with the state's monopoly of coercion (demobilization, disarmament, and reintegration, or DDR); and building new security forces, called security sector reform (SSR), which enables the state to exercise that monopoly of coercion. Completion of DDR and SSR allows the international security force to depart. These tasks are essential for developing legitimate rule, as they permit what Anthony Giddens describes as the "extrusion" of violence from politics and administration. This is the process through which military and police functions are distinguished, separating the inside of the state, regulated by rule of law, administration, and policing, from the external relations, regulated by diplomacy, military violence, and balance of power.[8]

COERCION AND SECURITY

The initial distribution of the means of violence in these operations varies. In cases of civil war or failed states, the lack of an effective, legitimate monopoly of force constitutes the problem. The foreign military defeat of incumbent regimes destroys a preexisting monopoly of violence, claimed by the invader to be illegitimate. Generally

---

[6] Ghassan Salamé, *Appels d'Empire. Ingérences et Résistances à l'âge de la mondialisation* (Paris: Fayard, 1996).
[7] Brahimi Report.
[8] Anthony Giddens, *The Nation State and Violence* (Berkeley/Los Angeles: University of California Press, 1987).

such interventions provoke an insurgency, which a new regime must co-opt or destroy, or which must succeed itself in implementing its own statebuilding agenda.

One can characterize the preoperation security situation as Tilly characterizes challenges to statebuilding, namely, the degree of accumulation and concentration of violence. "Accumulation" refers to the amount of means of violence available, and "concentration" to how widely control over them is distributed. Afghanistan, for instance, had a high degree of accumulation and a low degree of concentration (many armed groups with a lot of weapons), whereas East Timor had a low degree of accumulation and a high degree of concentration (few armed groups with few weapons). Low accumulation and high concentration of weapons combined with a high degree of legitimacy or consent constitutes the most favorable environment for peacekeeping. Higher accumulation, lower concentration, and less consent require more international forces with a more robust mandate.

Peacekeeping mandates in the early part of the 1990s presumed full agreement among warring parties and full legitimacy of the operation among all parties. This is the case of "warlord democratization," under which armed groups voluntarily demobilize in order to resolve a security dilemma, requiring confidence-building measures and transparency enforced by peacekeepers.[9]

When the agreement enjoys less consent, where some armed groups are outside the agreement, or where there is no agreement, the intervener's role cannot be one solely of resolving a security dilemma. The military intervention to defeat the Taliban and al Qaeda enjoyed broad legitimacy both internationally and domestically in Afghanistan, but the consent of the Northern Alliance factions to power sharing in the December 5, 2001, Bonn Agreement was obtained under pressure. The deposed groups (al Qaeda and Taliban) were not parties to the Bonn Agreement, and successful statebuilding requires eliminating or co-opting them. The Iraq invasion was far less legitimate, as the Security Council did not endorse it, significant portions of the Iraqi population continue to fight it, and even parts of the population who have consented to the invasion's political results appear now to want the invaders to leave.

Statebuilding operations following internal armed conflict must include measures for demobilization, disarmament, and reintegration of combatants and for changes in government security agencies (SSR). In cases of repressive, ethnicized, or racialized states (El Salvador, South Africa, Burundi), the security forces must be depoliticized and constrained to operate within the rule of law; in cases of state collapse (Afghanistan), security forces must be created, trained, and empowered to act within the rule of law.

All of these processes are intensely political. The provision of security, to some, means making those who threaten it insecure. In Afghanistan, different actors have

---

[9] Barbara F. Walter and Jack Snyder, eds., *Civil Wars, Insecurity, and Intervention* (New York: Columbia University Press, 1999). See also Leonard Wantchekon, "The Paradox of 'Warlord' Democracy: A Theoretical Investigation," *American Political Science Review* 98, no. 1 (2004), pp. 17–33.

had different security missions. The coalition came to assure the security of Americans from al Qaeda and then the Afghan government from the Taliban, initially with the assistance of local commanders and warlords. The International Security Assistance Force (ISAF) was supposed to provide the Afghan administration with security from warlord pressure, while helping the government to create new security agencies and administer a political transition to fully representative government. The UN, aid agencies, and NGOs define security as safe access to areas by civilian aid workers. Afghan civilians expected a "security assistance force" to provide them with security of their person and property, but no international force has had a mandate to provide such protection to Afghans.

Demobilizing militias and building security agencies are intimately related to the development of new political institutions. Where states and political institutions are weak, armed groups are simultaneously political, military, and economic actors – the last by necessity if they are to survive. In a model of implementation of a peace agreement, groups agree to disarm in return for guarantees of nonviolent political participation. Often, however, they cannot exercise as much power in the civilian realm and must be confronted with force or compensated. Senior leaders can receive state positions or become political leaders. Rank-and-file fighters may enter the new security forces, but that is a highly fraught political decision, as they are likely to politicize or corrupt the new forces, and it is difficult to retrain guerrillas as lawful security agents.

Training and reforming security agencies are equally political. The intense, quasireligious esprit de corps of military organizations derives from the human need to believe intensely in something for which one risks one's life. Forming effective armies and police requires formation of a national authority that can command such loyalty, not just technical training. The formation of an officer corps particularly depends on coherence and spirit in service to a mission. Hence, though effective security is necessary to carry out credible elections and other political processes, political processes that build credible, legitimate national leadership are essential to building effective security forces. It is no wonder that first elections almost invariably require international security forces.

If the state cannot sustain the recurrent cost of its security forces, its stability will always be at risk. Nor can any state long survive the funding of its army and police by foreign powers. The "Afghan National Army," fully paid for by the United States and deployed with embedded U.S. "trainers," can be only a transitional measure. States must eventually develop an economic and fiscal capacity to pay for their security forces. Economic development, capital accumulation, the collection of revenue, and the suppression of illegal, nontaxable parallel economies (such as trafficking in narcotics and other forms of smuggling) all require effective security forces. Hence among the tasks of transitional international security providers should be some they are often reluctant to assume, in particular, strengthening the government's fiscal capacity and providing security for property rights.

PUBLIC FINANCE, ASSISTANCE, CAPITAL ACCUMULATION

When peacebuilding or stabilization operations begin, local economies and the capacity of the state to deliver services are damaged by war. Many people need humanitarian assistance to return to their homes and survive. Basic assets such as roads, schools, power supplies, and financial institutions have to be built or rebuilt for economic recovery to start. To varying degrees, war-torn societies need massive building of human capital through education, training, and health care. States have often lost the capacity – to the extent that they ever had it – to mobilize even modest amounts of resources and to supply even the most basic services. Much of the economy may be informal or illegal, producing incomes for mafias or patronage networks that capture parts of the state but do not contribute to it. These economic actors use illicit force and official corruption to seize assets and exclude competitors, stifling investment.

Just as the provision of security requires transitional international security provision, so the development of state capacity to deliver public services and foster economic development requires transitional international assistance. But just as various international and local actors define security differently, so they also define economic strategy according to different models.

In the language of donors, aid must start with humanitarian assistance, move on to reconstruction, and then move on to development. The dominant modes of assistance delivery, however, ignore and indeed often undermine the fundamental strategic goal of economic assistance to statebuilding: strengthening sustainable state capacity to mobilize resources to deliver services, which requires the growth of licit economic activity, which in turn requires public services such as security, rule of law, fiscal and monetary management, and education. The mobilization of resources, finally, requires that the state develop both legitimacy (partly through service delivery) and capacity.

The central state institution that coordinates mobilization of resources, provision of services, and legitimation of state power is the budget. And it is the process of mobilizing those resources domestically, and particularly the struggle over the budget, which is at the center of the process of state formation and legitimation.

In postconflict situations, however, international donors provide most of the resources for public services. These donors are reluctant to support recurrent expenditures and usually fund other expenditures directly, through their own implementing agencies. Rather than disbursing money from a common account under the control of a political authority that can be held accountable to the nation receiving the aid, each donor country or agency maintains its separate spending mechanisms and procedures that are accountable to its own political authority. In the 2005 budget presented by the Afghan authorities, for instance, less than a quarter of all expenditures were channeled through the Afghan government's budget.[10] The creation

---

[10] Abdullah Abdullah, Minister of Finance of Afghanistan, presentation at the Afghanistan Development Forum, April 2005.

of what Ashraf Ghani has called the "dual public sector" constitutes the problem of dual legitimacy in the fiscal realm. The internationally sponsored public sector operates according to its own rules. Its salary scales tend to suck capacity out of the national government by drawing most qualified nationals into the service of international organizations. Its inflationary effect on price levels may further depress the real value of state salaries.

Accountability also suffers. As far as donor states are concerned, aid money is "spent" when it is disbursed to an agency, not when the agency implements a program. Hence multilateral statebuilding operations keep no accounts of what has been spent before projects are completed. Because citizens of the recipient countries, who hear reports of huge figures unmatched by what they think of as proportionate results, have no way to demand accountability for the funds, the frequent result is populist politics. The Afghan government passed legislation forbidding nongovernmental organizations (NGOs) from receiving government contracts just before an important donor meeting in April 2005. Former Minister of Planning Ramzan Bachardost has become one of the most popular politicians in the country by campaigning against NGOs, which he has said are more dangerous than al Qaeda.

This method of giving "aid" fails to build the legitimacy and capacity of the recipient government. The government cannot make decisions about what services are to be provided, track expenditures, or gain experience in providing public goods. Multilateral operations risk creating elected governments that are fragmented among clienteles of different aid agencies, with no political authority having the authority to pursue a coherent strategy for building sovereignty. Elected governments without budgetary authority or control over security provision hardly merit the term "democracies."

Of course, governments of countries emerging from war or violence are often incapable of exercising such responsibilities. International organizations have created a number of mechanisms to enable governments to increase their responsibility and build capacity. The most common such mechanism is a trust fund for categories of expenditure. Donors deposit nonearmarked funds in return for a voice in the management of the fund. The recipient government must provide full documentation of expenditure for approval by the fund's governors. The joint governance of the fund institutionalizes dual legitimacy transparently by providing both aid donors and the recipient government with a voice in accounting for expenditure, while empowering the government to make decisions and learn by doing. This method does not, however, enable donors to plant flags on projects or impose agendas.

The problem of dual legitimacy can also occur in the area of economic policy. War economies lead to hyperinflation; parallel economic activities as both survival strategies and funding mechanisms for militias; and the capture of productive assets (including land), state enterprises, and regulatory bodies by "mafias" linked to armed groups. The standard international response is development of the rule of law, shrinking the state to core functions, and privatization. Some criticize the international imposition of this liberal development model in ways that preclude societies from formulating their own economic policies through political processes. International development institutions (and some recipient governments, such as Afghanistan) support these liberalization measures on the grounds that they are not dismantling the institutions of a welfare state, but of corrupt networks. Just as the alternative to a corrupt state based on patronage, cronyism, and corruption is a democratic state based on transparency and the rule of law, so the alternative to the criminalized economy that supports the corrupt state and armed groups is a market system based on transparency and the rule of law.

The problem in implementing such policies is that they contrast an actually existing economy (what Duffield calls "actually existing development") with an idealized model of a market economy, including government-sponsored social safety nets and markets devoid of "illicit" power.[11] The "actually existing economy," criminalized as it may be, is providing livelihoods for many people, and those who are benefiting the most from that economy are liable either to control the process of marketization or to see it (possibly correctly) as a political plot by their opponents. The criminalized economy is at least nationally owned and operated.

LEGITIMACY, TRANSITIONAL GOVERNANCE, AND DEMOCRACY

Almost by definition, international statebuilding operations begin under conditions where states lack not only capacities to provide security and services but also legitimacy. Legitimacy begins with that of the international operation. At one extreme, few contest the legitimacy of UN operations requested by all parties to a conflict to assist in implementation of a peace agreement and approved by the Security Council. At the other extreme lies the war in Iraq, conducted with neither consent of parties nor approval by the Security Council. International legitimacy of such operations appears to increase domestic legitimacy. Involvement by the UN provides a more neutral and credible interlocutor for political groups than an occupying power, as the George W. Bush administration found to its apparent surprise in Iraq. International approval also communicates to opponents of the operation (called "spoilers" by those who support it) that they are less likely to gain external support.

The next stage is the establishment of a transitional administration. Besides a UN transitional administration or a foreign occupation regime, this may take the form of a coalition among national forces pursuant to an agreement or a monitored government consisting of previous incumbents. The main purpose of the transitional government is to preside over a process that establishes a legitimate legal framework for political contestation and rule (generally, a constitution) and to administer the first stages of the implementation of this framework.

[11] Mark Duffield, "Reprising Durable Disorder: Network War and the Securitisation of Aid," in Bjorn Hettne and Bertil Oden, eds., *Global Governance in the 21st Century: Alternative Perspectives on World Order* (Stockholm: Expert Group on Development Initiatives, Swedish Ministry for Foreign Affairs, 2002).

Though the UN, unlike some regional organizations, has no clear standards for the type of government that is legitimate for its members, its operational doctrine requires that the transition lead to adoption of a constitution providing for at least an appearance of liberal democracy, with elections constituting the principal benchmark. The United States even more explicitly has made "democracy" (defined as a government elected by universal adult suffrage) as the goal of such operations. International actors also require that any constitution or basic law profess adherence to international standards of human rights. Diplomats note that their parliaments at home may refuse to allocate aid funds without such adherence. This insistence may cause conflict with local elites, whether because of their belief in competing standards such as some interpretations of sharia law or because of their preference for more authoritarian limits on rights.

Elected governments, more so than interim governments of dubious legitimacy, presiding over a society that visibly supports them, however, will be better able to mount campaigns for empowerment by international actors. Hence the first election of a legitimate government, although a key step in the statebuilding process, is far from its termination point and may mark its true beginning. After his election, Afghan President Hamid Karzai openly opposed U.S. plans for aerial eradication of opium poppy, showing greater independence than previously.

POLITICS OF STATEBUILDING

Studies of statebuilding operations often try to identify "best practices" without asking for whom they are best. Although actors can learn how better to achieve their goals, every step of the process of internationally sponsored statebuilding generates political conflict.

Nonetheless, in a strategic environment where the goals of actors are interdependent, negotiation may lead to convergence among actors with different motivations. The Bush administration entered Afghanistan committed not to engage in nation building. Eventually, though, it needed an "exit strategy," which would be sustainable only if the United States and other international actors helped Afghans build institutions that would serve common interests of Afghanistan and the international community.

Hence although there is no purely technical solution to the political debate over the conditions for legitimacy of operations, the nationalist concept of exit strategy and the globalist concept of "sustainability" may at times converge on a mission of building a legitimate and capable state. Doing so effectively requires transitional governance institutions that incorporate the inescapable need for dual legitimacy transparently, as does governance of a trust fund, rather than in a fragmented and secretive way through ad hoc pressures. The Peacebuilding Commission, Peacebuilding Support Office, and Peacebuilding Fund proposed by the High-level Panel on Threats, Challenges, and Change, and endorsed by the UN Secretary-General, would provide an institutional framework to make this possible.[12] These institutions would create a single counterpart for the national sovereign of the recipient countries that would provide a forum for donors and troop contributors as a well as a fund through which they could coordinate their decisions.

Providing such a forum is only one such step. The Commission and the Peacebuilding Support Office will have to develop appropriate strategic and operational doctrines for postconflict statebuilding. International actors often try to introduce ready-made institutions from outside, trying to impose a model of a liberal democratic state without regard for the specific social relations and institutional history of a nation or territory, and without concern for whether the society will be able to sustain those institutions over the long run. Poor countries, unfortunately, need institutions that are cheap to operate, but that also can grow and become more sophisticated as economies expand. Learning these lessons will not be easy, but the establishment of these institutions within the UN will at least provide a location where the lessons can be learned and transmitted.

Above all, though, if donors and troop contributors treat the Peacebuilding Commission as simply another avenue for some of their aid, it will not serve its purpose. Instead it will simply add one more voice to the cacophony of actors that states emerging from conflict have to try to harmonize. Analyses of "failed states" or humanitarian emergencies often argue that the interdependence of security means that sovereignty carries with it responsibilities, not just rights. The Secretary-General has supported the concept of a "responsibility to protect" that can at times override sovereignty. But it is not only the sovereignty of the states enduring conflict that may have to be compromised. In order to place statebuilding at the center of the multilateral security agenda, as many now recognize is necessary, donor countries too must accept negotiated delegation of their sovereign functions. They will better serve their own needs by giving aid in ways that are more accountable to the global community and the reconstructed country's citizens, not just their own.

---

[12] UN High-level Panel on Threats, Challenges and Change, *A More Secure World* and "In Larger Freedom."

12

New Arrangements for Peace Negotiation[1]

Teresa Whitfield

In the fifteen years following the end of the Cold War, the landscape in which peace negotiations are conducted was transformed quite comprehensively as a result of a number of different factors. These include a change in the conflicts in which settlement was attempted through mediation – notably a move away from the Cold War conflicts whose proxy nature left open the possibility of leverage on contending parties by their former patrons – but also a change in the nature of mediators. Thus developments in the global security environment, including the launch by the United States of the "war on terrorism" in the aftermath of the attacks of September 11, 2001, were in many instances accompanied by a shift away from great power or United Nations (UN)-led negotiations to much more complex scenarios in which a variety of peacemakers, or would-be peacemakers, pressed for involvement.

From the mid-1990s a profusion of peacemakers saw multilateral and great power mediators working alongside or in partnership with small and middle powers, or "helpful fixer" peacemakers as well as regional and subregional organizations, and an increasing array of nongovernmental or private actors. This reflected a global context – widely analyzed elsewhere in this volume – in which the culture, distribution, and use of power were both dominated by the assertion of the might of the United States and diffused by the roles assumed by new actors and forces in international peace and security. One consequence was the emergence of a wide array of new arrangements for peacemaking, most notably informal mini-coalitions of states or intergovernmental organizations that provided support for resolving conflicts and implementing peace agreements – an innovation in many instances referred to as groups of "Friends." Between 1990 and 2006, Friends, Contact Groups, Core Groups, and the like, established to support or work alongside UN peacemaking

---

[1] This chapter draws on work developed by Teresa Whitfield for *Friends Indeed? The United Nations, Groups of Friends and the Resolution of Conflict* (Washington, DC: United States Institute of Peace Press, 2007).

and peace operations mushroomed from four to more than thirty, in a larger than sevenfold increase.

The *Human Security Report* has identified the global surge in conflict resolution activity after the end of the Cold War, of which these groups formed a part, as being the single best explanation for a decline of more than 40 percent in armed conflicts and 80 percent in civil wars in this period.[2] But it was also an inherently messy business. More actors' involvement brought greater potential for leverage on recalcitrant conflict parties, as well as more resources to support implementation of any agreement reached. But "multiparty mediation" as well as processes led by a single mediator nominally supported by a variety of other third-party actors and those in which no obvious lead mediator emerged all had inherent drawbacks. Foremost among them was the challenge of developing and sustaining a coordinated strategy in circumstances in which the interests, capacity, and resources of the third parties involved varied widely. It was to this challenge that Friends and related mechanisms struggled to respond.

Comparative analysis of these different arrangements is complicated by three distinct factors. The first is the self-selecting basis on which they tend to occur: the sustained involvement of an informal group of Friends is, after all, the result of significant external interest in a peace process. A second is the diversity of the groups themselves: this extends from the conflicts with which they have engaged to the various arrangements' composition, purpose, functions, and efficacy. And the third is the difficulty of establishing a clear relationship between the performance of a group of Friends or other mechanism and the outcome of a peace process – in itself a function of the fact that the success or failure of peace processes is determined by so many elements that establishing relationships of causality is difficult. It is, of course, as easy to attribute the "good" performance of one group to the relatively propitious conditions for conflict resolution with which it became involved, as it is to assign blame for the failings of another mechanism to the adverse circumstances in which it finds itself.

With these caveats in mind, and a concentration on the peacemaking of and through the United Nations, this chapter briefly explores why the proliferation of new peacemakers and peacemaking arrangements occurred, and how and where such arrangements took shape, before attempting some broad observations regarding possible elements for a successful engagement in diverse contexts. Emphasis is placed on the somewhat paradoxical relationship of the United States to the trajectory of peace negotiations. Although in all instances positions assumed by the United States played a determinant role in ensuring a peace effort's fortunes (it being hard to identify an international peace effort that has prospered in defiance of U.S. policy),[3] the

---

[2] Human Security Centre, *Human Security Report 2005: War and Peace in the 21st Century* (New York, Oxford: Oxford University Press, 2005).

[3] The veteran UN mediator, Lakhdar Brahimi, is wont to observe that the "international community" in any given conflict environment can be defined as the relevant regional and outside actors, plus the United States.

New Arrangements for Peace Negotiation 229

arrangements themselves – the most effective of which developed in arenas that were not at the very highest level of U.S. attention and/or interest – in many cases represented the utility to the United States of a supporting, rather than a leading, role in a peace effort.

PEACEMAKING AFTER THE COLD WAR

The end of the Cold War facilitated the negotiation and resolution of many conflicts. It both staunched the flow of resources from the United States and the Union of Soviet Socialist Republics (USSR) to parties in "proxy" wars across the developing world and largely removed, or at least undermined, the ideological causes of the conflicts themselves. It had a profound effect on the UN, liberating the Security Council from the shackles imposed on it by the politics of the Cold War and allowing it to play the role its founders had intended. But it also removed barriers to the involvement of other actors in international peace and security, both within the framework of the UN and outside it.

These actors were motivated by a complex set of factors. The factors were far from consistent with each other and defy easy generalization, but they contributed to the emergence of "peace" as an enduring goal of an increasing number of states as well as a plethora of nongovernmental organizations (NGOs). That there were no disinterested mediators is of course axiomatic; rather motives for mediation included a complicated mix of classic strategic and economic interests, some of them deriving from colonial or other ties; concerns regarding regional security and governance; and, particularly in the post–9/11 period, preoccupation with terrorism and its propensity to flourish in the context of conflict or weak and failing states. Meanwhile, after the end of the Cold War more traditional interests increasingly came to be complemented by "softer" interests related to human rights and humanitarian issues. In an ever-more connected world, these gathered greater significance for domestic constituencies, and thus, for many governments, became a more pressing subject for foreign policy attention.

At the UN, the thawing of the Cold War began in January 1987, as Secretary-General Javier Pérez de Cuéllar began his second term in office with the public suggestion that members of the Security Council should work together to end the war between Iran and Iraq. The five permanent members of the Council, as he put it, "had an obligation to try to reach agreement on the solution of problems related to peace and security."[4] The process that their cooperation on Iran and Iraq set in motion was to have lasting consequences for the way that diplomacy at the UN would be conducted and for the organization's capacity to help resolve a range of conflicts in southern Africa, Southeast Asia, and Central America. It established the "permanent five" (P5) as the most powerful of "groups" in the UN and provided the

[4] UN Press Release, SG/SM/3956, January 13, 1987.

basis for them to work together in response to Iraq's invasion of Kuwait in August 1990, eventually authorizing coalition forces to use "all necessary means" to reverse it.

Progress in untangling the Cold War conflicts was evident as early as 1988, which saw a ceasefire between Iran and Iraq, the signing of UN-mediated agreements on the withdrawal of Soviet troops from Afghanistan, and forward movement in both southern Africa, where the UN had long been engaged in efforts to secure the self-determination of Namibia, and Southeast Asia, where it had for a decade pursued the elusive goal of peace in Cambodia. In both these cases interaction between the UN and evolving groups of the most involved external actors had been critical. In Namibia, a Western Contact Group composed of Canada, France, the United Kingdom (UK), the United States, and West Germany that dated back to the mid-1970s engaged with a frontline group of African states (Angola, Botswana, Mozambique, Tanzania, Zambia, and Zimbabwe). The Contact Group had succeeded in putting forward a plan that became the framework for a Namibia settlement (contained in Security Council Resolution 435 of September 29, 1978), but progress stalled in the early 1980s. Negotiations led by the United States would consume much of the decade, but only come to fruition as the tensions of the Cold War eased.

Meanwhile, long-standing regional and other efforts – including those by the UN Secretary-General – to promote dialogue in Cambodia were gradually overtaken by evolving dynamics within the P5 and the efforts of concerned regional actors such as Australia, Indonesia, and Japan. Implementation of a peace plan agreed to in October 1991 was led by the United Nations Transitional Authority in Cambodia (UNTAC), but the P5 remained key players within informal mechanisms to support and finance UNTAC's operation. With the original five states "extended" outward to include others that had been integrally involved in the negotiations, a group that became known as the "Core Group" functioned as a sounding board for the exchange of information and ideas and an important source of financial and political support for the UN mission.[5]

A deliberate effort to create a mechanism to provide support to peace negotiations led by the UN was seen in El Salvador. Peace talks between the government and the guerrillas gathered in the Farabundo Martí National Liberation Front (FMLN) were conducted by Alvaro de Soto as the Secretary-General's personal representative. Throughout a two-year process he consulted regularly with a number of countries. Some of these – such as the United States and Cuba – had an obvious political stake in the outcome of a conflict whose escalation had been fueled by its international dimensions and others, such as the Nordic countries, did not.

The countries de Soto assembled as Friends of the Secretary-General (Colombia, Mexico, Spain, and Venezuela), however, represented states with a demonstrated interest in the region, like-minded in their concern to reach a negotiated settlement

---

[5] The Core Group in Cambodia bore some relationship to a distinct Core Group established in Mozambique to support the efforts of the UN operation established to implement the peace agreement reached in October 1992 under the auspices of the nongovernmental Community of Sant'Egidio.

of the conflict, but with no direct stake in its outcome. The three Latin American countries had been involved in the earlier efforts of the Contadora Group to foster peace in Central America, whereas Spain, with its historic ties to the continent, was an important bridge to the European Union. Part of the Group's purpose was to provide a counterweight to the United States and other members of the Security Council with clearly defined bilateral positions on El Salvador. It both reassured the insurgents engaged in negotiations and bolstered the independence of the Secretary-General with respect to the power politics of the Council. During implementation of the agreements, ties among the Friends and the Council were strengthened by the addition of the United States to the Group of "Four plus One," as the Friends became known.

External and internal circumstances aligned to create favorable conditions for the resolution of the conflict in El Salvador.[6] But the Salvadoran process also exemplified the functional benefits that can be gained from the involvement of an informal group of states. The Friends brought leverage over the parties to the Secretary-General and his representative; legitimacy to a privileged involvement in the peace process to the members of the Group themselves; a measure of equilibrium to the parties to the conflict; and coordination, resources, and informal guarantees to the process as a whole.[7] Implicit and explicit agreement that acceptance of the Secretary-General's invitation to be a Friend precluded unilateral initiatives also ensured that would-be rival mediators were harnessed to the UN's effort. The pressure on the parties exerted by the Friends – reinforced in the latter stages of the negotiations by the United States – proved an important element in the confluence of circumstances that led to the signing of agreements in the final minutes of Pérez de Cuéllar's term in office on December 31, 1991.

So positive an example did the Friends for El Salvador represent that the idea of Friends was quickly replicated. Between 1992 and 1995, as the post–Cold War demands on the UN rose, Friends were established to support the organization's efforts to reach and sustain peace in a range of situations including Georgia, Guatemala, Haiti, Tajikistan, and Western Sahara.[8] Less auspicious circumstances for peacemaking than those presented in El Salvador contributed to the mixed performance of some of these groups, but did not diminish their members' enthusiasm for the mechanism. An appreciation of the Friends of the Secretary-General for Haiti as a means to ensure that U.S. policy on Haiti was implemented in a multilateral framework (notwithstanding the checkered history of the resulting international effort) led

---

[6] See Alvaro de Soto, "Ending Violent Conflict in El Salvador," in *Herding Cats: Multiparty Mediation in a Complex World*, eds., Chester A. Crocker, Fen Osler Hampson and Pamela Aall (Washington, DC: United States Institute of Peace Press, 1999), pp. 345–85.

[7] These were first noted in Michael W. Doyle, Ian Johnstone, Robert C. Orr, eds., *Keeping the Peace: Multidimensional UN operations in Cambodia and El Salvador* (Cambridge, UK/New York: Cambridge University Press, 1997).

[8] Only the Haiti group was constituted as Friends "of the Secretary-General" from the outset. The "Friends of Georgia" became the "Friends of the Secretary-General for Georgia" in 1997.

directly to the decision by the United States to encourage the creation of the group of Friends of Western Sahara. Similarly, it was in reflection of an internal review of U.S. involvement in the Salvadoran negotiations – which the review suggested had been impeded by a lack of direct access to the Salvadoran guerrillas – that U.S. officials actively pursued a place within the Friends of the Guatemalan Peace Process.[9]

The path taken by some of these groups illustrated the difference between a mechanism's utility in managing a process – including within the Security Council – and its ability to help move that process forward. The Friends of both Western Sahara and Georgia, for example, openly prioritized interests of their members over the resolution of the conflict concerned. The big powers within the Friends of Western Sahara (France, Spain, Russia, and the UK joined the United States as its core members) placed more emphasis on their relationships with Morocco and Algeria than on the implementation of the settlement plan with which the UN was charged. Meanwhile divisions among the Friends impeded progress toward settlement of the conflict between Georgia and Abkhazia. Western states (France, Germany, the UK, and the United States) were indeed friends of Georgia, staunchly opposed to Abkhaz aspirations for independence. Russia – both a Friend and "facilitator" of the peace process – was above all a regional hegemon with complex and abiding interests of its own that contributed to its role as the Abkhaz's protector.

UNCHARTED TERRITORY

Difficulties in some of these cases, as well as those presented by conflicts raging across parts of Africa, challenged the emerging norm that conflicts should and could be addressed by mediation and negotiation.[10] The strings they had left to be pulled by the powerful states on the Security Council had helped resolution of the Cold War conflicts. But in their wake came conflicts in weak, new states, where freedom from the former colonial or metropolitan power had unleashed a series of contending forces that the traditional tools of the UN were poorly suited to address. These conflicts were characterized by multiple nonstate armed actors, many of them undisciplined or criminal in nature; a preponderance of civilian rather than combatant victims; massive movements of refugees and of the internally displaced; increasingly complex (though widely varying) conflict-sustaining economies; the

---

[9] Marilyn McAfee, "The Search for Peace in Guatemala: Ending a 36-year Conflict," March 1997, mimeo 14 (McAfee served as U.S. Ambassador to Guatemala from 1993 to 1996), and telephone interview, John Hamilton, June 18, 2003.

[10] Chester A. Crocker, "Peacemaking and Mediation: Dynamics of a Changing Field," *Coping with Crisis* Working Paper Series (International Peace Academy, New York, March 2007), pp. 5–6; and Charles King, "Power, Social Violence and Civil Wars," in *Leashing the Dogs of War: Conflict Management in a Divided World*, eds., Chester A. Crocker, Fen Osler Hampson, Pamela Aall (Washington, DC: United States Institute of Peace Press, 2006), p. 126.

New Arrangements for Peace Negotiation   233

presence of spoilers; and a ready access to weapons of all kinds and particularly small arms. Conflicts proliferated not only within states but also across borders to create regional clusters of conflict or vulnerability to conflict such as the Balkans, the Great Lakes, the Horn of Africa, West Africa, Central Asia, and the Caucasus.

The extent to which these represented "new wars" or forms of conflict, quantifiably distinct from those that preceded them, or harkened back to earlier forms of "criminal war" has been widely debated.[11] But they were certainly new to the UN, and it struggled to provide an adequate response. Public failures in Somalia, Rwanda, and the former Yugoslavia contributed to a marked drop-off in the number of peace operations on which the organization embarked in the mid-1990s. Yet this was rapidly countered by broader conflict trends. These saw a sharp decline in the numbers of wars, genocides, and international crises after a steady rise for more than four decades and a notable growth in the number of conflicts that ended, and ended in negotiated peace agreements rather than in victory.[12] Indeed, between 1990 and 2005 more civil wars ended through negotiation than in the preceding two centuries – although mediation led to settlement in only about 25 percent of cases, and approximately half of these "successful" cases slid back into conflict within a decade.[13] This confluence of circumstances underpinned an increased demand for peacekeeping and reconstruction, but also encouraged further attempts at mediation of even the most intractable conflicts.

The UN remained the preeminent international actor in the pursuit of peace. But its engagements were increasingly alongside or in parallel to other multilateral institutions, regional organizations, ad hoc "coalitions of the willing," individual states, NGOs, and private peacemakers. With the exception of conflicts long present on the UN agenda, such as Cyprus, East Timor, and Western Sahara, there was a natural shift away from peacemaking in which the Secretary-General had a clear lead. In some situations parties voiced an express preference to keep the UN out; in others, the UN was involved without a clearly established mandate, providing a fig leaf for international inaction or, across Africa in particular, working "from below" to support peacemaking efforts led by other actors. The many UN envoys, offices,

---

[11] Mary Kaldor, *New and Old Wars: Organized Violence in a Global Era* (Stanford, CA: Stanford University Press, 1999); the Research Note by Stathis N. Kalyvas, "'New' and 'Old' Civil Wars: A Valid Distinction?" *World Politics* 54 (October 2001), pp. 99–118; and John Mueller, *The Remnants of War* (Ithaca, NY: Cornell University Press, 2004), p. 86.

[12] *Human Security Report*; Mikael Eriksson and Peter Wallensteen, "Armed Conflict, 1989–2003," *Journal of Peace Research* 41, no. 5 (2004), pp. 625–36; and Monty G. Marshall and Ted Robert Gurr, *Peace and Conflict 2003: A Global Survey of Armed Conflicts, Self Determination Movements and Democracy* (College Park: University of Maryland Center for International Development and Conflict Management, 2003).

[13] Report of the High-level Panel on Threats, Challenges and Change, *A More Secure World: Our Shared Responsibility* (New York: United Nations, December 2004), paras. 85–86; Paul Collier et al., *Breaking the Conflict Trap: Civil War and Development Policy* (Washington, DC: World Bank and Oxford University Press, 2003), p. 7.

and peace operations were in themselves testament to the central importance of the organization's contribution to the long-drawn-out efforts required to bring conflicts to a self-sustaining peace. But how the UN Secretary-General and those who worked on his behalf managed their relations to the many other actors involved had never been so pressing.

In the post–Cold War period individual states involved in peace negotiations included both powers of global reach and projection, such as the United States and other permanent members of the Security Council, and regional actors motivated by immediate concerns within their own security environment. States such as Australia, Kenya, Malaysia, Mexico, Nigeria, and South Africa emerged as prominent peacemakers in their respective neighborhoods, both individually and through their regional organizations. Their assumption of responsibility was widely appreciated by more distant states reluctant to assume burdens in far-off places where their own security and economic interests were not directly engaged. This was particularly true of the United States, which welcomed participation in group structures – such as the Core Group on East Timor, or the International Contact Group on Liberia – in which other actors (Australia in the former, the Economic Community of West African States [ECOWAS], and the European Union [EU] in the latter) had more prominent roles. The groups ensured that essential U.S. policy concerns were met without placing strain on diplomatic and other resources. As the international standing of the United States fell in the aftermath of the war on Iraq launched in 2003, some U.S. officials gained new appreciation of the value to the United States of cooperation with others in environments less contentious than the Middle East.

New actors in conflict mediation and negotiation encompassed states whose avowed disinterest in the outcome of the conflicts with which they were engaged represented one of their principal advantages as well as an increasing number of nongovernmental, or private, mediators. Foremost among "disinterested" states were Norway and Switzerland, which developed peacemaking as a central pillar of their respective foreign policies and assumed widely varying, but nonetheless critical roles in efforts to reach peace in contexts as diverse as Colombia, Guatemala, the Middle East, Nepal, the Philippines, Sudan, and northern Uganda. Not far behind, other states such as Canada, the Netherlands, Spain, and Sweden became increasingly engaged in conflict management as well.

Meanwhile the involvement of nongovernmental or private entities – most effective, as the Roman Catholic organization the Community of Sant'Egidio had demonstrated through its leadership of negotiations on Mozambique, when reinforced by state support – expanded exponentially. In some cases, organizations such as the Carter Center or the Crisis Management Initiative headed by Martti Ahtisaari, the former president of Finland, drew on the personal status, as well as skills, of individual leaders (a parallel development to the prominence of elder-statesmen mediators in Africa, where former presidents Julius Nyerere of Tanzania and Nelson Mandela of South Africa led efforts on Burundi while Ketumile Masire of Botswana did so on the Democratic Republic of the Congo). Others, such as Sant'Egidio, or the Geneva-based Centre for Humanitarian Dialogue, relied more explicitly on the private capacity with which mediation was conducted, even as they maintained close ties to the key states involved in any peace effort. Unlike state actors they had no political power or economic resources and thus offered neither direct leverage nor the promise of resources. However, in some circumstances – particularly the early stages of a peace process or in situations in which the state affected by conflict feared the implications of outside states engaging with nonstate armed actors – these characteristics worked to their advantage. They were able to engage, with varying results, in Aceh (Indonesia), Darfur, Nepal, the Philippines, southern Thailand, northern Uganda, and elsewhere.

The consequence of the involvement of these distinct actors was peacemaking efforts of unparalleled complexity, involving interventions by single and multiple mediators acting in representation of a state, multilateral organization, or NGO, as well as other formally or informally constituted composites. They were engaged simultaneously or in sequence, within structures that sought to bolster coordination or more diffusely. Problems with "competitive peacemaking" remained real and were rarely addressed explicitly. But the very proliferation of peacemakers – and a natural tendency to form partnerships to promote a united international community, provide essential leverage on the parties in conflict, and share the considerable diplomatic and financial burdens involved – contributed directly to the increasing frequency with which groups and other ad hoc coalition arrangements to support negotiations were formed.

WHERE FRIENDS ARE FOUND

Certain geographic tendencies could be discerned in the occurrence of Friends and other group arrangements. This was both a consequence of the perceived success of the earliest mechanisms in Central America and a reflection of the incidence of UN peace operations.[14] Thus, there was a predisposition toward Friends in Latin America; away from them in Europe, the Middle East, and Asia; and toward groups of some kind, although not necessarily Friends, in Africa. Group arrangements rarely engaged in the "hottest" phase of a conflict's activity, nor did they play prominent roles in negotiations addressing the most deadly conflicts of the post–Cold War period (such as Rwanda, and the Democratic Republic of the Congo). However, they were present both in conflicts recognizably easier than others to settle, such as those in Central America, and in some of the most intractable (Georgia/Abkhazia, Colombia, and Cyprus), involving issues of territory as well as government and sustained by the presence of illicit resources and ideology.

The self-selecting nature of Friends featured prominently in their occurrence. "We should not imagine," as Stephen Stedman put it in 2002, "that all civil wars are

---

[14] See Michael Gilligan and Stephen John Stedman, "Where Do the Peacekeepers Go?" *International Studies Review* 5, no. 4 (2003), pp. 37–54.

equally likely to have Friends."[15] Yet although Friends are the product of external interest in a conflict, the groups formed to support UN mediation in particular also suggest the absence of overriding interest in a conflict's outcome from the major powers. These powers are not likely to relinquish their role in conflicts at the top of the international agenda to an informal group of states working in support of a UN peacemaker. Indeed international action toward the Balkans, Iran, Iraq, the Middle East, and North Korea was driven by the direct diplomacy of the states most immediately involved. Large groups of Friends were occasionally formed for briefing purposes, but policy was set by the major states involved acting bilaterally, through mechanisms such as the Contact Group on the former Yugoslavia (France, Germany, Italy, Russia, the UK, and the United States) or, in the case of the Middle East, the Quartet of the European Union, Russia, the United States, and the UN. Consequently, conflicts in which more informal Friends structures were found were neither those in which "high politics" were engaged nor orphan conflicts such as Burundi and Somalia, where the big powers had no security and other interests.[16] Rather, Friends and other informal structures were most prevalent in those conflicts that command a middle level of international attention.

Outside the UN, groups ranging from the Group of Eight (G8) industrialized countries, to shifting configurations of states within regional organizations in Africa have also taken leading roles in conflict resolution. The Contact Group referred to earlier was originally created in response to a Franco-German initiative in February 1994. It had a long and varied history as a central actor in efforts to address the Balkan wars but remained essentially a mechanism within which differences among its powerful members could be addressed outside the public forum of the UN Security Council. In this respect it was perhaps the closest equivalent in this period to the great power "Concert" of the past. Its six members (France, Germany, Italy, Russia, the UK, and the United States) divested themselves of Russia to address the Kosovo crisis in 1999 as the "Quint," but reemerged in the mid-2000s as efforts to move Kosovo toward talks on its final status quickened.

States worked together in the Minsk Group on the Nagorno-Karabakh and the Friends of Albania to support peacemaking conducted by the Organization for Security and Cooperation in Europe. The four Guarantor States established within the 1942 Rio de Janeiro Protocol between Ecuador and Peru successfully oversaw the peaceful resolution of the two countries' border dispute more than half a century later. And a group of "Friends of Venezuela" was formed in 2003 to support the

---

[15] Stephen John Stedman, introduction to *Ending Civil Wars: the Implementation of Peace Agreements*, eds., Stephen John Stedman, Donald Rothchild, and Elizabeth M. Cousens (Boulder, CO: Lynne Rienner Publishers, 2002), p. 16.

[16] A Burundi Partners Forum was created in September 2005 at a late stage in the country's peace process. Discussion of the creation of a possible "Committee of Friends" of Somalia in the early 2000's fell prey to Somali complaints that some of the states of the region considered for the group were more enemy than Friend. A larger Contact Group was formed instead, but it had so little impact that when a new International Contact Group was formed in 2006, it was without reference to the former's existence.

Secretary-General of the Organization of American States as he sought a solution to the internal crisis provoked by attempts to force President Hugo Chávez from power. Meanwhile a complex array of group mechanisms in Africa – most notably within ECOWAS – had a mixed degree of success in addressing the conflicts that arose in their own neighborhoods.

Nongovernmental peacemakers in their turn developed a variety of arrangements to reinforce their efforts. The Core Group that worked with the United Nations to implement the peace agreement in Mozambique, for example, developed directly out of the group of international observers that had lent their support to the Community of Sant'Egidio during negotiations. In an early period of peace talks on Aceh, the Centre for Humanitarian Dialogue established a group of "Wise Men" that, although composed of individuals, implicitly brought with it the engagement of significant states.[17] At a later date a critical element in the successful effort on Aceh led by former President Ahtisaari was the extent to which his private mediation was able to pave the way for a monitoring mechanism established by the EU, Norway, Switzerland, and five contributing countries – Brunei, Malaysia, Philippines, Thailand, and Singapore – from the Association of South East Asian Nations (ASEAN).

Within the UN uncoordinated initiatives taken by Secretariat officials, member states, and even the parties to a conflict themselves led to the creation of an extraordinary number and range of mechanisms, overwhelmingly composed of states or other state-based organizations. Friends directly engaged in peace negotiations were joined by groups formed with the broader goals of increasing both the attention paid and the resources allotted to otherwise neglected conflicts as well as a slew of monitoring mechanisms. Collectively the groups highlighted both the operational limitations of the structures, most prominently the Security Council, charged with maintaining international peace and security, and also their surprising resilience in the face of a world quite transformed since the end of World War II. The workload of the Security Council was so heavy, and the composition established by the UN Charter more than fifty years before so obviously unrepresentative, that the creation of groups in some cases brought it welcome expertise and flexibility.[18] In other instances groups maintained, or were kept at, a greater distance from the decision-making process, while nevertheless providing a forum for engaging interested states from the region and elsewhere.

UN PEACEMAKING

In the UN context, the groups that were active within peace processes could be divided into two broad categories: the ad hoc mechanisms created or encouraged by

---

[17] Among the Wise Men were General (ret.) Anthony Zinni, whose involvement stemmed from a request from the State Department, and Dr. Surin Pitsuwan, the former Foreign Minister of Thailand, and Secretary-General of ASEAN.

[18] Teresa Whitfield, "Groups of Friends," in David M. Malone, ed., *The UN Security Council: From the Cold War to the 21st Century* (Boulder, CO: Lynne Rienner Publishers, 2004), pp. 311–24.

officials involved in peacemaking or negotiations outside Africa, largely as a result of the diplomatic predilections of the individuals involved, and the multiple groups formed to address conflicts in Africa.

The first category of groups included the Core Group on East Timor – which played a central role in supporting the UN's efforts to implement a popular consultation on the future status of the territory in August 1999 and in assisting in its transition to the independent state of Timor Leste – and low-key and informal structures on Afghanistan, Cyprus, and Colombia, directly informed by individual UN officials' experience with earlier groups elsewhere, as well as the anomalous mechanism of the Quartet established to help coordinate positions on the Middle East peace process if, most specifically, not to engage in negotiations. The groups in Africa, in contrast, reflected an emerging approach to the region's peace and security broadly shared in the international community as its representatives struggled to find in their interventions an appropriate balance between African ownership and international partnership. In this context, Secretary-General Kofi Annan offered his public encouragement – most notably in a recommendation endorsed by the Africa Action Plan adopted in July 2002 by the G8 – of the creation of groups to marry the influence and resources of international actors to the legitimacy and expertise available in the continent.[19]

The prime mover behind the creation of the Core Group on East Timor – originally composed of Australia, Japan, New Zealand, the UK, and the United States – was Francesc Vendrell, a senior UN official who had worked as Alvaro de Soto's deputy in Central America. In the mid-1990s, Vendrell became increasingly involved in supporting tripartite talks among Indonesia, Portugal, and the UN regarding the future of East Timor. He resisted suggestions to recommend the formation of a group of Friends until 1999, when a change in policy by Indonesia for the first time opened up the possibility of the Timorese achieving their self-determination. (Before then the fear had been that powerful states' support of Indonesia would cause any group formed to exert pressure on Portugal to let the territory go.)[20] A tendency to form groups would again be evident in 2000 when Vendrell assumed responsibility for the UN's good offices in Afghanistan. Although conditions for any peace process were not auspicious – not least because of the persistence with which some members of a "Six plus Two" group of neighbors, Russia, and the United States continued to fuel the conflict parties – he encouraged the creation of a variety of group mechanisms that might bring leverage, support, and the promise of resources to his efforts.

It took the attacks of September 11, 2001, to bring home to the international community the cost of its neglect of Afghanistan, transforming the terms with which it

---

[19] The Action Plan specifically endorsed a proposal by Annan to establish "contact groups and other similar mechanisms to work with African countries to resolve specific African conflicts." Africa Action Plan, available at http://www.g7.utoronto.ca.

[20] Interview, Francesc Vendrell, November 19, 2003.

engaged with the country comprehensively. Yet Afghanistan after September 2001 notably lacked a Friends group. This was in part a reflection of the diplomatic style of Lakhdar Brahimi, who was reappointed the Secretary-General's special envoy to Afghanistan in October 2001, having served an earlier term in the job from 1997 to 1999. Brahimi had worked closely with the group of Friends on Haiti, while heading the peacekeeping operation in the country in the mid-1990s. In Afghanistan, however, he was to demonstrate a preference for less structured arrangements through which to interact with the UN's many more diverse partners, maintaining privileged channels of communication with the United States in particular. Suggestions to form a group of friends came up periodically, but were consistently resisted, as any small – and therefore effective – group would have involved the exclusion of key donors and/or regional actors. Accordingly, more flexible methods of consultation, with different interlocutors, sounding boards, and partners for different issues, were pursued.

De Soto's experience in El Salvador and elsewhere had left him fully aware of the benefits to be gained not only from the leverage of key interested states but also from the risks posed by a proliferation of would-be mediators or a formally constituted group that might develop a life of its own. When he assumed responsibility for the UN's good offices on Cyprus in late 1999 he therefore viewed the multiplicity of special envoys already in place with some trepidation.[21] The international context offered conditions more favorable to a negotiated settlement than had been seen in the past, but to create a "group" of friends would have involved a large and incoherent structure or potentially damaging exclusion. De Soto instead worked closely with layers of unspecified Friends of the Secretary-General, as well as with the EU. The UK and the United States were the UN's closest partners, providing close and consistent support. That success was thwarted by Greek Cypriot rejection of a UN plan for Cyprus in April 2004 provided a sober reminder of the limits of even a carefully managed process, strongly backed by the coordinated support of powerful states and multilateral actors.

A peacemaker working without a clearly established lead in a peace process faces limitations quite distinct from the problems that may beset a lead mediator (who may at least have some choice over how to structure international support). Yet in widely differing circumstances in the Middle East, Colombia, and across Africa, Annan and his colleagues encouraged the formation of groups as a means to promote international coherence, increase leverage on the conflict parties, and engage the UN in circumstances in which it might otherwise have been relegated to a process instrument.

An innovative – and quite atypical – example of this approach was represented by the Quartet, a grouping of the most powerful external actors involved on an issue, the

---

[21] The envoys included officials from Australia, Canada, Finland (President of the European Union at the time), Germany, Russia, Sweden, the UK, and the United States. Interview, Alvaro de Soto, June 12, 2003.

Middle East peace process, at the very top of the international agenda. Developed by Annan and his personal representative, Terje Rød-Larsen, the Quartet consists of the EU, Russia, the United States, and the UN. Although the UN did not aspire to lead a mechanism so evidently dominated by the United States, it played a significant role in coordinating Quartet business, at times brokering the diverging views of the EU and the United States behind the scenes. However, the structure of the mechanism was not without considerable risks for the UN. These became evident, as it was increasingly perceived to be beholden to policies determined by the United States.[22] More closely related to earlier Friends' initiatives was the strategy adopted by the Secretary-General's special adviser on Colombia, the Norwegian diplomat Jan Egeland. With his encouragement, separate groups of Friends were formed to support talks between the government and the two largest guerrilla organizations involved in the country's long-running internal conflict. However, the proliferation of mechanisms not anchored to the support of any third-party lead, the weakness of the process itself, and the continuing ambivalence of the UN's role in it all adversely affected their utility.

Meanwhile, UN officials across Africa worked with regional mediators and other involved diplomats to encourage the formation of a wide variety of groups. Perhaps unsurprisingly, given the complexity of the situations they engaged with, the course taken by these mechanisms was mixed.

From the late 1990s on, initiatives variously pursued by the Secretariat and, more often, member states had led to groups' appearance in Angola, the Central African Republic, Guinea-Bissau, and Ethiopia-Eritrea. These groups, like those that would follow them – the International Contact Group on Liberia cochaired by ECOWAS and the EU, the informal Troika that emerged to support the regionally led negotiations on southern Sudan, the Core Group supporting efforts to bring peace to Northern Uganda, the International Working Group, and the smaller Mediation Group created by the African Union for Côte d'Ivoire in late 2005 or the International Contact Groups on Guinea-Bissau and Somalia created in 2006 – differed in many respects from Friends groups elsewhere. One, the Friends of the UN Mission in Ethiopia and Eritrea, espoused formal "friendship" of a peacekeeping operation.[23] Others, such as the groups on Guinea-Bissau, had a broader interest in promoting international support for peacebuilding and development, whether working from New York or more specifically anchored in the field, as was the case of the Commission to Accompany the Transition in the Democratic Republic of Congo (CIAT) or the Burundi Partners Forum created in September 2005.

---

[22] Chris Patten, the former European Commissioner for External Relations, describes how, after 2003, "some of our moderate Arab friends understandably began to refer to the 'Quartet, *sans trois.*'" *Not Quite the Diplomat* (London: Penguin Books Ltd., 2005), p. 111.

[23] This reflected the objections of Ethiopia and Eritrea to a group engaged with the political process, but also the priorities of the Netherlands, which established the Friends to safeguard its own interests in an operation to which it was contributing troops.

New Arrangements for Peace Negotiation   241

UN officials and other international actors pursued the formation of groups on the basis of a broad consensus on what best practices might look like. This was determined, on the one hand, by the political imperative of a strong African role in the pursuit of solutions to Africa's conflicts, and on the other, by a perennial need for resources and capacity, at times including political leverage, from outside. In most circumstances, mechanisms that might be able to combine regional and African ownership with the partnership of the international community were perceived to represent an optimum form of organization of interested external actors. However, creating and maintaining groups of this kind was not easy. The very nature of the United Nations' post–Cold War engagement with African conflicts – which, with a few notable exceptions, has been characterized by the relative scarcity of UN-led peacemaking but a proliferation of forms in which the organization has supported the peacemaking of others and then been asked to establish peace operations – ensured that its influence on the many different structures varied widely. Meanwhile, the regionally entwined nature of many African conflicts created a range of problems with neighbor states that, while actively involved in conflicts across the Horn of Africa and the Great Lakes Region, for example, were clearly unwelcome in mechanisms that sought to end them.

The peace process for southern Sudan reinforced the value of informality when the formal structures in place proved unwieldy and contentious. Frustrated by the challenges of coordinating with the regional organization leading the negotiation process, the Intergovernmental Authority on Development (IGAD) and other international partners – committed individuals in Norway, the UK, and the United States – informally agreed to work more closely together. Their grouping became known as the Troika. Assisted by renewed U.S. interest in Sudan in the aftermath of September 11, 2001, some of it a consequence of increasing pressure from the Christian right, the Troika assumed a critical role in support of the Kenyan mediator, General Lazaro Sumbeiywo, and became an effective bridge to other actors in the international community, including the UN.[24] Indeed as negotiations moved forward Secretariat officials maintained regular contact with the Troika in New York and elsewhere and joined its members, the African Union, and Italy as formal "observers" of the process.

The efficacy of international support to the negotiations on southern Sudan would stand in marked contrast to the incoherence of the effort on Darfur that concluded with the signing of the Darfur Peace Agreement (DPA) in Abuja, Nigeria, on May 5, 2006. Led by the African Union, the negotiations were attended by officials from the UN and European Union, Nigeria, Chad, Libya, and Eritrea; and a changing cast of

---

[24] J. Stephen Morrison and Alex de Waal, "Can Sudan Escape Its Intractability?", in *Grasping the Nettle: Analyzing Cases of Intractable Conflict*, eds., Chester A. Crocker, Fen Osler Hampson, Pamela Aall (Washington, DC: United States Institute of Peace Press, 2005), pp. 161–82. See also Mark Simmons and Peter Dixon, eds., "Peace by Piece: Addressing Sudan's Conflicts," *Accord Issue 18* (London: Conciliation Resources, 2006).

representatives of individual states (among them the United States, the UK, Canada, France, the Netherlands, and Norway) that varied in number and level. Problems were rooted in a lack of willingness among the conflict parties to engage in substantive negotiations and a marked disparity – in negotiating capacity as much as military force – between the government of Sudan and the increasingly fragmented Darfurian rebels. But they were exacerbated by competing levels of interest and commitment from the outside "partners" that directly encouraged the parties' intransigence, the inability of the African Union to impose any discipline upon the process, and the increasingly muscular use of "deadline diplomacy" by the United States and United Kingdom in particular to force through an agreement – in the end only signed by two out of four of the parties it was intended for – that was doomed from the start. Many of those involved would come to see the peacemaking effort as "a case study in how not to do it."[25]

ELEMENTS FOR SUCCESS

This brief account of the emergence and trajectory of a variety of different arrangements suggests quite how difficult it is to quantify the contribution made by mechanisms that are structurally limited to playing an auxiliary role and take different forms and functions in relation to different peace negotiations. This is not least because of the difficulty of analyzing the counterfactual – the impact of the UN's efforts, Mexican diplomacy in Central America, or Russia's policy toward Georgia in the absence a group of Friends, let alone, say, what peacemaking in the Democratic Republic of the Congo might have looked like if the key external actors had been able to work together from an early stage in a unified structure.

The groups' amorphous nature and the varied elements involved in their formation and performance – not least the preferences, commitment, and abilities of the individuals concerned – suggest the risks involved in treating the fact of their engagement as a variable with causal implications for a process's outcome. But this is not to deny that comparative analysis of the performance of groups of Friends and other informal structures may point to some factors that can be identified as contributing to the likelihood of their success. Five, in particular, emerge as particularly salient: the *regional environment* in which the conflict takes place; the *conflict parties'* demands, practices, and interaction with the various third parties mediating or in a group structure; a group's *composition* and the resources that this may bring with it; questions of *leadership* encompassing a group's relationship to the lead peacemaker, be it a representative of the UN Secretary-General, individual state or nongovernmental peacemaker; and *timing* or the *phase of the process* with which the group may be involved.

---

[25] Interview, UN official, November 21, 2006. See contributions by Laurie Nathan and Alex de Waal to Alex de Waal, ed., *War in Darfur and the Search for Peace* (Harvard, MA/London: Global Equity Initiative and Justice Africa, 2007).

The importance of *regional environment* to the success of a peace process is widely acknowledged.[26] Indeed, conflicts at the heart of what Barnett Rubin and others have dubbed "regional conflict formations" – such as Afghanistan and the Democratic Republic of Congo – like those that take place under the shadow of the pronounced interests of a larger and more powerful neighbor, such as Somalia or Sri Lanka, have generally been Friend-less.[27] Where the regional environment is more propitious to the conflict's settlement, Friends or other arrangements, on the other hand, have been found to be highly effective vehicles for engaging regional actors, as the role played by Mexico in the Central American cases, or Australia and other regional actors in East Timor, demonstrate. Indeed, the provision of a vehicle for the central involvement of regional actors not consistently present on the Security Council emerges as one of the principal benefits of such arrangements.

In considering the conditions for the successful involvement of group structures, the nature of the *conflict parties* emerges as more significant than the conflict's typology. Individual members of Friends and other groups are generally representatives of governments with bilateral relations with the governments involved, often with clearly held positions on the issues at stake. In most cases, they are likely to encounter problems in engaging directly with nonstate armed actors.[28] As composite bodies with ill-defined roles in the process, these problems have tended to be even more marked in the case of groups of states than those encountered by the UN Secretariat or individual state mediators, both of which regularly run into government reluctance to accept parity at the negotiating table with rebel or secessionist forces they hold as illegitimate, subversive, and perhaps terrorist. In countering this bias, critical factors for constructive engagement include the nonstate actors' demands (ideological, decolonialist, or secessionist), practices (more or less abusive of human rights or identified as "terrorist"), and the degree of international engagement they have pursued in the conflict and efforts to end it (bringing with it the potential for leverage by third parties).

The *composition* of any group is all important. Like its formation in the first place, it will also be directly related to the strategic purposes pursued by its architects, and the distinct contributions made within each process by different Friends and kinds of Friends. In most cases the question of size has been perceived to be key to a group's efficacy. Groups formed at the UN have generally involved some mixture of Security Council permanent members (including the United States), interested

---

[26] See, for example, George Downs and Stephen John Stedman, "Evaluation Issues in Peace Implementation," in *Ending Civil Wars*, ed., Stedman et al., pp. 43–69.

[27] The Center on International Cooperation's work on "Regional Conflict Formations," led by Barnett R. Rubin, is available at http://www.nyu.edu/pages. No group of Friends was formed on the DRC during the active years of the conflict; on Somalia, see note 16, previously. Meanwhile, Norway, the facilitator of talks between the government of Sri Lanka and the Tamil Tiger rebels, considered and then rejected the creation of a Friends group, although took part in a donor mechanism known as the Cochairs composed of the EU, Japan, Norway, and the United States.

[28] See Robert Ricgliano, ed., "Choosing to Engage: Armed Groups and Peace Processes," *Accord Issue 16* (London: Conciliation Resources, 2005).

regional actors, and midsized donor states or "helpful fixers" (such as Norway) with experience of the conflict. Such a membership brings the promise of different combinations of resources to the table: diplomatic leverage with one or more of the conflict parties, financial assistance for relief and reconstruction, and the possible commitment of troops in a UN peace operation or alongside it. In all cases the essential prerequisite is that the members of a group structure are like-minded in holding the settlement of the conflict as their highest goal – as opposed, for example, to preserving the stability of one or other conflict party or their own access to political leverage and/or natural resources.

Issues of *leadership* go to the heart of what or who Friends or other group structures are created for, as well as – in the case of UN peacemaking – the delicate relationship between the Secretary-General as a peacemaker acting with the implied consent or overt support of the Security Council and the UN's member states. Groups have interacted in distinct manners with the Secretary-General or, more frequently, the senior official representing him in a peace process. In some circumstances they helped to bridge the gap between the fragile independence of the Secretary-General and the power politics of the Security Council. But in other processes this has not proved possible, and states' conflicting interests have complicated the relationship between the Secretary-General and his representative and other members of groups of Friends. Peacemaking conducted without UN mediation (as in Aceh or southern Sudan) underlines the importance of a coherent lead, rather than the issue of who, or what organization, may actually hold it.

The *timing* of a group's formation has had a central bearing on both its functions and incidence in a given process, as distinct operational needs have led to varied relationships with the actors involved. Most obviously, the relationship between the mediator and a group of Friends that has been involved in peacemaking will change on the signing of an agreement and establishment of a peace operation to monitor or assist in its implementation. Whether the Security Council mandates such an operation, peacebuilding will require the allocation, commitment, and coordination of resources that are likely to benefit from structures established to try to pursue these ends. (One curious footnote with regard to timing is the observation that while group structures engaged with peacemaking or peacebuilding have multiplied exponentially, and a large grouping of states [fifty-three at last count] meets at UN headquarters in New York as "Friends of Conflict Prevention," it is difficult to identify examples in which a group of states has effectively engaged in the prevention of a conflict.)

INTO THE FUTURE

No lesson has emerged more starkly from international experience in conflict management since the end of the Cold War than that ending wars, and particularly civil wars, is difficult. The rise in international attention to the resolution of conflicts has contributed directly to the decline in global conflict in this period documented by

New Arrangements for Peace Negotiation 245

the *Human Security Report*. But there is no room for complacency, either in the prospects for the future – conflicts will continue to be widespread, in a context, as other chapters in this book point out, in which the global security agenda as a whole is more complex than it has been in the past – or in the means by which international actors have lent their support to the negotiation and implementation of peace agreements.

The proliferation of actors motivated to become involved in peace processes is in itself to be welcomed. The support, interest, and engagement of outside actors have proved critical complements to the fundamentally internal factors that will contribute to the potential for a conflict's resolution. But that same proliferation has also brought with it its own challenges. This chapter has outlined not only the growth in the number and kind of arrangements that have been instituted as a means to harness the various actors involved in a given conflict but also some of their drawbacks. Any group mechanism will be vulnerable to the extent that its members' interests may differ. Moreover even the most well-aligned group is not well placed for "collective mediation"; rather its efficacy will depend on the capacity, caliber, and legitimacy of a lead mediator, for whom management of the external actors involved is in many instances almost as critical as his or her relations with the conflict parties.

With a growing realization of the problems presented by uncoordinated or even competitive peacemaking has come recognition of the benefits that might be gained by greater organization of the practice, and practitioners, of peacemaking and mediation. A series of retreats for senior mediators, cohosted by the government of Norway and the Centre for Humanitarian Dialogue, has become a useful forum for the informal exchange of perspectives and expertise between peacemaking professionals of all kinds.[29] The establishment by the UN Secretariat of the Mediation Support Unit represents a welcome – if tardy – attempt to adopt a more considered and strategic approach to the organization's peacemaking. The Unit has the ambitious goal to "serve as a central repository for peacemaking experience" as part of a determined effort to strengthen the UN's capacity for good offices and mediation.[30] Meanwhile, the burgeoning nongovernmental sector has also shown signs of attempting what is probably the impossible: identification of who works where in order to enhance the possibilities for complementarity and collaboration.[31]

There is certainly room for improvement in the means by which peacemakers of all stripes interact with each other, and all can benefit from the extent to which the UN improves the quality and preparedness of its own mediators, while refining the support it is able to offer others. But the likelihood of any coherent organization of

---

[29] Information on the Mediators' Retreats held in Oslo since 2004 is available on the website of the Centre for Humanitarian Dialogue, http://www.hdcentre.org.

[30] UN peacemaker Web site, http://peacemaker.unlb.org/.

[31] "Private Diplomacy Network: Mapping of Member Organisations," Crisis Management Initiative, Helsinki, Fall 2006.

the conflict management field emerging would appear slim. This being the case, the proliferation of ad hoc arrangements – Friends, Contact Groups, or more informal structures that at times may deliberately avoid the creation of any recognizable group – seems inevitable, and greater attention to how the various resources and capacities of the third-party actors involved in a given peace effort might best be drawn on will be required.

13

International Humanitarian Cooperation: Aiding War's Victims in a Shifting Strategic Environment

Abby Stoddard

The act of extending aid to foreign peoples in crisis may be as old as the nation-state system itself. The cooperative institutions of international humanitarian aid are young, however, and they comprise a relatively new sphere of international cooperation. The current network of state and nonstate entities that allows for the large-scale delivery of relief aid came into being less than two decades ago.

This chapter explores the evolving institutions of the international humanitarian system as they relate to the shifting security landscape and U.S. political priorities.[1] Overwhelmingly the world's largest humanitarian donor, the United States has in effect always carried, but at no time led, the international system for humanitarian response. Its engagement over the years is characterized by a steady permissiveness, and a tendency to observe and follow trends rather than drive institutional and policy change. At the same time, a leadership mantle in humanitarian institution building has been taken up by Great Britain, which seems to have found a niche in this issue-area to promote a values-based agenda and advance its policy goals in the developing world. As put forward in this chapter, impartial humanitarian assistance may in fact depend on the United States keeping to its more modest role.

The modern history of international humanitarian action includes a post–Cold War boom and crisis, followed by early reform and institution building; and later a second phase of reform that took on a United Nations (UN)-centric emphasis on strategic coherence for peacekeeping and peacebuilding objectives. Throughout these stages, as this chapter seeks to illustrate, cooperation for humanitarian assistance has been gradually shaped and increasingly driven not by a hegemon, but by midlevel national powers, on the one hand, and midlevel government and

---

[1] This chapter focuses on the subset of international assistance that meets the "humanitarian" or emergency response needs of victims of war and natural disasters. Although it is not possible to speak about humanitarian action in complete isolation from development and postconflict reconstruction/transition assistance, humanitarian action's place in foreign policy and the multilateral institutions that frame it are conceptually, legally, and operationally distinct.

international agencies, on the other. The trend suggests a "functionalist" dynamic at work that maintains the international humanitarian system, flaws and all, and supports cooperation within a defined and to some extent protected policy space. The post–9/11 policy environment presents a complicating overlay to these institutional developments, rather than a significant departure. Though the operational environment has unquestionably changed for humanitarian action in areas relevant to the U.S. strategic agenda, there is no evidence that humanitarian financing and institutional arrangements have been directly affected by these new security priorities – at least not yet. The one seemingly significant change on the horizon, however, is the rise of the U.S. military as a potentially significant humanitarian donor and implementer in the near future.

THE DISTINCTIVE NATURE AND FUNCTIONING OF THE HUMANITARIAN SECTOR

In comparison with other cooperative regimes, humanitarian action hardly exemplifies broad multilateralism. In terms of state participation, it remains a small club of northern (and – with the exception of Japan – largely Western) governments, with just ten countries contributing 90 percent of global funding for the international humanitarian system.[2] Efforts to engage "emerging" donor nations from the other regions in the institutions and systems of humanitarian action remain largely in the rhetorical phase.[3]

If humanitarian cooperation is not widespread across the world's governments, however, it nonetheless goes inordinately deep. The provision of relief aid in humanitarian emergencies involves multiple layers of public, private, and civil society entities, all of which play integral, functional roles – as opposed to merely being stakeholders, advocates, or interested parties. More than any other sphere of international activity covered in this volume, humanitarian action comprises and requires the efforts of a dense tangle of institutions and informal networks of governmental, intergovernmental, and nongovernmental actors. State donors, UN bodies, international organizations, nongovernmental (NGOs) and community-based organizations, and other civil society actors all play key implementation and operational roles. Above all, the system is characterized by a profound interdependence. The scale of humanitarian crises in the developing world over the past twenty years has underscored the reality that no one agency – whether public or private, or even the strongest national military – possesses both the capacity and the skills to launch a sufficient response on its own.

---

[2] The countries, by size of contribution, are the United States, the UK, Germany, Sweden, the Netherlands, Japan, Norway, Italy, France, and Switzerland (Development Initiatives, *Global Humanitarian Assistance 2003*, http://ocha.unog.ch/fts/exception-docs/FTSDocuments/Global_Humanitarian_Assistance_2003.pdf).

[3] With the possible exception of the United Arab Emirates, which in 2006 joined the Donor Support Group of the UN Office for the Coordination of Humanitarian Assistance.

International humanitarian assistance can be placed apart from most other types of interstate cooperation by virtue of its "third-party beneficiaries" (the populations in crisis). Institutions for humanitarian action may be colored by the interests of the participating states, but they are not primarily designed to serve them in the way trade, nonproliferation, or collective security regimes directly serve the collective interests or needs of their members. This is not to say that all nations do not benefit from meeting a crisis-affected population's dire needs in order to stave off widening regional instability, massive refugee flows, and so forth, but these are secondary concerns and in most cases not compelling by a realist assessment. In this way humanitarian assistance parallels some instances of international peacekeeping. Peacekeeping, however (when it is organized through the UN), is funded by assessed, obligatory contributions by member states, whereas all humanitarian contributions are voluntary. The humanitarian institutions are essentially altruistic by design, even if they can be self-serving in usage and execution.

THE POST–COLD WAR HUMANITARIAN ERA: A LEADERLESS SYSTEM UNDERGOES GROWTH, CRISIS, AND EARLY REFORM

The late 1980s marked the beginning of greatly expanded humanitarian reach into conflict areas, starting with the 1989 negotiated access of a group of aid organizations to war zones in Sudan, and brought with it a host of new mechanisms, and operational and ethical challenges that shape the international humanitarian system today. These developments in the 1990s reflected what has been called the "humanitarianization" of developing world conflicts, whereby the geostrategic security lens of the superpower rivalry was replaced by a far broader notion of global security that depended on stable, functioning states.

The 1990s saw an upsurge in both demand and supply in the humanitarian sector. The decade brought with it a wave of massive, conflict-driven humanitarian emergencies beginning with the Kurdish refugees in northern Iraq, followed in rapid succession by the Somalia, Bosnia, and Rwanda crises (and punctuated by natural disasters such as the Bangladesh cyclone, Hurricane Mitch, and the earthquake in Kocaeli, Turkey). Global humanitarian funding abruptly doubled in 1991 and continued to rise fairly steadily throughout the decade, whereas the population of aid organizations ballooned.

Institutional growth in international humanitarian action was more organic than engineered and developed into what is today a patchwork of coordination instruments of varying degrees of formality. The system formed around three main pillars. One of these is comprised of the government donors who fund the relief efforts through voluntary contributions. Second, a core group of UN agencies[4] began

---

4 These include the UN High Commissioner for Refugees (UNHCR), the World Food Program, UNICEF, and, to a lesser extent, the UN Development Fund and the World Health Organization.

routinely engaging in crisis response, and the UN system itself became an institutional locus for humanitarian operations. Finally, a dozen or so NGOs joined the Red Cross in providing the bulk of humanitarian service delivery in the field.

The rapid and uncoordinated growth of aid actors and activities, spurred by increasing bilateral funding flows from donors, led to a widely perceived crisis in coordination and performance failures of aid in some of the high-profile emergencies – particularly in the Rwandan refugee crisis in 1994. Bad press and donor dissatisfaction then precipitated international efforts to standardize, professionalize, better coordinate, and institutionalize humanitarian response. Among the most notable were UN General Assembly Resolution 46/182 which established a Department of Humanitarian Affairs (later reorganized as the Office for the Coordination of Humanitarian Affairs [OCHA]), as well as an Emergency Relief Coordinator with the rank of Under Secretary-General, and a norm-setting and coordination mechanism known as the Inter-Agency Standing Committee (IASC) that comprised the relevant UN aid agencies along with Red Cross and NGO representatives. From the NGO side, a multiagency endeavor known as the Sphere Project developed comprehensive operational guidelines and common performance standards for relief work.[5]

The coordination crisis coincided with an ethical crisis, as humanitarian actors at this time also began to be alarmed at how their actions could potentially fuel conflict or promote specific political interests. This prompted the development of norms and guidelines for ensuring principled humanitarian action, often led by nongovernmental actors. The Code of Conduct for the International Red Cross and Red Crescent Movement and NGOs in Disaster Relief, and the Humanitarian Charter that emerged from the Sphere Project embodied the norms and principles of the international humanitarian regime.[6]

It is fair to say that all these coordination instruments and common codes for principle and practice were prompted by donor dissatisfaction with results on the ground, but not created by the donor governments. Rather they were designed and driven by the operational humanitarian agencies themselves, and this has remained the case until very recently.

SECOND PHASE REFORM: NEW INSTITUTIONS AND GROWING STATE INVOLVEMENT

A second wave of humanitarian reforms and major new institutional mechanisms for financing and coordination were initiated starting in the late 1990s, and picked up steam after 2003. The Secretary-General's 1997 UN reform package corralled the thirty-odd UN departments, programs, and funds in the areas of peace and

---

[5] Humanitarian Charter and Minimum Standards in Disaster Response.

[6] Core principles for humanitarian providers include humanity (the preeminence of the humanitarian imperative over other concerns), impartiality, neutrality, and independence.

security, economic and social affairs, development, and humanitarian affairs under three Executive Committees.[7] At the field level, the UN entities would behave as a more cohesive team under a strengthened Resident/Humanitarian Coordinator, and utilize common premises and services whenever possible.

As regards humanitarian action, the UN reform process initiated in 1997 had mainly to do with getting the UN's own house in order, and as a result it in many ways ran counter to the earlier strand of humanitarian reforms. Those reforms, embodied in Resolution 46/182 of December 1991, and subsequent resolutions in 1991 and 1993,[8] established the current institutional architecture for humanitarian coordination comprising a wide range of UN and non-UN actors alike. They emphasized that the UN was but one, albeit central, player, which relied on nongovernmental actors and civil society to implement the work of humanitarian response. The Secretary-General's reform process, in contrast, was geared primarily to make the UN leaner, more efficient, and more unified in its field presence. The goal was a UN that speaks with one voice and acts accordingly, incorporating humanitarian, political, and military objectives within a single coherent mission strategy. "Integrated missions" of this sort have become the UN's preferred way of operating in countries where peacekeeping or peacebuilding missions are deployed. In the humanitarian sector the result has been an increasingly UN-centric discussion and orientation of instruments. Such developments appear to endanger the greater universality that the IASC and the spirit of 46/182 brought to UN humanitarian action, namely, the acknowledgment of the importance of NGOs, Red Cross, and other non-UN actors, which, for their part, have noted their exclusion from these processes with mounting concern. They also seem to leave little room for independent humanitarian advocacy, necessarily separate from (at times in opposition to) political actors and processes.

IDPs and R2P – How the Idea of Protecting Civilians within States Has Influenced the Humanitarian Endeavor

As governance collapsed and internal conflict surged in an expanding number of developing countries, the international community became aware of a growing problem of internally displaced people (IDPs). Unlike refugees, who by definition have managed to cross a border, IDPs had no special rights enshrined in international law, were harder to identify and track, and were inherently much more difficult politically to assist, as it required intervention within borders of a state whose government, as often as not, bore some responsibility for the displacement. International aid officials began observing that in some of the same countries, refugee camps enjoyed a significantly higher level of management, security, and services than nearby camps for IDPs. On the provider side, it often came down to a problem of mandate: there was no

---

[7] *Renewing the UN: A Programme for Reform*, Report of the Secretary-General, A/51/950 (14 July 1997).
[8] A/RES/46/182 (1991) and A/RES/48/57 (1993).

one agency charged with addressing the special needs and vulnerabilities of IDPs the way UNHCR was designated as the agency responsible for refugees. Moreover, the donor architecture of governments, particularly the United States, tended to favor refugees, with dedicated budgets and funds, but had no financing or programmatic mechanisms that focused on the internally displaced.

The recognition of the issues around aiding internally displaced people represented a small part of a broader shift in international norms. At the start of the twenty-first century, the new conceptual framework of "human security" had come about, which shifted the focus in security from the state to the individual. This concept, promoted by western states, in particular Canada,[9] begat "the Responsibility to Protect" in a resolution and report on which Kofi Annan pinned his legacy. The responsibility to protect ("R2P" in the international shorthand) reflected a willingness to intervene in sovereign states when governments had abdicated their duty of care to their own citizens.

Longstanding frustration with the IDP mandate gap, compounded by a slow and poor initial response by the international aid community to the emergency in Darfur, led to the establishment of a new coordination process known as the cluster approach. The cluster approach designates lead agencies for key sectors of emergency response. It includes a protection cluster, which focuses, among other forms of civilian protection, on the needs of IDPs. UNHCR, by assuming the lead agency position for both the protection cluster and the emergency shelter cluster (for conflict-related crises), has undertaken a dramatic expansion of its mandate to encompass IDPs in conflicts. The lead agency, in addition to coordinating all aid organizations working in the sector, also serves as the "provider of last resort" when their critical needs are going unmet.

In addition to the cluster approach, which has already led to significant field operational changes in countries where it has been rolled out, other new humanitarian coordination instruments were created after 2000. Unlike their predecessors, these new mechanisms owed more to the initiative and increasingly active involvement of donor governments.

The Dawn of the "Good Donor"

At the same time as donors were criticizing the aid agencies on the ground for lack of coordination, donor policies and activities were themselves poorly coordinated, leading to duplication and gaps and a surprising lack of formal and informal interaction between donor counterparts. Humanitarians had long complained about the competitive pressures that uncoordinated donor policies caused among agencies on the ground, posing obstacles to coordination. They urged reform of the donor practices

---

[9] The Canadian government established the International Commission on Intervention and State Sovereignty (ICISS) whose report, *The Responsibility to Protect* (Ottawa: International Development Research Centre, December 2001), became the foundation of the subsequent UN resolution.

Aiding War's Victims in a Shifting Strategic Environment 253

that made humanitarian funding overall unpredictable, slow to arrive, and uneven across countries. In 2003, sixteen donor governments,[10] including the world's major humanitarian funders, took up this challenge by signing a joint statement pledging to abide by a set of principles and good practices in their humanitarian financing, and to jointly pursue common objectives. The Good Humanitarian Donorship (GHD) initiative, as it is known, is a voluntary agreement with a series of action steps aimed to improve donor behavior and coordination. The agreement enshrined twenty-three principles and best practices of "good humanitarian donorship," which among other things call upon donors to

- "Allocate humanitarian funding in proportion to needs and on the basis of needs assessments.
- Strive to ensure that funding of humanitarian action in new crises does not adversely affect the meeting of needs in ongoing crises.
- Recognizing the necessity of dynamic and flexible response to changing needs in humanitarian crises, strive to ensure predictability and flexibility in funding to United Nations agencies, funds and programs and to other key humanitarian organisations
- While stressing the importance of transparent and strategic priority-setting and financial planning by implementing organisations, explore the possibility of reducing, or enhancing the flexibility of, earmarking, and of introducing longer-term funding arrangements."[11]

Donor representatives to the GHD process brooked no illusions that the agreement meant an end to politically motivated humanitarian funding of the type that inflated the response budgets for some emergencies (Kosovo), while starving others (Democratic Republic of Congo). However, it also signaled unprecedented political will to institutionalize humanitarian best practices while becoming more closely engaged with the execution of humanitarian assistance on the ground. Particularly surprising has been the relatively active participation of the U.S. government in the GHD process, discussed later in this chapter.

Humanitarian organizations, especially the NGOs, have displayed deep ambivalence about the Good Humanitarian Donorship movement. While in principle lauding the objectives, they privately express doubt that donor behavior will change. And though they cannot but welcome an initiative that purports to address all the donor shortcomings that they have criticized for so long, they are discomfited by a stronger governmental hand in their activities, and the feeling they are being pushed into new modes of operation and coordination structures to the potential loss of their independent action.

---

[10] These were Australia, Belgium, Canada, Denmark, ECHO, Finland, France, Germany, Ireland, Japan, Luxembourg, Netherlands, Norway, Sweden, Switzerland, UK, and the United States, all members of the OECD Development Assistance Committee (OECD/DAC).

[11] "Principles and Good Practice of Humanitarian Donorship," Endorsed in Stockholm, 17 June 2003.

"Friends" Groups

Another way donors and agencies have added to the creeping institutionalization of humanitarian affairs is through the creation of quasiformal coordination fora where they can oversee and help steer the workings of humanitarian entities. As in other areas of international cooperation, these "friends groups" serve as a channel for influence without formal lines of accountability. One example is the eighteen-nation OCHA Donor Support Group (ODSG).

Although officially an office of the UN Secretariat, the Office for the Coordination of Humanitarian Affairs receives only 12 percent of its funding from the UN regular budget. For the remainder, it relies on the contributions of the donor nations – putting it in a similar position to the operational humanitarian agencies it is tasked with coordinating. ODSG provides a forum for donors to engage with OCHA on its work as well as to coordinate with each other. Another, similar platform is provided by the Humanitarian Liaison Working Group (HLWG), which convenes regular meetings in New York and Geneva of the humanitarian agencies together with donor nations, and is chaired by the donors on a rotating basis.[12]

New Financing Mechanisms

Potentially the most far-reaching developments in international humanitarian action have been in the area of financing. As an outcome of the Secretary-General's reform process, and strongly supported by a few key donors, the UN's Central Emergency Response Fund (CERF) was expanded from its original, seldom used revolving loan fund to include a grant component of $500 million. Government donors contribute these funds into the central pool over which the Emergency Relief Coordinator exercises discretion and can draw down at the request of field-level humanitarian coordinators for new emergencies, and on the advice of staff for chronic, under-funded emergencies.

Common Humanitarian Funds at the country level were an idea that did not emerge from the reform process; rather they were driven by donors, notably Great Britain. Beginning in 2005, the funds were piloted in two countries – the Democratic Republic of Congo and Sudan – and have since been replicated in a handful of other countries. Something like the CERF at the country level, participating donors put contributions into a single pot, from which the Humanitarian Coordinator can make strategic allocations according to his or her own decision making. These funding instruments were pushed forward by Britain, along with the Scandinavian countries, the Netherlands, and Canada, which provide the bulk of the financing.

---

[12] Australia, Austria, Belgium, Canada, Denmark, Finland, France, Germany, Greece, Iceland, Ireland, Italy, Japan, Luxembourg, Netherlands, New Zealand, Norway, Portugal, Russian Federation, Spain, Sweden, Switzerland, Turkey, the UK, the United States, the EU Commission, and the EU Council.

Beyond a token contribution to the CERF,[13] the United States has declined to channel its funding through either of these mechanisms, citing requirements that stipulate its funding bilaterally, except through global budgetary support of the major international organizations such as the ICRC. Privately, officials express concern that both mechanisms, while sound in principle, have been pushed forward too fast, with some serious start-up problems and lingering unanswered questions. In particular they are concerned with OCHA and the Emergency Relief Coordinator effectively taking on the role of a humanitarian donor before they are capable of doing so.

Outside the Club: "Nontraditional Donors" and Different Visions of Humanitarian Aid

The donors who traditionally supply the core of the major (counted) contributions to humanitarian emergencies form a small and fairly homogeneous group, all belonging to the Development Assistance Committee of the Organization for Economic Cooperation and Development (OECD/DAC). Humanitarian actors see wealthy non-Western countries such as the Gulf states as a large and largely untapped resource, and have long made calls to diversify this club, though with little concrete action or accomplishment to show. A notable exception was the recent induction of the United Arab Emirates into the OCHA Donors Support Group.

For their part, these states, dubbed "nontraditional," "non-DAC," or "emerging" humanitarian donors, have shown neither antipathy nor for that matter much eagerness for signing on to the joint mechanisms and normative codes that characterize the Western-based humanitarian system. Most non-DAC humanitarian contributions flow directly to the affected state government, and have only recently begun to be reported and tracked by the UN. In two recent emergency settings, moreover – the tsunami-affected countries and Lebanon after the Israeli offensive – these states made significant humanitarian contributions, and after their own fashion. In Lebanon in particular, the donations from non-DAC countries outstripped those of many traditional Western donors, even as contributions in general exceeded the actual humanitarian needs.[14] Some donor states adopted whole villages in South Lebanon to rehabilitate. Hezbollah's large direct cash donations to families were widely reported.

In Pakistan, which in 2006 suffered a catastrophic earthquake, non-DAC countries fund many large and active Islamic NGOs that reportedly coordinate effectively among each other and receive large quantities of in-kind donations from neighboring countries. Though some non-DAC countries give to UNICEF and other "traditional" humanitarian operators, for the most part they have chosen to pursue

---

[13] "Token" is how a U.S. government official described the U.S. contribution, which at $10 million was the seventh largest contribution after Britain, the Netherlands, Sweden, Norway, Canada, and Ireland.

[14] U.S. officials describe an atmosphere in Lebanon where they and other donors were scrambling to find traditional humanitarian activities on which to spend their large allocated funds.

256   *Abby Stoddard*

their own humanitarian objectives without overmuch interest in the institutional structures that comprise the international humanitarian system, as it is known in the West.

PUNCHING BENEATH ITS WEIGHT? U.S. ENGAGEMENT
IN THE HUMANITARIAN INSTITUTIONS

The United States contributes far and away the greatest share of humanitarian resources of any nation. In 2004, U.S. humanitarian funding ($2.5 billion) was greater than the contributions of the next four largest bilateral donors combined.[15] In 2005, it was greater than the total of the next six donors.[16] That year, flush with tsunami relief contributions, humanitarian aid from DAC donors reached $8.7 billion, of which the U.S. contribution ($2.995 billion) accounted for more than a third.[17]

If one expects that the world's most powerful nation will create and advance institutions that reinforce the status quo, and exercise preponderant influence within those institutions, then U.S. behavior in the humanitarian sector breaks the mold. Washington has not exhibited a drive to create, shape, or lead international humanitarian institutions in any way approaching its relative weight as a humanitarian donor. Since its first major humanitarian campaign in postwar Europe (the Marshall Plan of 1947–1951), it has been both passive observer and permissive participant, but never took the reins of setting and leading humanitarian policy, despite the influence inherent in the volume of its financing. In contrast, the United States has been much more active in forging and directing the multilateral institutions of economic development assistance. In addition to the Bretton Woods institutions, the United States was instrumental in establishing the OECD and DAC.

While showing consistent growth in its level of bilateral humanitarian funding (to specific agencies for specific emergencies), the multilateral funding from the United States fluctuates from year to year, and a recent OECD/DAC peer review found that the share of overall U.S. assistance that went through multilateral channels lately declined.[18] In this and in other ways, the United States has tended to be somewhat out of step with the other primary DAC donors. The U.S. government has serious doubts regarding the readiness and effectiveness of the new common funding mechanisms – the CERF and Common Humanitarian Funds – as alluded to earlier. Even in the absence of such concerns, however, such instruments will naturally be

---

[15] Development Initiatives, *Global Humanitarian Assistance 2006*, p. 177.
[16] OECD/DAC Statistics, http://www.oecd.org/statisticsdata.
[17] Total U.S. official aid that year hit an all-time high of $27.6 billion, albeit this figure counts Iraq reconstruction aid and over $4 billion in debt relief. Critics of U.S. aid policy are quick to point out that irrespective of these large sums, U.S. contributions represent just 0.22 percent of GNI, whereas the average for the other DAC members is 0.48 percent, and the UN's target goal for donors is 0.7 percent.
[18] Organization for Economic Cooperation and Development, *The United States: Development Assistance Committee (DAC) Peer Review* (OECD, 2006), pp. 12, 13.

Aiding War's Victims in a Shifting Strategic Environment 257

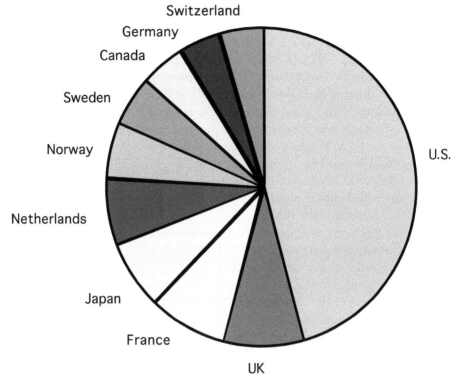

FIGURE 13.1. *Top ten government humanitarian donors by share, 2005*
(Source: OECD/DAC).

of greater value to smaller donors seeking to leverage their contributions and reduce their transaction costs by making fewer, larger contributions to multilateral pots, and barely relevant to the United States, which contributes more than the total all by itself. In this area, in the words of a USAID official, the United States will continue to stand aside, retaining the role of "interested and supportive observer."

The peer review notes the differing audiences and motivations between the United States and its DAC counterparts: "The US Government sees results-based management of its bilateral system as synonymous with aid effectiveness and the best way to address Congressional insistence on 'value for money.' The DAC views aid effectiveness as an international issue, involving interaction between partner countries and the donor community, as much as a bilateral one."[19]

The need to continually justify the humanitarian endeavor to the legislature and the broader public is indeed a key feature of U.S. multilateral behavior in the humanitarian sphere. Unlike Britain, which has established a permanent legal basis for its ongoing humanitarian action, the major government entities rely on congressional

[19] Ibid., 14.

allocations year to year, some of which hinge on particular representatives and their staff, and could in theory change on a dime. In addition, the comparative mass of the U.S. donor machinery and the fact that its contribution is divided among separate government bodies – USAID, State Department, the Departments of Agriculture, and, increasingly, the Department of Defense – mean that a great deal of time must be spent coordinating among itself, leaving little time for harmonization with external counterparts. This is also true in the field, as noted by the OECD/DAC peer review: "At country level, understandable preoccupations with bilateral efficiency may cause the US to bypass opportunities for productive collective action with the broader donor community."[20] At the end of the day, the United States may be so large a presence in international humanitarian assistance that it does not perceive the need or added value of engaging in the multilateral humanitarian institutions.

Even so, however, both U.S. and non-U.S. humanitarian officials alike attest to the fact that since 2000 the United States has become gradually more active within multilateral donor processes. It recently served for the first time as chair of the ODSG, and during its tenure secured the participation of the first non-DAC donor in the group – the United Arab Emirates. The United States has also proven the most insistent of all the donors for greater transparency and efficiency on the part of the UN humanitarian agencies. As a participant in the Good Humanitarian Donorship initiative, the United States surprised skeptics by joining the initiative seriously and with vigor, and ultimately committing the U.S. government "to a multilateral process that aims to harmonize its policies and practice with those of its counterparts, potentially subject them to peer review and ground them more firmly in objective humanitarian principles..."[21] It must be said, however, that the principles and implementation items of GHD have not been taken up, nor have they been invoked by the most senior officials or mainstreamed into U.S. humanitarian policy. Engagement in the multilateral processes and institutions of humanitarian assistance remains the purview of midlevel officials of USAID and the State Department.

TAKING A LEAD HUMANITARIAN ROLE ON THE WORLD STAGE: BRITAIN AS INSTITUTIONAL DRIVER AND INNOVATOR

In 2005 the United Kingdom (UK) was the second largest bilateral contributor of humanitarian assistance after the United States. At roughly one-sixth that of the U.S. contribution, the British contribution is by no means a close second, and it contributes at roughly the same level as Japan and the Netherlands. (It leads, however, in contributions to the common humanitarian funding mechanisms.) Britain's funding alone does not accord it an automatic position of influence, yet

[20] Ibid., p. 84.
[21] Abby Stoddard, "Too Good to be True? US Engagement in the GHD Initiative," *Humanitarian Exchange*, No. 29 (March 2005).

it has emerged as an undisputed leader of humanitarian reform and champion of multilateral cooperation in this field.

Foreign aid policy in general appears to be a policy area where Britain has carved its niche, and in which former Prime Minister Tony Blair sought to leave his personal stamp. The UK has made global poverty reduction a national priority, and its Department for International Development (DFID) is headed by a cabinet-level minister (Secretary of State for International Development).[22] A tight consensus between the secretary of state, the prime minister, and the chancellor of the exchequer has allowed significant forward movement on the complex issues of foreign aid.[23]

The UK government's approach to humanitarian assistance is strategic, emphasizing institutions, and is grounded in established policy. The guiding policy document entitled "Saving Lives, Relieving Suffering, Protecting Dignity" defines three primary goals in humanitarian assistance: (1) improving humanitarian effectiveness; (2) "delivering adequate, predictable, and flexible funding according to need," as per the Good Humanitarian Donorship agreement; and (3) reducing risk and extreme vulnerability. The policy also invokes the core humanitarian principles of humanity, impartiality, neutrality, and independence.[24]

According to a former U.S. State Department official, Britain, among all the donors, is the most "intellectually serious about the humanitarian job." The Good Humanitarian Donorship initiative was born in the UK (midwived by a British think tank, the Overseas Development Institute/Humanitarian Policy Group, which provides a good deal of DFID's analytical input), and after its signing in Stockholm it was Britain that proposed its formal acceptance by the DAC. Regarding the other strands of humanitarian reform, Britain set itself the following objectives, all of which involve strengthened multilateral cooperation:

- Establish the UN Central Emergency Response Fund (CERF).
- Empower country-level Humanitarian Coordinators.
- Strengthen the development of Common Humanitarian Action Plans.
- Establish Common Humanitarian Funds at the country level.
- Establish benchmarks for monitoring performance and accountability.
- Increase funding levels for underfunded emergencies.[25]

A review of progress in the GHD initiative found that very few donor governments had developed policy frameworks or implementation plans pursuant to their GHD commitments, and only Britain could show uptake of GHD at the highest levels of

---

[22] In terms of overall foreign aid volume, the UK ranks fourth in the world, and with recent increases has achieved an aid to GNI ratio of nearly 0.5 percent. In 2004 it committed to reaching the UN target of 0.7 percent by 2013.

[23] Organization for Economic Cooperation and Development, *The United Kingdom: Development Assistance Committee (DAC) Peer Review* (OECD, 2006), p. 10.

[24] Ibid., 86.

[25] Ibid., 87.

government.[26] UK Foreign Secretary Jack Straw and other top-level British officials have attested to the UK's commitment to GHD in their public statements.[27] A large part of Britain's humanitarian agenda is to catalyze reform and achieve greater cooperation among the major humanitarian actors. The OECD/DAC Peer Review of the UK notes this, observing that "British strategic interest in promoting more effective approaches to aid includes a role to motivate bilateral and multilateral donors to act similarly," and adds that Britain has sometimes overstepped in its efforts, and other donors have seen it as trying to foist a British model on the entire community as opposed to forging consensus.[28] The UK also supports multilateralism in humanitarian action through its funding patterns, in contrast to the United States and many other donors.

Historically the UK has channeled about 60 percent of its humanitarian allocations through multilateral agencies, in contrast to the United States, which has seen its multilateral contribution drop over the years as a portion of its overall aid flows to just 8 percent in 2005 – the lowest of any DAC donor.

In 2001, the British government embarked on an interagency strategic initiative known as the Global Conflict Prevention Pool, which seeks to unite the efforts of DFID, the Ministry of Defense, and the Foreign and Commonwealth Office toward preventing and managing conflict in developing countries around the world.[29] Similar in its cross-government approach to the new U.S. National Security Strategy described next, it nonetheless takes a very different angle: prioritizing human security in conflict-prone foreign nations as opposed to bolstering national security by stabilizing conflicts abroad. Although the underlying national interests may not be dissimilar, the British approach speaks to its government's ability to present and promote foreign assistance as a worthy endeavor for its own sake. Although surely not immune to domestic political pressures, DFID seems less constrained by them than some other donors. The UK government's activities in international assistance have a firm legislative basis in the 2002 International Development Act, and DFID does not have the same onus of justifying its spending and programs each year as does, for instance, USAID's Office of U.S. Foreign Disaster Assistance.

Perhaps because it is not singing for its supper to a domestic audience, DFID, in the words of a British official, is also "less worried about visibility than other donors" (i.e., getting public credit for its largesse) and can afford to support multilateral instruments without needing to fly the Union Jack over them. At the same time,

---

[26] Adele Harmer, Lin Cotterell, Abby Stoddard, "From Stockholm to Ottawa: A Progress Review of the Good Humanitarian Donorship Initiative," *HPG Research Briefing* No. 18 (Overseas Development Institute, London, October 2004).

[27] See, for example, "Shaping a Stronger United Nations," Speech by UK Foreign Secretary Jack Straw, Chatham House, London, September 2, 2004, www.fco.gov.uk.

[28] OECD/DAC Peer Review, p. 11.

[29] The high-conflict region of sub-Saharan Africa was given a special, separate entity – the Africa Conflict Prevention Pool.

DFID's program enjoys a good deal of domestic public support due to what many consider a highly effective communications strategy. The U.S. donor agency has for years struggled to convey its message and correct misperceptions among the American public about how and how much the United States assists foreign nations.

Despite its multilateralist ambitions in this sector, it was not until recently that DFID sought to develop a sustained interface capacity to deal with and try to influence the U.S. humanitarian agenda. Many at DFID were daunted by the size and complexity of the U.S. donor mechanism, and its complicated relationship with Congress. Instead it spends much of its time talking to other midlevel donors such as Norway and Sweden, creating its own "coalition of the willing" on these issues, within which it can test drive certain new initiatives. Having begun piloting the Common Humanitarian Funds in Sudan and the Democratic Republic of Congo, for instance, one DFID officer mused that it was perhaps for the best that the large donors, the United States and the European Commission's Humanitarian Aid Office, did not contribute, as it would have made the risks even higher and put more pressure on the mechanism working without a hitch in the first year. Arguably, however, without the muscular support, if not leadership, of the United States in this endeavor, the sort of far-reaching change sought by Britain will be impossible and they will be left tinkering at the margins. This is acknowledged by those involved in the GHD process, who believe the United States could have flipped the kill switch on GHD by not participating.

HUMANITARIAN ACTION IN THE POST–9/11 ENVIRONMENT

The events of 9/11, by many accounts, galvanized a formerly rudderless U.S. foreign policy into an assertive and encompassing new doctrine, originally under the now-discarded term "global war on terror." Starting in the days immediately after the towers went down, members of the assistance community began speculating that U.S. foreign aid, both development and humanitarian, would be hijacked into the service of counterterror priorities. Humanitarian practitioners and observers have warned of dangers in this regard since the inception of Washington's war on terror. A 2006 *New York Times* editorial warned of "worrying signs" that antipoverty programs in the developing world will be scaled back to pay for increasing numbers of projects focused on building stability and democracy in "front-line" Islamic states, to the detriment of poor countries not seen as geopolitical priorities in the war on terror.[30] Though numerous changes can be seen in U.S. aid mechanisms and rhetoric, such fears so far have not materialized in any clear or substantial way.

So what has actually happened to the way the United States provides humanitarian aid to crisis victims around the world? When surveying the panoply of changes in government that would affect how it engages in the international aid system, it is useful to unpack which of these are rhetorical or conceptual, which are

---

[30] "Foreign Aid, Revised," *New York Times*, Editorial, November 25, 2006.

architectural/bureaucratic, and which are operational – that is, amounting to concrete changes in financing and programming on the ground. A close examination reveals that despite a sweeping overhaul in bureaucratic planning and budgeting in the U.S. government, the actual delivery of humanitarian aid and functioning of the key offices of the U.S. government remain mostly unchanged. One large change looming on the horizon, whose effects have not yet made themselves known, is the dramatic rise in military funding now being allocated for humanitarian purposes. In the space of just a year or two, the Department of Defense has become a major humanitarian provider within the U.S. government, with allocations comparable to the budgets of USAID and the State Department humanitarian wings.

Rhetorical Shifts

One possibly counterintuitive development in the post–9/11 U.S. policy arena has been the increased rhetorical emphasis placed on international assistance. Development aid has been elevated to a key pillar of U.S. foreign policy. A 2004 U.S. policy White Paper prepared by USAID declares, "Development is now as essential to US national security as are diplomacy and defense."[31] These "three-Ds" provide the foundation for the U.S. National Security Strategy. Under this rubric, assistance is deemed critical to the U.S. strategy of "transformational diplomacy" that seeks to "to build and sustain democratic, well-governed states that will respond to the needs of their people and conduct themselves responsibly in the international system."[32]

The U.S. counterparts in the DAC have expressed concern that poverty alleviation as a goal in itself is deemphasized in this framework; that prior to 9/11 the U.S. government used both needs and U.S. interests to justify foreign aid (to Congress and the citizenry), but that since then its aid policy – at least the rhetorical rationale behind it – has taken on an all-encompassing political and security rubric. As regards the specifically humanitarian component of foreign assistance, however, meaning that which is geared to respond to urgent needs on an impartial basis as they occur, it has undergone no marked change in definition or emphasis.

Changes in the U.S. Aid Architecture

For many years, U.S. humanitarian assistance was split between its two main institutional pillars, USAID's Bureau for Democracy Conflict and Humanitarian Response (DCHA) and the State Department's Bureau for Population, Refugees, and

---

[31] "U.S. Foreign Aid: Meeting the Challenges of the 21st Century," White Paper, USAID Bureau for Policy and Program Coordination (January 2004), p. 3.

[32] Keynote Address by Ambassador Randall L. Tobias, U.S. Director of Foreign Assistance and Administrator of USAID – "The New Approach to U.S. Foreign Assistance," Woodrow Wilson International Center for Scholars Gala, Harry S. Truman Building, Ben Franklin Room, Washington, DC, November 17, 2006.

Migrations (PRM). The former serves as the channel for the bulk of the U.S. bilateral humanitarian funding to NGOs and UN agencies, whereas the latter funds the multilateral organizations such as the International Committee for the Red Cross and the global budget of UNHCR. The bifurcation of humanitarian funding has been the subject of many critiques and attempted reforms of the U.S. donor architecture. Although proposals to consolidate the two channels into one entity failed to get off the ground, some recent institutional changes have resulted in the furthest reaching efforts yet to bring the two together. The government created a new position of Director of Foreign Assistance with the rank of deputy secretary of state and added this as a second hat to the USAID administrator, creating a more direct line management over USAID from the secretary of state, and ostensibly facilitating more strategic coherence and leadership. The first USAID administrator to take on the Director of Foreign Assistance role was Randall Tobias, who launched a sweeping revision of the budgeting and planning process. The "F Process," as it is known, attempts to consolidate nearly twenty different aid budgets from State and USAID offices into a single planning, budgeting, and operational framework. The end goal is to match funding with strategic priorities. In April 2007, Randall Tobias resigned amid personal scandal, and the future of the "F Process" was unclear.

Funding Patterns

Despite many worries, no clear evidence has emerged that the preexisting U.S. humanitarian aid programs and funding have been significantly affected by new security priorities and the post–9/11 political environment. In terms of total official U.S. aid flows, the numbers show the following trends[33]:

- Greater flows to Middle East (thanks to large Iraq reconstruction bills and debt forgiveness).
- Less core budget funding for U.S. government aid bodies, compensated by greater congressional earmarks and emergency supplemental funding.
- Lower share of funding going through multilateral aid channels.
- More to the reconstruction sector (again, due to Iraq bills).
- More funding to the governance sector, reflecting a heightened emphasis on "fragile states."

When shown as a percentage of total official aid flows, it appears that aid is now being shifted to the Middle East at the expense of Africa and other regions. In fact, a breakdown of official U.S. assistance by region and sector shows that funding increases in some areas do not correspond with decreases in others. In other words, new priorities seem to be funded by new money. Civilian aid flows to the Middle

---

[33] OECD/DAC Peer Review United States, Table C3 "Bilateral ODA Allocable by Region."

East grew more than twentyfold from 2002 to 2005, and took the biggest leap from 2004 to 2005, when aid rose from $3.76 billion to $11.13 billion.[34] This, however, did not preclude a rise in aid funding to sub-Saharan Africa (from $1.5 billion in 2002 to $4.2 billion in 2005, in constant dollar terms) and a 20 percent overall average annual increase to South and Central Asia.

USAID/DCHA and State Department/PRM officials attest that neither their overall spending levels nor their relief aid programming has changed dramatically, and although representatives of the State Department refugee bureau note that their budget has had uncharacteristic declines recently, these were made up for by supplemental funding allocations from Congress. These same officials do not think it reflects "anything more than the overall budget environment," but the OECD/DAC peer review also found that the U.S. core budget for aid has been diminishing across the board, and that this is a danger.

Fragile states were a growing concern even before 9/11. The term refers not only to states undergoing civil conflict but also to those in early postconflict recovery and those whose weak governance renders them particularly vulnerable to instability and crisis. Such states, even if not in active conflict, tend to have a larger ratio of humanitarian to development needs, and roughly 30 percent of aid funding is typically delivered as humanitarian. Thinking on fragile states within USAID emphasized the need to address governance and democratization issues around conflict-affected states as opposed to simply providing aid. This culminated in the reorganization and broadening of the Bureau for Humanitarian Response into the Bureau for Democracy, Conflict and Humanitarian Assistance in 2001, predating the al Qaeda attacks. U.S. policymakers can now point to fragile states as demonstrable security risks, as breeding and staging grounds for international terrorism, in their rationale for a more sustained and holistic approach to crisis management that DCHA tries to bring. As the DCHA director explained, "All crises, even natural disasters and famines, have a governance component to them" that needs to be addressed.

USAID released its "Fragile States Strategy" in 2005. This policy white paper defines failed or failing states as a critical national security problem, stating that the attacks of 9/11 "profoundly demonstrated the global reach of state failure."[35] It calls for the United States to engage all of government – diplomatic, military, and aid entities – in addressing failed states. This emphasis on fragile states is shared throughout much of the donor community – Great Britain released a similar policy paper and strategy on the issue at the same time[36] – and OECD/DAC has served as a forum to convene international actors on the issue.

---

[34] Ibid.
[35] USAID, *Fragile States Strategy* (January 2005), p. 1.
[36] UK/DFID, "Why we need to work more effectively in fragile states," DFID Policy Paper, January 2005.

In sum, the U.S. humanitarian programming as it was proffered before 9/11 did not change dramatically after. Multilateral funding as a percentage of the total may have gone down, but as the OECD/DAC peer review noted this was due to a number of factors rather than a conscious policy decision. And the United States in fact has shown slightly *more* engagement in humanitarian multilateral institutions over the past few years. Regarding the post–9/11 security and democratization emphasis, humanitarian officials within USAID have spoken of this as more of a conceptual and management overlay, and a way of communicating and justifying their work to Congress, than a change to its core business.

It would be a mistake to conclude, however, that just because USAID and the State Department humanitarian entities were unaffected that there have been no dramatic developments in the humanitarian sphere. The U.S. military now seems poised to take on a substantial new humanitarian role.

The U.S. military: a major new humanitarian provider? Although the humanitarian budgets of the State Department and USAID have stayed relatively stable, over the past few years the Department of Defense has allocated vastly more funding to do humanitarian activity within insurgency and counterterrorist operations. Whereas the Department of Defense accounted for 5.6 percent of total U.S. aid flows in 2002, it now accounts for nearly a quarter.

The department funds humanitarian activities from several different accounts. The best known of these is the Overseas Humanitarian Disaster and Civic Aid (OHDCA) program, which received $49.4 million in appropriations in 2002, rising steadily to $63 million in 2006.[37] Other funds go through combatant commands and training budgets. (Not all of this funding tagged as humanitarian is devoted to traditional relief response. For instance, the humanitarian label is used to cover "sympathy/condolence payments" to the families of civilians accidentally killed by combat operations.) A new mechanism, the Commander's Emergency Response Program (CERP), provides a special pot of money to commanders in the field to undertake humanitarian and reconstruction activities. Originally developed for use in Iraq, the CERP mechanism was then used in Afghanistan as well, and new authorization legislation seeks to make it available to military commanders everywhere, in addition to the humanitarian activity they may already be engaged in. In 2006 U.S. military commands undertook to implement more than five hundred humanitarian projects in ninety-nine countries.[38]

Although military engagement in humanitarian operations is not new (e.g., Operation Provide Comfort for Kurdish refugees in 1991) humanitarian action appears to have been seized on with new interest by the military in recent years – not only

---

[37] U.S. Defense Budget, FY2004 (http://www.defenselink.mil/comptroller/defbudget/fy2004/budget_justification/pdfs/operation/Overview_Book/18OHDACA.pdf); USG interviews; OECD/DAC Peer Review: United States.

[38] Elizabeth Kelleher, "U.S. Military Humanitarian Efforts Planned for 99 Nations," U.S. Department of State, 15 July 2006 (article archived at www.usinfo.state.gov).

TABLE 13.1 *The key foreign aid funding channels U.S. and their share of official aid flows in 2005*

USAID	Department of State	Department of Defense	Department of Agriculture	Other (including Peace Corps and Treasury)
38.8%	13.4%	21.7%	13%	13.1

Source: OECD/DAC, *The United States: Development Assistance Committee (DAC) Peer Review* (2006), p. 21.

as part of military operations in Iraq and Afghanistan but also in recent natural disasters such as the tsunami and Pakistan earthquake. The consensus in government (bolstered by international opinion polls) is that military humanitarianism is highly effective for "hearts and minds" objectives and improving the U.S. image across the Muslim world. A "humanitarian adviser" now sits in the National Security Council to counsel the president and the principals on these matters.

Humanitarian operations were also seen to be central to the planning for the new regional Africa Command (AFRICOM), which the U.S. military announced it was forming in 2007 (the continent of Africa was formerly covered by three different commands). AFRICOM was envisioned, among other things, as a major platform for humanitarian assistance as a preventive and stabilizing measure, within operations the military has termed SSTR – "Stability, Security, Transition, and Reconstruction."[39] Apart from the sad distinction of being host to some of the world's worst crises and greatest humanitarian needs, Africa is also growing in geostrategic concern to the United States as a potential new nexus of failed states and international terrorism. The conflict and governance elements of the U.S. humanitarian bureaucracy have already been brought to bear in this regard, when USAID participated in a counterterrorism assessment of the Sahel, together with the Departments of Defense and State in October/November 2006.[40]

The heightened profile of the military in humanitarian assistance creates significant operational and ethical difficulties for traditional humanitarian workers, who depend on neutrality and clear boundaries between themselves and military entities – both for their effectiveness and increasingly for their security. USAID humanitarian officers, for their part, have greatly increased their liaison and communication with the military and have established two offices in USAID for the purpose. USAID has made efforts to educate the military on humanitarian performance standards, particularly after the first rounds of CERP projects proved effective in terms of PR and visibility but disappointing in terms of impact and results. USAID participates in

---

[39] DoD Directive 3000.05, "Military Support for Stability, Security, Transition, and Reconstruction (SSTR) Operations," November 28, 2005.

[40] "Counter-Terrorism Assessment in Mauritania," accessed March 2, 2007, at: http://www.usaid. gov/our_work/cross-cutting_programs/conflict/in_the_spotlight.html.

training and orientation. The military is funding USAID/DCHA to provide humanitarian training and orientation money for every Department of Defense group that goes out to Iraq or Afghanistan. Their military counterparts, they say, do not feel confident in their skill set for this work and would prefer to leave it to the traditional aid operators, but they step in when the job is too large or the environment is too insecure for humanitarian actors. The USAID officials give the impression of walking a fine line between being helpful and proactive in reaching out to the military, on the one hand, and protecting their own humanitarian mandate, on the other. They claim the relationship and mutual understanding have advanced a great deal since the 1990s, but the relative tininess of USAID next to the U.S. military makes it difficult to have the sort of influence they would aspire to, not to mention to affect the scale of operations that the military, with its enormous manpower and logistical capacity, is capable of conducting.

CONCLUSION: A FUNCTIONAL HUMANITARIANISM

The institutional and legal architecture of the USAID, foreign aid system both mandates and depends on a low U.S. profile to retain a functional capacity for neutral humanitarian response. Whereas development assistance can and has been openly conditioned and instrumentalized for political ends, to a very real extent U.S. humanitarian assistance remained immune to the vagaries of the foreign policy agenda. This immunity was made possible by the bureaucratic architecture of the USAID, in particular its primary humanitarian office within DCHA, the Office of U.S. Foreign Disaster Assistance (OFDA). OFDA automatically triggers an aid response to an emergency, whether the country has diplomatic relations with a particular government, and can waive certain cumbersome government regulations when they slow down the aid response. OFDA's personnel are largely career humanitarian professionals, many of whom have come out of the NGO world.

Protecting the bailiwick of this rather technical, functional office turns out to be critically important from the standpoint of principled, apolitical humanitarian action. In the words of one official, OFDA has managed to build "constituencies all over the Hill" and can use the humanitarian nature of its work "as a defense shield" to keep other parts of government and the military at bay. To do this they are absolutely willing, they say, to "talk the talk" and use national security as a way to rationalize it to the public. Such a stance is anathema to many humanitarian NGOs, of course, as it flagrantly violates the principles of neutrality and independence. Although USAID personnel maintain they are committed to the separation of political/military and humanitarian activities, they argue that pushing more forcefully for this separation would only hurt the effort. One USAID officer described it as a need to get closer to the military in order to clearly define the lines. As he put it, "the purists are the ones who will end up killing us." In a paradoxical and largely unrecognized way, therefore, these U.S. government agency personnel are allied with the principled humanitarian NGOs in the effort to protect humanitarian action from being completely subsumed by political and strategic interests of the world's largest power.

Thus have midlevel powers (Britain and Canada) in recent years helped innovate, and midlevel functionaries maintained and solidified, the international humanitarian system. It is a system that remains largely owned and operated, however, by the humanitarian providers themselves – the broad range of agencies and NGOs that continue to undertake relief efforts, and coordinate their actions with varying degrees of success. The absence of high-level engagement of the superpower may mean the international institutions of humanitarian action are necessarily more informal, ad hoc, and slow to get off the ground, but a classic hegemon-driven institution in this case would arguably result in a politicized endeavor that would not resemble the ideal of impartial, needs-driven humanitarian action in any way.

Evidence in the humanitarian sphere would seem to suggest taking a fresh look at the functioning of individuals and bureaucracies within international institutions, and perhaps reviving some of the ideas associated with functionalist theories of international relations, which posits that midlevel actors and networks create their own momentum for continued cooperation. If indeed "institutions matter" to state behavior, the functionalist frame would suggest that sometimes what matters to institutions is protected space to work under the great power radar.

14

The Evolution of Regional and Subregional Collective Security Mechanisms in Post–Cold War Africa

A. Sarjoh Bah

Although it was widely believed that the end of the Cold War significantly reduced Africa's strategic importance, few commentators acknowledged the unique opportunities it offered for regional cooperation – not least in the field of security. At the same time, the violent internal conflicts that erupted during this period exposed the lack of effective African response mechanisms. In West Africa, the Economic Community of West Africa States' (ECOWAS) intervention in Liberia and Sierra Leone in the 1990s demonstrated the complex challenges of invoking Cold War-era institutions to deal with domestic conflicts. The cooperative security instruments that were developed during the Cold War mirrored the primacy of the "state-centric" approach to security, with its primary focus on interstate security. But, most of the conflicts that erupted in Africa in the 1990s were internal, though with wider regional effects. To adequately respond to and address the new forms of conflict, existing entities were restructured and new ones established. In Africa, the restructuring of ECOWAS, the Southern African Development Coordination Conference (SADCC), and the Organization of African Unity (OAU) are some of the most notable efforts at developing effective conflict management mechanisms. Similar processes took place in East Africa with the transformation of the Inter Governmental Authority in Drought and Desertification (IGADD) and the revamping of the Economic Community of Central African States (ECCAS).

The structural transformation of these institutions was underpinned by a paradigm shift in the understanding of security, from state-centric to a more people-centered approach, in other words, human security. Most of these developments took place at a time of relative disengagement by the United States, especially after its failed humanitarian mission in Somalia in 1993. However, the September 11, 2001, terrorist attacks heralded a dramatic shift in U.S. policy, with a new interest in conflict situations involving failed or failing states. This interest is driven primarily by the fact that Afghanistan – a failed state – provided sanctuary for al Qaeda as it planned and executed the 9/11 attacks. Hence, conflicts in hitherto remote corners of the world now feature prominently in U.S. security considerations, as was captured in the 2002 National Security Strategy, which stated that "the events of September 11, 2001, taught us that weak states . . . can pose as great danger to our national interests as strong states."[1] But the U.S. "reengagement" in Africa raised concerns about the extent to the administration of George W. Bush's preoccupation with the "war on terror" would introduce an "overlay"[2] reminiscent of the Cold War years when security was viewed through the lens of the superpowers. The competing sides to the Cold War dumped huge quantities of weapons across Africa; propped up authoritarian regimes in Liberia, Zaire (now Democratic Republic of Congo), and Ethiopia; and supported white-minority governments and the apartheid regime in South Africa. Consequently, there was concern that the Bush administration-led war on terror could have similar effects as the United States entered into alliances that were solely driven by its counterterrorist agenda.

Additionally, the fact that the United States increasingly views Africa as an alternative source of energy from an increasingly troubled Middle East raises further questions about the real imperatives driving its policies on the continent. In 2007, the United States imported more crude oil from Africa than from the Middle East, and it is estimated that by 2015, Africa will account for more than 25 percent of U.S. energy supplies.[3] The thirst for African oil brings the United States into direct competition with China, which has also turned to the continent for oil to lubricate its burgeoning economy. Hence, some including this author argue that current U.S. Africa policy is partially driven by its desire to checkmate the aggressive Chinese penetration of African markets, especially as it relates to energy supplies.

This chapter therefore takes a cursory look at the evolution of collective security mechanisms in Africa during and after the Cold War and contextualizes these developments in the changing discourse and approach to security during this period. Underlying the structural transformations of African security cooperation mechanisms was a normative shift in the understanding of security. The shift from noninterference to nonindifference is perhaps the most significant change in Africa's

---

[1] See *National Security Strategy of the United States of America*, September, 2002. The 2006 NSS identified Africa as a high priority for the Bush administration with a focus on partnering with Africans to deal with fragile and weak states.

[2] For a detailed analysis of the concept of an "overlay," see Barry Buzan, *People, States and Fear: An Agenda for International Security Studies in the Post-Cold War Era*, 2nd edition (Boulder, CO: Lynne Rienner, 1991). Buzan defines an overlay as when the direct presence of outside powers in a region is strong enough to suppress the normal operation of security dynamics among local states. For more on the West African security complex, see Alhaji M. S. Bah, "West Africa: From a Security Complex to a Security Community," *African Security Review* 4, No 2 (2005). This article can be found at: http://www.iss.co.za/index.php?link_id=29&slink_id=2184&lamp;ink_type=12&slink_type=12&tmpl_id=3.

[3] See John Authers, "The Short View: African Oil," *Financial Times* (April 24, 2007). The 2015 estimate is based on a Central Intelligence Agency Report, *Global Trends 2015: A Dialogue about the Future with Non-governmental Experts* (December 2000). See: http://infowar.net/cia/publications/globaltrends2015/. In the past two years, a combination of oil imports from Nigeria and Angola has surpassed that from Saudi Arabia.

international relations in the post–Cold War era. The crux of the analysis focuses on how the security architectures of SADC, ECOWAS, and African Union (AU) have been adapted, with an in-depth look at ECOWAS and the AU primarily because of their operational experiences. The role of the United States or lack thereof in shaping these institutions will be investigated, especially in light of its seeming reengagement and its policy shift toward regional and subregional organizations.

THE SECURITY DISCOURSE IN AFRICA

Security discourse and cooperation in Africa took a dramatic turn at the end of the Cold War. As with most parts of the world, the Cold War had a far-reaching impact on security and the kinds of collective security arrangements that were developed. The climate of suspicion and mistrust engendered by the rivalry among the superpowers influenced the security mechanisms that emerged during this period. This, coupled with concerns over "Balkanization," led the newly independent African states to embrace the principle of nonintervention as was evidenced by the Charter of the Organization of African Unity (OAU), which forbade intervention in the internal affairs of member states. The outcome was to sanction a state-centric approach to security. For instance, although a number of African leaders were pleased with Tanzania's unilateral decision to oust Idi Amin's regime from Uganda in 1979, others were not so enthused. President Julius Nyerere was publicly criticized at the OAU summit in July 1979 by some of his peers. The Tanzanian action was condemned as a "dangerous precedent of unimaginable consequences."[4]

But strict adherence to nonintervention has been increasingly questioned since the end of the Cold War, with Africa, which played host to several brutal domestic conflicts including the genocide in Rwanda, being at the forefront of the debate. It is therefore not a coincidence that this period witnessed a paradigm shift in the understanding of security as reflected in the interventionist posture of the collective security instruments that emerged on the continent.

Paradigm Shift

Just as World War II marked a turning point in Europe, the genocide in Rwanda had similar effects as it galvanized the discourse about the need to develop effective prevention and response mechanisms. The impact of the genocide was captured by former South African President Nelson Mandela, when he openly challenged his peers at a Summit of Heads of State and Government of the OAU in Tunis in June 1994 for failing to act to stem the tide of death and destruction that engulfed Rwanda.

---

4 Quoted in Robert H. Jackson, "Negative Sovereignty in Sub-Saharan Africa," *Review of International Studies* 12, (October 1986), p. 253; and Zdenek Cervenka and Colin Legum, "The Organization of African Unity in 1979," in Colin Legum, ed., *Africa Contemporary Record: Annual Survey and Documents*, 1979–1980 (New York: Africana, 1981), p. A62.

Emphasizing the interwoven nature of democracy, human rights, and development, Mandela reminded his peers that

> Rwanda stands out as a stern and severe rebuke to all of us for having failed to address these inter-related matters . . . As a result of that, a terrible slaughter of the innocent has taken place and is taking place in front of our very eyes. We know it is a matter of fact that we must have it in ourselves as Africans to change all this. We must, in action, assert our will to do so.[5]

In essence, President Mandela challenged the African leadership to play an active role in preventing and mitigating the effects of conflict by, among other things, improving cooperation and developing effective response mechanisms.

However, prior to the genocide, the adoption of the Kampala Document, which called for the establishment of a Conference on Security, Stability, Development and Cooperation in Africa (CSSDCA) had signaled a shift in the security discourse. The CSSDCA points to the fact that peace, security, and stability are the pillars of development and cooperation in Africa. It emphasized that the security, stability, and development of African states are interlinked and that the erosion of security and stability is a major cause of conflicts and has impeded development efforts on the continent.[6]

In its principles, the exercise of responsible sovereignty was presented as the key to security, failing which cooperation among neighbors is required to deal with conflicts. It called for measures to be put in place to assure the security of both states and people, thereby creating a security community among African states where war is no longer envisaged as a tool of national policy and where the basic necessities of life are assured to their citizens. Stability, on the other hand, calls for the rule of law, accountable democratic procedures, the free participation of the citizenry in governance, and the full protection of human rights. Finally, development calls for an open, competitive economy to assure the satisfaction of basic human needs, and the full growth of the African potential.[7] The CSSDCA emphasized that the "security, stability and development of African countries are inseparable. So, instability in one country affects the stability of neighboring countries and has serious implications for continental unity, peace and security."[8] The principles espoused by the CSSDCA, which among others include good governance, have been incorporated in the new policy and legal frameworks such as the Constitutive Act of the African Union. The

---

[5] African Rights, *Rwanda: Death, Despair and Defiance*, revised edition, August 1995, p. 1138.

[6] Ayodele Aderinwale, "The Conference on Security, Stability, Development and Cooperation in Africa – Framework and the Role of Regional Institutions," in Moufids Goucha and Jakkie Cilliers, eds., *Peace, Human Security and Conflict Prevention in Africa* (Paris/Pretoria: ISS/UNESCO, 2000).

[7] For information and analysis of the CSSDCA process, see William I. Zartman, "Security, Stability, Development and Cooperation in Africa: A Regional Expression of a Global Policy Network in Formation" (Washington, DC: The Johns Hopkins University). This article can be found on the internet at www.gppi.net/cms/public/.

[8] Ibid.

Collective Security Mechanisms in Post–Cold War Africa

273

adoption of the African Peer Review Mechanism is the most recent example of a broader approach to security to include good governance.

The paradigm shift in Africa coincided with similar trends at the global level, where there was a growing perception especially among middle powers that the concept of security needed to be redefined to include nonmilitary issues. In other words, human security should take precedent over the state-centric approach that held sway throughout the Cold War. Calls for the redefinition of security took on a more serious turn when the United Nations Development Program (UNDP) released its 1994 Annual Human Development Report (HDR).[9] The report defined human security as "... a child that did not die, a disease that did not spread, a job that was not cut, an ethnic tension that did not explode into violence, a dissident who was not silenced."[10] Human security was simply described as freedom from fear and want. The publication of the 1994 HDR reinforced efforts that were already under way in Africa to shift from the traditional state-centric approach to a people-centered approach to security. The shift precipitated a process of restructuring existing institutions to reflect the true security realities on the ground. Hence, ECOWAS, SADCC, and the OAU – the focus of the ensuing section – were restructured to bring them in line with the security landscape and the emerging norm.

THE ECONOMIC COMMUNITY OF WEST AFRICAN STATES

Following its establishment in 1975, ECOWAS member states soon realized that the attainment of its core objectives – socioeconomic development through integration – could not be achieved without a stable political environment. Good interstate political and security relations were seen as a prerequisite for development.

The Protocols on Nonaggression and Mutual Assistance on Defense

ECOWAS adopted the Protocols on Non-Aggression (PNA) and Mutual Assistance on Defense (PMAD) in 1978 and 1981, respectively. A separate defense agreement, the Accord de Non-Aggression et d'Assistance en Matiere de Defense (ANAD), was adopted by the exclusive francophone organization, Communaute Economique L'Afrique de l'Ouest (CEAO) in 1977.[11]

The main objective of the PNA was to ensure an atmosphere free of fear of attack or aggression by an ECOWAS member state against a fellow member. It invoked

9 For details see, "New Dimensions of Human Security," *UNDP Human Development Report* (New York: Oxford University Press, 1994).
10 Ibid.
11 For more information on ANAD see Gani Joses Yoroms, "Mechanism for Conflict Management in ECOWAS," ACCORD Occasional Paper, No. 8, 1999. Note that in order to avoid duplication of functions ANAD was incorporated into the ECOWAS Conflict Resolution Mechanism following the adoption of the Protocol on Conflict Prevention, Management, Peacekeeping, and Security in 1999.

274 A. Sarjoh Bah

the Charters of the UN and OAU to emphasize the significance of respecting the territorial integrity and independence of member states and to refrain from taking actions that are inconsistent with the Charters of the UN and OAU.[12]

The PNA's focus on the protection of the territorial integrity of member states demonstrated the suspicion and fear that characterized interstate relations in postindependence Africa. However, lack of political will rendered the protocol a mere political declaration because no implementation mechanisms were put in place. Critics of the protocol saw it as an aspiration that failed to tackle the growing political tensions among member states.[13]

To deal with the weaknesses of the PNA, ECOWAS adopted PMAD in 1981. PMAD declared that "... any armed aggression directed against any member state shall constitute a threat or aggression against the entire community"[14] and committed member states to give mutual aid and assistance for defense against such threats. The most significant innovation of this protocol was its reference to internal conflicts and calls for member states to extend mutual aid and assistance "in case of internal armed conflict within any member state engineered and supported actively from outside likely to endanger the security and peace of the entire Community."[15]

The significance of this clause was demonstrated ten years later, when it was invoked to justify the deployment of the ECOWAS Ceasefire Monitoring Group (ECOMOG) – ECOWAS' first peace operation – in Liberia in 1990. The deployment was, however, mired in controversy from the start as member states were divided into two camps: the intervening states and those who opposed it. For their part, the intervening states – Ghana, Nigeria, Sierra Leone, Guinea-Conakry, and The Gambia – justified their action on the basis that both Côte d'Ivoire and Burkina Faso supported the Liberian dissidents, and the National Patriotic Front of Liberia (NPFL) invaded Liberia from Ivorian territory, in violation of PMAD. Those opposed to the intervention – Burkina Faso and Côte d'Ivoire – questioned the mandate of the Standing Mediation Committee (SMC), which had been set up to deal with the Liberian crisis, to take a decision to send troops without fully consulting with other members.[16]

The ensuing controversy made it evident that by the time of ECOWAS' first deployment, there was no mechanism for resolving intrastate conflicts. Although the PNA and PMAD were in place they were nothing more than policy proclamations as they lacked enforcement mechanisms, and references to intrastate conflicts were

---

[12] ECOWAS Protocol on Non-Aggression, Lagos, April 22, 1978.

[13] See Clement Adibe, "Managing Arms in Peace Processes: Liberia," Geneva: UNIDIR, 1996 p. 5. Cited in Eric G. Berman and Katie E. Sams, *Peacekeeping in Africa: Capabilities and Culpabilities* (Geneva/Pretoria: UNIDIR/ISS, 2000), p. 81.

[14] ECOWAS A/SP5/5/81 Relating to Mutual Assistance on Defense, Freetown, Sierra Leone, May 1981. Also reprinted in *The West African Bulletin* No. 3 (June 1995), pp. 23–27.

[15] Ibid.

[16] For more on the mandate of the SMC and the controversy, see ECOWAS Standing Mediation Committee, Banjul, Republic of Gambia, Final Communiqué of the First Session, August 7, 1990.

Collective Security Mechanisms in Post–Cold War Africa 275

somewhat ambiguous. And because none of PMAD's organs were ever put in place, ECOMOG was based on ad hoc arrangements, such as the SMC that resulted in fractious legal and political acrimony, in the face of difficult operational challenges.

A New Mechanism for Conflict Prevention

Following the Liberian experience, ECOWAS launched a process of reforms to reflect the new security realities on the ground. The first step was the revision of the 1975 ECOWAS Treaty to expand the mandate of the organization from its narrow economic integration focus to a holistic approach that embraces security.[17] This was succinctly captured by the preamble to the revised treaty, which states that

> the integration of the Members into a viable regional community may demand the partial and gradual pooling of national sovereignties to the Community within the context of a collective political will, emphasizing . . . the need to face together the political, economic and socio-cultural challenges of the present and the future, and to pool together the resources of our peoples while respecting our diversities for the most rapid and optimum expansion of the region's productive capacity.[18]

Taking its cue from the Kampala Document and other developments, ECOWAS adopted a set of political principles including but not limited to the promotion and consolidation of a democratic system of governance.[19] The enunciation of these principles was significant as it was the first time that the issue of good governance was directly linked to security. This presented unique opportunities for developing a collective security framework with prevention and response capacities in line with the emerging norm of nonindifference.

Subsequently, ECOWAS adopted a more substantive Mechanism for Conflict Prevention, Management, Resolution and Security in December 1999.[20] Unlike previous arrangements, the new mechanism is not limited to interstate conflicts; it provides for intervention in internal conflicts that pose a threat to human rights and the general peace and security of the subregion. Chapter V Article 25 states that the mechanism will be applied in any of the following cases: (1) internal conflict that threatens to trigger a humanitarian disaster; or (2) that poses a serious threat to peace and security in the subregion; and in the event of serious and massive violation of human rights and the rule of law.[21]

---

[17] Ibid.

[18] See *Revised Treaty of the Economic Community of West African States* (ECOWAS), Cotonou, Benin, 24 July 1992.

[19] Declaration A/DCL.1/7/91 of Political Principles of the Economic Community of West African States, Abuja, July 1991. This document can be found at: http://www.iss.co.za/AF/RegOrg/unity_to_union/pdfs/ecowas/7DecPolPrin.pdf.

[20] Yoroms, op. cit., 1999, pp. 3–4.

[21] See Protocol on Conflict Resolution, op. cit., p. 17.

To reinforce the Conflict Resolution Mechanism, a supplementary Protocol on Democracy and Good Governance was put in place in December 2001.[22] Among other things, the protocol established the following principles: every accession to power must be made through free, fair, and transparent elections; and there is zero tolerance for power obtained or maintained by unconstitutional means, among others.[23] ECOWAS' adoption of these principles was a clear recognition of the link among democracy, good governance, security, and the perennial problem of military coups in the region. But although ECOWAS' attempt to deal with the democratic deficit through this protocol and other mechanisms is laudable, to date not all member states have ratified it. Moreover, it failed to prescribe any framework for dealing with civilian misrule, as was the case with Guinea under the late president, Lansana Conte.

Meanwhile, to bolster its conflict prevention and management capabilities, an early warning mechanism, headquartered in Abuja, Nigeria, with four zonal bureaus in Benin, Burkina Faso, The Gambia, and Liberia, has been established. The early warning mechanism is aimed at strengthening ECOWAS' ability to undertake effective conflict prevention, a move away from the reactive responses that characterized its interventions in the past. But a major challenge for ECOWAS is how to ensure that early warning is matched by early and adequate response.

ECOWAS in Togo and Guinea

Operationally, ECOWAS has deployed two peace operations since the adoption of the protocol in 1999: the ECOWAS Mission in Côte d'Ivoire (2003) and the ECOWAS Mission in Liberia (2003). ECOWAS collaborated with the United Nations (UN), France, and the United States in the two deployments, with troops from both missions subsequently rehatted to the follow-on UN-led missions. Despite the huge attention given to ECOWAS' collaboration with the UN and others for its deployments in these countries, ECOWAS' roles in resolving the political crisis in Togo (2005) and Guinea (2007) are its most prominent forays into conflict prevention since 1999. Unlike Liberia and Côte d'Ivoire, where ECOWAS intervened to deal with the aftermath of violence, its engagement in Togo and Guinea is credited for averting the eruption of violence in those countries.

In Togo, the death of President Gnassingbé Eyadéma in 2005 threatened to plunge that country into chaos. Members of the opposition and ECOWAS rejected Faure Gnassingbé's assumption of power at the death of his father as unconstitutional and unacceptable. However, having changed the constitution and with the country's

---

[22] For details see "Protocol A/SP1/12/01 on Democracy and Good Governance – Supplementary to the Protocol relating to the Mechanism for Conflict Prevention, Management, Resolution, Peacekeeping and Security," Dakar, Senegal, December 21, 2001.

[23] For ECOWAS' recent invocation of the Protocol on Good Governance see, "Stepping up to the Plate," *Africa Today* 9 No. 10 (October 2003), pp. 20–22.

Collective Security Mechanisms in Post–Cold War Africa 277

military on his side, Faure initially appeared determined to succeed his father, a move that threatened the stability of the country. This prompted ECOWAS to intervene by calling for an immediate end to the unconstitutional "father-to-son" transition, and restoration of the old constitution, or Togo would risk sanctions and even military intervention, with Nigeria's National Assembly endorsing the latter.[24] Invoking the Togolese constitution and its zero-tolerance policy against unconstitutional change of government (and that of the African Union), ECOWAS succeeded in brokering a deal that saw Faure step aside, and the deputy speaker of the National Assembly assume the presidency, as provided for by the Togolese constitution. Presidential elections, subsequently won by Faure Gnassingbé, were held in sixty days – in line with the constitution but in the face of complaints by the opposition about the short notice as the sixty days included time spent negotiating with Faure to relinquish power. ECOWAS' success in resolving the crisis can be attributed to three main factors: first, it invoked the Togolese constitution as an entry point to justify its pressure on Faure to relinquish power; second, it invoked its zero-tolerance policy against unconstitutional change of government to justify its intervention; and third, its close collaboration with the AU added legitimacy to its actions.

On a separate note, in late January 2007, Guinea was gripped by strike action as calls by the nation's trade union and civic movements for improved working and broader socioeconomic conditions metamorphosed into demands for the country's then ailing president, Lasana Conté, to resign. The government reacted with half-measures by appointing a long-time ally of the president as prime minister. The government's move further inflamed the civic opposition, leading tens of thousands of protesters to take to the streets to protest the appointment. The president responded by declaring a "state of siege" and unleashed the country's military on the protesters, resulting in a high death toll with thousands injured across the country. ECOWAS, the UN, and bilateral partners unanimously condemned the government's heavy-handedness and warned the military of the repercussions of their actions. ECOWAS dispatched a high-powered mediation team, led by former Nigerian president General Ibrahim Babangida and ECOWAS Commission president Dr. Mohamed Ibn Chambas, to mediate between the parties. The ECOWAS mediation culminated in the appointment of a new prime minister with extensive powers. The appointment of Lansana Kouyaté, a long-time Guinean diplomat and former Executive Secretary of ECOWAS, was supported by Guinean civic groups and members of the opposition and welcomed by the wider international community.

Unlike previous attempts at mediation, the 2007 efforts were believed to have succeeded largely because the government of President Conté realized that its options were dwindling as even some of its parliamentarians voted against an extension of

---

[24] "Nigeria National Assembly Endorses Military Action against Togo," Letogolis.com, Lagos, February 10, 2005. This article can be found at: http://www.letogolais.com/article.html?nid=1520. Last accessed December 17, 2007.

the "state of siege." Although ECOWAS' mediation averted Guinea's descent into chaos, President Conte's refusal to step down until his sudden death in December 2008 – with no clear succession plans – and ECOWAS' failure to convince him to do so expose the limits of the "carrots and sticks" at the disposal of the subregional body.

Carrots and Sticks

Thus, ECOWAS' lack of effective carrots and sticks to deal with recalcitrant civilian heads of state remains a big challenge. It is thus not surprising that the initial ECOWAS interventions in both Togo and Guinea were reactive, rather than heading off the crises in advance. That ECOWAS wielded a big stick in its engagement with the crisis in Togo compared to its approach with Guinea manifests its lack of an effective strategy to deal with entrenched civilian dictatorships.

The limit of carrots and sticks at the disposal of ECOWAS becomes even starker when one considers Nigeria's preponderant position in the region. If ECOWAS has been timid in enforcing some of the political principles on smaller and weaker member states, it remains to be seen how member states can ensure that Nigeria adheres to these principles. Nigeria's military muscle, population, and economic power are unmatched in the region. Although Nigeria can muster the necessary political, diplomatic, and military resources to deal with conflicts in member states, the same cannot be said for any of the other remaining fourteen members. It is, however, hoped that as Nigeria helps to develop a rules-based system, often through its direct intervention, it would be forced to adhere to the emerging norms.

As stated previously, ECOWAS' limited entry points and leverage over entrenched dictatorships and civilian misrule remain a major weakness. ECOWAS should therefore explore more options for engaging civilian dictatorships as that would deal with one of the fundamental causes of conflicts in the region. To this end, it needs a more substantive peer review mechanism that involves the relevant regional institutions, including the regional parliament, regional court, and civil society organizations. Such efforts will be complemented by similar developments in other parts of the continent such as southern Africa, where similar efforts are underway to develop a collective security framework, which mirrors the new dynamics in the subregion following the end of apartheid.

THE SOUTHERN AFRICAN DEVELOPMENT COMMUNITY

The end of both the Cold War and apartheid presented unique opportunities for security cooperation in southern Africa.[25] During the Cold War, the subregion

---

[25] Some aspects of this section have been adapted from the author's Martello Paper: "Toward a Regional Approach to Human Security in Southern Africa," Queen's Center for International Relations, 2004.

Collective Security Mechanisms in Post–Cold War Africa

was the center of international attention as liberation wars were waged against white-minority governments in Zimbabwe, Namibia, the two former Portuguese colonies of Mozambique and Angola, and the apartheid regime in South Africa. The active involvement of the superpowers contributed to prolonging the conflicts and complicated the political dynamics in the subregion. But the presence of white-minority regimes served as a coalescing agent for the various states and liberation movements, culminating in the establishment of the Front Line States (FLS) by Tanzania, Mozambique, and Zambia in 1974. Liberation movements such as the African National Congress (ANC) and the South West Africa Peoples Organization (SWAPO) were granted seats at FLS meetings. The FLS became both the symbol and the mechanism through which the struggle to liberate the people of the region was coordinated. The FLS had as its central objective the liberation of Zimbabwe, Angola, and Namibia and the campaign to tighten economic sanctions against apartheid-South Africa.

The Inter-State Defense and Security Committee (ISDSC) implemented FLS policies. The ISDSC was created to deal with various individual and collective security issues. The FLS like the ISDSC had no governing Charter or secretariat and functioned informally, holding meetings on an ad hoc basis, but at least once a year.[26] The ISDSC coordinated training assistance and venues for freedom fighters both within Africa and abroad during its early days.

The Southern African Development Coordination Conference (SADCC)[27] was established in 1980 to reduce the economic dependence of its members on apartheid-era South Africa. With Namibia's independence in 1990 and the increased prospect for majority rule in South Africa, SADCC was transformed into the Southern African Development Community (SADC) in 1992. The treaty and declaration establishing the Southern African Development Community (SADC) were signed in Windhoek, Namibia in 1992. The treaty set out a broad spectrum of objectives from economic development to security.[28] Currently, SADC consists of all the original member states of SADCC with South Africa, Mauritius, and the Democratic Republic of Congo (DRC) becoming members in 1994, 1995, and 1997, respectively. The new SADC differs from the previous one because its goals extend beyond economic coordination to encompass issues of high politics.

For instance, between 1992 and 1994, SADC adopted various legal and policy instruments on peace and security. Drawing on the principles espoused by the Kampala Document, the SADC Framework and Strategy document called for the development of common political values based on democratic norms, the creation of a nonmilitaristic security order, and the need to address nonmilitary sources

---

[26] Berman and Sams, op. cit., pp. 16–161.

[27] The founding members of SADCC were Angola, Botswana, Lesotho, Malawi, Mozambique, Swaziland, Tanzania, Zambia, and Zimbabwe; with Namibia joining the group on attaining independence in 1990.

[28] See *The Treaty and Declaration* establishing SADC, in Windhoek 1992.

of conflict and threats to human security, such as poverty and domestic political repression. The Framework and Strategy document further proposed the adoption of a new approach to security that emphasizes the security of people, the creation of a forum for mediation and arbitration, reduction in force levels and military expenditure, the introduction of confidence and security-building measures and nonoffensive defense doctrines, and the ratification of key principles of international law governing interstate relations.[29]

The Organ on Politics, Defense, and Security

In June 1996, SADC established an Organ on Politics, Defense and Security (OPDS) mandated to promote peace and security in the region. Its mandate included protecting the region from instability, encompassing everything from a breakdown of law and order to external aggression. But the fact that the Organ was to operate independently of other SADC structures generated intense divisions among those member states – led by South Africa – that preferred a more structured approach and others – led by Zimbabwe – that preferred a loose arrangement, rendering it ineffective from 1996 to 1999. However, the disagreements were resolved with the adoption of the Protocol on Politics, Defense and Security Cooperation in August 2001.[30] Under the protocol, the Organ will operate as an integral part of SADC. A Mutual Defense Pact followed this in 2003, with the primary objective of operationalizing the "mechanisms of the Organ for mutual cooperation in defence and security matters."[31] A Strategic Indicative Plan for the Organ (SIPO) was also established.[32] The SIPO provides a framework for the implementation of the region's broader peace and security agenda. The adoption of the SADC *Principles and Guidelines Governing Democratic Elections*, in August 2004 was a milestone in efforts to link governance to security.[33] Despite criticisms of the SADC principles on elections, its value rests on the fact that for the first time member states committed themselves to proper elections, although mechanisms for holding member states accountable are lacking.[34]

Operationally, rifts over the Organ contributed to conflicting interpretations of the "SADC" interventions in Lesotho and the Democratic Republic of Congo in

---

[29] Laurie Nathan and Joao Honwana, "After the Storm: Common Security and Conflict Resolution in Southern Africa," Centre for Conflict Resolution, University of Cape Town, January 1995, p. 10.

[30] See *The Protocol on Politics, Defence and Security Co-operation*, Blantyre, Malawi, August 2001.

[31] For in-depth analysis of security cooperation in Southern Africa, see Naison Ngoma, "SADC: Towards a Security Community?" *African Security Review* 12(3) (2003).

[32] Strategic Indicative Plan for the Organ on Politics, Defence and Security Cooperation (SIPO), Maseru, Lesotho, August 2004.

[33] *SADC Principles and Guidelines Governing Democratic Elections*, Mauritius, August 2004.

[34] For a critical analysis of the SADC Principles see, Khabele Matlosa, "Democratization at the Crossroads?: Challenges for the SADC Principles and Guidelines Governing Democratic Elections." *ISS Paper* 118 (October 2005).

1998.[35] In September 1998, South African and Botswanan troops entered Lesotho at the invitation of the country's prime minister to stabilize the crisis that had erupted in that country. Operation Boleas, the joint South African/Botswanan operation, triggered controversy among member states. But the intervention that polarized SADC member states more than anything else was the Angolan, Namibian, and Zimbabwean intervention in Democratic Republic of Congo in the name of SADC. In August 1998, the government of President Laurent Kabila was faced with a rebellion in the northeastern part of the country that threatened his government. President Kabila, feeling the increasing pressure from the Congolese Rally for Democracy (RCD) rebels and their Rwandan and Ugandan allies, turned to SADC for help to stave off what Kinshasa viewed as a foreign invasion. Angola, Namibia, and Zimbabwe responded and sent troops to support Kabila.[36] The controversy that surrounded the intervention raised questions about the extent to which a common ground existed among SADC members on how to promote its human security agenda. As with the rift over the Organ, South Africa and Zimbabwe found themselves on opposing ends, an indication of a power struggle between the two subregional hegemons. Thus, the Lesotho and DRC interventions exposed differences among member states on how to collectively enhance regional human security.

Nonetheless, the adoption of the Protocol on the Politics, Defense and Security, the Mutual Defense Agreement, and other related frameworks brings the region closer to a common understanding and approach to collective security.[37] Although some observers have criticized SADC for failing to deal with the deteriorating situation in Zimbabwe, its resistance to "megaphone diplomacy" is perhaps an indication of the lingering suspicion and mistrust that characterized interstate relations throughout the Cold War. Despite criticisms of its handling of the crisis in Zimbabwe, SADC has made significant progress in dealing with the "confidence gap" that resulted from decades of conflict and destabilization often engineered by the apartheid regime. Meanwhile, the establishment of the AU is perhaps the most positive development for security cooperation on the continent.

THE AFRICAN UNION

Since its establishment in 2002, the AU has embarked on a process of developing a comprehensive security architecture primarily aimed at preventing conflicts and dealing with those that have already erupted. Although its predecessor, the OAU,

---

[35] For more on the OPDS and the interventions in Lesotho and DRC, see Alhaji M. S. Bah, "Toward a Regional Approach to Human Security in Southern Africa," *Martello Paper Series* 26, Queen's Center for International Relations, Kingston, Canada, 2004.

[36] Berman and Sams, op. cit.

[37] For more on this, see Naison Ngoma, "Prospect for a Security Community in Southern Africa: An analysis of Regional Security in the Southern African Development Community," Institute for Security Studies: Pretoria, 2005.

was governed by the principle of noninterference, the AU is driven by the principle of nonindifference.[38] This is manifested in the Constitutive Act, which authorizes the AU to intervene either at the invitation of a member state or without in situations involving gross violations of human rights, war crimes, crimes against humanity, and genocide. However, the origin of the current AU security architecture dates back to the OAU Mechanism for Conflict Prevention and Resolution.

Prior to the genocide in Rwanda, the OAU had established its Mechanism for Conflict Prevention, Management and Resolution,[39] which was adopted at the Cairo summit in 1993. The Mechanism was an attempt to move away from the ad hoc approaches that had characterized previous efforts in the past and was therefore hailed as a bold and positive initiative that would give the OAU a prominent role in dealing with the brutal conflicts on the continent.

The Mechanism had two main structures: the Central Organ and Conflict Management Division. The Central Organ, which was comprised of sixteen Heads of State and Government, was the Mechanism's main decision-making instrument. From the start, it was clear that conflict prevention was the primary focus of the Mechanism but that meant little to the thousands of civilians who were already trapped in violent intrastate conflicts.

Nonetheless, the OAU initiated several conflict prevention and/or mediation efforts in Burundi, and Comoros, and collaborated with the Regional Economic Communities with varying degrees of success.[40] But most tellingly, the OAU watched helplessly as hundreds of thousands perished in the space of one hundred days during the genocide in Rwanda in 1994.

By the early to mid-1990s, some African states – led by Nigeria, Libya, Senegal, and South Africa – recognized that the changing nature of conflicts, from interstate to intrastate wars with a large number of nonstate actors who largely disregarded international humanitarian law, required a robust response. This was difficult to achieve through the Mechanism due to institutional capacity and normative constraints that were built around adherence to nonintervention. Hence, the constraints imposed by the Charter, and the desire to provide adequate responses to the brutal conflicts paved the way for the AU, which was launched in Durban, South Africa, in July 2002.

The Constitutive Act: An Interventionist Regime

The Constitutive Act establishing the AU was adopted in July 2000, replacing the OAU Charter, which was out of sync with developments on the ground. Since

---

[38] The policy of nonintervention was clearly spelled out in Article III of the Charter of the Organization of African Unity, Addis Ababa, May 25, 1963.

[39] See *Declaration of the Assembly of Heads of State and Government on the Establishment within the OAU of a Mechanism for Conflict Prevention, Management and Resolution*, AHG/DECL.3(XXIX).

[40] Monde Muyangwa and Margaret A. Vogt, "An Assessment of the OAU Mechanism for Conflict Prevention, Management and Resolution 1993–2000," *International Peace Academy Report*, 2000. Report can be accessed from http://www.ipacademy.org.

Collective Security Mechanisms in Post–Cold War Africa 283

then, the AU has been developing its preventive and responsive capacities. The Constitutive Act, perhaps the most interventionist regime anywhere in the world, provides for the AU to intervene in inter- and intrastate conflicts. For instance, although Article 3(b) of the Constitutive Act pledged to "defend the sovereignty, territorial integrity and independence of its member states," the Act gives member states the prerogative to intervene in cases of genocide, war crimes, or other gross violations of human rights. In this respect, Articles 4(h) and (j) stipulate "the right of the Union to intervene in a Member State . . . in respect of grave circumstances, namely war crimes, genocide and crimes against humanity," and the right of member states to request intervention from the Union to restore peace and security.[41]

The Peace and Security Council (PSC)

To implement its ambitious peace and security agenda, the first Summit of the AU held in Durban, South Africa, in July 2002, adopted the Protocol Relating to the Establishment of the Peace and Security Council of the African Union.[42] The PSC was established as the "standing decision-making organ for the prevention, management and resolution of conflicts"[43] and is meant to act as a collective security and early warning instrument for timely and efficient response to both existing and emerging conflicts and crises in Africa.

The PSC is comprised of fifteen member states elected on the basis of equal rights. Ten of the members are elected for a two-year period, whereas the remaining five are elected for three years. The election of members of the PSC is to be guided by the principle of equitable representation of the five regions: North, West, Central, East, and Southern Africa.[44]

Unlike the UN Security Council where the five permanent members wield the veto, none of the fifteen members of the PSC has a veto; all members are entitled to one vote each. The protocol, however, took account of the need for regional balance so as to increase cooperation, and also factored in the power balance among its membership by emphasizing the need for members to possess the political, military, financial, and diplomatic muscle to execute their mandate. This was identified as a major shortfall of the OAU Mechanism because it failed to specify the criteria for membership to the Central Organ. This meant that some of the most influential powers on the continent such as Nigeria, South Africa, Algeria, Senegal, Ghana, Kenya, and Egypt could be potentially left out of the Organ. Under the new arrangement, these countries could be considered for a three-year membership, a pseudo-UN Security Council but without the veto.

---

[41] *Constitutive Act of the African Union*, Lomè, Togo, July 2000, p. 5. The Constitutive Act was formally adopted by the AU at its first Summit Meeting in Durban, South Africa, in 2002.
[42] *Protocol Relating to the Establishment of the Peace and Security Council of the African Union*, Durban, South Africa, July 9, 2002.
[43] Ibid., p. 4.
[44] Ibid., p. 8.

The PSC is to be supported by the African Commission, a Panel of the Wise, a Continental Early Warning System, an African Standby Force (ASF), and a Special Fund. A Panel of the Wise consisting of prominent Africans was established in 2006. At the time of this writing, plans were also under way to operationalize the African Standby Force and the continental early warning system. Efforts to operationalize the ASF have registered varying degrees of progress, with most subregions adopting the policy and legal frameworks for establishing the regional standby brigades, the pillars of the ASF. Similar progress has been registered in establishing the continental early warning system linking the AU and the Regional Economic Communities (RECs).

The AU recognizes the need for collaboration with RECs, the UN, and other multilateral institutions. Its relationship with the RECs will be guided by the principles of subsidiarity and comparative advantage. For instance, the AU will allow RECs to take the lead in situations where they possess a strong comparative advantage. In this vein, although the AU has been involved in attempts to resolve the crisis in Côte d'Ivoire, it has allowed ECOWAS to take the lead and has provided political support to bolster ECOWAS' role. The interface between ECOWAS and the AU in this instance adhered to the principle of comparative advantage because ECOWAS has more leverage in this case than the AU. In fact, the Ivorian crisis has involved a trilateral linkage involving the ECOWAS, the AU, and the UN, and provides useful lessons for future cooperation between the UN and regional entities, and between the AU and the RECs.

However, the AU has taken the lead in Burundi and Somalia, where the subregional organizations were either weak or the neutrality of some of the member states could not be guaranteed. In 2004, the AU deployed its first peace operation in Burundi due to the weakness of the subregional entities. And in 2006, it deployed the AU Mission in Somalia (AMISOM) because the neutrality of Somalia's immediate neighbors – Kenya, Ethiopia, and Djibouti – who are also members of the Inter Governmental Authority on Development (IGAD), the subregional body, could not be guaranteed and would undermine the credibility of the operation.

But although the AU can fill the void in some regions due to the reasons discussed earlier, it will have a limited operational role in regions with strong entities such as West and Southern Africa. The AU's role in these regions is likely to be limited to a legitimizing role through its support for initiatives undertaken by ECOWAS or SADC. In June 2008, the AU, RECs, and Coordinating Mechanisms signed a Memorandum of Understanding to guide their interactions, which among others will address questions of coordinating the activities of the decision-making organs of the AU and these subregional entities.[45] As a first step, in 2007 it was agreed that the

---

[45] See The Memorandum of Understanding on Cooperation in the area of Peace and Security between the African Union, the Regional Economic Communities and the Coordinating Mechanisms of the Regional Standby Brigades of Eastern Africa and Northern Africa, Addis Ababa, Ethiopia, June 2008. This document can be found at: http://www.africa-union.org/root/AU/publications/PSC/MOU-AU%20and%20RECs.pdf.

RECs would send representatives to the AU headquarters in Addis Ababa, a process that was well underway by the time of this writing.

The AU's relationship with the UN will be guided by Chapter VIII of the UN Charter, which makes provision for regional organizations to participate in the maintenance of international peace and security. At the time of this writing, the AU and the UN have collaborated on a broad range of issues from capacity-building to hand-over missions, and joint or hybrid operations. However, the relationship between the two institutions in the area of peacekeeping is likely to be shaped by the outcome of the hybrid UN–AU mission in Darfur, the first joint deployment between the two.

To date, the AU has deployed peace operations in Burundi (2004), Darfur (2004), Comoros (2006, 2007), and Somalia (2006). That these missions have put the AU on the radar as an important player in maintaining peace and security in Africa is beyond dispute. But they have also revealed serious capacity gaps, especially with respect to the AU's ability to undertake effective multidimensional peace operations. The AU's deployments thus far have demonstrated several important points. First, AU decisions enjoy a great deal of legitimacy among its members, manifested by the widespread support for its interventions, except for Somalia where member states have been reluctant to contribute troops. Second, these operations have demonstrated a "willingness and capability" gap as was brought to fore by its mission in Sudan (AMIS). Despite a strong commitment by member states, AMIS suffered from a perennial shortage of finances and other crucial mission-enabling elements. Third, the AU has some capacity to undertake small-scale missions such as Comoros or act as a bridgehead for a larger UN force as was the case in Burundi – especially where one country is prepared to take on the role of lead nation, as South Africa did in Burundi and Tanzania has done in Comoros. Fourth, the Darfur operation has demonstrated the limits of the ad hoc financial and logistics support systems that were organized to support AMIS, thereby calling for a more structured division of labor between the AU and its international partners.

U.S. POLICY IN AFRICA

The failed U.S. humanitarian intervention in Somalia in 1993 was a turning point in its involvement on the continent. When the United States withdrew from Somalia it was clear that it would not easily return to Africa in an operational role.

Presidential Decision Directive 25 (PDD-25)

Immediately after the Somali debacle, the administration of President Bill Clinton adopted Presidential Decision Directive 25: the Clinton administration's Policy on Reforming Multilateral Peace Operations in May 1994. PDD-25 addressed six major issues that the administration identified as crucial in determining U.S. support and improving the overall efficacy of peace operations. Among others, the issues included making disciplined and coherent choices about which peace operations the United States should support – both in voting at the Security Council and in participating in such operations, defining clearly U.S. policy regarding command and control of American forces in UN peace operations, and reforming and improving the UN's capability to manage peace operations.[46]

With respect to the first point about making "disciplined and coherent choices," PDD-25 outlined stringent standards that were to be applied in determining U.S. support for a particular peace operation and enumerated even stricter standards in situations that may involve the deployment of U.S. personnel especially in Chapter VII robust operations. However, although the Clinton administration acknowledged that "peace operations can be a useful tool to advance American national interests . . . " it also declared that the "US cannot be the world's policeman,"[47] despite emphasis that it will not act as a bystander in situations of internal strife that may have a cumulative effect on U.S. national interests.[48]

Thus, PDD-25 marked a dramatic shift in U.S. policy as Washington became more cautious and reluctant to either directly intervene or support UN interventions in situations where U.S. national interests were not directly threatened. Herman J. Cohen, former Assistant Secretary of State for African Affairs, argued that with the adoption of PDD-25, "assertive multilateralism," a cornerstone of President Bill Clinton's early days in power, was abandoned for a more cautious and prudent approach, and lamented the policy shift.[49] Although Cohen agreed with the Clinton administration's application of "national interest" as a "litmus test" for the deployment of U.S. troops, he criticized the administration for using it as a standard test for all peace operations, even those that did not include U.S. military deployments.[50] The consequences of such a broad approach were immediately felt in Rwanda with the outbreak of the genocide in April 1994.

Less than a year after the U.S. withdrawal from Somalia, and the adoption of PDD-25, Rwanda was embroiled in a genocide that left an estimated 800,000 people dead in the space of one hundred days. The genocide raised serious moral dilemmas for the international community, especially in relation to humanitarian

---

[46] For more information see, *The Clinton Administration's Policy on Reforming Multilateral Peace Operations PDD-25*, White Paper. This document can be found at: http://clinton2.nara.gov/WH/EOP/NSC/html;.document/NSCDoc1.htm1.

[47] Ibid., p. 13.

[48] Ivo H. Daalder, "Knowing When to Say No: The Development of US Policy for Peacekeeping," in Bill Durch, *UN Peacekeeping, American Politics, and the Uncivil Wars of the 1990s* (New York: St. Martin's Press, 1996).

[49] See Madeleine K. Albright (then U.S. Permanent Representative to the United Nations), "Myths of Peacekeeping," Statement before the House Subcommittee on International Security, International Organizations, and Human Rights, House Committee on Foreign Affairs, Washington DC, June 24, 1993.

[50] Herman J. Cohen, "US-Africa Policy as Conflict Management," *SAIS Review* XXI, no. 1 (Winter-Spring 2001), pp. 240–1; *Intervening in Africa: Superpower Peacemaking in a Troubled Continent* (New York: St. Martin's Press, 2000).

intervention in the face of long-standing nonintervention norms. To most observers, however, U.S. policy during the Rwanda genocide was largely shaped by its experience in Somalia, which had ended with the humiliating collapse of the United Nations Operation in Somalia (UNOSOM). According to Boutros Boutros-Ghali, then Secretary-General of the UN, Somalia had a particularly negative impact on the response of the international community. In his own words: "Disillusion set in. Where peacekeepers were asked to deal with warfare, serious setbacks occurred. The first came in Somalia, and weakened the will of the world community to act against genocide in Rwanda."[51]

It was therefore not surprising that the Clinton administration refused to label the killings as "genocide" or heed pleas for reinforcements of the United Nations Assistance Mission in Rwanda (UNAMIR). Instead, the mission was scaled down, leaving only a skeletal force with no capacity to change the course of events on the ground.

Although the United States disengaged from Africa at the strategic level, it remained engaged at the tactical level, primarily by providing support to develop the capacities of African countries to keep the peace on the continent. Throughout the 1990s, capacity-building efforts were largely bilateral with minimal focus on the regional and subregional entities, although U.S. policy toward these institutions has changed over the past five years, as manifested by its appointment of an ambassador to the AU Commission in 2006.

The African Crisis Response Force (ACRF), launched immediately after the genocide in Rwanda, was the first in a series of capacity-building initiatives. The ACRF was to comprise African forces that could be rapidly deployed in a theater of conflict. The initiative did not gain traction as it was viewed by some African leaders, most notably former president Nelson Mandela, as a knee-jerk reaction by the Clinton administration for its failure to intervene in Rwanda and an excuse to establish a foothold on the continent.[52] Consequently, it failed to muster support among African governments who saw it as an imposition from outside that smacked of colonialism. The ACRF evolved into a new initiative known as the Africa Crisis Response Initiative (ACRI), retaining some elements of the ACRF.

The Africa Crisis Response Initiative

The ACRI's main objective was to train African contingents on a bilateral basis for future peacekeeping missions on the continent. Although ACRI was initially

[51] Cited in Ingrid A. Lehmann, *Peacekeeping and Public Information – Caught in the Crossfire* (London: Frank Cass, 1999), p. 90. For an in-depth analysis of U.S. policy during the genocide see Samantha Powers, "Bystanders to Genocide," *The Atlantic Monthly* (September 2001), which can be accessed at: http://www.mtholyoke.edu/acad/intrel/power.htm; and Powers, *A Problem from Hell: America in the Age of Genocide* (New York: Basic Books, 2002).

[52] Brian J. Hesse, *The United States, South Africa and Africa: Of Grand Foreign Policy Aims and Modest Means* (Aldershot: Ashgate, 2001).

designed to operate on a bilateral basis, the United States explored the possibility of allowing subregional entities such as ECOWAS to receive direct military assistance through ACRI.[53] But although some countries like Uganda, Ethiopia, and Senegal embraced ACRI, Nigeria and South Africa remained opposed to what they viewed as a foreign initiative that did not necessarily address African concerns. However, troops from Ghana, Senegal, Uganda, and Tanzania trained under the ACRI initiative and served in Liberia as part of the expanded ECOMOG in 1997.

The Africa Contingency Training Assistance

Meanwhile, ACRI was succeeded by the Africa Contingency Training Assistance (ACOTA), which was initiated by the Bush administration. ACOTA like its predecessor is based on bilateral agreements between the United States and recipient states, although there is reference to providing support to strengthen the capacities of regional and subregional organizations. Perhaps ACOTA's most significant innovation is the inclusion of training for "offensive" military operations and the provision of participating countries with weaponry to undertake such operations. The inclusion of offensive training in ACOTA can be explained by the growing trend of robust peace operations, a shift from traditional peacekeeping. The existence of a large number of spoilers who are often not parties to a peace agreement has led in some instances to a blurring of the line between peace operations and war fighting as in DRC and potentially Darfur (as well as non-African examples such as Afghanistan). ACOTA also moved away from the "one-size-fits-all" approach that characterized earlier programs. Under this initiative, training modules were tailored to suit the needs of the recipient states, thereby taking into consideration the varied training needs among African countries.[54]

Global Peace Operations Initiative

In 2005, the United States launched the Global Peace Operations Initiative (GPOI) aimed at improving the supply of peacekeepers, which is currently outpaced by rising demand. The central objectives of GPOI are, among others, to train at least 75,000 peacekeepers globally, with a strong focus on Africa at the initial stages, and enhance the ability of countries and regional and subregional organizations to train, prepare for, plan, manage, conduct, and learn from peace operations by providing technical assistance, training, and material support to enhance institutional knowledge at headquarters.[55] One of GPOI's innovations is its recognition of the strategic

---

[53] For more information on ACRI and other U.S. initiatives see Berman and. Sams, op. cit., pp. 267–90.

[54] See Russell J. Hardy, "Africa Contingency Operations Training Assistance: Developing Training Partnerships for the Future of Africa," *Air & Space Power Journal* (Fall 2003).

[55] More information on GPOI can be found at: http://www.state.gov/t/pm/ppa/gpoiteam/gpoi/c20337.htm. Last accessed April 24, 2007.

significance of developing the capacities of regional and subregional institutions. It is envisaged that developing the capacities of these institutions will ensure "sustainability and self-sustainment," which is at the core of the program. Moreover, GPOI will also provide support to centers of excellence like the Kofi Annan International Peacekeeping Training Center in Ghana; the Peace Support Training Center in Karen, Kenya; and the Peacekeeping School in Koulikoro, Mali. GPOI provides support to operationalize the African Standby Force (ASF) and regional and subregional logistics depots.

The shift in U.S. approach to regional and subregional organizations could be explained by several factors. First, it is recognition of these organizations as valuable partners in the maintenance of peace and security on the continent. Despite acute financial and logistical challenges, these organizations have demonstrated a commitment to the maintenance of peace in Africa dating back to the ECOWAS deployments in the early 1990s. Second, the exponential growth in the demand for peacekeepers in the face of continued reluctance by Western nations to deploy troops to UN-led peace operations on the continent often leaves the burden of peacekeeping on a handful of African troop contributors. It is therefore imperative to provide support to develop the capacities of these organizations. Third, these organizations have put in place the necessary legal frameworks that give legitimacy to their actions. The adoption of the protocol establishing the Peace and Security Council is the most significant move in this respect.

Like its predecessors, GPOI faced daunting funding challenges. Budget support for these initiatives has been inadequate and has often been cut to cater to other competing demands for resources. In fiscal year 2006, the request for support for the State Department's Voluntary Peacekeeping Operations account was under $200 million. This account includes support for Africa and GPOI, which has a global mandate. Funding requested for the Africa regional account was a paltry $41 million.[56] Such low budget figures raise question about the level of U.S. commitment to developing the capacities of African troop contributors. Nonetheless, the shift in U.S. policy toward these entities is a significant development.

CONCLUSION

Efforts to develop collective security instruments in post–Cold War Africa have resulted in remarkable progress. The paradigm shift in the understanding of security paved the way for the establishment of mechanisms that addressed both interstate and intrastate security. The instruments adopted by ECOWAS, SADC, and, most importantly, the AU serve as useful platforms to deal with intrastate conflicts. For instance, West Africa has moved from its ad hoc interventions of the early 1990s to

---

[56] See Victoria K. Holt, hearing on "African Organizations and Institutions: Positive Cross-Continental Progress," *Subcommittee on African Affairs, Senate Foreign Relations Committee*, US Senate, Washington DC, November 17, 2005.

an institutionalized system designed to deal with the political, legal, and diplomatic controversy that arose from those interventions. Southern Africa has emerged from decades of violence and destabilization to develop robust mechanisms to deal with conflict. Progress in southern Africa has been remarkable as it has moved from being one of the most unstable subregions to perhaps the most stable and prosperous on the continent.

At the continental level, the establishment of the AU has significantly improved the chances of developing broader continental response mechanisms like the African Standby Force. The AU has been proactive in finding solutions to some of the intractable conflicts on the continent, though not without its challenges. The AU mission in Darfur and Sudan brought to the fore its capacity and resource constraints as it embarks on implementing its ambitious peace and security agendas. The shortage of resources has often led to close partnerships with multilateral and bilateral partners like the UN and the United States. The United States, which was not an active player in the formation of these organizations, has moved from being a skeptical observer to a proactive partner. But care should be taken to ensure that the security concerns on the continent are not subsumed by U.S. security interests, reminiscent of the Cold War years when African security concerns were overshadowed by superpower rivalry.

15

International Courts and Tribunals

Cesare P. R. Romano

One of the most visible changes brought about by the end of the Cold War to the structure, institutions, and discourse of international law and relations is the remarkable multiplication of international courts and tribunals and their increasing specialization and diversification.[1] This chapter aims to verify the extent to which the evolution of the array of international courts since the end of the Cold War has followed the two major lines of development suggested in this volume's introduction (the adaptation of existing institutions and the creation of new ones), and how far it has matched the three phases identified by the editors as characterizing international relations (the end of the Cold War to 9/11, the phase between 9/11 and the invasion of Iraq, and the period from the fall of Saddam Hussein to the present day, at the time of this writing).

It is necessary to make some initial general observations and then delimit the scope of the analysis. The first general remark is that it is apparent that the development of international courts and tribunals has been largely haphazard and unplanned – perhaps inevitably so. Every court was born out of highly contingent situations, sometimes trying to replicate the success of previous experiments, and at other times, in reaction to past failures or the need to provide alternatives. Key players also have different attitudes and behaviors, changing from court to court and over time. It is all highly contextual. It is also apparent that the only significant catalytic event in the

---

[1] For some explanations of why international courts have proliferated, see, in general: the issue of *International Organizations* devoted to "Legalization and World Politics" (Vol. 54, No. 3, summer, 2000); José E. Alvarez, "The New Dispute Settlers: (Half) Truths and Consequences," *Texas International Law Journal* 38 (2003); and Romano, "The Proliferation of International Judicial Bodies: The Pieces of the Puzzle." For a comprehensive listing of international adjudicative bodies, see Cesare P. R. Romano, "The Proliferation of International Judicial Bodies: The Pieces of the Puzzle," *NYU Journal of International Law and Politics* 31 (1999), pp. 709, 715–9. An updated version, 3d edition, is reprinted in Jose Alvarez, *International Organizations as Law-makers* (2005), pp. 404–7. Available at http://www.pict-pcti.org/publications/synoptic_chart/Synoptic%20Espanol.pdf.

modern history of international adjudication is the end of the Cold War, and there is little sign – perhaps besides the case of the criminal courts – that the 9/11 events and the war on Iraq have had any impact. Only some very broad general trends can be discerned. There is really no single factor driving development or reform common to all international courts.

Second, between international adjudication, on the one hand, and peace and security, on the other, there is not a straightforward causal relationship, not even in the case of international criminal courts. Although advocates of international courts and tribunals rightly claim that no lasting peace can exist unless justice has been done, at least for the most egregious war crimes and crimes against humanity, it is equally a well-known fact that justice cannot be properly administered while guns are roaring. International courts can help defuse a diplomatic crisis, stabilize countries, or prevent further deterioration of a situation, but they need a high degree of security, stability, and peace to operate credibly, particularly because they lack enforcement powers of their own and are highly dependent on the cooperation of all involved states.

To illustrate the complexity of the relationship between peace and justice, one can note that although the International Criminal Tribunal for the former Yugoslavia (ICTY) was established in 1993 and started operating in earnest in 1994, it did not prevent, by its mere existence, the massacres in Srebrenica, Goradze, and other Bosnian towns in 1995. It was only after the Dayton agreement and the ensuing peace in Bosnia-Herzegovina that the ICTY had access to the crime scenes, could carry out investigations, and obtain arrest of some (but not all) of those most responsible. On the other hand, had the ICTY not indicted Slobodan Milosevic he would probably still be in power in Belgrade, making any long-term stabilization of the region doubtful. Again, some argue that the issuing of arrest warrants for crimes against humanity and war crimes by the ICC Prosecutor against five senior commanders of the Lord's Resistance Army rebel movement in Uganda undermined attempts to reach a negotiated settlement of the civil war.[2] At the same time, there is little doubt that the ICC's indictments were a significant factor in creating pressure on the Lord's Resistance Army to cease its campaign of mayhem and terror in northern Uganda.[3]

Subject to this qualification, the scope of this analysis is limited to those courts that might have an impact on peace and security issues. International criminal courts are obviously central to this analysis, but there is more. The International Court of

---

[2] See, in this book, Malone, at Chapter 4. See also, William W. Burke-White, "Double-Edged Tribunals: Domestic Politics and the Relationships among National and International Courts," in *International Institutional Reform: Proceedings of the Seventh Hague Joint Conference Held in The Hague, the Netherlands, June 30–July 2, 2005*, (The Hague: T.M.C. Asser Press, 2006), pp. 203–12.

[3] See Nick Grono, "What Comes First, Peace or Justice? Uganda's Dilemma," *International Herald Tribune* (27 October 2006).

Justice (ICJ), although a court of general jurisdiction, has time and again decided disputes arising out of situations threatening international peace and security, and the legality of the use of force.[4] Being the principal judicial organ of the United Nations (UN), the universal organization devoted to maintenance of international peace and security, it cannot be ignored.

Human rights courts, too, can play an important role. True, the relationship between these courts and issues of peace and security is only indirect. Human rights courts rarely face situations of widespread chaos and violence, and when they do, they are largely toothless. But international human rights courts facilitate maintenance of peace and security because governments that grossly abuse human rights often either become belligerent toward their neighbors or face domestic insurrections and civil wars. They might help prevent governments from following this path to chaos and strife. In other words, if international criminal courts are the fire brigade, human rights courts are the fire alarm and sprinkler system.

Other courts, like the European Court of Justice, or the dispute settlement system of the World Trade Organization, will not be treated, as their connection with peace and security issues is very indirect – unless, of course, one takes a very broad approach to the concept, arguing that without an "international rule of law" administered by an impartial third-party adjudicator, international peace and security cannot be guaranteed.

Finally, this chapter considers also the influence that key players, such as the UN, the United States, and Europe, as well as other major powers, have in the development of international courts and how they relate to them. However, when we speak of "European" attitudes, policies, and behaviors, the adjective is used as shorthand for the European Community/European Union (EC/EU). At other times, it is used in the large geographical sense to indicate countries that are not or were not yet, at the time we refer to, members of the EC/EU but are on the European continent. (Russia is, however, treated separately.) The reader should also remember that the composition of the EC/EU has changed over time, and as with the UN, there can be a difference between attitudes and behaviors of EC/EU institutions and those of its member states. Indeed, the UN plays a role of its own in – and has its own attitudes toward – international courts and tribunals that is somehow different from the mere sum of the positions of its most influential members.

---

4 For example, Corfu Channel (United Kingdom v. Albania); Temple of Preah Vihear (Cambodia v. Thailand); United States Diplomatic and Consular Staff in Teheran (United States v. Iran); Military and Paramilitary Activities in and against Nicaragua (Nicaragua v. United States); Border and Trans-border Armed Actions (Nicaragua v. Costa Rica and Nicaragua v. Honduras); Aerial Incident of July 3, 1988 (Islamic Republic of Iran v. United States); Territorial Dispute (Libyan Arab Jamahiriya/Chad); Oil Platforms (Islamic Republic of Iran v. United States); Land and Maritime Boundary between Cameroon and Nigeria (Cameroon v. Nigeria); Armed Activities on the Territory of the Congo (Democratic Republic of Congo v. Uganda, Rwanda and Burundi).

EVOLUTION, ADAPTATION, ATTITUDES, AND BEHAVIORS

The International Court of Justice

The end of the Cold War and subsequent world events have had only marginal impact on courts that settle legal disputes among sovereign states, the oldest genus of all international courts, whose roots can be traced back to the practice of international arbitration. International courts to hear disputes among sovereign states were born (or at least conceived) during, or even before, the Cold War. The ICJ was created in 1945, and it was largely the continuation of the Permanent Court of International Justice, (PCIJ) established in 1921. No new court to decide classical disputes among sovereign states at the global level was established at the end of the Cold War, and there are no signs that any has been considered since.[5] If institutional innovation has taken place in this particular genus of international relations, it has only been marginal. After all, a two-century-long practice has crystallized structures and categories in this field.

What has changed with the end of the Cold War, however, is the frequency of the resort to the ICJ or international arbitration. The number of cases litigated in these fora during the forty-one years of the Cold War is a fraction of those litigated in the eighteen years since its end. Fifty of the 109 cases submitted to the ICJ in its entire history have been started since 1990. Also, the Permanent Court of Arbitration, the oldest of existing international dispute settlement bodies, having been founded in 1899, underwent a true renaissance since the end of the Cold War.[6] It was largely abandoned after World War II, its facilities and services unused for decades, but has gotten back in business since the early 1990s, with several cases now on its docket, and its services in demand.[7]

---

[5] The only exception being, at the regional level, the OSCE Court for Conciliation and Arbitration, which was created in 1995. Yet, it was hatched toward the end of the Cold War and in its history and structure reflects quintessential Cold War concerns. It has never been used. For a detailed analysis of the history of the creation of the OSCE Court, see Patricia Schneider and Tim J. Aristide Müller-Wolf, "The Court of Conciliation and Arbitration within the OSCE: Working Methods, Procedures and Composition," Center for OSCE Research, University of Hamburg, Working Paper 16 (2007), pp. 5–18, available at: http://www.core-hamburg.de/documents/CORE_Working_Paper_16.pdf.

[6] It was established by the 1899 Hague Convention on the Pacific Settlement of International Disputes, subsequently revised in 1907. For the text of the Convention of July 29, 1899, see C. I. Bevans, ed., *Treaties and Other International Agreements of the United States of America 1776–1949* (1968), Vol. I, pp. 230–46. For the text of the Convention of October 18, 1907, see id. at pp. 577–606.

[7] The point has been well made that the name "Permanent Court of Arbitration" is not a wholly accurate description of the machinery set up by the Hague conventions. Indeed the PCA is neither a "court" nor "permanent." It is rather an institutional framework open to parties to a dispute to avail themselves of at their choice. It provides them with all legal, administrative, and secretarial services necessary to have an effective settlement of the dispute, including providing an updated list of leading scholars and practitioners to be appointed as arbitrators or conciliators; acting as a channel of communication between the parties, holding and disbursing deposits for costs; ensuring safe custody of documents;

International Courts and Tribunals 295

Moreover a larger and more diversified group of states use these courts than in the past. During the Cold War they were mostly used to litigate disputes either among Western countries or between the West and developing countries; since the end of the Cold War developing countries have also increasingly resorted to them to litigate disputes among themselves.[8]

The UN is, of course, central to the fortunes of the ICJ, because the "World Court," as it is dubbed, is the principal judicial organ of the UN.[9] Although the UN itself cannot bring disputes before the World Court, time and again it has used the advisory jurisdiction of the court to "litigate disputes" with certain UN members or attempted to use it to change the dynamics of issues that had reached a dead end within political organs of the organization (like occupation of South-West Africa,[10] or Palestine,[11] or nuclear weapons[12]). However, the UN is arguably the reason why the ICJ has been highly resistant to change, to the point of having its relevance to international relations questioned. The Statute of the ICJ is part of the UN Charter, and the UN Charter has proven to be all but nonreformable.[13]

Since World War II, the attitude and practice of the United States toward the ICJ have been far from consistent. Specifically, one can identify four distinct phases.[14] The first one, from its inception to 1959, was characterized by high hopes. The United States championed carrying the prewar PCIJ over to the new UN, in the form of the ICJ. This period was marked by several efforts by the United States to invoke the jurisdiction of the Court, without success, against countries of the Communist bloc while, at the same time, it managed to avoid the Court's jurisdiction. As a result, the second phase, between 1960 and 1979, was a lengthy period where the United States viewed the Court as a failure or, at least, as inconsequential. The third phase, between 1980 and 1987, was the period of the return to the Court. During those years, the United States accepted the Court's jurisdiction to handle

---

arranging for efficient secretarial, language, and communications services; and providing a courtroom and office space.

[8] See, in general, C, Romano, "International Justice and Developing Countries (cont.): A Qualitative Analysis," *Law and Practice of International Courts and Tribunals* 1 (2002), pp. 539–611; idem, "International Justice and Developing Countries: A Quantitative Analysis," *Law and Practice of International Courts and Tribunals* 1, (2002), pp. 367–99.

[9] UN Charter, art. 92.

[10] Legal Consequences for States of the Continued Presence of South Africa in Namibia (South-West Africa) notwithstanding Security Council Resolution 276 (1970), Advisory Opinion, 1971 *I.C.J.* 16.

[11] Legal Consequences of the Construction of a Wall in the Occupied Palestinian Territory, Advisory Opinion, 2004 *I.C.J.* 136.

[12] Legality of the Threat or Use of Nuclear Weapons, Advisory Opinion, 1996 *I.C.J.* 226 (July 8).

[13] For some of the literature on UN and ICJ reform, see ABILA Committee on Intergovernmental Settlement, "Reforming the United Nations: What about the International Court of Justice?", in ABILA Committee on Intergovernmental Settlement of Disputes, Report, *Chinese Journal of International Law* 5 (2006), pp. 39–65, note 4.

[14] Murphy, S., "The U.S. and the International Court of Justice: Coping with Antinomies," in C. Romano, ed., *The Sword and the Scales: The US and International Courts and Tribunals* (Cambridge University Press, 2009).

both a territorial dispute[15] and a major political crisis,[16] only to be followed by bitter rejection of the Court after losing a politically charged Cold War case (the so-called *Nicaragua* case).[17] Finally, since the dawn of the post–Cold War era (about 1988) to present, the attitude has consistently been merely defensive. The United States has declined bringing any cases, while aggressively defending against cases brought by others. During this phase, it has resisted the Court without breaking from it and has turned to other fora, particularly for what concerns issues of trade and economics.

The attitude of the Europeans toward the ICJ has probably been equally ambiguous. This might sound surprising given that Europeans have the reputation of being enthusiastic supporters of the idea of an international rule of law administered through international courts. However, this reputation seems to be due more to the success of regional courts, like the European Court of Justice and the European Court of Human Rights, in replacing power politics with a rule-based system, rather than any commitment to the ICJ. There is definitely a need for a better understanding of European policies (or lack thereof) in this field.

Subject to the caveat at the beginning of this chapter about the use of the adjective "European," it can be safely said that European states in general have not been particularly supportive of the ICJ, surely no more than other states or regions. If support is measured not by number of judges on the bench and funding (which, in any event, are not elective but both depend on the UN structure), and not by words and rhetoric, but by actual behaviors, the European record is mixed. Like the United States, Western European states have long kept the ICJ at arm's length, trying to avoid appearing before it, both as plaintiffs and as defendants, if possible. The number of cases initiated, or submitted with the agreement of the other party, by West Europeans is relatively small,[18] and in some of these they did so as part of "the West" and not individually.[19] The United States has been involved in twenty-one cases before the ICJ (nine as applicant, eleven as respondent, and one consensually), more than the UK (seven, five, and one),[20] France (six, six, and two),[21] Germany

---

[15] Delimitation of the Maritime Boundary in the Gulf of Maine Area (Canada/United States), 1984 *I.C.J.* 246 (Oct. 12).

[16] United States Diplomatic and Consular Staff in Tehran (United States v. Iran), 1980 *I.C.J.* 3 (May 24); 1979 *I.C.J.* 7 (Dec. 15) (provisional measures).

[17] Military and Paramilitary Activities in and against Nicaragua (Nicaragua v. United States), 1991 *I.C.J.* 47 (Sept. 26) (removal); 1986 *I.C.J.* 14 (June 27); 1984 *I.C.J.* 392 (Nov. 26) (jurisdiction).

[18] Out of 109 cases submitted to date to the ICJ, the number of cases started by, or litigated by agreement including, a European State (i.e., the fifteen Western EC members, before the last two recent enlargements), is 24.

[19] For instance, in the case of the dispute arising out of the bombing of Pan Am flight 103 over Lockerbie, Libya filed cases both against the UK and the United States. In the case of the NATO bombing campaign over Kosovo in 1991, Yugoslavia filed cases against the United States, the UK, Spain, Portugal, Netherlands, Italy, Germany, France, Canada, and Belgium.

[20] The last time the UK submitted a case to the ICJ was in 1972, against Iceland.

[21] The last time France submitted a case to the ICJ was in 1959, against Norway.

International Courts and Tribunals

(four, two, and zero),[22] and Italy (one, two, and zero).[23] These figures do not suggest a particular European predilection for the ICJ. Moreover, although everyone seems to remember how the United States refused to participate in the proceedings in the *Nicaragua* case, and withdrew its acceptance of jurisdiction, few seem to remember that France and Iceland had essentially done the same a few years before.[24] Currently, of the twenty-seven members of the EC/EU only eighteen have declared acceptance of the jurisdiction of the ICJ,[25] and often with extensive reservations.[26] Even more remarkably, three out of the "big four" members of the Union – Germany, Italy, and France – have no "optional declaration" standing.

It is a fact that since the *Nicaragua* case at least,[27] and surely since the end of the Cold War, the ICJ has increasingly become a favorite for developing countries. In particular, it is becoming a forum of choice for medium and small developing countries, whereas large powers (e.g., China, India, Brazil, Nigeria, Mexico, and also Russia) have either been absent or have had mixed records. This phenomenon can be explained both by the indifference of developed countries, which, as we just explained, appear seldom and grudgingly, and by a certain tendency (conscious or unconscious) of the ICJ to pander to the majority of the UN General Assembly (made up of developing countries) when interpreting international law.

In recent years, the ICJ has decided a few cases that touch on post–9/11 anxieties and sensitivities. One is the question of the legality of the wall in Palestine, which is the cause célèbre in Islamic countries[28]; another is the question of the use of force to respond to low-intensity, hit-and-run attacks or asymmetric warfare[29]; and yet another is the question of sovereign immunity from jurisdiction for international crimes.[30] In all of these, the ICJ's answers have been criticized in the United States, but surely also perplexed many in Europe.

Human Rights Courts

The second genus of international courts to emerge historically is the one of human rights courts. As in the case of courts that can only hear disputes between sovereign

---

[22] The last time Germany submitted a case to the ICJ was in 1999, against the United States.

[23] The last time Italy submitted a case to the ICJ was in 1953, against France, the UK, and the United States.

[24] Fisheries Jurisdiction (United Kingdom v. Iceland), 1973 I.C.J. 3 (jurisdiction); Fisheries Jurisdiction (United Kingdom v. Iceland), 1974 I.C.J. 3 (Merits); Nuclear Tests (Australia v. France), 1974 I.C.J. 253; Nuclear Tests (New Zealand v. France), 1974 I.C.J. 457.

[25] Austria (declaration filed in 1971); Belgium (1958), Bulgaria (1992), Cyprus (2002), Denmark (1956), Estonia (1991), Finland (1958), Greece (1994), Hungary (1992), Luxemburg (1930), Malta (1966 and 1983), Netherlands (1956), Poland (1996), Portugal (1955), Slovakia (2004), Spain (1990), Sweden (1957), and the UK (1969).

[26] For example, the UK.

[27] See note 17 earlier.

[28] See note 11 earlier.

[29] Oil Platforms (Islamic Republic of Iran v. United States), 2003 I.C.J. 161 (Nov. 6), 1996 I.C.J. 803 (Dec. 12) (prel. obj.).

[30] For example, Certain Criminal Proceedings in France (Democratic Republic of Congo/France).

states, the courts belonging to this group are only a few. All had been created before the end of the Cold War, and their basic structure has changed a little. There are three of them: the European Court of Human Rights (ECHR), the Inter-American Court of Human Rights (IACHR), and the African Court of Human and Peoples' Rights (ACHPR), belonging, respectively, to the Council of Europe, the Organization of American States, and the Organization of African Unity (now African Union [AU]). The ECHR emerged in the late 1950s; the IACHR, in the 1970s; and the ACHPR, at the start of the current decade.

The main exception to the relative stasis that characterizes this group is the European system, which was substantially transformed in the early 1990s, as a result of the end of the Cold War and the need to accommodate former Soviet Republics and their satellites in the Council of Europe. With the entry into force of Protocol 11 to the European Convention, in 1998, the filter of the Commission has been abolished, and the Court now faces a staggering number of more than 700 million potential plaintiffs in forty-six countries.[31] The practical challenges facing a court with such a wide jurisdiction have prompted, in recent years, discussion about the need for further reform to avoid gridlock, sometimes invoking the need to reestablish some sort of filter between individuals and the court, but so far no radical solution has been implemented.[32]

The ECHR has long been regarded as the archetype of the human rights court, and a success; and Europe has fundamentally contributed, by both example and knowledge sharing, to the establishment of the other two regional systems. Over the years, the ECHR gained legitimacy and acceptance by European governments and domestic courts.[33] It entrenched the transition of countries like Spain, Portugal, and Greece from dictatorships to full-fledged democracies. It helped prevent Turkey from slipping down a dangerous authoritarian slope during the fight against the Kurds and the Islamists and over the question of Cyprus. As its footing became increasingly secure, it waded into contentious territory at the limit of the textual interpretation of the European Convention – like human rights in the private sphere – and away from traditional hard-core human rights issues – like forced disappearances, extrajudicial killings, and torture – which remain a significant part of the docket of the other human rights courts.

Nowadays, its jurisdiction extends to Eastern Europe, including the whole of the Russian Federation, and as far as Turkey's borders with Iran and Iraq. Hard-core

---

[31] Protocol No. 11 to the 1950 European Convention for the Protection of Human Rights and Fundamental Freedoms, May 11, 1994, E.T.S. 155.

[32] See, generally, Alastair Mowbray, "Proposals for Reform of the European Court of Human Rights," in *Public Law* 2 (2002), pp. 252–64; András B. Baka, "The Problems of the European Court of Human Rights and its Reform," in *L'état actuel des droits de l'homme dans le monde: défis et perspectives* (Paris: Pedone, 2006). Some reforms were implemented in the (yet to enter into force) Protocol 14 to the European Convention of Human Rights. See, generally, Paul Lemmens, Wouter Vandenhole, eds., *Protocol no. 14 and the Reform of the European Court of Human Rights* (Antwerpen: Intersentia, 2005).

[33] See, generally, Michael Goldhaber, *A People's History of The European Court of Human Rights* (New Brunswick, NJ: Rutgers University Press, 2007).

International Courts and Tribunals

human rights issues are coming back to the ECHR docket. In a world agitated by the moral dilemmas imposed by the U.S.-declared war on terrorism, and the invasion of Afghanistan and Iraq, one can wonder whether the ECHR can, wants, and would play a role in the maintenance of peace and security in a significant part of the globe. If it manages, if not to stop, to at least make Russia think harder before resorting again to ham-fisted tactics like those it used in Chechnya, that would be a significant achievement.[34] It remains to be seen whether and to what extent the ECHR will scrutinize the antiterrorism measures taken by European states (governments and legislatures) and the assistance they have given the United States in the war on terror.

In the Americas, there has been no change comparable to the one that took place in Europe in the aftermath of the Cold War. Looking hard for signs of change, one might notice that in recent years the Inter-American Court has put greater emphasis on following up its judgments and ensuring compliance with them by dedicating a significant part of its scarce resources to this task.[35] This is probably because with the waning of dictatorships in much of the continent (which had been justified by one bloc or the other during the Cold War), it has felt it could tackle with more confidence the issue of compliance with its own decisions. Like the ECHR in the 1980s, it is also slowly moving away from hard-core human rights issues. Until the mid-1990s most of its docket was made of cases arising out of the "dirty wars" (such as Guatemala, Nicaragua, El Salvador, and Colombia), as the conflicts fueled by the Cold War in Latin America were known, and the heritage of dictatorships (such as Argentina, Chile, and Peru). Since then, it has gradually moved into the terrain of economic, social, and cultural rights.

---

[34] Several cases brought by Chechen civilians against Russia have been decided by the ECHR in the past few years. See, for example, Khashiyev and Akayeva v. Russia, App. Nos. 57942/00 and 57945/00; Gasan v. Russia, App. No. 43402/02; Kolstov v. Russia, App. No. 41304/02; Petrushko v. Russia, App No. 36494/02; Isayeva v. Russia, App. No. 57950/00; Isayeva, Yusupova and Bazayeva v. Russia App Nos. 57947/00; 57948/00, 57949/00 (all Feb. 24, 2005); Timishev v. Russia App Nos. 55762/00 and 55974/00 (Dec. 13, 2005); Bazorkina v. Russia App No. 69481/01 (July 27, 2006); Estamirov and Others v. Russia, App No. 60272/00 (Oct. 12, 2006). Tarik Abdel-Monem, "Chechens Win First Claims in the European Court of Human Rights in Khashiyev & Akayeva v. Russia," *Cornell International Law Journal* 39 (2006) p. 171; Erika Niedowski, "Russians Find Justice Scarce," *The Baltimore Sun*, August 27, 2006, p. 21A. There are hundreds of cases involving human rights abuses in Chechnya currently pending before the ECHR. Joshua Pantesco, "Europe Rights Court Holds Russia liable for Death of Chechen," *Jurist Legal News & Research* (July 27, 2006), http://jurist.law.pitt.edu/paperchase/2006/07/europe-rights-court-holds-russia.php (last visited Oct. 27, 2006); "Russia Censured over Chechen Man," *BBC News* (July 27, 2006), http://news.bbc.co.uk/2/hi/europe/5219254.stm (last visited Oct. 27, 2006); "Russia Condemned for Disappearance of Chechen," *Human Rights Watch* (July 27, 2006), (last visited Oct. 27, 2006).

[35] The first decision on compliance with judgments of the IACHR was in 2001. I/A Court H.R., Case of Castillo-Páez v. Peru; Loayza-Tamayo, Castillo-Petruzzi, et al., Ivcher-Bronstein and the Constitutional Court. Monitoring Compliance with Judgment. Order of the Court of June 1, 2001. On the issue, see, generally, Morse Tan, "Member State Compliance with the Judgments of the Inter-American Court of Human Rights," *International Journal of Legal Information* 33 (2005) pp. 319–44; Mónica Pinto, "NGOs and the Inter-American Court of Human Rights," in Tullio Treves (ed.), *Civil Society, International Courts and Compliance Bodies* (The Hague: T.M.C. Asser Press, 2005), pp. 47–56.

It should be remarked that, between 2002 and 2006, the Inter-American Commission on Human Rights has questioned repeatedly the treatment of the detainees of the war on terror at Guantanamo Bay by the United States. Although the United States is not a state party to the American Convention on Human Rights, the Commission exercises jurisdiction over the United States on the basis of its mandate under the OAS Charter, to which the United States is a party. In such cases, the Commission applies the standards set forth in the American Declaration of the Rights and Duties of Man.[36] The Commission issued provisional measures urging the United States to close the Guantanamo Bay facility without delay; to remove the detainees in full accordance with international human rights law and international humanitarian law; to investigate, prosecute, and punish any instances of torture or other cruel, inhuman, or degrading treatment or punishment that may have occurred; and to take the necessary measures to ensure detainees a fair and transparent process before a competent, independent, and impartial decision maker.[37] This foray into the legal and moral quagmire of the war on terror did not have, unsurprisingly, much impact on U.S. policies and attitudes. It was probably the high mark of IHCHR criticism, as the United States was already showing signs of reconsidering its general war on terror strategy, but it makes clear that human rights bodies will not be silent witnesses to the war on terror.

Finally, Africa is the third continent to equip itself with a regional human rights agreement guaranteed by a commission and a court. Although the African Commission on Human and Peoples' Rights has now been active for twenty-one years, the Court came into being only in 2004, and it has yet to start operating.[38] The contribution of the African Commission to peace and security in the continent is, admittedly, very small – and, of course, that of the African Court is still only a hypothesis; yet, as we said earlier, peace and stability are often a prerequisite for the rule of law and not the consequence.[39] Considering the number, scale, and intensity of conflicts that have marred the region since at least the 1960s, no international organization, not even the UN itself, can claim a good record in Africa, least of all a Commission that does not have binding powers.

As concerns players in human rights courts, one should note that all human rights courts are regional and are attached to regional international organizations of a general competence (the Council of Europe, Organization of American States, Organization of African Unity/African Union). They have given the opportunity to regional powers to play an important role, both in their establishment and their

---

[36] American Declaration of the Rights and Duties of Man, O.A.S. Res. XXX, adopted by the Ninth International Conference of American States (1948), reprinted in *Basic Documents Pertaining to Human Rights in the Inter-American System*, OEA/Ser.L.V/II.82 doc.6 rev.1 at 17 (1992).

[37] Inter-American Commission on Human Rights, Resolution No. 1/06 of July 28, 2006.

[38] Protocol to the African Charter on the Establishment of the African Court on Human and Peoples' Rights. OAU/LEG/MIN/AFCHPR/PROT.1 rev.2 (1997).

[39] On compliance with recommendations of the African Commission, see, in general, Frans Viljoen and Lirrete Louw, "State Compliance with the Recommendations of the African Commission on Human and People's Rights – 1994–2004," *American Journal of International Law* 101 (2007), pp. 1–34.

functioning. Thus, the UN has played no role in their creation or functioning. Nor does it assist them. At the universal level, there are no comparable human rights mechanisms, unless one argues that the UN Human Rights Council, which has no binding powers, can be compared to an international tribunal.

The lack of UN participation can be explained by the fact that, for different reasons, neither the United States nor many Asian and Middle Eastern countries favor the idea of being submitted to the jurisdiction of human rights tribunals. The attitude of the United States can be best described as benign disinterest. It has nodded favorably to the Council of Europe for decades and welcomed its expansion eastward. It has supported, financially and politically, both the Inter-American Commission and – albeit less – the Court, while at the same time, it has resisted being subject to their scrutiny. Typically, it has applauded developments, while convinced that it is blessed by the best judiciary in the world, one that does not need second-guessing.

International Criminal Courts

The international criminal courts comprise the last genus to emerge in the kingdom of international adjudicative bodies, but they have broken onto the scene suddenly, massively, and loudly, awing some and rattling others. This is the area marked by the greatest innovation and expansion.

The rise of international criminal courts has been sudden, at least when compared to the glacial pace with which international legal regimes and institutions emerge. Yugoslavia started breaking apart in the summer of 1991. The war in Bosnia started in April 1992, by which time experts were already busy drafting the statute of the International Criminal Tribunal for Yugoslavia (ICTY). UN Security Council Resolution 827 created the ICTY in May 1993, and it started operating (slowly) by the end of the year.[40] When hell broke loose in Rwanda between April and July 1994, a template for a criminal court was already in place, and the Yugoslav model was adopted, *mutatis mutandis*, by Resolution 955, in November 1994, creating the International Criminal Tribunal for Rwanda.[41] As soon as the two ad hoc tribunals had been established, the idea of a permanent international criminal court was resurrected and immediately gained traction among governments and at the UN. The Statute of the ICC was adopted in Rome in July 1998, and by 2002 it had entered into force.[42]

Yet, as the ICC does not have retroactive jurisdiction,[43] a number of other criminal courts were created to address crises where multiple international crimes had been committed that could not be referred to it: Sierra Leone, East Timor, Kosovo, and Cambodia. The entry into force of the Rome Statute did not exhaust the need for ad hoc prosecution – for procedural and political reasons – leading to

[40] Statute of the International Criminal Tribunal for the former Yugoslavia, U.N. Doc. S/RES/827 (1993).
[41] Statute of the International Criminal Tribunal for Rwanda, U.N. Doc. S/RES/955 (1994).
[42] Rome Statute of the International Criminal Court, 2187 U.N.T.S. 90, entered into force July 1, 2002.
[43] Rome Statute, art. 11.

negotiations to establish a tribunal for Lebanon,[44] and one for Burundi.[45] And, finally, the completion strategy that will force the shutting down of the ICTY and ICTR by 2010 at the earliest has also spurred the imposition of international oversight on domestic courts that are, or will be, taking over from where the ICTY and ICTR have left off.[46]

In sum, in the span of about fifteen years a dozen new international institutions, commanding considerable resources and attention, have been created. Given broad powers, and relying on their necessary independence, these institutions have swiftly proceeded to rewrite or add entire chapters to the book of international law. For instance, the doctrine of sovereign immunity, which had barely changed for centuries, has been radically altered – and for good. The notions of war crimes and crimes against humanity have greatly expanded and morphed. Heads of state and prime ministers have been put under pressure by international investigations, then forced to step down and finally arrested and put to trial (including Slobodan Milosevic, president of Yugoslavia; Charles Taylor, president of Liberia; Jean Kambanda, prime minister of Rwanda; and Ramush Haradinaj, prime minister of Kosovo). This is not the first time in history that top-level politicians have been removed, but it is the first time that they have lost power because an international tribunal has indicted them for crimes they committed to seize and hold on to power.

There are few precedents for similarly broad grants of powers to international institutions in such a short period. The idea that justice is necessary to achieve peace is radical and revolutionary, but it is inevitable. The fall of the Berlin Wall has been accompanied – and some might claim caused – by a level of mass access to information having no precedent in human history, in terms of scope and quantity. While for centuries war and peace was a business of a handful of decision makers, and the logic of it was apparent only to them, mass-media society and, even more, the age of the internet have changed forever how states justify going to war and making peace (or, at least, how they sell war and peace to the people). The logic and dictates of justice and accountability have increasingly crept in, and eventually started interfering with, classical balance of power considerations.[47] There is no way back. Cynical dictators used to boast that if one kills a man, one goes to jail, but if one million are killed, one goes to peace talks. Now there is an alternative scenario: having one's trial broadcast all over the planet.

---

[44] UN Doc S/RES/1644 (December 15, 2005) and UN Doc S/RES/1664 (March 29, 2006) on the situation in the Middle East.

[45] UN Doc S/RES/1606 (June 20, 2005).

[46] In the former Yugoslavia this led to the establishment of the War Crimes Chamber in Bosnia-Herzegovina.

[47] On the role played by civil society in pushing for the establishment of international criminal courts, see Marlies Glasius, *The International Criminal Court: A Global Civil Society Achievement* (New York: Routledge, 2006). See also chapters by M. Colitti, P. De Cesare, F. Trombetta-Panigali, C. Ragni, and M. Politi, in *Civil Society, International Courts and Compliance Bodies*, see note 35 earlier.

International Courts and Tribunals 303

The role of the United States in this revolution cannot and should not be understated. It has provided the media that brought about this revolution, from CNN to the internet. It is a country built on the very idea of justice for all and the rule of law, and it regards its own legal system and its judiciary almost as a supernatural gift rather than a perfectible human institution. The attitude of the United States toward international criminal courts has been very well chronicled, and it is far from as clear as its detractors claim it to be.[48] To begin with, there is really no coherent U.S. policy on international criminal courts in general. Although the Clinton administration created the position of the Ambassador at Large for War Crimes Issues within the U.S. State Department, this person is nothing like an "International Criminal Tribunals Czar." There is no single mind, no single master plan, in Washington, D.C., that includes all international criminal courts. This is in part due to the multifaceted nature of international criminal courts, and more generally to the fact that the U.S. perspective is an amalgamation of diverse views reduced in some cases to written form, which might itself be subject to varying interpretations.

At most, a historical survey would reveal certain consistent themes underlying U.S. attitudes toward international criminal courts. First, the United States is traditionally and in principle committed to justice and accountability for all. This dates, at least, back to the Nuremberg and Tokyo Trials, which took place largely at the insistence of the United States and, famously, in spite of the contrary opinion of the UK, not to mention the USSR. Granted, the United States never sought accountability at any cost. Even in cases where the U.S. attitude toward international criminal courts is at its most favorable, these institutions are not viewed as ends in themselves. The U.S. approach is better described as "pragmatic," or "hardheaded" as its critics might say. Each institution is assessed mostly, if not solely, in terms of its ability to advance U.S. interests, which include, but are not limited to, promoting accountability and the rule of law on the international level.[49] Of course, prosecution of American nationals by an international criminal court is not and has never been an option. Those can be taken care of, effectively and impartially – from the U.S. perspective – by the superior U.S. judicial system (military or civilian).

Second, according to the United States, it is best to prosecute crimes – including international crimes – at the national level. Prosecution by any other court (international or even domestic courts of other countries) should be the absolute last resort. To be fair, there is some merit to that. Many wonder whether, and to which degree, the ICTY and ICTR have been successful in making affected populations feel a sense of ownership of the justice that has been done. This objection is one of the favorite arguments of those who oppose the ICC. Considering that the first cases

[48] For a detailed account of U.S. attitude and practice toward international criminal courts, see, in general, J. Cerone, "U.S. Attitudes toward International Criminal Courts and Tribunals," in C. Romano, ed., *The Sword and the Scales*, see note 14 earlier.

[49] For an account of the official U.S. government position, see J. Bellinger, "International Courts and Tribunals and the Rule of Law," in C. Romano, ed., *The Sword and the Scales*, see note 14 earlier.

before the Court (and those likely beyond that) all originated from appalling African conflicts, while the ICC sits thousands of miles away in the The Hague, one has to admit that there is the risk some might see in the whole exercise a repetition of the infamous "white man's burden" approach.

Third, and probably decisively, the United States is strongly interested in maintaining the primacy of the Security Council in matters of peace and security, including accountability for international crimes. It is obvious that this is due to the status of the United States as a permanent and veto-wielding member of the Council. Indeed, there seems to be a direct correlation between the degree of U.S. support for international criminal prosecution and the degree of control it has over the institution that will do it. The ICC is far too independent from the Security Council for U.S. comfort. The ICTY and ICTR have largely benefited from the benevolence of the United States. Being creatures of the Security Council, they are unlikely to do anything against one of its permanent members, as the decision of the ICTY Prosecutor not to investigate the bombing of Yugoslavia by NATO in 1999 suggests.[50] And, finally, the hybrid courts are so fragile and dependent on international support and powerful patrons, and tread such a narrow ground, that the chances of them straying are close to nothing.

Of course, these are only broad trends. Ideological leanings – between institutionalists and realists, Democrats and Republicans, and all possible cross-combinations – determine, case by case, the ultimate U.S. attitude. In general, it is probably correct to say that the United States has been heavily involved in – in favor or against – the creation of each international criminal court for essentially two reasons. In favor, because it stands for accountability for international crimes, and its people demand so. Against, because, being the ultimate superpower, by definition, it has stakes, diplomatic or military, in any conflict around the globe. It is more exposed than any other state because the more situations it is involved in, the greater the chances that some of its personnel might be indicted for crimes.

All international criminal courts existing today have been created within or with the support of the UN (hence, with the support or acquiescence of the United States). There is no international criminal court that has been created, and works solely, with support of a regional organization. This does not necessarily mean that the UN, per se, is enthusiastic about each. The UN is, of course, more than the algebraic sum of its members; it has an agenda and will of its own. Various organs and offices within the UN have different opinions about the desirability, functioning, and ideal design for the numerous courts that have been hatched over time.

To illustrate, in the early days of the ICTY and ICTR, Western countries showed support of the ad hoc tribunals by generously seconding a large number of gratis

---

[50] Final Report to the Prosecutor by the Committee Established to Review the NATO Bombing Campaign against the Federal Republic of Yugoslavia (June 2000), http://www.un.org/icty/pressreal/nato061300.htm.

International Courts and Tribunals 305

personnel from their own bureaucracies (including prosecutors, attorneys, officials, and intelligence operators). One might be cynical and say that they wanted to make sure these courts worked and did not get bogged down in the "geographically correct" policies of the UN. Yet, the UN, being a truly universal organization, and one that goes to great lengths and pains to ensure its own personnel are concomitantly diverse, as of 1998 started phasing out gratis personnel and relying on its own procedures and criteria to staff them.

Also, it is well known that the UN Secretariat – especially former Secretary-General Kofi Annan – and member states have been divided by the issue of how to finance criminal courts, particularly hybrid international/domestic courts.[51] The considerable budgets of the ICTY and ICTR ($276 and $250 million, respectively, for the biennium 2006–2007) have attracted a lot of criticism by member states, which have blamed the UN bureaucracy and its way of doing things, for much of those costs. Because of that, when the creation of hybrid criminal courts for Sierra Leone first, and then for Cambodia, was discussed, member states opted for voluntary funding by donors and not underwriting those costs in the UN budget (either for regular or for peacekeeping operations). But this has shifted the onus of raising those funds on the Secretary-General, forcing him to spend considerable time and political capital, and exponentially increasing the unwillingness of the UN bureaucracy to create any such tribunal (at least so funded) in the future.

Let me give one last example of how the UN might have an attitude of its own toward international criminal courts. The UN has entered into negotiations with Cambodia to create an international (hybrid) mechanism to try the few surviving Khmer Rouge leaders very grudgingly and only after it was literally ordered to do so by the Security Council.[52] The UN and its staff are perfectly aware that there is a substantial risk that the trials will turn out to be just a tool for domestic Cambodian score-settling and political intrigue. Because it is a hybrid court, and because the Cambodians have a say greater than any other "host country" of a hybrid court, the UN has no way to effectively control trials and their outcome except in the bluntest, and most awkward, way: by pulling the plug. But, should that happen, it would be the first to be blamed for having made it possible for the remaining Khmer Rouge leaders to die free and safe in their beds and not be held to account for their actions. And, if trials are held and sentences are passed and people actually go to jail, it will be blamed anyway for the high selectivity of the trials (only a handful of people will be indicted) and the delays. It is the scapegoat of an announced public relations disaster.

---

[51] On financing of international courts in general and the ICTY and ICTR in particular, see C. Romano, "The Price of International Justice," *The Law and Practice of International Courts and Tribunals* 4 (2005), pp. 281–328.

[52] See, generally, C. Etchenson, "The Politics of Genocide Justice in Cambodia," in C. Romano, A. Nollkaemper, and J. Kleffner, eds., *Internationalized Criminal Courts and Tribunals: Sierra Leone, East Timor, Kosovo and Cambodia* (Oxford: OUP, 2004), pp. 181–206; D. Shraga, "The Second Generation UN-Based Tribunals – A Diversity of Mixed Jurisdictions," ibid., pp. 15–38.

Finally, as to the European role in international criminal courts, are Europeans really such "international criminal courts huggers" as everyone, including themselves, seem to believe? They might be, but probably not by their own merit, when compared not only to the attitudes of other major players, the United States foremost, but also to the dismal attitudes of Russia and China.

The ICC was not a European creation – suggesting that would be revisionism. At the outset, it had a constituency much larger than Europe and the countries that benefit from its generous foreign aid. It became a European darling once the United States pulled out when it did not obtain what it wanted during negotiations of the statute in Rome, when China, Russia, and India failed to get on board, and Japan hesitated on the fence. Then, Europe found itself to be the only wealthy parent of this neglected child, with so much political capital invested in its success.

Besides much rhetoric, there is no sign that European states might be more ready than the United States to see some of their service-members, or even politicians, being indicted by the ICC, not even "their" ICC such as this one. When key national interests of major and minor European nations have been threatened by international adjudication – like in the case of France with nuclear tests, Iceland with fisheries, UK with Libya over Lockerbie, to mention some – those states have not hesitated to assume guarded attitudes or even quickly turn their back on those same institutions they claim to support. Likewise, if one reads in the U.S. support of hybrid courts an attempt to undermine the ICC, what does the support by the Europeans mean? The UK and, to a lesser extent, the Netherlands have been promoters and constant supporters of the Special Court for Sierra Leone. France has been a driving force behind the Cambodian Chambers and now the Hariri Tribunal (in which Italy is also very active). The EU has supported, both politically and financially, all hybrid courts.

The truth is that the ICC was never intended to indict and try citizens of developed democracies. (Europeans are aware of that, while the United States for other reasons pretends not to know it.) Those countries have viable judicial systems that can take care of the occasional war criminal. They have rarely (at least since 1945) been visited by genocide. It is no secret that the ICC was thought of and created for those developing countries that are under a double-curse: that of having too frail national institutions and being prone to violence and conflict, and not being important enough for someone else to care enough to step in and take the risk (and losses) to restore order and peace, and try criminals. It turns out most of those are in Africa.

At the end of the day, there is really not much difference between attitudes toward international criminal courts of the United States and Europe. It is only the behavior that changes, with the Europeans playing a far shrewder game than the Americans.

CONCLUSIONS

In sum, the single most influential event in the development of contemporary international courts is, undoubtedly, the end of the Cold War. The end of the bipolar confrontation between the two antagonistic blocks has led to an increase in the number of cases litigated, and to participation by more diverse groups of states. It has opened the way for the expansion of the European Court of Human Rights' jurisdiction to the East, triggering its reform. It has opened the way for the establishment of the African Court of Human and Peoples' Rights. It has lessened the resistance of Latin American governments to having their actions (past and present) questioned by the Inter-American Court of Human Rights. Most significantly, the end of the Cold War has opened the way for accountability for war crimes and crimes against humanity, causing the emergence of a new genus of international courts, and subsequent mutations, branching out in three separate subgenera: ICC, ad hoc international tribunals, and hybrid courts.

There is little sign that 9/11, the war on terror, and the invasion of Iraq have had an impact on the structure, development, and pattern of utilization of international courts at large. Granted, some of the measures taken by certain states, including the United States, and even by the Security Council itself, have been an object of judicial scrutiny, but rulings (mostly adverse to those measures) have not produced much visible effect on either states' policies and behaviors or patterns of utilization or neglect of international adjudicative bodies. If they had any effect, they probably only made the United States shy away even further from international judicial scrutiny of its actions. There is no indication that post–9/11 events have spurred either the creation of new or the modification of existing international judicial structures.

As concerns attitudes and behaviors of key players, much of the judicialization of world politics has happened despite the United States and not because of it. Unlike many other areas of international law and relations, U.S. participation in international adjudication and the building of the international judiciary is not essential. Although the United States has been a force behind the ad hoc tribunals and some hybrid courts, and has broken new ground with other forms of quasi-judicial justice, like compensations commissions,[53] it has otherwise been largely absent. This aloofness is due to several structural factors (e.g., the U.S. Constitution, tradition, ambivalence; the fact that it is a superpower, hence, it has alternatives, and so on), which can only be mitigated or exacerbated, but not altered, by the ideological bent of those in control of the White House and Congress.

Europe has played a much greater role in shaping the development of the array of international courts. It has been instrumental in the creation of and support to criminal tribunals (ad hoc and hybrid), and it has become the champion of the ICC, it has grandfathered the IACHR and ACHPR, and it has provided the basic template for many regional economic courts. Interestingly, it has shown that this

---

[53] In this category, one can mention the Iran-US Claims Tribunal, the United Nations Compensation Commission, created by the UN Security Council to decide on damages arising out of the 1990–1991 Gulf War, and the Holocaust victims compensation mechanisms. On the history of the U.S. role in the establishment and operation of these bodies, see, generally, John Crook, in C. Romano, ed., *The Sword and the Scales*, see note 14 earlier.

is one of the fields in which it does not need U.S. or UN support to achieve its goals, and indeed, that it can do so even in the teeth of U.S. opposition. Even more interestingly, the opposite is not true. When the United States tried to set up a sort of international tribunal without UN or European support, as in the case of the Iraqi Special Tribunal, the result has been, by any standards, poor.

The UN is irrelevant in the case of international courts with regional scope. It is, however, essential in the case of all international criminal bodies. Only the UN can provide legitimacy to any attempt to try individuals for crimes that offend the whole of humanity. To date, there has not been any significant attempt to administer international criminal justice at the regional level, outside the framework of the UN.

Regional courts of any flavor have provided regional powers an opportunity to raise their profile by spearheading efforts to create judicial bodies and support them. Japan and Australia are driving forces behind the Extraordinary Chambers in the Courts of Cambodia. Argentina and Brazil have championed the judicialization of the Mercosur dispute settlement system. South Africa has played a fundamental role in the entry into force of the protocol establishing the African Court of Human and Peoples' Rights. Norway is the giant in the three-nation EFTA Court (the other two members being Iceland and Liechtenstein). Trinidad and Tobago have been in the forefront of the creation of the Caribbean Court of Justice.

Although there are signs that the breakneck expansion of the array of international courts during the 1990s and early 2000s is leveling off, it is certain that international courts are here to stay. They have become a fundamental feature of several international regimes. It is difficult to see how demand for accountability for international crimes might diminish. As long as states, and the UN, continue engaging in nation-building it is equally hard to see how that could be properly achieved without also building or rebuilding national judicial structures, and at least during the first stages, an international component is indispensable. It is equally difficult to imagine the creation of new regional integration agreements without at least some form of compulsory dispute settlement system and judicial oversight of the actions both of states and of community institutions.

Overall, the most interesting, and also perplexing, aspect of international courts and tribunals is probably the fact that not only the successes but also the failures of experiments in international justice have provided reasons to establish even more of them. In a sense, the development of international courts and tribunals might have acquired a logic and drive on its own not subordinate to, or dependent on, the interests of a specific government, but propelled by deeper public opinion forces, which are incarnated in the many nongovernmental organizations (NGOs) that have campaigned for and supported the creation of many of these judicial bodies.

IV

Conclusions

16

Conclusion: International Institutions and the Problems of Adaptation

Richard Gowan and Bruce D. Jones

In 1979, the evolutionary biologists Stephen Jay Gould and Richard Lewontin gave a conference paper that was soon recognized as a classic in their field. At first, it seemed to have nothing to do with evolution at all. "The Spandrels of San Marco and the Panglossian Paradigm: A Critique of the Adaptationist Programme" opens by observing that "the great central dome of St. Mark's Cathedral in Venice presents in its mosaic design a detailed iconography expressing the mainstays of the Christian faith."

> Three circles of figures radiate out from a central image of Christ: angels, disciples and virtues. Each circle is divided into quadrants, even though the dome itself is radially symmetrical in structure. Each quadrant meets one of the four spandrels in the arches below the dome. Spandrels – the tapering triangular spaces formed by the intersection of two rounded arches at right-angles – are necessary architectural by-products of mounting a dome on rounded arches. Each spandrel contains a design fitted into its tapering space. An evangelist sits in the upper part flanked by the heavenly cities. Below, a man representing one of the four Biblical rivers (Tigris, Euphrates, Indus and Nile) pours water into the narrow space below his feet.[1]

This is noteworthy not only because the artistry in the spandrels is beautiful but also because its beauty can fool a tourist or art historian "to view it as the starting point of any analysis, as the cause in some sense of the surrounding architecture." That is the reverse of reality. The spandrels are actually a matter of architectural necessity – given the design of St Mark's, they had to be there. They could have been left blank, but they would still have played their architectural role. The mosaics distract us from

---

[1] Stephen Jay Gould and Richard C. Lewontin, "The Spandrels of San Marco and the Panglossian Paradigm: A Critique of the Adaptationist Programme," *Proceedings of the Royal Society of London, Series B*, 205, No. 1161 (1979), pp. 581–2.

that role. We are still inclined to ascribe the shape of the building to its art rather than to its architectural needs.

Gould and Lewontin drew an analogy between this error and a recurrent mistake across academic disciplines. This is the tendency to assume that all the traits of a particular object or project serve a necessary purpose. Their target was the "adaptationist programme" in evolutionary theory. This assumed the "omnipotence of natural selection in forging organic design and fashioning the best among possible worlds."[2] Put simply, this means observing an organism's traits and assuming that they have all evolved to do something useful. A nonspecialist example was provided by the sign next to a Fiberglas tyrannosaurus in a Boston museum: "how tyrannosaurus used its tiny front legs is a scientific puzzle; they were too short even to reach the mouth. They may have been used to help the animal rise from a lying position."[3] This is silly. If a species evolved front legs to help it get up in the morning, why would it only evolve miniature limbs? More likely, Gould and Lewontin noted, is that the tyrannosaurs developed large heads and hind limbs over millennia, while their front legs did not evolve. To explain the front limbs in isolation is like focusing on St. Mark's mosaics but ignoring its (literally) overarching structure.

Any argument by analogy has obvious limits – and while evolutionary experts might nod to Gould and Lewontin's argument, it has come under successful attacks by Richard Dawkins and others.[4] But their analogy is useful to us in concluding this volume. It leads us back to the problem we set our authors and set out in our introduction. Can we explain the form and functioning of existing international security institutions in terms of the overarching realities of international politics in the immediate post–Cold War era, and especially the preeminent reality of U.S. hegemony? Pundits and serious commentators are declaring that hegemony to be passing, but for the period covered in this book, it was real (and trumpeted by many of the same pundits). American military strength and economic heft set the rules of the era.

There are two vulgar ways of thinking about how international institutions relate to power politics. The first is the normative assumption that even superpowers should obey the norms, rules, and legally binding dictates of institutions without question or exception. We do not need to review the chapters in this volume to realize that this does not happen in reality. The polar opposite of this assumption is that institutions should simply bend to power and, in conditions of hegemony, do what the hegemon wants. But this (equally normative) assumption is also not borne out by the experiences of the last decade.

Somewhere in between these positions, there is an "adaptationist programme" for international institutions. This has two pillars. First, if the behavior of major powers – even hyperpowers – remains fairly consistent with the rules of international

[2] Ibid., p. 584.
[3] Ibid., p. 587.
[4] See Tim Flannery, "A New Darwinism?", *New York Review of Books* 49, No. 9 (May 23, 2003).

International Institutions and the Problems of Adaptation 313

institutions most of the time, the institutions will maintain a minimum of credibility with other states. Second, if international institutions are fairly useful to those major powers most of the time, their governments will continue to work through them. The net result, filtered through complex intergovernmental and institutional interactions, is that institutions change gradually over time to survive. Major powers will adapt the institutions' rules and direct their operations, overtly or indirectly. Because there are multiple actors and obstacles to negotiate, the outcomes are never optimal for anyone. But they are sufficient unto the day.

These basic assumptions have two significant implications. One is about the institutions themselves: if an organization persists, it must have at least some utility, even if it is hard to identify. The second is about how we study institutions: we assume that, if we perceive organizations surviving and changing, there is some form of correlation, however tortuous, between the ongoing distribution and redistribution of power in the international system and institutional evolution. In *Imperfect Unions* (a study that informed much of our thinking in developing this volume, as we stated in our introduction) Helga Haftendorn, Robert O. Keohane, and Celeste A. Wallander argue that "all preliminary findings indicate that the ability of an institution to thrive, or even to survive, depends on its adaptability" and that "adaptation requires that organizations be sensitive not only to general changes in their environments, but specifically to the interests and foreign policy preferences of their most important members."[5]

In the terms of reference for authors of this volume, we specifically asked them to contrast examples of "innovation" (the creation of new international institutions) and "adaptation" (the realignment of existing ones to deal with new threats and power dynamics). We assumed that, with some exceptions, adaptation would predominate. We also assumed that we would find that U.S. interests and choices had been decisive in shaping both innovations and adaptations, although this would far from completely obscure the role of European and other middle powers.

This second assumption has not been borne out. Instead, we have found the United States notable by its absence from many reform processes (in the Clinton era as well as under George W. Bush). All too often, middle powers have obscured the United States, not vice versa. This implies a disconnect between international power and institutional innovation – a flaw that potentially challenges the credibility of international institutions as regulative and operational mechanisms.

If this sounds unduly nihilistic, it is worth asking four supplementary questions. Which continents have seen the most complex institutional evolutionary processes since the Cold War? The answer must be Europe, with Africa second. Which continent's governments have given most impassioned support to international institutions in this period? Again, Europe is to the fore. But which continent is agreed by virtually every commentator in every region to be gathering power at

---

[5] Helga Haftendorn, Robert O. Keohane, and Celeste A. Wallander, *Imperfect Unions: Security Institutions over Time and Space* (Oxford, 1999), p. 12.

Europe's expense? Asia. And how many truly significant and successful international institutional reforms have been driven from Asia in the period since the end of the Cold War? The answer – roughly none – suggests some sort of disconnect. Might international institutional reform be something similar to the spandrels of San Marco: "a secondary epiphenomenon representing a fruitful use of available parts, not a cause of the entire system"?[6]

The extent of this problem emerges when we look at the diverse ways in which the institutions analyzed in this volume have altered over two decades. There are cases of inertia (as in many aspects of international justice discussed by Cesare Romano in Chapter 15) and organizations evolving against the explicit will of the United States (as often with the International Criminal Court). There has been a great deal of innovation, but this has most often been led by middle powers rather than by the hegemon – as Abby Stoddard shows in her study of British influence over the humanitarian system (Chapter 13). In this case, it is as if a cathedral architect had called mosaic artists together and announced that he was not that bothered by what they designed for the spandrels – the result has been impressive, but not essential to the overall shape of international order.

So, if this volume has one basic lesson for international relations students (a lesson that is hardly new but requires repetition), it is this: there is no necessary correlation between balance of power in international politics and the structure, or even the behavior, of international institutions. Another case of this, only briefly touched on in this volume, has been the creation of the UN Human Rights Council (HRC) to replace the widely discredited Commission on Human Rights. As we note in our introduction, the HRC was formed in 2006 over U.S. objections. It has been a platform for a variety of countries to bash American allies and liberal principles heartily (American diplomats even gave up observing its proceedings toward the end of the Bush administration, although the Obama administration immediately engaged with the HRC, winning a seat there in 2009).[7] The dynamics of the HRC bear little relation to real-world political calculations: India and many African and Asian countries that aim for closer ties to the United States are fierce opponents of the West in Geneva. China is a vastly more assertive power in the HRC than in the Security Council.

It is possible to interpret this as one indicator of a post-American order in the making, and one can learn a good deal about ideology as a motivational force in international affairs by observing the HRC at work. But the best explanation for the HRC may be one of intentional redundancy. The countries engaging in it can use it to vent and posture without risking any real damage to their relations with the United States or the West more generally. When EU members grew particularly unhappy

---

[6] Gould and Lewontin, op. cit, p. 584.
[7] See Richard Gowan and Franziska Brantner, *A Global Force for Human Rights? An Audit of European Power at the UN* (European Council on Foreign Relations, 2008), pp. 37–46.

International Institutions and the Problems of Adaptation   315

with Chinese tactics at the HRC in 2007, they threatened their nuclear option: walking off the HRC. This international institution may persist (like the old Commission on Human Rights that it was meant to improve on) precisely because it *is* redundant.

So it is possible for international institutions to emerge and evolve without having to adapt to the will of a hegemonic power. Stewart Patrick (Chapter 2) and Stephen J. Stedman's (Chapter 3) contributions to this volume provide evidence for the argument that the Bush administration's confidence in its hegemony actually created permissive conditions for other powers to experiment with forms of international cooperation unmolested by Washington D.C. Sarjoh Bah's (Chapter 14) description of the variety of African security institutions (which arguably benefited from not only American aid but also a certain degree of American strategic disinterest) shows that international institutions developed on the margins of "mainstream" international politics do not need to be as redundant as the HRC. Ian Johnstone's (Chapter 10) discussion of norms at the United Nations (UN) and Teresa Whitfield's (Chapter 12) analysis of new arrangements for peace negotiation (in which the United States plays a surprisingly small role) also show how useful ideas and mechanisms can develop while the hegemon nods.

These studies, like Stoddard's (Chapter 13), lead to the intriguing conclusion that the chances of creativity in international institutional cooperation may sometimes reflect *detachment* by a major power or powers. But this conclusion comes with an immediate qualification: if such bursts of creativity are essentially disconnected from the overall shape of international order, the lessons they offer often do not travel well.

A case in point is the Responsibility to Protect (R2P), raised by Johnstone in Chapter 10. Although R2P can be linked to European arguments for intervention in the Balkans in the 1990s – and was developed under the auspices of the Canadian government with a former Australian foreign minister as its best known standard-bearer – it is nonetheless rooted in the African experience of genocide and large-scale warfare in the 1990s. The term was coined by an African scholar-politician, Francis Deng, and encoded in the Constitutive Act of the African Union. Insofar as it has provided part of the logic for international engagement in Darfur and robust UN peacekeeping elsewhere in Africa, it has done some good. Johnstone notes that it has also informed a "proactive" approach by the UN in Haiti. But efforts to encode R2P in the law and practice of the international community as a whole – peaking in the inclusion of the concept in the 2005 World Summit outcome document, as described by Stedman (Chapter 3) – have done the concept unforeseen damage. The General Assembly has pressured UN Secretary-General Ban Ki-moon to confine R2P to conflict prevention activities, while an effort to cite it in the Security Council by France after the 2008 Burmese cyclone crisis was an abject failure – and probably hardened China against it.

R2P is not dead yet. But the fate of R2P to date is a sobering reminder of the sort of mistake identified by Gould and Lewontin. Just as one might be tempted to explain the architecture of St. Mark's starting with the artistry in its spandrels, one might see

R2P at work in the African context and attempt to build a theory of international obligations and action around it. But try to raise it to the level of an international ordering principle and it may fail.

What of the adaptation of international security institutions in which the United States has maintained a clear interest, even if it has sometimes ignored them, like NATO and the Security Council? Here we would expect to see a much greater tendency to adapt to American wishes, and to some extent we do. But in no case has adaptation proved easy. Indeed, the most striking feature of what we called the "first world" of multilateralism in our introduction is exactly how closely it resembles the structures that protected the First World in the Cold War. NATO's Article V, the Security Council, and the NPT are all still here – while NATO and the UN have changed vastly, the fundamentals of the Cold War order remain the same.

This leads to further qualifications of our idea of adaptation in international cooperation, and a further analogy with Gould and Lewontin's 1979 paper. After poking fun at the "adaptationist programme" with their exploration of spandrels (and Aztec cannibalism) the biologists set out a series of detailed objections to various arguments about adaptation in nature that we are in no way competent to discuss. They conclude by turning to "another, and unfairly maligned, approach to evolution" advocated by continental European scientists. This does not reject all ideas about adaptation, but focuses on its constraints:

> It holds instead that the basic body plans of organisms are so integrated and so replete with constraints upon adaptation that conventional styles of selective arguments can explain little of interest about them. It does not deny that change, when it occurs may be mediated by natural selection, but it holds that constraints restrict possible paths and modes of change so strongly that the constraints themselves become the most interesting aspect of evolution.[8]

The most obvious of these constraints are "phyletic": simply put, these dictate that organisms of a certain descent are not able to diverge wildly from the characteristics of their ancestors. Humans may stand upright, but they are still not "optimally designed" for doing so because they are descended from quadrupeds – similarly, "no molluscs fly in air and no insects are as large as elephants." Although biologists who focus on the role of natural selection in driving adaptation are always looking for signs of change, Gould and Lewontin wanted them to take into account what endured. A vandal might chip the mosaics off the spandrels in St. Mark's, in other words, but the spandrels would stay there.

Our account of international security institutions similarly pushes us to the question of how to balance the study of change in international organizations with an awareness of their inherent constraints. Mats Berdal, David Ucko, Richard Gowan, and Sara Batmanglich bring this question on European security, and NATO in

---

[8] Gould and Lewontin., p. 594.

particular, into focus in their chapters. The evolution of NATO is open to very distinct adaptationist and constraint-based interpretations. The "adaptationist" narrative, adopted by most of the organization's American advocates, goes like this: NATO has been transformed from a Western defensive alliance into a security framework capable not only of including former members of the Warsaw Pact but also of taking on the war on terrorism in Afghanistan. In so doing it has fundamentally, if grumpily, adapted to the post-Soviet and post–9/11 world. In this, it has served the United States well. The constraints-based version runs thus: although it has engaged in expeditionary operations, NATO still rests on the basic desire of European states to remain under a U.S. security umbrella and Article V of the North Atlantic Charter. The former Warsaw Pact states that have signed up are far more attracted to this very traditional guarantee than the Afghan campaign, and that campaign has also shown the constraints that result from Europe's aversion to paying for new weaponry or having its troops killed. NATO has failed to meet U.S. needs, which have proved insufficient motivational forces to overcome its inner constraints.

The reality, as Berdal and Ucko show in Chapter 6, is somewhere in between these two narratives (just as Gould and Lewontin conclude their 1979 article by admitting that any understanding of evolution actually has to rest on intellectual pluralism). However, the North Atlantic Treaty Organization (NATO) case is a reminder that although this volume has analyzed institutional change in the post–Cold War era, many of the basic security calculations shaping that change are of far older stock. A similar lesson can be drawn from Christine Wing in Chapter 7 on nuclear issues. Wing notes that the antiproliferation regime has altered somewhat since 1990, with the Security Council and IAEA increasing their role – simultaneously, there is interest in mechanisms outside the framework of the NPT. And yet the basic architecture of the NPT remains in place, and the failure of the 2005 Review Conference suggests that the constraints on realigning the international community to handle a world containing a nuclear Pakistan and North Korea (let alone Iran) are extremely powerful indeed. In this case, however, it is harder to set up a compelling dichotomy between American interests and "institutional constraints," as the United States has unfortunately played a declining role since the early 1990s.

The problem of institutional constraints on change inevitably brings us back to the UN. A large number of the authors in this volume were involved in the efforts to reform the UN through the 2005 High-level Panel on Threats, Challenges and Change and the 2005 World Summit, either working within the UN (Stedman, Jones, Rosand, and von Einsiedel) or assisting from the immediate periphery (Forman, Malone, and Rubin). Having been involved in that process, they have been accused of failing to think enough about constraints on change (by Berdal, and Edward C. Luck, who advised us when we started this project, among others).[9] But

---

9 See Edward C. Luck, "How Not to Reform the United Nations," *Global Governance* 11 (2005); and Mats Berdal, "The UN's Unnecessary Crisis," *Survival* 47, No. 3 (2005).

as Stedman notes in Chapter 3, those directly involved in the reform process felt all too sensitive to the limitations they met daily. One advantage of this book is to bring together veterans of that reform process and give a sense of how they feel about institutional reform "having come out the other side." They emphasize constraints. Stedman highlights "mixed results." Malone (Chapter 4) combines a positive account of the Security Council's transformation in the immediate post–Cold War phase with warnings of growing divisions among China, Russia, and the United States on the Council in the future. Rubin (Chapter 11) concludes his study of peacebuilding and statebuilding with a very cautious assessment of what the Peacebuilding Commission, a flagship product of the 2005 World Summit, can achieve.

In contrast to NATO where fairly clear American interests are observable, it is hard to see much evidence of the United States having any effective strategy to adapt the UN to its interests in these pieces. As Wing notes in Chapter 7, and Fiona Simpson (Chapter 9) also perceives in the case of mechanisms to handle chemical and biological proliferation, the Clinton administration did have strategies in some areas – but for the reasons atomized by Stewart Patrick in Chapter 2, their successor had no desire to follow suit. Perhaps suitably for an administration that flirted with promoting "intelligent design" in public education, the Bush administration's attitude to most prospects for the evolution of international security cooperation at the UN level has ranged from benign ignorance to disruption. Eric Rosand and Sebastian von Einsiedel (Chapter 8) demonstrate that the United States has only developed a partial strategy to promote a multilateral response to terrorism, although here the UN and other organizations have repeatedly indicated a degree of desire to adapt to take on the challenge.

The largely detached attitude of the George W. Bush administration only reinforces our warning that we should not try to understand the nature of international politics through a narrow focus on international institutions. It also points to the conjecture that U.S. power is not a force for change in the international system, but rather the primary constraint on change. The advantages that the United States enjoys in the international system – predominance in the Security Council and North Atlantic Council, a privileged status under the NPT, and so forth – are so great that they may indeed "restrict possible paths and modes of change so strongly that the constraints themselves become the most interesting aspect of evolution." This is hardly a new insight, being a standard critique of international order from the Left and South, but it is relevant to the adaptationist approach to international institutional reform: one reason that the UN and other institutions have not altered to meet all U.S. interests may be the very fact that American diplomats are wary of trading their established preeminence inside each organization in exchange for reform. There is a divergence between what the United States wants *from* international institutions and what it wants *within* them.

A growing number of American scholars and commentators have recognized the need to overcome this dilemma by negotiating on more level terms with other powers. Order "must be negotiated, not imposed," as Jones, Stedman, and Carlos Pascual have argued elsewhere (recapturing many of the arguments of Stanley Hoffmann cited by Gowan and Batmanglich in this volume).[10] But even if the United States enters into international negotiations in this spirit, the contributions to this volume suggest that it should temper its strategy with the following qualifications about how international institutions tend to evolve.

First, it should be clear that real shifts in the balance of power do not necessarily create institutional adaptation – the constraints inherent in existing security institutions mean that they are rarely as flexible as the moment requires (see NATO and the NPT). Second, not all institutional adaptation – even if it is well managed and well intentioned – is actually relevant to global order (see the African and UN cases highlighted previously), and this applies to concepts as well as mechanisms (see R2P). Third, institutional reform may lead to intentional redundancy, and this is not necessarily a disaster (see the HRC).

The overarching lesson is, however, that international security institutions will not be able to manage the coming shifts in global power if they are not more closely aligned with power itself. The crux of international institutional reform cannot be situated in Europe any more. If, for example, the UN Security Council proves to be a useful forum for bartering between China and the United States, the UN will remain relevant to global affairs. If not, it may still remain a significant conduit for humanitarian action, development aid, and peacekeeping in certain areas – but it will not have a central role in international peace and security. International institutions actually need a more deliberate "adaptationist programme."

But, as our analogy with Gould and Lewontin implies, fiddling with the internal structures of international organizations and assuming that the real world will respond to this tweaking cannot achieve adaptation. Too often, the international institutional agenda has focused on technicalities rather than major political issues. This book shows the result: an international security system with worthy refinements but a lack of strategic direction. If the United States and the emerging powers cannot agree on a role for international security institutions, asking how to improve them is like studying the arms of the tyrannosaurus.

---

[10] Bruce D. Jones, Carlos Pascual, and Stephen John Stedman, *Power and Responsibility* (Washington, DC: Brookings Institution Press, 2009), p. 14.

Afterword

The Changing Context for International Cooperation, 2006–2011

Richard Gowan

History is past politics; and politics present history.

Sir John Seeley

Cooperating for Peace and Security was designed to be a rough draft of history with political implications. The contributions all offer empirical evidence of the significance of multilateral cooperation to stability and security in the post–Cold War world. Our initial goal was simply to gather this evidence in one place. But we also wanted to communicate the importance of multilateral cooperation to America's status and interests – with the implication that the United States should be much more proactive in its approach to the evolution of the international system. This may sound like a well-intentioned but modest project. It is worth recalling that in the period in which *Cooperating for Peace and Security* was planned and written – the declining years of George W. Bush's second administration in 2006–8 – America's commitment to multilateralism appeared fragile. The 2003 invasion of Iraq was very recent history and both political and academic discussions of international cooperation were typically informed by partisan presumptions rather than hard facts. We wanted to restore a little empirical rigor to the debate.

This afterword is written near the end of President Obama's third year in office, offering a chance to reflect on the value of the volume's judgments, predictions, and recommendations after a period of intense global change.[1] It is divided into three main parts. First, it returns to the immediate political circumstances in which the volume came together, and notes how they affected some of its assumptions. It then looks at how the 2008 financial crisis upended some of these assumptions, not least concerning the respective roles of the United States and Europe in fostering international cooperation. It then turns its attention to how the United States has utilized multilateralism in its dealings with emerging powers (especially China),

---

[1] The author thanks Emily O'Brien and Francisca Aas, as well as the original contributors to this volume, for their advice on this afterword.

322   *Afterword*

new middle powers (such as South Korea and Mexico) and regional players in East and Southeast Asia during the Obama administration. It concludes with some brief thoughts on strategic priorities for the United States in the current, all too complicated context for international cooperation. The afterword draws frequently and extensively on the editors' other writings on these issues. These excerpts give some sense of how our thinking has evolved and may guide readers to some analyses that have built on *Cooperating for Peace and Security*.[2]

THE ORIGINAL CONTEXT: MALAISE

As we briefly noted in the acknowledgments, this volume emerged from a small conference held at New York University in December 2006. This was a period of political uncertainty. Nearly four years after the invasion of Iraq, the Bush administration's muscular foreign policy, with its in-built suspicion of multilateralism, was running out of credibility. The year 2006 had been the bloodiest one of the Iraqi civil war. That summer, the United States had accepted a large United Nations peacekeeping deployment in Lebanon to help end the war between Israel and Hezbollah, much to the chagrin of neoconservatives. The midterm elections had brought huge successes for the Democrats. But the 2008 presidential polls were still a long way off, and few could have guessed at how dramatic the campaign ahead would become. There was a general sense that the next administration would need to restore America's global standing, and that this would mean embracing elements of the international system that the Bush administration had distrusted and undermined. In the shorter term, the Bush administration itself had already shifted toward a more pragmatic attitude to the UN and international institutions than the one it had demonstrated from 2001 to 2005. But as of late 2006, foreign policy debates were listless and typically dominated by recriminations over Iraq.

Thus *Cooperating for Peace and Security* was first proposed at a liminal moment between the derailing of the Bush project and the rise of the Obama phenomenon. Traces of the mood of that moment are identifiable throughout the text. The chapters by Stewart Patrick and Stephen John Stedman capture the intellectual and policy battles over America and multilateralism that still felt raw and unresolved when we started out. An underlying sense of frustration is also evident in the volume's emphasis on the fact that the United States had been "passive at best" in promoting international cooperation, in the Clinton era as well as under Bush.

---

[2] *Cooperating for Peace and Security* has received a number of positive reviews. See Manuel Lafont Rapnouil, "Cooperating for Peace and Security," *International Journal*, Vol. LXV, No. 3 (Summer 2010), pp. 782–784; James H. Lebovic, "Cooperation in International Security," *International Studies Review*, Vol. 13, No. 3 (July 2011), pp. 488–494; and Kalliopi Chainoglou, "Cooperating for Peace and Security," *European Journal of International Law*, Vol. 22, No. 3 (August 2011), pp. 912–917. A transcript and recording of a launch event for the volume on March 24, 2010 at The Brookings Institution can be accessed at http://www.brookings.edu/events/2010/0324_un_nato_reform.aspx.

Afterword 323

The volume took some time to gestate, however. As it did so, Barack Obama established himself as a presidential candidate who appeared strongly committed to the revitalization of multilateralism. "No country has a bigger stake than we do in strengthening international institutions," he had written in his memoirs, "which is why we pushed for their creation in the first place, and why we need to take the lead in improving them."[3] Somewhat shamefully, it took us slightly longer to complete our editorial process than it took Barack Obama to capture the White House. But this meant that we were at least able to submit the final text at the start of 2009 confident that its arguments were broadly in line with those of the new administration (additionally, two contributors to the volume entered government service).[4]

THE SHOCK: THE IMPLICATIONS OF THE FINANCIAL CRISIS

It was also clear by the time the text was complete that some of our guiding assumptions were already open to challenge. The introduction and conclusion to the volume underline two broad points about the evolution of multilateralism in the post–Cold War era. The first is that this evolutionary process has been characterized by adaptation rather than innovation: the international order has been refashioned very significantly, but very few parts of it are entirely new, and large parts of the Cold War system have survived intact. The second assumption, sketched out more briefly, is that the processes of adaptation involved have rarely satisfied the interests of non-Western emerging powers such as Brazil, China, and India.

Yet the global financial crisis forced unexpected changes on the international system that defied both generalizations. In November 2008, the Group of Twenty (G20) met for the first time at the leaders' level to discuss the crisis in Washington DC. Its most striking feature was the prominent inclusion of non-Western leaders at the table. Moreover, it was an American initiative. Although French president Nicolas Sarkozy had originally proposed a summit, he had intended something based on the G8. It was George W. Bush who decided to convene the larger forum. Although this was technically one more example of adaptation – the G20 had been meeting at the level of finance ministers since the Asian financial crisis – it was generally recognized as a significant political *innovation* by the outgoing administration. President Obama seized on the G20 in his first year in office, hosting its third leaders' summit in

---

[3] See Bruce D. Jones and Richard Gowan, *Mr. Obama Goes to New York* (The Brookings Institution, September 2009), p. 6.

[4] Eric Rosand became the Senior Advisor on Multilateral Engagement in the State Department's Office of the Coordinator for Counterterrorism. Barnett Rubin was appointed Senior Advisor to the U.S. Special Representative for Afghanistan and Pakistan. For an earlier interpretation of the Obama administration's multilateral strategy by a contributor to *Cooperating for Peace and Security*, see Stewart Patrick, "Prix Fixe and à la Carte: Avoiding False Multilateral Choices," *The Washington Quarterly*, Vol. 32, No. 4 (October 2009), pp. 77–95.

324 *Afterword*

Pittsburgh and giving it explicit priority over the G8. Some of the assumptions at the core of *Cooperating for Peace and Security* now looked distinctly questionable. In the febrile atmosphere of the first twelve months of the financial crisis, multilateral innovation seemed not merely possible but absolutely essential, with the emerging powers on board and the United States in the lead.

It can be argued that a distinction should be drawn between innovations in economic cooperation such as the rise of the G20 and continuities in the types of security cooperation described in this volume. Both the Obama administration and the major emerging powers have ensured that the G20 has remained focused on economic affairs rather than the international security system. British officials wondered whether Security Council reform could be discussed in the margins of the second G20 summit in London in May 2009, but their American counterparts were not enthusiastic. President Sarkozy likewise suggested that France could use its presidency of the G20 in 2011 to stimulate new talks on the Council's future, but this proposal went nowhere. In the meantime, aspirants for permanent seats on the Security Council, including Brazil and India, have underlined that participation in the G20 is not a satisfactory alternative to enhanced status at the UN.

Nonetheless, experts on multilateralism have typically argued that the emergence of the G20 cannot be treated in isolation from debates about the UN and other elements of the international security order. Whereas many of the institutions and agreements described in *Cooperating for Peace and Security* have struggled to escape their organizational and political histories (a theme of the volume's conclusion), the G20 seemed to show that looser, top-level interactions between leaders could galvanize international action. The Obama administration made a high-profile effort to transfer this model to security cooperation in April 2010 when it hosted the first Nuclear Security Summit in Washington, bringing together leaders from forty-seven countries to discuss how to keep nuclear materials out of the hands of terrorists. This had the additional benefit of improving the diplomatic atmosphere in talks on the Non-Proliferation Treaty later in 2010. As Bruce Jones noted on the eve of the Nuclear Security Summit, the administration's initiatives had significant implications for the broader international security system.

> Now that informal "leadership clubs" have become the chief means of bringing together established and emerging powers, important questions arise regarding the future of global arrangements. Will power be concentrated within these informal great power mechanisms, or will they instead be used to spur decision making in other formal institutions? . . . Most important: will they develop implementation capacities, or will implementation remain in the hands of governments and other intergovernmental organizations? If so, how will the major power clubs relate to the formal institutions?[5]

---

[5] Bruce D. Jones, *Making Multilateralism Work: How the G-20 Can Help the United Nations* (The Stanley Foundation, April 2010), p. 3.

Other dilemmas lurked in the wings. One was how the American emphasis on engaging the emerging powers would affect the attitude of European and other Western powers to multilateralism. As *Cooperating for Peace and Security* underlines, European governments provided the "most impassioned support to international institutions" in the post–Cold War period, and other traditional friends of the United States such as Canada have also been keen multilateralists. Although all these powers had long acknowledged the importance of including the major emerging economies in international decision making, they were left uneasy in 2009 and 2010 by the Obama administration's focus on courting China in particular. The editors of this volume can take some pride in having identified this problem early. In an essay on "the Obama moment" published in 2009 (much of it based on the essays in *Cooperating for Peace and Security*), Jones questioned the widespread consensus that the new administration's commitment to multilateralism would naturally draw it closer to Europe. Highlighting America's interest in engaging non-Western powers, he countered that "the most likely scenario for the coming period is that the transatlantic relationship will be but one of several strands of a broader international order that shapes the management of a series of global challenges."

> In some areas, such as human rights, the U.S. and Europe may for a time stand shoulder to shoulder. In a few others, the U.S. and Europe will compete, or go their separate ways. In most areas, a broader constellation of powers will find formal and informal ways to join forces – sometimes literally – in the management of transnational and global threats. The U.S. itself, not the transatlantic relationship, will be at the hub of this process. And on the governance of global institutions, the U.S. and Europe will quietly clash – that is unless Europe makes the hard choices necessary to take a decisive leap forward towards coherence in its global presence.[6]

This prediction has largely been borne out by events. In the context of the G20, for example, the United States sided with the emerging powers to insist that European governments give up some of their voting rights and seats on the board of the International Monetary Fund to accommodate the fast-growing Asian economies. Although agreeing to this in theory, the Europeans procrastinated in practice, debating the problem internally and postponing a decision until the United States put irresistible pressure on them to act. Meanwhile, European officials were stung by President Obama's decision to negotiate an ad hoc deal to conclude the chaotic 2009 Copenhagen summit on climate change with the leaders of the BASIC group (Brazil, China, India, and South Africa) without any of their EU counterparts in the room.

---

[6] Bruce D. Jones, "The Coming Clash? Europe and U.S. Multilateralism Under Obama," in Álvaro de Vasconcelos and Marcin Zaborowski, eds., *The Obama Moment: European and American Perspectives* (EU Institute for Security Studies, 2009), p. 64.

As this author pointed out in 2010, many European observers were becoming concerned that "the US has embarked on a radical transformation of the international system without a clear grasp of the consequences."

> Rather like Lewis Carroll's White Queen, they complain, the Obama administration foresees "jam tomorrow" (i.e. a new era of international cooperation) but has yet to receive much "jam today" (i.e. Chinese support on climate change or Iran). Given the huge political obstacles in Washington DC to the approval of new international treaties, they worry that the administration will not be able to implement future agreements, weakening the credibility of its political commitment to multilateralism. Perhaps most galling for Europeans is the suspicion that the US has made a high-odds bet on reforming multilateralism, but Washington is largely gambling with European assets.[7]

In short, the multilateral order described in this volume – in which the United States played a largely passive or permissive role in multilateral affairs while its Western allies actively pursued reform – was breaking down. Now the United States was the active force, and the Europeans at least found this discomforting (Canadian and Japanese officials are also reported to have disliked the Obama administration's emphasis on the G20, as they feared that their influence in the G8 would be diluted.) The financial crisis and ensuing chaos within the Eurozone has also had a negative effect on the Europeans' ability to drive improvements to the multilateral system. By 2010, EU members including France and the Netherlands were making cuts to their humanitarian and development aid budgets, while the French and British (although committed to keep development spending high) were questioning their expenditures on UN peacekeeping. In 2011, the U.S. permanent representative to the UN, Susan E. Rice, accused her European counterparts of a "holier than thou" approach to enforcing austerity on the UN Secretariat.[8] For the time being, the Europeans were still significant players in the UN and other international institutions. But the presumption that their leverage was now in indefinite decline was a commonplace one.

ON THE RISE: NEW MIDDLE POWERS AND GREAT POWERS

The Europeans' loss of leverage has created space for a new generation of middle powers to play a more active role in multilateral affairs. Examples include South Korea (which presided over the G20 in 2010 and is set to host a second Nuclear Security Summit in 2012) and Mexico (which successfully facilitated talks on climate change in 2010, undoing some of the damage done at Copenhagen, and presides over

---

[7] Richard Gowan, *The Obama Administration and Multilateralism: Europe Relegated* (FRIDE, February 2010), p. 4.

[8] Colum Lynch, "U.S. and Europe fight over cuts in peacekeeping," *Foreign Policy* online, 10 October 2011, available at http://turtlebay.foreignpolicy.com/posts/2011/10/10/us_and_europe_fight_over_cuts_in_peacekeeping.

the G20 in 2012). Turkey has also put itself forward as a more important multilateral player than before, while Qatar has positioned itself as both an important player in the Middle East and a sponsor of mediation efforts such as that aimed at concluding the Darfur conflict. Singapore has stepped forward as a representative of small states' interests both in the UN and vis-à-vis the G20, while Chile has found a niche as a constructive and generally respected voice on human rights at the UN.

The rise of these new middle powers is one of the most positive developments in international cooperation in recent years. They are often more widely acceptable facilitators of multilateral processes than their European counterparts, as they carry neither the baggage of colonial history nor the burden of having to coordinate with other members of the EU on policy issue after policy issue (Norway and Switzerland, as the two main European states still outside the EU, are also still very active in UN affairs.)

Nonetheless, the new middle powers' stance on multilateralism continues to be overshadowed by the attitudes of the main emerging economies: China, Brazil, India, and to some extent South Africa.[9] These larger powers – and China in particular – were the main targets of the Obama administration's multilateral outreach. The consensus among policy analysts is that U.S. efforts have generated, on the most optimistic reading, very limited benefits. Chinese policy makers were reported to view American overtures as signs of weakness. Our colleague Thomas Wright argued in a July 2010 article that China's hard line was "nothing short of a revelation for much of the administration's foreign policy team."

> Instead of accepting the offer of a full partnership, China became far more antagonistic and assertive on the world stage. It expanded its claims in the South China Sea, engaged in a major spat with Google over Internet freedom, played an obstructionist role at the climate change negotiations in Copenhagen, regularly and openly criticized US leadership, and, sought to water down sanctions against Iran's nuclear program at the UN Security Council.[10]

If China's attitude was the primary challenge for the U.S, it was not the only one. Indian officials were nostalgic for the Bush administration, which had courted them assiduously as a counterweight to China – although President Obama improved this relationship by visiting New Delhi in 2010 and publicly endorsing the Indian quest for a permanent Security Council seat. Brazil also proved a complicated partner, working with Turkey to open a new track of negotiations with Iran over its nuclear ambitions and generally shifting away from cooperation with the West at the UN as its own influence increased.

---

9 See Andrew F. Hart and Bruce D. Jones, "How Do Rising Powers Rise?" *Survival*, Vol. 52, No. 6 (December 2010–January 2011), pp. 63–88. For a detailed discussion of India's diplomatic posture, see David Malone, *Does the Elephant Dance? Contemporary Indian Foreign Policy* (Oxford University Press, 2011).

10 Thomas Wright, "How China Gambit Backfired," *The Diplomat* online, July 28, 2010, available at http://the-diplomat.com/2010/07/28/how-china-gambit-backfired/.

328 *Afterword*

By mid-2010, President Obama's advisors were reevaluating their initial emphasis on multilateral cooperation. After playing an important role in restoring confidence after the financial crisis, the G20 went adrift in 2010 and 2011, as differences over how to manage the recovery became prominent. As Wright noted, a "vital debate" emerged in the Obama administration over how to redirect policy:

> On the one hand are those who wish to persist with cooperative strategic engagement so the international order is run by a concert of powers, with the United States and China at its heart. On the other are those who believe that, even as they cooperate, relations between the United States and emerging powers will be far more competitive and prone to limited rivalry than relations between members of the old Western order, meaning the United States will have no choice but to compete with emerging powers to shape the international order while maintaining a geopolitical advantage over its competitors.[11]

The argument over whether the future will be "competitive" or "cooperative" intensified in 2011, as the crises in Libya and Syria highlighted differences between the West and emerging powers over interventionism and sovereignty. By coincidence, Brazil, India, and South Africa all held seats on the Security Council in 2011. The first test of their positions was Libya's descent into civil war. The non-Western powers surprised some observers by supporting an initial Security Council resolution citing the Libyan government's "responsibility to protect" its people and putting pressure on the Gaddafi regime through sanctions. The resolution also ordered the International Criminal Court to investigate the crisis – demonstrating how some of the normative and legal innovations described by Ian Johnstone, David Malone, and Cesare Romano in this volume have gradually become embedded in diplomatic practice.[12] When the Libyan government failed to respond to these pressures, France, Britain, and (belatedly but decisively) the United States decided to push for military action through the Council. China and Russia refrained from using their vetoes, while Brazil and India abstained (as did Germany). South Africa voted in favor.[13] But as NATO aircraft swung into action over North Africa – embarking on a campaign that reinforced many of the questions about the Alliance's capabilities and goals raised by Mats Berdal and David Ucko in this volume – all five major non-Western powers criticized the Americans and Europeans for using excessive force and aiming to overthrow Gaddafi. As the situation in Syria deteriorated in mid-2011, China and Russia refused to countenance European proposals for even a Security Council resolution imposing sanctions, arguing that it would mark a step toward

---

[11] Ibid., p. 2.

[12] Johnstone and Romano have elaborated their thinking in two recent volumes. See Ian Johnstone, *The Power of Deliberation: International Law, Politics and Organizations* (Oxford University Press, 2011); and Cesare Romano (ed.), *The United States and International Courts and Tribunals* (Cambridge University Press, 2009).

[13] See Bruce D. Jones, "Libya and the Responsibilities of Power," *Survival*, Vol. 53, No. 3 (June–July 2011), pp. 51–60.

Afterword

another military intervention. India, Brazil and South Africa took a marginally more moderate approach, but were also opposed to putting serious pressure on Damascus.

Commentators were often too quick to draw lessons from this sequence of events. The Security Council's authorization of the use of force and invocation of the responsibility to protect was hastily greeted as a breakthrough in the debate over humanitarian intervention. The West's failure to win UN support for action against Syria was equally hastily declared to mark the end of interventionism. To some extent the U.S. debate over international cooperation has slipped backward as skeptics have argued that the Syrian case in particular shows that the emerging powers are untrustworthy. A more measured conclusion might be that the events of 2011 were characterized not by outright competition, but by *contestation*: an ongoing struggle between the established and emerging powers to define the precedents and norms of cooperation, in which states such as China and India have become increasingly forthright but only intermittently get their way. This distinction may seem minor, but it is important to recognize that the contest over how to act in Libya and Syria did not escalate into classical interstate competition in the region. European, Russian, and U.S. forces may have maneuvered in the Mediterranean, but the chances of them directly confronting one another – a very real risk in previous crises in the Middle East during the Cold War – always appeared infinitesimally low. Diplomatic contestation may be an exhausting business for diplomats, but it is distinctly preferable to more direct forms of expressing antagonism.

If the Mediterranean was one laboratory for international cooperation in 2011, Asia was another. On sending *Cooperating for Peace and Security* to press, we were already conscious that a chapter on Asian attitudes to regional security arrangements would have been a useful addition. As Jones and Forman noted in the introduction, it could be argued that the post–Cold War period had seen "the emergence of 'three worlds' of multilateralism, or at least three pathways forward: a world of institutions driven by U.S. policy and politics; a world of institutions friendly to but not inclusive of the United States; *and a world of institutions specifically designed to contain or constrain the United States, both at the global level and in Asia.*"[14] In the Asian context, China invested in the Shanghai Cooperation Organization, East Asian Summit (EAS), and ASEAN Plus Three mechanisms in an effort to place itself at the center of regional multilateral networks in which the United States had no part. It also forged trilateral talks with Japan and South Korea, again excluding their American patron. As of late 2008, it seemed possible that a regional security system could emerge in the Asia-Pacific in which the United States would be absent or peripheral.

Yet once the Obama administration had grown wary of Chinese intentions, it made a concerted effort to reinsert itself into regional forums. Secretary of State Hillary Clinton secured an invitation to the EAS in 2010, and President Obama attended the event in 2011. The administration also worked hard to revitalize the

---

[14] Page 18 in this volume, emphasis added.

330 *Afterword*

Asia-Pacific Economic Community (APEC), which had risked being marginalized, and launched a new Trans-Pacific partnership to promote economic cooperation. In an even more direct diplomatic challenge to Beijing, Washington advocated for the creation of a cooperative framework to manage incidents in the much-disputed South China Sea. Concerned by increasing Chinese assertiveness in the area, other regional players such as Vietnam and Malaysia welcomed this initiative. In a much-noted *Foreign Policy* article on "America's Pacific Century," Secretary Clinton noted that "we have emphasized the importance of multilateral cooperation, for we believe that addressing complex transnational challenges of the sort now faced by Asia requires a set of institutions capable of mustering collective action."

> A more robust and coherent regional architecture in Asia would reinforce the system of rules and responsibilities, from protecting intellectual property to ensuring freedom of navigation, that form the basis of an effective international order. In multilateral settings, responsible behavior is rewarded with legitimacy and respect, and we can work together to hold accountable those who undermine peace, stability, and prosperity.[15]

In spite of this ostensibly highly inclusive language, the new U.S. approach to cooperation in the Asia-Pacific has the potential to launch a new bout of contestation in the region, in which China and the United States will struggle diplomatically to develop multilateral frameworks that contain and constrain one another. This may lead to a significant amount of institutional innovation and adaptation, meaning that cooperation on specific issues among sets of states will be driven by a broader strategic competition. The new era of multilateralism in the Pacific, if it continues along this trajectory, will involve complications and tensions far greater than those seen in Africa and Europe in the 1990s and 2000s.

CONCLUSION: WHERE NOW?

There may be other strategic surprises ahead: at the time of writing, some commentators are predicting the breakup of the EU as a result of the Eurozone crisis. Even if this is alarmist, the EU's travails will surely affect the calculations of other regional organizations about the limits of cooperation. Nonetheless, the greatest challenge to effective international cooperation still remains the lack of consensus among the United States and major emerging powers on how to structure global order. In late 2011, Jones noted the prevalence of the question "Do the West and the Rest have common interests?"

> Two paradigms answer the question differently. The first was in vogue at the height of the global financial crisis: an "all in one boat" paradigm highlighting the global economy's deep realities of interconnection and a powerful set of associated

---

[15] Hillary Clinton, "America's Pacific Century," *Foreign Policy* online, November 2011, available at http://www.foreignpolicy.com/articles/2011/10/11/americas_pacific_century?page=0,3.

Afterword 331

shared interests that trumps all other sources of tension and facilitates cooperation between the West and the Rest. The second paradigm – traditional great power realism – asserts that the rise of a new power necessarily produces tension with the established power; even shared economic interests can be eclipsed by a combination of security dilemmas and nationalist sensitivities. History provides evidence for both paradigms.[16]

Jones's own conclusion is that no single paradigm applies to all areas of international relations. There are many areas, such as dealing with piracy and global health issues, where states behave in a "semi-cooperative" fashion. By contrast, there is a tendency toward contention over energy resources, and major powers are naturally inclined to compete over scare resources or for influences in their neighborhoods (as demonstrated by Russian policy toward Georgia and Beijing's efforts to assert itself in the South China Sea). International interventions and debates over human rights abuses inevitably involve "contention in real time" as major powers work out their policy options in dealing with crises, while the economic sphere is a mix of cooperation and competition in which "the United States and the major powers share a compelling interest to protect the global system from collapse, but within that system have every incentive to compete – and compete intensively – for political and economic gain."[17] Jones concludes his analysis by arguing that the ups-and-downs of the Obama administration's efforts at international engagement should not be used as an excuse for giving up on multilateralism:

> US strategy should put a premium, as it already does, on building up patterns of cooperation and, even more importantly, tools for effective governance in the realm of the global economy and global finance. It should press further and complement these with similar cooperation on those security issues, especially transnational threats, where we have shared interests (e.g. on maritime security with India and food security with Brazil).... Finding ways to maintain a balance of interests, or at least dampen conflict, on energy security questions will be a long game indeed, starting with protracted negotiations over climate change. Patient and multilevel diplomacy will be the name of the game in this policy sphere.[18]

This passage is reminiscent of another, older formula for American strategy cited elsewhere in *Cooperating for Peace and Security*. This is Stanley Hoffmann's argument from the 1970s for a U.S. strategy aimed at sustaining world order cited by Gowan and Batmanglich in the chapter on European security cooperation. As we noted, Hoffmann's guidelines for action include the need to "protect and support the elements of order that exist already" and the importance of accepting "ulterior progress, rather than perpetual competition."[19] The goal is "relationships that are

---

[16] Bruce D. Jones, *Beyond Blocs: The West, the Rest and Interest-based International Cooperation*, The Stanley Foundation, October 2011), p. 1.

[17] Ibid., p. 5.

[18] Ibid., p. 11.

[19] See pp. 82–83 in this volume.

only partially adversary and allow for sufficient cooperation to make order possible." These phrases feel all too relevant today.

While many of the assumptions that underpinned *Cooperating for Peace and Security* have been challenged in the five years since it was conceived – and these challenges have intensified in the two years since it was published – many of the basic problems of international cooperation remain the same. The many dimensions of cooperation can only be sustained in the context of an international order that requires constant renewal if it is to satisfy the interests and desires of major powers. In our conclusion, we expressed concern that the volume had described "an international security system with worthy refinements but a lack of strategic direction." Although the Obama administration set out to improve this situation, a sense of drift and uncertainty still persists, and it is far from clear if it will be dispelled.

New York, December 2011

Index

Accord de Non-Aggression et d'Assistance en Matiere de Defense (ANAD) (CEAO), 273
Acheson, Dean, 143–144
Afghanistan
  counterterrorism norm, impact in, 206
  Friends mechanism and UN peace negotiations, 238–239
  international aid, accountability for, 222–223
  ISAF in, 64–65, 98–100
  military humanitarian assistance to, 265
  post–9/11, 33, 112, 159–161
  security provisions in, 220–221
  statebuilding in, 225
  U.S.-NATO involvement, 7, 33, 112, 159–161
  U.S.-UN role in, 51
Africa/African Union (AU). *See also specific countries in*
  ACRF in, 287
  criminal courts and tribunals, 297–298, 300, 306–307
  institutional pluralism and EU-UN relations, 94–95
  military humanitarian assistance to, 266
  UN peace negotiations in, 240–242
Africa/African Union (AU), evolution of collective security mechanisms
  conclusions, 289–290
  introduction, 269–271
  post–Cold War, 271–273, 281–285
  Southern African Development Community (SADC), 278–281
  U.S. policy and, 269–270, 285–289
Africa Command (AFRICOM), 266
Africa Contingency Training Assistance (ACOTA), 288
Africa Crisis Response Initiative (ACRI), 287–288

Africa Mission in Sudan (AMIS), 67–68, 196–197, 285
African Commission on Human and Peoples' Rights, 300
African Court of Human and Peoples' Rights, 297–298, 300, 306–307
African Crisis Response Force (ACRF), 287
African Peace Facility, 94–95
Ahtisaari, Martti, 61, 87, 234–235
Albright, Madeleine, 22–23, 62, 172
Allied Command Transformation (ACT) (NATO), 113–114
al Qaeda, 33, 206–207, 220–221. *See also* Taliban
Al-Qaida/Taliban Sanctions Committee (1267 Committee) (UN), 146–147
al Sestani, Sayyed Ali, 52
American Convention on Human Rights, 299–300
American Court of Human Rights, 297–298
American Declaration of the Rights and Duties of Man, 299–300
Amin, Idi, 271
Annan, Kofi
  conflict management, normative innovations in, 14
  on the Council's antiterrorism agenda, 73
  counterterrorism actions, 149–154
  GWB administration relationship, 7–8, 34
  humanitarian intervention, 14–15, 67, 252
  international criminal courts financing position, 305
  oil for food scandal and, 51, 54
  peacekeeping and peacebuilding efforts, 13–14
Anti-Ballistic Missile (ABM) Treaty, 25, 122, 131
Argentina, 128
Armitage, Richard, 146

333

Index

arms control. *See* International Atomic Energy Agency (IAEA); nuclear nonproliferation institutions, evolution of; *specific treaties relating to*; weapons of mass destruction (WMD)

Arnault, Jean, 51

AU Mission in Somalia (AMISOM), 241, 284

Aum Shinrikyo sarin attacks, 181–182, 184

Australia, CWC leadership role, 179, 180–181, 183

Australia Group, 174, 179

axis of evil, 34, 134

Azerbaijan, 88–89

Babangida, Ibrahim, 277

Bachardost, Ramzan, 223

Balkan conflict, 85–92, 103

Belarus, 128, 131–132

Benjamin, Daniel, 144

Bin Laden, Osama, 205–206

Biological Weapons Convention (BWC)
Cold War years (1976–1990), 168–169
conclusions, 175–177
CWC compared, 166
failure of the protocol (2000–2006), 25, 173–175, 176
Fifth Review Conference, 173–175
First Review Conference, 168
Fourth Review Conference, 171–172
future of, 176–177
overview and early history, 166–168
post–Cold War (1991–2000), 175, 176
Second Review Conference, 168–169
Sixth Review Conference, 174–175
Third Review Conference, 169
UK draft proposal, 167–168
VEREX group established, 169–171
verification and compliance assurance, 25, 167–173, 176

Biological Weapons Convention (BWC), U.S. policy on verification and
Bush, G. W. administration, 173–175, 176
Clinton administration, 169–173, 176
Cold War years (1976–1989), 168–169
conclusions, 175–176
UK draft proposal, 167–168

biosecurity, 42. *See also* Biological Weapons Convention (BWC); Chemical Weapons Convention (CWC)

Blair, Tony, 37, 259

Bolton, John
BWC verification protocol, 173–174
Human Rights Council actions, 7
ICC and, 4, 5

Khalilzad replacement of, 62–63
Proliferation Security Initiative of, 41–42
UN reform package, involvement in, 52–54
UNSCR 1540, U.S. policy direction and, 148

Bosnia, 206–207

Bosnia-Herzegovina, 75

Boutros-Ghali, Boutros, 200, 204, 206–207, 286–287

Brahimi, Lakhdar, 7, 13, 16, 39, 51–52, 238–239

Brazil, 128

Bremer, Paul, 38

Bretton Woods Institutions, 31

Burundi, AU peace operations in, 284

Bush, George H. W. (GHWB), 178

Bush, George H. W. (GHWB), administration
BWC verification protocol position, 170
CWC leadership role, 179–181, 183
GWB policies compared, 30–31, 37–38
new world order vision, 24

Bush, George W. (GWB), 3, 29

Bush, George W. (GWB), administration. *See also* Iraq, U.S. invasion of; United Nations (UN) Security Council-GWB administration relations
Afghanistan, nation-building commitment, 225
Africa policy, 269–270, 287, 288–289
BWC verification protocol position, 173–175
CWC leadership, declining role in, 182, 184
Darfur policy, 39–40, 52
democracy norm, support for, 209–211
doctrine of preemption and primacy, 30–31, 35–36, 46, 208–209, 211, 215–216
EU relations and the Iraq war, 92–93
GHWB policies compared, 30–31, 37–38
hegemony, decline in, 3–7
ICC, opposition to, 4, 5, 76–77
nuclear nonproliferation and the, 122–123, 133–134, 184
R2P norm, support for, 209–210
Sudan policy (Khartoum regime), 5–7
Syria's withdrawal from Lebanon and, 5

Bush, George W. (GWB), administration, multilateralism and the
ad hoc approach to, 20, 30–31, 41–42
arms control and, 41–42
global war on terrorism, 31–33
hegemony in conflict with, 3–7
NATO role in Afghanistan, 33–34
post–9/11, 4, 28–30
pre–9/11, 25–28
treaties circumvented, abrogated, unsigned, opposed, 4, 25, 122, 143

Bush, George W. (GWB), administration, post–9/11

Africa policy, 269–270
axis of evil, 34, 134
biological weapons policy, 42, 174, 176
counterterrorism agenda, 143–144, 208–209, 211,
215–216
international security architecture, effect on,
16–17
nationalism, exploitation of, 29
National Security Strategy, 4, 35–36, 46, 209,
269–270
policy of military dominance, 4
war on terrorism, 31–33, 105, 120–121, 159–161,
261, 269–270, 299–300
Bustani, José Maurízio, 182

Cambodia, 69, 305
Canada, 172, 174–175, 194–196, 252
Central Emergency Response Fund (CERF)
(UN), 254–255
Chambas, Mohamed Ibn, 277
Chávez, Hugo, 236–237
Chechnya, 88–89
Chemical Weapons Convention (CWC)
BWC compared, 166
Cold War years (1976–1987), 177–178
drivers of change, 183
issues outstanding, 173
key aspects, 181
overview and early history, 166, 167
post–Cold War (1989–1993), 179–181
UNSCR 1540, impact on, 208–209
U.S. leadership role, 177–184
verification policy and challenge inspections,
177, 183
Chemical Weapons Treaty, 141
Cheney, Dick, 28, 34, 37, 181–182
Chesteman, Simon, 73
China, 61, 76–77, 128, 130–131, 211
Chirac, Jacques, 120–121
Clinton, William Jefferson (Bill), administration
African policy, 285–287
BWC verification protocol position, 170–171,
176
CWC leadership role, 181–182, 183
international criminal courts and the, 4, 76–77,
302–303
international security architecture policy, 9–10
multilateralism, commitment to, 24–25, 26
NATO expansion, commitment to, 85–86,
89–92
NPT, engagement in, 131–133, 137–138
prosperity and peace during, 3
Coalition Provisional Authority (CPA), 38–39
Cohen, Herman J., 286

Cold War, era post–. *See also* NATO, post–Cold
War evolution
Africa/African Union security architecture,
281–285
Biological Weapons Convention (BWC), 175,
176
Chemical Weapons Convention (CWC),
179–181
EU security architecture, 80–81, 84–89
international humanitarian cooperation, 11–12,
249–251
international security architecture, evolution
of, 9–11
Cold War era
Biological Weapons Convention (BWC),
168–169
Chemical Weapons Convention (CWC),
177–178
current terrorism threat compared, 143–144
U.S. leadership role, 31, 177–178
Commander's Emergency Response Program
(CERP) (US), 265, 266–267
Commonwealth of Independent States (CIS),
80–81
Communaute Economique L'Afrique de l'Ouest
(CEAO), 273
Comprehensive Test Ban Treaty (CTBT), 24–25,
129–132
Comprehensive Test Ban Treaty Organization
(CTBTO), 129
Conference on Security and Cooperation in
Europe (CSCE), 84–85, 86–89, 91
Conference on Security, Stability, Development
and Cooperation in Africa (CSSDCA),
272–273
Constitutive Act (AU), 282–283
constructivist international relations theory,
188–189
Conté, Lasana, 277
Convention on Human Rights (U.S.), 299–300
Convention on Nuclear Terrorism (UN), 205
Convention on Offences and Certain Other Acts
Committed on Board Aircraft (UN), 205
Convention on the Prohibition of the
Development, Production and Stockpiling of
Bacteriological (Biological) and Toxin
Weapons and on their Destruction. *See*
Biological Weapons Convention (BWC)
Conventional Forces in Europe Treaty, 84–85
Cooperative Threat Reduction (CTR) program,
130, 132
Cornish, Paul, 85–86
Council for Mutual Economic Assistance
(Comecon), 84

counterterrorism, multilateral cooperation
intelligence and law enforcement cooperation, 156–159
International Criminal Tribunals, 161–164
introduction, 143–145
NATO and military cooperation, 159–161
normative framework for, 192, 213
reshaping the architecture, 165
terrorist financing, 154–156
UN Secretariat and the General Assembly, 149–154
UN Security Council agenda, 145–149, 151
Counter-Terrorism Action Group (CTAG) (UN), 153
Counter-Terrorism Committee (CTC) (UN), 32–33, 39–40, 72, 145–149, 153
Counter-Terrorism Executive Directorate (CTED) (UN), 146
Counter-Terrorism Implementation Task Force (UN), 150–151
Counter-Terrorism Task Force (UN), 206
Court of Human Rights (U.S.), 297–298
crime, transnational, 74–75
Cyprus, 239

Daley, William, 172
Danforth, John, 52
Darfur
AU peace operations in, 94–95, 196–197, 285
ICC case relating to, 77, 162–164
R2P norm, effect in, 67–68, 197
UN and, 39–40, 51, 52, 67–68, 196–197, 241–242, 285
U.S. policy, 39–40, 52
Dayton Peace Accord, 87, 89, 103
Declaration of the Rights and Duties of Man (U.S.), 299–300
Declaration on the Granting of Independence to Colonial Peoples, 200
de Cuéllar, Javier Pérez, 59, 229–230, 231
Defence Capabilities Initiative (DCI) (NATO), 108–109
de Mello, Sergio Vieira, 6, 14, 39
Democracy Conflict and Humanitarian Response (DCHA) bureau (USAID), 262–267
democracy norm
depth of commitment to, 209–213
ECOWAS adoption of, 275–276
emergence of, 200–202
good governance and development assistance, impact on, 204–205
peace operations, impact on, 202–204
SADC adoption of, 279–280
U.S. responsibility for, 192

democracy stage in statebuilding operations, 224–225
Democratic People's Republic of Korea (DPRK)
Agreed Framework negotiations, 129–130, 133
International Atomic Energy Agency (IAEA) inspections, 133, 134, 139–140
NPT membership/ratification, 124, 129–130, 134–135
Six-Party talks, 60
UN Security Council actions against, 135
Democratic Republic of Congo, 93, 94–95, 196–197, 206–207, 280–281
democratization
decision-making driver of UNSC, 69–70
warlord, 220
Deng, Francis, 198–199
Department for International Development (DFID) (UK), 259, 260–261
Department of Humanitarian Affairs (UN), 250
de Soto, Alvaro, 230–231, 238–239
development assistance and democracy norm, 204–205
Development Assistance Committee of the Organization for Economic Cooperation and Development (OECD/DAC), 255
Dole, Robert, 26–27
Doyle, Michael, 202–203
Duffield, Mark, 224

E3/EU, 95–96
East Timor, 69, 238
Economic Community of Central African States (ECCAS), 269
Economic Community of West African States (ECOWAS), 65–66, 269, 273–278, 284
ECOWAS Ceasefire Monitoring Group (ECOMOG), 274
Egeland, Jan, 239–240
Eighteen-Nation Committee on Disarmament (ENDC), 167–168
Eisenhower, Dwight, 190
ElBaradei, Mohamed, 96, 137
Eliasson, Jan, 54
El Salvador, 69, 230–232
Emergency Relief Coordinator (UN), 12
European Court of Human Rights (ECHR), 296, 297–301, 306–307
European Court of Justice, 296
European Security Strategy (EU), 2003, 93–94
European Union (EU)/European Community (EC). See also institutional pluralism and the EU
Balkan conflict negotiations, involvement in, 86
BWC verification protocol position, 173, 176

Index

Democratic Republic of Congo operations, 93, 94, 95
formation of, 84–85
IAEA relations and the Iranian crisis, 95–96
ICJ, attitudes and practices toward, 296–297
international courts and tribunals, 293
international criminal courts and the, 305–306, 307–308
multilateral counterterrorism cooperation, 156–159
Russia relations, 80–81, 90–91
security architecture, 80–81, 84–89, 93–94
Evans, Gareth, 179, 180–181
evolutionary theory, adaptionist programme, 311–312
exceptionalism, U.S., 23–24, 190–191
Eyadéma, Gnassingbé, 276–277

FBI, multilateral counterterrorism cooperation, 156–159
Financial Action Task Force (FATF) (UN), 154
Finnemore, Martha, 188–189
Fissile Material Cut-off Treaty (FMCT), 130
Fleischer, Ari, 38
Founding Act on NATO-Russia relations, 90
"Fragile States Strategy" (USAID), 263–264
France, 5, 128
Friends mechanism in peace negotiations, 230–232, 235–237
Front Line States (FLS) (Southern Africa), 278–279
Fukuyama, Francis, 42

Garfinkle, Adam, 27–28
Gates, Robert, 10
G8, 156–159
General Agreement on Tariffs and Trade (GATT), 31
Georgia, 80–81
G4 countries, 48–49
Ghani, Ashraf, 222–223
Gingrich-Mitchell Panel on U.S.-UN reform, 51, 149
Global Conflict Prevention Pool (UK), 260
Global Counter-Terrorism Strategy (UN), 206
Global Health Security Action Group, 42
Global Peace Operations Initiative (GPOI), 288–289
global war on terror (GWOT), 31–33, 159–161, 261, 269–270. See also terrorism; war on terrorism, U.S.
Gnassingbé, Faure, 276–277
good governance agenda, democracy norm and, 204–205

Good Humanitarian Donorship (GHD), 253, 258, 259–260
Gould, Stephen Jay, 311–312
Greenstock, Jeremy, 146
Group of Friends of UN Reform, 164–165
G77, 54
G7/G8, 90–91, 156–159
Guantanamo Bay detention center, 299–300
Guinea, ECOWAS in, 276–278

Haiti, 52, 64, 66–67, 75, 197
Hariri, Rafik, 164
Haslam, Jonathan, 90
Hawke, Bob, 179
Helms, Jesse, 23–24
Hezbollah, 7, 95, 206–207
High-level Panel on Threats, Challenges and Change (UN)
purpose of, 40–41, 150, 215
R2P norm concept affirmed by, 194–195
support for, 46–47
threats defined by, 47
U.S., relevance to, 51
Hoffmann, Stanley, 81, 82–84, 88, 90, 93, 94, 97
humanitarian assistance
cluster approach to, 252
emergency assistance process, 252
evolution of the international system for, 11–12, 14–15
institutional architecture for coordinating, 249–251
military, 265–267
in peacebuilding/stabilization operations, 222–224
post–Cold War era crises and reforms, 249–251
R2P norm and, 193–199, 251–252
humanitarian cooperation, international
conclusions, 267–268
IDPs and R2P, influence on, 251–252
introduction, 247–248
post–9/11, 261–267
post–Cold War era crises and reforms, 249–251
state and civil society actors in, 248–250
UK leadership role, 258–261
U.S. engagement in, 247, 256–267
humanitarian cooperation, international, donors/funding element of
friends groups, 254
GHD initiative, 253, 258, 259–260
mechanisms of, 254–255
nontraditional/emerging, 255–256
post–9/11, 261–267
United Kingdom, 258–261
United States, 247, 256–258, 261

Index

humanitarian intervention, doctrine of, 66–68, 192, 193–195
humanitarian law, and counterterrorism efforts, 72–73
humanitarian sector, nature of, 248–249
human rights. *See also* international courts and tribunals
  Constitutive Act and, 282–283
  decision-making driver of UNSC, 68–69
  democracy norm, impact on, 200–202
  international courts and tribunals, 293, 297–301
  nonindifference principle and, 281–282
  nonintervention policy and, 271–272
Human Rights Commission (UN), 7
Human Rights Council (UN), 7, 50–51
human security, 252, 269, 273, 279–280, 281
Hussein, Saddam, 34, 36–38

Ikenberry, John, 191–193
Imperfect Unions (Keohane and Wallander), 8, 313
India, 124, 130, 137
institutional adaptation, conclusions, 311–319
institutional pluralism
  tensions inherent in, 88
  theoretical basis for, 82
institutional pluralism and the EU
  Africa and EU-UN relations, 94–95
  Balkan crisis effect on, 86–91
  established as norm, 93–94
  Iran and EU-UN relations, 95–96
  Iraq war and mechanisms of, 92–94
  Lebanon and EU-UN relations, 95
  maximizing influence through, 81–82
  NATO expansion and the failure in Russia, 89–92
Inter-Agency Standing Committee (IASC) (UN), 250
Inter-American Commission on Human Rights, 299–300
Inter-American Court of Human Rights, 297–298, 299–300, 306–307
Inter Governmental Authority in Drought and Desertification (IGADD), 269
Inter Governmental Authority on Development (IGAD) (AU), 241, 284
internally displaced persons (IDPs), 198–199, 251–252
International Atomic Energy Agency (IAEA)
  1990–2006 system-wide changes, 141–142
  DPRK inspections, 133, 134, 139–140
  Iran and the, 95–96, 135
  Iraq's nuclear program and, 139–140
  Libya case, 135–136

  and nonproliferation, 129–130, 139–140
  NPT, enforcement role, 123–125
  Safeguards Agreements, 124–125, 135
  UNSCR 1540, impact on, 208–209
  U.S relations, future of, 39–40
International Commission on Intervention and State Sovereignty (ICISS), 194–195
International Convention for the Suppression of the Financing of Terrorism (UN), 205
International Court of Justice (ICJ), 292–293, 294–297
international courts and tribunals. *See also specific bodies*
  conclusions, 306–308
  evolution of the international system for, 15
  human rights courts, 293, 297–301
  international criminal courts, 301–306
  introduction, 291–293
International Criminal Court (ICC), 5–7, 76–78, 162–164, 301–306
international criminal law
  GWB administration position on, 27
  UNSC role in development of, 78
International Criminal Tribunal (ICTY), 292, 301–302, 303–305
International Criminal Tribunal for Rwanda, 76, 301–302, 303–305
International Criminal Tribunals, 161–164
International Security Assistance Force (ISAF), 33, 64–65, 98–100, 159–160, 220–221
Inter-State Defense and Security Committee (ISDSC) (FLS), 278–279
Iran, 34, 95–96, 135, 137–138
Iraq
  counterterrorism norm, impact in, 206
  military humanitarian assistance to, 265
  nuclear weapons program/NPT membership, 129–130
  post–9/11, 34, 159–160
  postwar, NATO/UN involvement, 33–34, 38–39, 51–52
  UN sanctions against, 132–133
Iraq, U.S. invasion of
  democracy norm, effect on, 204
  doctrine of preemption as justification for, 137–138, 209
  EU cooperation and, 92–93
  GWB-GHWB policies compared, 37–38
  institutional mechanisms used by European states during, 92–94
  international criminal courts effect on, 307
  international opposition to, effect of, 4, 36–38, 62–63, 64, 143, 224
Iraq-Iran war, 229–230

Iraq-Kuwait war, 132–133
Israel, 124, 130
Israel-Hezbollah war (2006), 7, 95

Kabila, Laurent, 280–281
Kagan, Robert, 82
Kampala Document, 272
Karzai, Hamid, 51
Kazakhstan, 128, 131–132
Keohane, Robert, 8
Khalilzad, Zalmay, 62–63
Khan, Abdul Qadeer, 133, 135–136, 147
Khartoum regime (Sudan), 5–7, 71–72
Khmer Rouge, 305
King, Larry, 32
Kissinger, Henry, 24–25
Koh, Harold, 189–191
Kony, Joseph, 77–78
Kosovo, 61, 160, 193–194
Kouyate, Lansana, 277
Kuwait, Iraqi invasion of, 132–133
Kyoto Protocol, 24–25

League of Nations, 23–24
Lebanon
    counterterrorism norm, impact in, 206–207
    humanitarian assistance in, 255
    institutional pluralism and EU-UN relations, 95
    Syrian withdrawal from, 5, 52
    terrorist tribunals, 164
    U.S. and, 5, 7
legitimacy stage in statebuilding operations, 224
Lesotho, SADC intervention in, 280–281
Lewontin, Richard, 311–312
Liberia, 52, 274
Libya, 71, 135–136
Lodge, Henry Cabot, 22
Lord's Resistance Army rebel movement in Uganda, 77–78, 292
Lugar, Richard, 105

Maastricht Treaty, 84–85
Mandela, Nelson, 234–235, 271–272, 287
Masire, Ketumile, 234–235
McNamara, Thomas, 146, 148
Mead, Walter Russell, 29
mediation system, evolution of, 12–13, 14
Middle East, U.S. assistance to, 263–264
Middle East peace process, 52, 95, 239–240
Milosevic, Slobodan, 292
MINUSTAH. *See* United Nations Stabilization Mission in Haiti (MINUSTAH)

Mission de l'Organisation des Nations Unies en République démocratique du Congo (MONUC), 196–197
Mubarak, Hosni, 71–72
Mueller, Robert, 159
multilateral cooperation, U.S. and. *See specific administrations*; United States (U.S.)
Museveni, Yoweri Kaguta, 77–78
Mutual Assistance on Defense (PMAD) (ECOWAS), 273–275
Myanmar, 7

nationalism, U.S., 190
NATO
    in Afghanistan, 98–100
    Balkan conflict and, 86–91, 103
    budget, 108
    characteristics of the Alliance, 101–107
    EU relations, proposal for strengthening of, 93–94
    expansion, 85–86, 88–92
    future role of, 99–100, 101, 106–115, 117–121
    Iraq war and institutional rivalry, 92–94
    Kosovo crisis, intervention of, 193–194
    military power, common and deployable assets, 107, 108–109
    modernization, problems related to, 108–110, 114
    strategic vision, 110–113
    tensions within, history of, 99–100
NATO, post–Cold War evolution
    achievements and limitations, 107–117
    continuity and change in, 101–107
    institutional reforms, 84–85
    overview, 100–101
NATO Response Force (NRF), 109, 116–117
NATO-Russia Permanent Joint Council, 90–91
NATO-U.S. relations
    expansion, Clinton administration support, 85–86, 89–92
    overview, 104–106
    U.S. containment policy and, 31
    U.S. military imprint on, 111–114
NATO-U.S. relations, GWB administration
    on Afghanistan, 7, 33–34, 112
    counterterrorism cooperation, influence on, 159–161
    DCI and modernization of, 108–109
    on Iraq, 33–34, 112
    post–9/11 confidence in, 4, 105–106, 120–121
    relevance questioned by, 27
natural selection, 311–312
Nepal, 69–70
Nevers, Renée de, 105

Index

Nigeria, ECOWAS and, 278
Non-Aligned Movement, 54
nongovernmental organizations, 223, 250
nonindifference principle (AU), 281–282
nonnuclear weapons states (NNWS)
    challenges to NPT, 129–131
    Safeguards Agreements, 124–125
norms in international relations
    impact on state behavior, 188–189
    U.S. role in promoting, 190–193
norms in UN operational activities. *See also*
    democracy norm
    Annan's normative innovations, 14–15
    conclusions, 213–214
    counterterrorism norm, 192, 213
    durability of, 209–213
    introduction, 187
    Responsibility to Protect (R2P), 193–199
North Korea. *See* Democratic People's Republic
    of Korea (DPRK)
nuclear nonproliferation institutions, evolution
    of
    1990–2001, 125, 126–133
    1990–2006 overview, 125–127
    institutional implications, 139–140
    introduction, 122–123
    overview, 123–125
    periodization, 138–139
    post–9/11–2006, 133–138
    system-wide (1990–2006), 141–142
    U.S. leadership role, 136–139, 140–141
Nuclear Non-Proliferation Treaty (NPT), 41,
    123–126, 130, 137–138
Nuclear Suppliers Group (NSG), 123–124
nuclear weapons states (NWS)
    challenges to NPT, 129–131
    Safeguards Agreements, 124–125
Nyerere, Julius, 234–235, 271

Obama, Barack, administration, 55–56
OCHA Donor Support Group (ODSG), 254,
    255
Odom, William E., 90
Office for Disarmament Affairs (UN), 174–175
Office for the Coordination of Humanitarian
    Affairs (OCHA) (UN), 250, 254
Office of Drugs and Crime (UN), 39–40
Office of Reconstruction and Humanitarian
    Assistance, 38
Office of US Foreign Disaster Assistance (OFDA)
    (US), 267–268
oil for food scandal, 51, 54
Operation Artemis, 93, 94
Operation Boleas, 280–281

Operation Enduring Freedom, 159–160
Operation Iraqi Freedom, 37. *See also* Iraq,
    U.S. invasion of
Operation Provide Comfort, 193, 265–266
Operation Uphold Democracy, 64–65
Organ on Politics, Defense and Security (OPDS)
    (SADC), 280–281
Organization for Economic Co-operation and
    Development (OECD), 31, 255
Organization for the Prohibition of Chemical
    Weapons (OPCW), 166, 181, 182
Organization for Security and Cooperation in
    Europe (OSCE), 80–81, 84–85, 88, 93–94
Organization for the Prohibition of Chemical
    Weapons (OPCW), 173
Organization of African Unity (OAU), 202, 269,
    271, 281–282
Ottawa Convention, 22–23
Overseas Humanitarian Disaster and Civic Aid
    (OHDCA) (US), 265

Pakistan, 124, 130, 164–165, 255
Patten, Christopher, 34
Patterson, Anne, 52
Peace and Security Council (PSC) (AU), 283–285
Peacebuilding Commission (UN), 39–40, 50–51,
    215, 225–226
Peacebuilding Support Office (UN), 225–226
peace-justice relationship, 292
peacekeeping and peacebuilding. *See also specific*
    countries
    economic factors, 222–224
    evolution of the international system for, 13–14
    future of, 244–246
    obstacles to identified by UN, 215–216
    stabilization and, 217–219
    training peacekeepers for, 288–289
peacekeeping and peacebuilding, new forms of
    Friends mechanism, 230–232, 235–237
    introduction, 227–229
    new actors in, 234–235
    post–Cold War, 229–234
    success elements, 242–244
    UN groups, 237–242
    U.S. role, 228–229
peacekeeping operations. *See also specific*
    operations
    Clinton administration policy, 285–287
    internal conflicts and compliance
        enforcement, 65–67
    norms impact on, 195–198, 202–204, 206–208
    policing functions, 75
Perle, Richard, 28
Permanent Court of Arbitration, 294

Index

341

Permanent Court of International Justice, 294
P5, 229–230
Ping, Jean, 53
pluralism, Hoffmann on, 82–84, 88, 90, 94, 97
Population, Refugees and Migrations (PRM)
  bureau (US), 262–267
post–Cold War era. *See* Cold War, era post–
Powell, Colin, 5, 33, 34, 37
Prague Capability Commitments (PCC)
  (NATO), 109, 113, 160–161
Prendergast, John, 209–210
Proliferation Security Initiative (PSI), 41–42, 136,
  137, 174
Prosper, Pierre-Richard, 6
Protocols on Non-Aggression (PNA) (ECOWAS),
  273–275

Quartet and the Middle East Peace Process, 95,
  239–240

refugees, 66–67, 193, 251–252
Responsibility to Protect (R2P), normative
  framework for, 193–199, 251–252
Rice, Condoleezza, 26, 28, 36, 41, 96
Robertson, George, 107, 159–160
Robinson, Darryl, 77
Robinson, Mary, 68
Rød-Larsen, Terje, 52, 239–240
Rome Statute of International Criminal Court, 4,
  22–23, 25, 76–77
Roosevelt, Franklin Delano, 190
Roosevelt, Theodore, 190
Ruggie, John, 190
Rumsfeld, Donald, 32, 109, 117, 181–182
Russia
  chemical weapons policies, 177–178, 182
  democracy norm, support for, 211
  International Criminal Court (ICC), position
    on, 76–77
  NATO expansion as threat to, 88–92
  nuclear nonproliferation, 122–123, 130, 131, 132
  OSCE, influence over, 88
  post–Cold war and EU security institutions,
    80–81
Russian Federation
  chemical weapons disposal, 183–184
  P5 dynamics over Kosovo status, 61
Russia-U.S. relations
  Anti-Ballistic Missile Treaty, abrogation of, 25
  biological weapons noncompliance, 168
  chemical weapons disposal, 177–178
  NATO expansion and, 90–91
  nuclear nonproliferation, 122–123, 130, 131, 132
Russo-Georgian war, 80–81, 87

Rwanda
  international criminal courts and the genocide
    in, 64, 76, 301–302, 303–305
  nonintervention policy and, 271–272
  refugee crisis, 250
  UN failed strategies in, 64
  United Nations Assistance Mission in
    (UNAMIR), 287
  U.S. policy on, 286–287

Sambanis, Nicholas, 202–203
Sarkozy, Nicolas, 81
Schroeder, Gerhard, 37
Scowcroft, Brent, 37–38
security agencies, building and training,
  221
security architecture, evolution of international
  Annan's normative innovations, 14–15
  conclusions, 18–19
  humanitarian response, 11–12, 249–251
  international courts and tribunals component,
    15
  introduction, 8–9
  mediation system development, 12–13
  peacekeeping and peacebuilding component,
    13–14
  post–9/11, 16–17
  post–Cold War, 9–11
  solidification of regional structures excluding
    the U.S., 17–18
Security Sector Reform (SSR), 119
September 11, 2001 terrorist attacks. *See also* Bush,
  George W. (GWB), administration, post–9/11
  counterterrorism norm and, 205–206
  humanitarian aid funding, effect on, 261–267
  international criminal courts, effect on, 307
  UNSC efforts following, 72, 133–134
  U.S. policy in Africa post–, 269–270
Shea, Jamie, 117
Sierra Leone, 68, 76, 195–196, 206–207
Sikkink, Katherine, 188–189
Sistani, Grand Ayatollah, 39
Somalia, 64, 66–67, 206–207, 241, 284, 286–287
Soros, George, 4
South Africa, 128
Southern African Development Community
  (SADC), 278–281
Southern African Development Coordination
  Conference (SADCC), 269, 279
South Ossetia, 88–89
sovereignty, constructing for security
  coercion and, 219–221
  economic factors, 222–224
  historical context, 216–217

Index

sovereignty, constructing for security (*cont.*)
  introduction, 215–216
  politics of, 225–226
  resources required for, 217–219
  stages of, 224–225
  statebuilding, internationalized, 219
Soviet Union, post–Cold War, 84
"The Spandrels of San Marco and the Panglossian Paradigm" (Gould and Lewontin), 311–312
Special Trafficking Operations Program (STOP), 75
Sphere Project, 250
Stability Pact for South-East Europe, 87
statebuilding. *See also* sovereignty, constructing for security
  challenges to, 220
  extroverted, 218
  internationalized, 219
  politics of, 225–226
  resources required by a sovereign for, 217–219
Stedman, Stephen, 235–236
St. Mark's Cathedral in Venice, 311–312
Straw, Jack, 259–260
Sudan, 52, 67–68, 71–72, 196–197, 241, 285
Sumbeiywo, Lazaro, 241
Syria, 52

Talbott, Strobe, 90–91
Taliban, 33, 71–72, 98–99, 113, 205–207, 220–221. *See also* al Qaeda
Tanzania, 271
Taylor, Charles, 52, 68
terrorism. *See also* global war on terror (GWOT); war on terrorism, U.S.
  A.Q. Khan nuclear proliferation network, 133, 135–136, 147
  Aum Shinrikyo sarin attacks, 181–182, 184
  Cold War threat compared, 143–144
  defining, 162–163, 164, 205
  financing, 145, 154
  norms in addressing the threat of, 188
  UNSC role in the fight against, 59
Terrorism Financing Convention (UN), 145
Thomas-Jensen, Colin, 209–210
3+1 Group on Triborder Area Security, 158–159
Tilly, Charles, 220
Tobias, Randall, 263
Togo, ECOWAS in, 276–278
Traub, James, 43–44
Treaty of Versailles, 24
Truman, Harry, 190

Uganda, 77–78, 292
Ukraine, 128, 131–132

UN Commission on Human Rights, 26–27
UN Counter-Terrorism Committee (CTC), 32–33, 39–40
UN Emergency Relief Coordinator, 12
UN High Commissioner for Refugees (UNHCR), 12, 252
UN Human Rights Council, 50–51
United Kingdom, 167–168, 170, 173, 174–175
United Nations (UN)
  Afghanistan and the, 51, 238–239
  AU peace negotiations, 240–242
  in Balkan conflict negotiations, 86–91
  counterterrorism agenda, 205–206
  Darfur conflict and the, 39–40, 51, 52, 67–68, 241–242
  Democratic Republic of Congo and the, 93
  future reforms, U.S. role in, 55–56
  Haiti and the, 52, 64, 75
  history, 47
  humanitarian architecture, 11–12
  international criminal courts and the, 304–305, 308
  in Iraq, postwar, 51–52
  Iraq war and institutional rivalry, 92–94
  Lebanon and the, 5, 52
  Liberia and the, 52
  Middle East peace process involvement, 52
  multilateral counterterrorism cooperation, 149–154
  oil for food scandal, 51, 54
  Rwanda and the, 64, 287
  Somalia and the, 64
  Sudan and the, 52, 241
  Yugoslavia and the, 64
United Nations (UN), Annan reform agenda
  elements of, 45–46, 49–50
  globalization and collective security, 47–48
  importance of, 46–47
  results of, 49–55
  Security Council reform, 48–49
United Nations (UN) Security Council
  Clinton administration and the, 62–63, 64, 132–133
  counterterrorism focus post-9/11, 72, 133–134, 145–149, 165, 205–206
  effectiveness determinants, 48
  Iraq and DPRK, 134
  Kofi Annan reform agenda, 48–49
  NPT regime role, 123–125, 129–130, 140
  P5, Council dynamics, 61
  Russian relations, 87–88
  transnational crime focus, 74–75
  U.S. leadership role in reforms, 40–41

Index

United Nations (UN) Security Council Charter, 48

United Nations (UN) Security Council, evolution of
antiterrorism agenda, 71–74
conceptions of sovereignty, effect on, 78–79
democratization and, 69–70
humanitarian issues in, 66–68
human rights and, 68–69
internal conflicts and compliance enforcement, 65–67
international criminal law, role in development of, 78
legal and regulatory mode of decision making, shift to, 71
post–Cold War shifts in cooperation, 15–16, 59–60
regulatory overreach of legislation, 73–74
transnational crime, focus on, 74–75

United Nations (UN) Security Council-GWB administration relations
Annan's role in, 7–8, 34
doctrine of preemption and primacy, 35–36, 46
expansion opposition, 48–49
International Criminal Court and, 5–7
Iraq, invasion of, 4, 36–38, 62–63, 64, 137–138, 143
Myanmar resolution on human rights, 7
post–9/11, 16–17, 30, 31–32, 145–149, 165
war on terrorism and, 31–33

United Nations (UN) Security Council, post–9/11 Resolutions
UNSCR 1267, 212–213
UNSCR 1373, 145–146, 205–206, 208, 212–213
UNSCR 1535, 146
UNSCR 1540, 30, 136, 137, 147–148, 174, 205, 208–209, 212–213

United Nations-African Union Mission in Darfur (UNAMID), 195–196

United Nations Development Program (UNDP), 273

United Nations General Assembly counterterrorism strategy, 206, 212–213

United Nations Mission in Sierra Leone (UNAMSIL), 195–196, 206–207

United Nations Stabilization Mission in Haiti (MINUSTAH), 197

United Nations-U.S. relations
future of, 39–41, 46
GWB administration
Human Rights Council, 7
Kofi Annan UN reform agenda and, 51–54
on Lebanon, 7
position on, 26–27

postwar Iraq, negotiations for role in, 38–39
UN Peacebuilding Commission, 39–40

United States (U.S.). *See also* NATO-U.S. relations; *specific administrations*; United Nations-U.S. relations
Cold War leadership, 31, 177–178
energy supplies, African oil and, 269–270
exceptionalist tradition, 23–24, 190–191
human rights courts, attitude toward, 301
ICJ, attitudes and practices toward, 295–296
international criminal courts and the, 296–297, 302–304, 307
Iran's right to nuclear energy, position on, 96
multilateral cooperation and the, 20–26, 43–44, 191–192
post–Vietnam policy/post–Cold War policy, 22–23, 82–83
role in promoting norms, 190–193
rule of law, 302–303
Russian Federation relations, 61

United States, nuclear nonproliferation and the. *See also specific administrations*
ABM Treaty, 131
Cooperative Threat Reduction program, 130, 132
CTBT position, 24–25, 130, 131–132
domestic politics effect on, 138–139
DPRK Agreed Framework negotiations, 129–130, 133
India relations in, 137
Iraq, military action against, 132–133
leadership role, 30, 136–138
NPT ratification, 130
PSI established, 136, 137
Russia relations in, 122–123, 130, 131, 132

United States Agency for International Development (USAID), 262–267

Universal Declaration of Human Rights, 200

UN Mission in Iraq (UNAMI), 39

UN Office for Disarmament Affairs (UNODA), 174–175

UN Office on Drugs and Crime (UNODC), 39–40

UN Operation in Somalia (UNOSOM), 286–287

UN Peacebuilding Commission, 39–40, 50–51, 215

UN Relief and Works Agency (UNRWA), 11, 66–67

Vendrell, Francesc, 238
Villepin, Dominique de, 37

Wallander, Celeste, 8
Wang Guangya, 61

war on terrorism, U.S., 105, 120–121, 269–270, 299–300. *See also* global war on terror (GWOT); terrorism
Warsaw Pact, 84
Warsaw Pact countries, 167–168
Wasmosy, Jaun Carlos, 202
weapons of mass destruction (WMD), 37, 41–42, 208–209. *See also* Biological Weapons Convention (BWC); Chemical Weapons Convention (CWC)
West African states, economic community of. *See* Economic Community of West African States (ECOWAS)
Western EU, 86–91
Wippman, David, 77
Wolfowitz, Paul, 28, 159–160

Woodward, Susan, 86
World Bank, 204–205
World Court. *See* International Court of Justice (ICJ)
World Health Organization (WHO), 39–40
World Trade Organization (WTO), 91

Yeltsin, Boris, administration, 88–89
Yugoslavia
  collapse of, 85–92
  International Criminal Tribunal in, 64, 76, 292, 301–302, 303–305
  refugees, plight of, 66–67
  UN failed strategies in, 64

Zoellick, Robert, 26

For EU product safety concerns, contact us at Calle de José Abascal, 56–1°,
28003 Madrid, Spain or eugpsr@cambridge.org.

www.ingramcontent.com/pod-product-compliance
Ingram Content Group UK Ltd.
Pitfield, Milton Keynes, MK11 3LW, UK
UKHW020156060825
461487UK00017B/1436